Alberta's Day Care Controversy

Alberta's Day Care Controversy
From 1908 to 2009—and Beyond

Tom Langford

To Barry + Vanessa
with warmest comradely
regards,
Tom 13 August 2011

AU PRESS

© 2011 Tom Langford
Second printing 2011
Published by AU Press, Athabasca University
1200, 10011 – 109 Street
Edmonton, AB T5J 3S8

Library and Archives Canada Cataloguing in Publication
Langford, Tom
Alberta's day care controversy : from 1908 to 2009—and beyond / Tom Langford.

Includes bibliographical references and index.
Issued also in electronic format (978-1-926836-03-4).
ISBN 978-1-926836-02-7

1. Day care centers—Alberta—History. 2. Day care centers—Government policy—Alberta. 3. Child care services—Alberta—History. 4. Child care services—Government policy—Alberta. I. Title.

HQ778.7.C32A4 2011   362.71'2097123   C2010-905425-3

Cover design by Natalie Olsen, kisscutdesign.com.
Book design by Marvin Harder, marvinharder.com.
Printed and bound in Canada by Marquis Book Printing.

This project was funded in part by the Alberta Foundation for the Arts.

Contents

Tables

Abbreviations

AAYC Alberta Association for Young Children (1971–99)

ACCAP Alberta Child Care Accreditation Program (2005–)

ACCN Alberta Child Care Network (1987–2009; succeeded by Alberta Child Care Association)

ADCAC Alberta Day Care Advisory Committee (1980–86)

ADCTF Alberta Day Care Task Force (1977)

AFWUF Alberta Federation of Women United for Families (1981–)

AHS Aboriginal Head Start

AHSTF Alberta Heritage Savings Trust Fund (1976–)

ATRC Alberta Tax Review Committee (1998)

B-MDCA Bowness-Montgomery Day Care Association (Calgary, 1968–)

CA Calgary Archives, City of

CAFRA Child and Family Resource Association (Greater Edmonton Area)

CAFSAC Community and Family Services Advisory Committee (Edmonton)

CAP Canada Assistance Plan (1966–96)

CAPC Community Action Program for Children (1992–)

CCFRC Child Care Family Resource Centre (Edmonton)

CDN Community Day Nursery (Edmonton, 1964–2001)

CDNC Calgary Day Nursery Committee (1943–44)

CFSA Child and Family Services Authority (regional authorities, from 1998)

CSA Council of Social Agencies (Edmonton and Calgary, 1940s)

CSS Calgary Social Services

CSSC Children's Services Sub-Committee (Edmonton, 1986–92)

CUPE Canadian Union of Public Employees

CWL Catholic Women's League

DCAC   Day Care Association of Calgary (1967 to early 1980s)

DCSA   Day Care Society of Alberta (1982– ; preceded by PDCS)

EA   Edmonton Archives, City of

ECA   Early Childhood Academy (of Calgary) (1983–late 1990s)

ECD   Early Childhood Development

ECE   Early Childhood Education

ECFS   Edmonton Community and Family Services (municipal department from 1989; succeeded by Edmonton Community Services)

ECS   Early Childhood Services

EDCC   Edmonton Day Care Committee (1943–44)

EDCC   Edmonton Day Care Council

ELCC   Early Learning and Child Care (federal program, 2004–7)

ESS   Edmonton Social Services (municipal department; renamed ECFS in 1989)

EWC   Edmonton Welfare Council

FCSS   Family and Community Support Services (1981–)

FDH   Family Day Home

FSA   Family Service Association (of Edmonton)

FSS   Family and Social Services (provincial department, 1989–99)

HSD   Health and Social Development (provincial department, 1971–74)

IOA   Independent [Day Care] Operators' Association (of Medicine Hat and District)

Kids First   Kids First Parents Association (1987–)

KPMG   Accounting, audit, and consulting firm. A limited liability partnership. Initials come from principal founders: Klynveld, Peat, Marwick, and Goerdeler.

MADC   Municipally Approved Day Care (Edmonton)

MHDC   Medicine Hat Day Care (1969–81)

NAC   National Archives of Canada

NCB   National Child Benefit (1998–)

NDP   New Democratic Party

NFFRE   National Foundation for Family Research and Education

NSS   National Selective Service

OOSC   Out-of-School Care

PAA   Provincial Archives of Alberta

PC   Progressive Conservative (the political party in Alberta officially known as the Progressive Conservative Political Association of Alberta)

PDCS   Private Day Care Society (of Alberta) (1977–82; succeeded by DCSA)

PLAY   People Looking After Youth (a day care in Calgary, 1974–)

PQCC   Parents for Quality Child Care (Edmonton)

PSS Preventive Social Service (1966–81)

PTF Preschool Task Force (Edmonton, 1995)

REAL Realistic, Equal and Active for Life (Women) (1983–)

RFD Request for Decision (prepared by minister for provincial cabinet)

SPC Social Planning Council (of Edmonton or Calgary)

SPC Social Planning Committee (of the Alberta cabinet)

SSCH Social Services and Community Health (provincial department, 1974–86)

UCCA United Child Care Association (of Alberta) (1987)

UCCB Universal Child Care Benefit (2006–)

UCF United Community Fund

VFM Value for Money (Audit)

Timeline

1908   First charitable day nursery is established in Edmonton.

1912   Children's Aid Society of Edmonton runs a day care, 1912–17 (approx.).

1930   Edmonton Creche is established on a charitable basis.

1935   Edmonton College, Inc. is established, with kindergarten and day nursery divisions.

1943   Wartime day nurseries cost-sharing agreement is signed by Alberta and Ottawa.

1944   Advisory committee votes four to three against establishing wartime day nurseries.

Demonstration day nursery in Calgary opens and then closes.

1941–60s   Strong kindergarten programs are run in Calgary as part of school system until 1954 and later by community groups or commercial operators.

1959   Province agrees to enforce its licensing regulation for day cares.

1960   First provincial civil servant is hired to be responsible for day care.

1961   First provincial standards for day care are put in place.

1964   Edmonton Creche Society decides to close the Edmonton Creche.

Community Day Nursery (CDN) succeeds the Edmonton Creche.

1965   For the first time, the province agrees to finance a day care (CDN).

1966   Preventive Social Service (PSS) program begins.

Canada Assistance Plan (CAP) begins.

Mary Hull introduces a play-oriented program at CDN.

1967   Howard Clifford is hired as Edmonton's first day care director.

Edmonton adopts the Child Welfare League of America's day care standards.

Alf Hooke rejects use of PSS funds for Edmonton's Glengarry Day Care.

Day Care Association of Calgary is formed by commercial operators. A parallel group in Edmonton is headed by Hilde Bloedow.

1968   Province reverses Hooke's decision on PSS funding for Glengarry Day Care.

1969 Al Hagan is appointed Calgary's first day care counsellor.

Calgary adopts high day care standards much like Edmonton's.

First PSS day care opens in Medicine Hat.

Ray Speaker rejects Lethbridge's request for PSS funds for a day care after commercial operators protest.

1970 Day care opens at Mount Royal College, the first at a college in Canada.

Bowness-Montgomery Day Care opens in Calgary.

First cohort of early childhood education (ECE) students enters Mount Royal College in Calgary.

1971 Calgary's first municipal day care (Shaganappi) opens.

First cohort of ECE students enters Grant MacEwan College in Edmonton.

Red Deer City Council votes against supporting a PSS day care.

First change in provincial government in thirty-six years occurs. Peter Lougheed becomes premier.

Alberta Association for Young Children has founding conference.

1972 Red Deer reverses 1971 rejection decision: first PSS day care opens.

First PSS day care opens in Grande Prairie.

1974 First PSS day care opens without publicity in Lethbridge.

First cohort of ECE students enters Grande Prairie Regional College.

1976 Medicine Hat operates a network of five municipal day cares. There are no commercial day cares in the city.

1977 Report of the Alberta Day Care Task Force.

Formation of Private Day Care Society of Alberta (PDCS), a province-wide lobby group led by large commercial operators.

First cohort of early childhood development students enters Medicine Hat College.

1978 Province imposes new system involving portable day care subsidies and relatively weak day care standards.

Commercial centres become eligible to take subsidized children.

Calgary and Lethbridge join new system.

Edmonton, Medicine Hat, Grande Prairie, and Red Deer delay.

Province announces plan to phase out funding to former PSS day cares.

1979 Medicine Hat, Grande Prairie, and Red Deer join new day care system.

1979–96 Alberta loses at least $255 million (2006 dollars) in CAP transfers from Ottawa because it allows subsidized children to attend commercial centres.

1980 January: Edmonton joins new day care system.

February: Review of day care by Tory MLAs favours commercial interests.

April: Province assumes responsibility for out-of-school care (OOSC) and then returns it to municipalities in September.

August: Municipal involvement in provincial day care system ends.

September: Universal operating allowances are announced, along with significant improvements in staff-to-child ratios, group size, and indoor space.

September: First appointments are made to Alberta Day Care Advisory Committee (ADCAC).

Autumn: Maximum facility size for day cares is set at eighty spaces.

1980–90s   Lighthouse day cares and family day home (FDH) projects are supported by municipal governments across Alberta in opposition to provincial system.

1981   Operating allowances for infants and toddlers are substantially increased.

Special provincial payments to PSS day cares end.

1982   Minister Bob Bogle funds an alternative staff training program sponsored by the PDCS.

Province abandons plan to establish training requirements for day care staff.

Canadian Union of Public Employees (CUPE) boycott threat stops the U.S.-based corporation KinderCare Learning from opening day cares in Alberta.

1983   Municipalities begin to receive CAP flow-through payments for their lighthouse child care programs.

New regulation sets ownership cap at five hundred spaces; it is never enforced.

1984   Glengarry Day Care is transferred from city service to not-for-profit board.

1986   Operating allowance freeze occurs; new spaces do not qualify.

Province discontinues ADCAC.

1987   Kids First Parents Association is formed in Calgary.

Alberta Child Care Network holds its first meeting.

1988   Province considers providing a subsidy to stay-at-home parents. The idea is rejected because of the projected cost.

Canada Childcare Act dies when federal election is called.

1989   Commercial operators' "war chest" defeats CUPE union drive in Calgary.

Medicine Hat and District Independent Day Care Operators' Association is established.

1990   Cutbacks to the size of operating allowances begin, but freeze is lifted.

Staff training requirements are added to the Day Care Regulation.

1991   Number of day cares and number of licensed spaces peak.

1992   New right-wing majority on council approves the planned phase-out of Medicine Hat's municipally run day cares over four years.

1994   "Klein Revolution" budget cuts to social services begin.

Bankruptcy of Dennis Sorensen's Kindercare chain in Calgary.

Value for Money audit leads to the end of Calgary's municipal day care program (effective 1995).

Province deregulates FDHs with four to six children.

1995   Edmonton uses Preschool Task Force to shift its emphasis from municipally approved day cares to programs for "children and families in poverty."

Grande Prairie council votes to privatize the city-run FDH program.

1996   CAP ends. Flow-through payments to Alberta municipalities end.

Dedicated funding for municipally approved day cares in Edmonton ends.

1998   Relaxation of standard: a single staff member is now allowed to look after six children as young as eighteen months at beginning and end of day.

Child and Family Services Authorities begin administering day care.

1998–2001   Province implements pro-family reprivatization tax measures: income-tested child tax credit, doubled spousal exemption, and flat provincial tax rate.

1999   Operating allowances are eliminated.

Red Deer City Council votes to phase out its subsidies to the old PSS day cares.

2001   CDN in Edmonton closes.

2002   Wage enhancements begin. Accreditation program is announced.

2003   Alberta sits last among the provinces in per capita spending on child care.

Not-for-profit child care programs become eligible for gaming licenses.

2005   Accreditation program begins for day cares and FDH agencies.

Wage enhancements more than double for all trained staff.

Alberta signs an Early Learning and Child Care (ELCC) agreement with the federal Liberal government.

2006–8   Federal Conservative government pursues pro-family agenda by cancelling ELCC agreements with provinces, beginning a $100-per-month "baby bonus" for children under six, and passing two tax measures: a child tax credit and a higher spousal exemption.

2007   Wage enhancements increase by 40 percent.

Capital grants of $1,500 per new space are created.

Maximum facility size for day cares is deregulated.

123 Busy Beavers corporate chain buys centres in Calgary and Edmonton.

2008   Wage enhancements increase by 60 percent.

Infant space operating allowance of $150 is introduced.

Municipal involvement in OOSC ends.

Provincial subsidy program for OOSC begins.

Capital grants are provided to buy modular buildings for OOSC programs near schools.

2009   Accreditation program is announced for OOSC.

Wage enhancements are extended to workers in OOSC centres.

Alberta Child Care Association is founded.

Edleun Inc., backed by venture capital, acquires the 123 Busy Beavers chain.

Acknowledgements

I worked on this book for more years than I care to remember, and yet I never grew bored with the topic. For that I owe a debt of thanks to the many talented and dedicated Albertans who have worked tirelessly to put young children on the political agenda and to build high-quality child care options for young children and their families. Your efforts and successes continually inspired me and renewed my enthusiasm when it flagged after yet another long day spent sifting through archival photocopies and squinting at the computer screen.

My research was generously supported by the citizens of Canada through grants from the Social Sciences and Humanities Research Council (standard research grant 410-94-0477) and the University Research Grants Committee of the University of Calgary. This financial support allowed me to hire a number of graduate and undergraduate students who served as stellar research assistants or research associates at different points in the project: Gillian Anderson, Janine Bauman, Chris Frazer, Kristin Lozanski, Robin MacAulay, Lynne Malmquist, and Rachael McKendry. After contributing to this project, all of these students went on to finish one or more graduate degrees, and three of them now hold professorial appointments at universities across Canada. It was my good fortune to have worked with such skilled and committed social scientists.

One of Canada's national treasures is our system of public archives. For my research, I spent considerable time at the National Archives of Canada in Ottawa, the Provincial Archives of Alberta in Edmonton, the City of Calgary Archives, and the City of Edmonton Archives. I appreciated the opportunity to visit these archives and thank the staff members for their good spirit, courtesy, and public-mindedness. Many other individuals and organizations helped by providing me with copies of key documents that had not yet found their way into archives.

In this regard, I owe particular debts of gratitude to the City of Medicine Hat Children's Services, the City of Edmonton Community and Family Services, the Clifford E. Lee Foundation, and the Alberta Association for Young Children.

Evelyn McCallen, my partner, and I have been committed to our version of co-parenting since 1985. Our life journey didn't make work on this book any easier, but it certainly helped me keep the academic endeavour in its proper perspective. Our three children have made our lives richer and more interesting than we could have ever imagined. I especially thank my children for muting their teasing in recent years about the slow pace of my progress on the manuscript.

Almost seventy individuals were interviewed during the course of the research. Except for the few who wish to remain anonymous, they are listed in Appendix B. I thank each of the interviewees for generously contributing their time and attention to the study. I also thank Patricia and Eoin Lalor for graciously hosting me during an extended research trip to Edmonton and both Bob Hawkesworth and Karen Charlton for supporting my application for a book-publishing grant from the Historical Preservation Partnership Program of the Alberta Historical Resources Foundation.

The final stages of my work on the manuscript consisted in cutting out extraneous chunks of text. I was skillfully assisted in this process by Scott Anderson. I then had the distinct pleasure of working with the staff of AU Press. In particular, I would like to thank Joyce Hildebrand, whose careful and thorough copy-editing not only improved the construction of many sentences and eliminated repetitive phrasings but also corrected several errors and omissions in the citations; and senior editor Pamela Holway, who expertly managed the entire process.

Finally, the experiences and insights of three individuals were especially helpful to me as I oriented myself to a vast amount of research materials. They bear no responsibility for the shortcomings of my work but certainly helped me do the best I could. Special thanks go to Sheila Campbell, Howard Clifford, and the late Judy Padua. In recognition of their careers of distinguished accomplishment, all royalties from book sales will be assigned to the Alberta Child Care Association.

1. Introduction
Research Strategy, Themes, and Scope

The history of caring for young children in Alberta is one of unexpected and often paradoxical turns of policy, of vigorous arguments and counterarguments about issues such as the appropriateness of mothers' employment and the desirability of commercial rather than not-for-profit day care, and of competing sentiments of indifference toward and passionate concern about the quality of children's care. It is also a story of countless hours of hard work by undervalued and often unacknowledged caregivers, the vast majority of whom have been women. Therefore, investigating day care in Alberta requires an exploration of the "gendered social worlds" in which caring work has been accomplished (Ribbens 1994, 14) as well as the world of policy struggles involving governments and bureaucrats, movements and countermovements, experts and parents.

Alberta's approach to child care has long been recognized as anomalous relative to that of other Canadian provinces. For instance, in 1992 substantially more licensed centre-based spaces in Alberta were found in commercial than in not-for-profit facilities (65 percent to 35 percent); in the rest of Canada, commercial spaces constituted only 25 percent of the total (CRRU 1994, 87). In Calgary, where I had moved in 1989, commercial day cares were typically located on commuter routes. They sought new customers by distributing discount coupons in nearby neighbourhoods, promoting their brand names, and (in some cases) maintaining an attractive playground to create curb appeal for potential new customers. This decidedly commercialized approach to day care had more in common with developments in states like Texas and Florida than with what was happening elsewhere in Canada.

Alberta was indeed an anomalous case at that time, but not in any simplistic or easily categorized way. For instance, in the early 1990s, the Government of

Alberta modestly subsidized the care of every child in a licensed day care centre. This universal funding program allowed Alberta day cares to keep parental fees relatively low and meant that licensed day care was more accessible to full-fee–paying parents in Alberta than anywhere else in Canada. Another feature of the day care landscape in Alberta was the extraordinary variation in day cares among communities—a vestige of the 1970s, when municipal governments were delegated the authority to initiate subsidized day care services (although through cost sharing with the other levels of government, municipalities only had to pay twenty cents on the dollar for new services). From the mid-1970s to the mid-1990s, Medicine Hat was the most active of Alberta's municipal governments in planning and delivering day care services. So significant were its efforts that the national advisor on child care for Health and Welfare Canada, Howard Clifford, stated in 1993 that Medicine Hat was not only "the most progressive community in Alberta in terms of child care" but "the equal of any community in Canada" (221).

This particular history of child care in Alberta begins in chapter 2 with the establishment of Alberta's first day nursery in Edmonton in 1908. Subsequent developments, especially during World War II, are given considerable attention in chapter 2. Alberta, like Ontario and Quebec, signed an agreement with the federal government to participate in the Dominion-Provincial Wartime Day Nursery Program but, unlike the other two provinces, never established any day nurseries at that time. The core of the book, however, consists of chapters 3 to 8, which focus on developments in day care between the mid-1960s and the late 1990s. Remarkable twists and turns in provincial policies and programs occurred during this relatively short time period. Indeed, the controversies over day care reveal a great deal about the patterns of power and inequalities in Alberta society in the last third of the twentieth century. Chapter 9 concludes the book with an examination of how day care in Alberta changed through the first decade of the new millennium and links historical developments to contemporary policy questions.

The purpose of this introductory chapter is to outline the research strategy, themes, and scope of the book. My analytical focus is on group care of young children while the adults who are normally responsible for them (usually one or two parents) work or go to school. Although this sort of group care existed in Alberta over the entire period in question, the name used to designate it shifted over time. In the early decades, "day nursery" was a favourite term. Between the 1960s and 1980s, "day care" replaced "day nursery" to the extent that the latter now evokes images of a bygone era. In the 1980s, many people working in the field started to use "child care" instead of "day care." More recently, "early learning and child care" or "early childhood education and care" have been the favourite terms of experts and policy makers. Despite these shifts in terminology, I have used "day care" in the title of this book and throughout the remaining pages. I do so for two reasons.

First, even though the term "day care" is widely understood, it often evokes strong and divergent opinions among Albertans. An important goal of this history is to explain what lies behind the strong reactions of so many people to the seemingly innocuous descriptive term "day care." Second, much of this book is concerned with struggles over the character of government regulation and the funding of what the provincial government has officially called "day care centres" or "day care programs." The title of this book is therefore consistent with Alberta's regulatory language.[1]

RESEARCH STRATEGY

As a sociologist engaged in historical scholarship, I have drawn upon themes and concepts grounded in particular theoretical perspectives and debates. To my mind, the advantages of this approach are twofold. First, the historical narrative may attract the interest of a broader group of people, including those who are only marginally concerned with the development of day care in Alberta but who are keenly interested in the conflict between social conservatives and free market conservatives (neo-liberals) over the agenda of the conservative political movement. Second, the researcher is given the opportunity to consider the broader theoretical relevance of a historical narrative and to engage in what Michael Burawoy calls the "reconstruction of theory" (1998, 20–22) in order to advance our knowledge of social processes that operate in many social fields and settings in addition to the care of young children in Alberta. This book's theoretical contribution, found in the concluding chapter, involves a discussion of the social mechanisms that have created recurring patterns of events and discourse.

This history also includes a comparative focus. It is impossible to appreciate the broader significance of developments in Alberta without reference to day care in other jurisdictions. Among the many useful categories of comparators is other Canadian provinces and territories, particularly those with relatively strong economies and large urban populations. These comparators are part of the same set of federal-provincial relations as Alberta and are consequently useful for highlighting how day care in Alberta has developed in distinctive ways despite pressures to follow the policy guidelines of the federal government or the policy initiatives of other provinces. Another category is American states where, like Alberta, a marked expansion of commercial day care chains took place in the 1980s, notably Texas, California, Florida, and North Carolina (Neugebauer 1989, 16). These comparators are valuable in that they enable me to identify the extent to which day care in Alberta has developed in ways parallel to the most commercialized of the American states.

Alberta is an oil-and-gas producer, and it is thus useful to compare the development of day care in Alberta with another oil-and-gas-producing jurisdiction in order to gauge the impact of the economic boom-and-bust cycle on child care. Texas is the comparator in this category, and I pay particular attention to child care developments in Houston and Calgary when oil prices collapsed in the mid-1980s. Finally, certain select countries and regions have developed exemplary systems of early childhood education and care. Unlike the other three categories of comparators, these exemplars are not similar to Alberta on either the dependent variable (nature of the day care system) or key independent variables (political system and character of the economy) and thus cannot be used to explain developments in Alberta. I discuss one of these exemplars, Sweden, in order to highlight the unique features of Alberta's approach to day care at the end of the 1970s and beginning of the 1980s. The consideration of Sweden also serves as a concrete reminder that the care of young children in Alberta could have been organized on a much different basis than it eventually was.

This is a case study rather than a work of systematic comparison. In the latter, equivalent data for two or more cases are presented and analyzed, usually in order to test hypotheses based upon theory or previous research findings. An example of such a comparative research design is a study by Linda A. White, who systematically compared child care policy development in Alberta and Ontario from 1980 to 1996. Her goal was to assess the hypothesis that in times of fiscal crisis, right-wing governments will attempt to change the nature and limit the scope of social programs at the same time as they cut spending, while left-wing governments will simply cut spending (1997, 8).

I decided against a systematic-comparison research design for two reasons. First, I felt it important to undertake detailed, labour-intensive research on day care in Alberta so as to avoid arriving at superficial or incomplete conclusions and to ensure that I did not ignore important sources and perspectives. Given this commitment to primary research, it was impossible to contemplate equivalent research for other jurisdictions (and hope to complete the project sometime in this lifetime). Second, I am unconvinced that testing hypotheses using data from comparable cases is the most effective way to develop understandings of historical processes. Hypotheses are usually stated in terms of a small set of variables and proceed by abstracting those variables from the complex, historically specific relations they have with other variables. A great deal is lost in this abstraction process, as has been noted in prominent critiques of variable-type analysis over the years (e.g., Abbott 1992; Blumer 1956). This loss can be justified in studies of structural patterns over a large number of cases. However, when the goal is to understand process rather than structural pattern, and when few rather than many cases are being studied, variable-type, case-comparison analysis limits rather than furthers knowledge.

Nevertheless, variable-type analysis can be useful in case-study research when it is applied to units that are embedded within the primary case. For the Alberta day care system, the embedded units include municipalities (where there are a few dozen cases) and licensed day cares (where there are hundreds of cases). I comparatively analyze these embedded units not as an end it itself but rather to build up a richer understanding of the historical development of day care in Alberta. In Robert Yin's terms, my study has an embedded, single-case research design (2009, 47–53).

KEY CONCEPTS AND THEMES

The history of day care in Alberta involves a complex conjunction of economic, social, and political processes. At any single point in the story, I am interested in explaining why a particular policy decision on day care was made and not another. Economic, social, and political factors must all be considered when trying to explain such decisions. Furthermore, I am concerned with understanding the consequences of crucial policy decisions for subsequent developments in day care.

In studying the influence of economic factors on the history of day care, I have drawn upon insights from the field of political economy. In line with my training as a sociologist, my conception of the "social" begins by identifying major social inequalities in Alberta society. In this history, I consider how patterns of social inequalities have influenced developments in day care. As a political sociologist, my understanding of politics encompasses both societal groups and state groups. I examine how social movement organizations and interest groups have mobilized resources to shape the direction of day care in Alberta. I also pay attention to how divisions within and between states have figured in the development of day care in Alberta. The purpose of the rest of this section is to outline briefly the key concepts and themes that I have drawn from each of these areas of scholarship.

Political Economy of Day Care

Conventional economic analysis of day care is concerned with issues such as the effect of day care costs on women's decision making about employment, the efficiency of the day care market, and the economic rationale for government subsidies of day care (see, for example, Blau 1991; Cleveland and Krashinsky 1998). In contrast, political economy has a broader focus: how day care fits into the overall operation of the economy on local, regional, national, and international scales. In addition, political economy differs from conventional economic analysis because it analyzes and critiques, rather than takes for granted, the different types of power relations that structure day care's place in the economy.

Because of the importance of commercial day care in Alberta, the political-economic concepts of commodification and de-commodification are of particular relevance. A service like child care can be supplied through markets or, alternatively, by family members, friends, community groups, or state organizations. Child care has been organized in Alberta such that monetized exchange pervades all forms of provision and a market logic must be implemented to some extent by all providers because of the strength of the market-based commercial sector. Nevertheless, it would be inaccurate to conclude that, as a consequence, child care in Alberta is wholly commodified. As has been recently noted by Colin Williams (2009, 68), a service is commodified only when it is delivered to make a profit. As a consequence, monetized exchange is not synonymous with commodification, and services organized under the auspices of state agencies or community groups are definitely not commodified. Williams even argues that, in some circumstances, private businesses are driven by a rationale other than profit (72). This is relevant to the field of child care in Alberta since some commercial owners appear to have a track record of putting children's interests ahead of return on investment. Therefore, from a political-economic perspective, Alberta is an interesting case for study because of the relative parity of the commercial and non-commercial day care sectors and the consequent tension between the processes of commodification and de-commodification. Further complicating the politics of day care in Alberta is a strong pro-family movement that supports child care within family units along with the "pre-commodified" dependency of women that such an approach entails (Esping-Andersen 1999, 45).

This case study can also be used to raise broader questions about the character of Alberta's form of the welfare state. More than two decades ago, Gøsta Esping-Andersen proposed three ideal types to aid in analyzing the empirical character of welfare state regimes: liberal, corporativist (later renamed "conservative"), and social democratic. Canada was identified as one of the "archetypical examples" of the liberal regime type as characterized by means-tested rather than universal benefits, strict entitlement rules, and promotion of welfare through private rather than public plans (1989, 25–27).

Esping-Andersen's specification is a useful first approximation of Canada's approach to social welfare. However, Gerard Boychuk (1998) has demonstrated how his designation ignores important provincial variations in social assistance provision and changes in provincial social assistance regimes over time. Furthermore, Rianne Mahon (2008) has convincingly argued that three varieties of liberalism are currently contending to become "the dominant organizing principle" of the Canadian welfare regime: (1) a social liberalism that has an orientation toward program design that is very similar to social democracy, (2) a neo-liberalism with strong roots in classical liberalism, and (3) an inclusive liberalism that combines many broader neo-liberal perspectives with a stress on the empowering of individuals through education and training (343–45). These three varieties of liberalism are particularly apparent in the field of child care in Canada, where social liberal proposals for universal early learning programs contend with neo-liberal emphases on privatization (for example, the federal government's $100 monthly payment for each child under six years of age) and with inclusive liberal programs such as early learning opportunities for young children "at risk" (358). Mahon's schema is a useful tool for specifying the shifting and contested character of Alberta's approach to child care over the past fifty years.

Social Inequalities

This book identifies inequalities of gender, class, immigrant status, and generation as being central to an understanding of the history of day care in Alberta.

Day Care and the Gender Order

A gender order is the "historically constructed pattern of power relations between men and women" in an entire society, along with the historically extant notions of masculinity and femininity (Connell 1987, 98–99). It is a concept that describes an overall pattern of gender relations, not necessarily the situation in every group or institution, and certainly not the experience of every individual. In Alberta throughout the period in question, the gender order was one of institutionalized male domination, which means that this domination could be observed in face-to-face settings like workplaces and homes, and in the normal operation of societal institutions like the mass media and religion (Connell 1990, 514). Nevertheless, between 1908 and 2009, important changes occurred in the gender order such that the overall level of societal male domination decreased and the particular character of male domination changed in all institutional sites. How day care fits into that changing gender order over time is one of the central thematic questions of this book.

Many feminists have argued, in the words of Sonya Michel, that "the key to women's disadvantaged position in liberal polities and market economies lies in their cultural and social assignment to the family, specifically to the role of mother" (1999, 2). In this type of analysis, governmental support for child care by someone other than a mother is seen as an important extension of social citizenship rights: it allows women to escape the reality and expectation of compulsory motherhood and, as a result, gain greater opportunities for success and advancement in other fields of life (Orloff 1993, 318–19).

But not all types of publicly supported child care are equal in their capacities to transform the gender order. Child care by nannies may enhance the opportunities of higher-income women, but it does so by exploiting the limited opportunities of the women who work as nannies (Wrigley 1999). Exactly the same point applies when middle- and upper-income women place their children in low-wage family day homes (FDHs), day care centres, and out-of-school care (OOSC) centres; such low-wage workplaces predominated in Alberta prior to the establishment of an effective provincial wage enhancement program between 2005 and 2009. Furthermore, when government support for day care is organized as a low-cost alternative to welfare payments, the mother who is using day care does not necessarily benefit since she may be stuck working in a low-wage female job ghetto.

This critique also applies at the level of what children learn about gender while partaking in day care. The gender order, as defined above, includes cultural definitions of masculinity and femininity. When day care takes place in social worlds where care is overwhelmingly an activity of women and men are largely absent, and when societal support for day care (in places such as church basements and crowded private homes) is clearly marginal compared to societal support for almost everything else, highly differentiated and hierarchically ordered notions of masculinity and femininity are learned.

Class Struggles in Day Care

A class is a category of people who bring distinctive sets of resources to the production of goods and services. Class is a salient element of human experience and identity since people who occupy a similar structural location over time may participate in class subcultures and, as a consequence, develop broad similarities in outlook and political commitment (Langford 2002). Classes struggle with one another over the distribution of resources in day care and over competing visions of the future of the day care system.

All of the major classes in contemporary capitalist societies are important players in child care in Alberta.[2] First, there is the working class, defined as people who are paid to look after young children but who have no ownership or managerial role in a day care operation. It includes employees in day care centres, OOSC programs, and satellite FDHs; frontline government employees such as licensing inspectors; and nannies.[3] The second and third classes constitute two distinct types of commercial owners. The first is owner-operators of commercial services who, although they may employ some workers, primarily depend upon their own labour and the labour of family members to keep their business going. This class includes the owners of small day care centres and of independent FDHs. For brevity, this group of small business owners can be termed the old middle class in day care.[4] The second class of owners comprises the investors in large commercial centres or chains of centres, some of whom are involved in the management of day care operations while others are not. These capitalists employ day care workers in order to generate a return on their investment.

A fourth class involved in day care is the new middle class. It is made up of a somewhat diverse group of employees who, like workers, have no ownership stake in day care but who have some say over the direction of either a particular day care program or a day care policy. This new middle class includes the directors of day care centres and agencies, civil servants involved in managing the participation of governments in day care, the administrators of early childhood education programs, and the outside consultants and academics who periodically evaluate the day care system.

Immigrant Status and the Ownership of Commercial Day Cares

There has been a boom in immigrant ownership of small businesses in Western Canadian cities since the early 1970s. New immigrants are typically drawn to investing in businesses "that require relatively small capital outlays, no specific educational qualifications and where technical barriers are low" (Kloosterman 2000, 94). Prior to 30 November 1990, Alberta did not require directors of day care centres to have any educational qualifications. Furthermore, small day cares can be purchased fairly cheaply and are often attached to a residence where a proprietor's family can live; day care is also a decidedly "low-tech" activity. As a consequence, in response to the strong demand for day care in the late 1970s and 1980s, many new immigrants invested in commercial day cares in Alberta. This changed the racial/ethnic face of the ownership of commercial day care in Alberta since, starting in the late 1970s, immigration from Asia surpassed immigration from Europe (Kalbach 2000, 26–27).

Gender and class inequalities have been integral to the history of day care in Alberta from the very beginning. Inequalities involving racialized and ethnicized groups, in comparison, were of secondary importance in shaping policy developments in the early years.[5] Changes in the ownership patterns of commercial day cares in the 1980s, however, increased the importance of racialization and ethnicity as factors affecting developments in day care. This importance was further extended by government emphasis on early intervention programs for "at-risk" children beginning in the 1990s; as documented in chapter 9, this led to an increase in the number of day cares in Aboriginal communities at the same time as the overall number of day cares in Alberta declined.

Forgotten Generational Inequalities

The final type of inequality to be singled out for special attention in this study involves generations. In conceptualizing "generation," I follow McDaniel (2001, 197), who detaches the notion from birth cohort and argues that people are part of a generation by virtue of their social roles (e.g., mother, grandfather). In general terms, intergenerational relations involving young children are dependent upon both cohort processes and historical change. In studying the history of day care in Alberta, I have paid attention to how successive cohorts of young children have experienced day care in light of the changing patterns of intergenerational relations. Fundamental to understanding these social relations are intergenerational inequalities, particularly in regard to human rights and social citizenship benefits.

This study assumes that contemporary states are shaped by the balance of forces in society (Jessop 1982, 221–24) but also have the legal, institutional, and political power to develop original policy responses in any particular conjuncture. It further assumes that divisions within and between states are consequential for the development of social policy. Given this perspective, the key issues in analyzing state actions are (1) to identify the possible policy courses given the existing balance of forces, (2) to ascertain both the societal groups and state actors that favour each possible policy course, and (3) to explain why one policy prevailed over others.

Societal Groups Compete to Influence Social Policy
The balance of forces in society is dynamic. Although it certainly depends upon the patterns of inequalities in a society, it is also affected by the relative success of societal groups in marshalling available resources to influence civil servants, political parties, government leaders, and the public. One of the defining features of day care as a policy issue in Alberta is that it has often engendered strong positions and hard lobbying/mobilizing efforts from a surprisingly wide variety of social groups.

My analyses of the actions and effects of societal groups draw upon concepts taken from the sociological literature on social movements (e.g., McAdam 1996) and the political science literature on interest groups (e.g., Maloney, Jordan, and McLaughlin 1994). Social movement organizations and interest groups both engage in conventional types of advocacy like lobbying and public education, and also undertake organizational activities like membership drives. What distinguishes social movement organizations from interest groups, however, is that they enjoy support from a significant number of ordinary citizens who are willing to engage in contentious as well as conventional political action and whose commitment to the movement's cause spans an extended period of time (Tarrow 1998, 4). The movement for quality day care has waxed and waned over the years in Alberta; as a consequence, at particular points in the history (e.g., the 1970s), an organization like the Alberta Association for Young Children fits the definition of a social movement organization while at other times (e.g., the 1990s), it could be defined as an interest group. It is probably futile to try to classify an advocacy organization as either one or the other (Andrews and Edwards 2004, 483); nevertheless, it is still useful to recognize that when an organization enjoys widespread public support and is part of an organizational field that includes many like-minded groups, its capacity to influence policy is much different than when it is narrowly based and relatively isolated.

This book describes many instances where societal groups engaged in conventional lobbying efforts with municipal or provincial politicians. There are also a number of examples of groups mobilizing to counter the efforts of other groups. For instance, commercial operators in Calgary tried to disrupt the formation of the Bowness-Montgomery Day Care Association in 1968 (see chapter 3), and the pro-family movement that took shape in the 1980s can be seen as an attempt to counter significant changes in the gender order, including growing public investments in day care (see chapter 7). Indeed, just as some groups can be depicted as movement organizations, others can be described as countermovement organizations.

Divisions Within and Between States

"The State" is a complex of institutions concerned with governing a territory. Furthermore, there are overlapping states with different scales of operation, namely, federal, provincial, and municipal. Divisions within and between states are crucial elements of the history of day care in Alberta. The main years of this study coincide with a period when state institutions became much more complex and when the provincial state expanded its jurisdiction vis-à-vis both municipal states and the federal state. Therefore, this book is an examination of the changing nature of governance in Alberta seen from the vantage point of day care policy.

This study records a surprising number of cases where civil servants and elected officials strongly disagreed over day care policy or administration, demonstrating just how controversial day care has been in Alberta. The tension over the years also reflects the fact that many civil servants remained attached to the social liberal model of high-quality, not-for-profit day care that was supported by the provincial government in the 1970s but abandoned thereafter.

A second type of division involves different departments of the provincial state. For instance, in the early 1980s, the Department of Education supported higher standards of training for day care workers than did the Department of Social Services and Community Health. This aligns with the research finding that social movements may win support from one state agency but be opposed by others (McAdam, McCarthy, and Zald 1988).

Given the decentralized nature of the Canadian federation, it is not surprising that federal-provincial conflict is a recurring element of this history. Nevertheless, I also record important examples of federal-provincial collaboration, most notably in the mid-1960s when the Canada Assistance Plan (CAP) was developed. "CAP was a product of multilateral executive federalism," notes Michael Prince, "and the pattern of intimate intergovernmental consultation and interaction continued well into the 1970s" (2001, 797). Prince has identified "interprovincial/territorial collaboration" as a second model of federalism that has arisen in Canada in conjunction with the growing demands of provincial governments like Alberta for autonomy in social policy (805–9). This history pays close attention to the mode of federalism in play at different junctures. It is noteworthy that important policy and funding initiatives in day care in Alberta have sometimes been initiated by the federal government (in periods of executive federalism) but have at other times been the product of autonomous action by the Alberta government.

Finally, from the mid-1960s to the early 1980s, conflict between municipalities and the province dominated the politics of day care in Alberta, with municipalities supporting demands for strong standards and generous funding. The province terminated this conflict in 1980 when it arbitrarily ended municipal participation in the provincial day care system. These events fit a pattern noted by a group of British sociologists in the late 1980s:

> The exigencies of local situations will lead to local state managers developing
> policies in particular ways, possibly ways inappropriate from the viewpoint
> of those groups dominant at the centre. Furthermore, social relations are also
> unevenly developed and particular social groups which are not well represented
> in the power bloc dominating the national [or provincial] state may be locally
> important. The necessary degree of local state autonomy gives such groups
> leverage; they can begin to use state power to further their own interests and
> develop their own local interpretations of policy. (Goodwin, Duncan, and
> Halford 1988, 124)

This generic process helps to explain why the day care systems developed in various Alberta municipalities in the 1970s were so different from one another. It also aligns with Peter Saunders' observation that central governments tend "to remove 'contentious', 'strategic' or 'expensive' aspects of public policy from the local level" (1986, 302). When this is done, as was the case with day care in Alberta in 1980, democratic channels of control over public policy are reduced.

While this is the first book-length history of day care in Alberta, a number of reports and articles have already appeared on the subject. There is a fairly large body of evaluations of the state of day care in Alberta at particular points in time, and I use these critiques as source material throughout the book. In order to fill gaps in my own research, I have used a historical paper by Sheila Campbell (2001) on day care in Edmonton up until 1970. Finally, between the mid-1980s and mid-1990s, a number of valuable academic studies appeared: Bagley (1986), Friesen (1995), Hayden (1997), Read et al. (1992), and White (1997). I have used these to orient my own research and as secondary sources of information.

2. Early Efforts to Organize Day Nurseries, 1908–45

A real, although usually unacknowledged, need for day care arose in Alberta in the years prior to World War II since women with young children were sometimes forced to work outside the home in order to shelter, feed, and clothe their families. These women were largely left to their own devices when trying to arrange for the care of their children. Indeed, not only did the provincial government fail to provide any funding for day care, but it was renowned for seizing children from parents who were unable to provide the means of subsistence and quickly making those children available for adoption to families in Alberta, other provinces, and the United States. Consequently, it is little wonder that the need for day care was not a major public issue in Alberta prior to the early 1940s: poor working-class families were better off trying to organize day care privately rather than involve a government bureaucracy that was primed to take away their children.[1]

EDMONTON'S FIRST DAY NURSERIES, 1908–17

Edmonton's first day nursery was an initiative of the Local Council of Women. In October 1908, the group "decided to undertake the establishment of a creche, patterned after the highly successful day nurseries of eastern cities, where the children of working women are properly cared for from 7:30 a.m. until 6:30 p.m., leaving their mothers free to work with an easy mind knowing that their little ones will be warm, well fed and happy during their absence." The Edmonton Creche was operational by the end of 1908. According to the *Edmonton Bulletin*, it was situated in a leased house near the Immigration Hall since it was intended to serve the children of new immigrants. Between 1906 and 1910, 216,000 immigrants arrived in Alberta. At the time of the census of 1911, these new immigrants constituted a majority of the province's population of 375,000.[2]

At the time of the founding of the Edmonton Creche, a handful of day nurseries in Eastern Canadian cities and a widespread network of day nurseries in the cities of the northeastern United States had already been established. The day nurseries in the United States "were part of a broad social reform movement ... aimed at improving the lives of children and their families, which included the establishment of settlement houses, charity kindergartens and children's aid societies." In cities where orphanages and children's aid societies were well established, day nurseries developed a distinctive identity (Prochner 2000, 40–41). Since there was no Children's Aid Society in Alberta in 1908, however, the Edmonton Creche was forced to immediately become a residential home on top of a day nursery and was soon renamed the Edmonton Creche and Children's Home. In April 1909, it had fourteen children in residence but continued to provide "a daily home to little ones whose mothers go out working by the day or are unable, through illness or other causes, to attend to their children during their waking hours." Associated with the day nursery was "a free employment bureau." Women desiring domestic work could register at the creche; in turn, the creche provided the list of registrants to any "ladies requiring workwomen" who telephoned.[3]

That same year, the provincial government passed an act that required all communities with populations of ten thousand or more to have a children's shelter (Prochner 2000, 46). This led to the establishment of a Children's Aid Society in Edmonton that, in early 1910, assumed the work of "the ladies of the Creche." The original Edmonton Creche and Children's Home was closed and a new residential shelter for neglected and delinquent children was opened.[4]

Even though Edmonton's first day nursery closed in 1910, the need for day care had hardly dissipated. Immigration to Alberta between 1911 and 1915 (at 170,000 people) was almost as high as between 1906 and 1910, and there was also considerable migration to Alberta from Central Canada and the Atlantic provinces. The population of the City of Edmonton jumped from 25,000 in 1911 to an astounding 73,000 in 1914, before falling back to 59,000 in 1915. Clearly some new immigrants and migrants were stopping in Edmonton for a short time before moving on to rural areas; many others, however, put down roots in the city and contributed to the strong demand for day care in the years immediately before and during World War I.

In response to this demand, the Children's Aid Society established a stand-alone day nursery in 1912 and moved the facility to successively larger premises on four occasions between 1912 and 1916; the last of the moves was to a building that had previously been the location of the Caledonian Hotel. In early 1917, this day nursery looked after thirty-two children with a staff of three. It is noteworthy that the staff at Alberta's first dedicated day care suffered from exactly the same plight as the tens of thousands of workers (almost all women) who have worked in day cares in Alberta in the last ninety years: wages that fell far short of the value of the work. An *Edmonton Bulletin* story in early 1917 commented, "No high salaries are paid at the Nursery, and in this respect the total salaries do not represent the work that is actually done by the staff."[5]

I have not located a record of what happened to this day nursery after 1917.[6] We do know that no mention of it was made in 1930 at the time when a new Edmonton Creche was organized by the Local Council of Women. The most likely guess is that the day nursery in the old Caledonian Hotel closed shortly after the end of World War I because of the combined effects of two developments.

First, in 1919 Alberta followed the lead of Manitoba and Saskatchewan and introduced a mothers' allowance program (Guest 1980, 217n12). Although the term "mothers' allowance" is a misnomer for the program in Alberta since the only eligible mothers were those whose husbands had died or who had been committed to a mental hospital, the program did somewhat reduce the demand for day care in Alberta. Among the mothers who were ineligible for mothers' allowance payments in Alberta were the unmarried, separated, or divorced, and those whose husbands were disabled, in jail, or had deserted the family (Cohen 1927, 23).[7] However, the mothers' allowance program meant that some of the mothers who could in no way be blamed for their plight no longer required day care. This change undoubtedly lessened the interest of elite charitable organizations in supporting a day nursery since they generally believed that parents and their kin should be held responsible for young children.

Second, Edmonton's population was much more stable in the early 1920s than a decade earlier. Only 54,000 immigrants arrived in Alberta between 1921 and 1925, less than one-third the number that had flooded the city between 1911 and 1915; Edmonton's 1925 population of 65,000 was still less than the population in 1913–14 at the outbreak of World War I.[8] This stability may well have lessened elites' anxieties about social change and caused them to pay less attention to the social needs of working-class immigrant families.

In both 1921 and 1931, Alberta contained slightly less than 78,000 children under the age of five. By 1941 this number had fallen slightly to 75,000. Most of these young children were part of husband-wife families and were cared for by their mothers on a full-time basis. During these years, most women exited the labour force after they married; as a consequence, in 1931 there were only 2,200 husband-wife families in Alberta where the wife was in the paid labour force, representing less than 2 percent of all husband-wife families (Alberta Bureau of Statistics 1981, tables 1 and 23).

Nevertheless, when a woman had to support her young children on her own or when her husband's wages were insufficient to sustain the family, she was forced to work for pay and, in order to do so, to make arrangements for the care of her children. A sufficient number of women needed child care in Drumheller in the mid-1920s to prompt a women's organization associated with the communist movement to organize a day care. The Women's Labour League saw this day care in political terms: it was depicted as "free from bourgeois influence" (quoted in Seager 1981, 378). The proletarian day care in Drumheller, however, was a lonely exception throughout Alberta. The vast majority of mothers had to make their own child care arrangements as best they could, taking into account convenience and cost. Often these arrangements were satisfactory but sometimes they were horribly inadequate.

In 1929 in Edmonton, "five small children, left home alone while their mother worked, were barely rescued from their burning home by a passerby." This prompted Lady Rodney, convenor of child welfare in the Local Council of Women, to personally investigate the care of young children in the inner city. She reported finding "unsanitary conditions, children locked in rooms while their mothers worked, irresponsible caregivers, overcrowded care situations and, in one case, six or seven babies in a home, some lying on the floor holding their bottles" (Campbell 2001, 82). Lady Rodney's research helped to mobilize action by prominent citizens, supported by the municipal government. In 1930 the Edmonton Creche and Day Nursery Society was formed and opened a new Edmonton Creche.

Twenty years later, the society claimed that its founding in 1930 was meant "to meet the appalling situation then existing in Edmonton due to the depression." But while the depression may have exacerbated the situation, it is undoubtedly the case that dismal care arrangements were a standard feature of the day care landscape in Alberta's largest cities in the years before the depression. Lacking resources and fearing the loss of their children, working-class mothers sometimes had no option but to leave their young children in care environments that were less than the best. What was "appalling" in this situation was not the mothers' neglect of their children but rather the deep-seated economic and social inequalities that gave mothers no other viable options. Seen in this light, the response of the ladies of the Creche was meant to salve the consciences of Edmonton's elites rather than to seriously address the condition of the children of Edmonton's poorest families: given what Lady Rodney had found, a creche that accommodated merely eighteen children was in no way a serious attempt to meet the needs of the children.[9]

While the new Edmonton Creche was the only subsidized day nursery in Edmonton, and indeed in all of Alberta, in the 1930s, the city had at least one commercial day nursery during that decade: Edmonton College Inc. was established in 1935 with both kindergarten and day nursery divisions. The day nursery offered both full-day and half-day care and would have attracted enrolment from parents who had a steady and decent income. Poorer families would have continued to rely upon relatives, neighbours, or nearby family day homes to look after their young children.[10]

The outbreak of World War II greatly increased the demand for female labour in Canada: not only did it lead to a rapid expansion of many industries, but it also choked off the supply of immigrant labour. Most of the federal government's war contracts were placed with firms in Ontario and Quebec, with Vancouver and Manitoba being secondary war-production centres. As a consequence, single Albertan women were actively recruited by war industries in other provinces, and the National Selective Service (NSS) facilitated their relocation. A total of 15,000 civilians left Alberta during the war, a great many of them women recruited by war industries. As a result of this exodus of civilians and enlistment into the military, Alberta's population declined from 796,000 in 1941 to 776,000 in 1942 (apparently its low point between the 1941 and 1946 censuses). But at the same time as many young men and women left the province, the demand for industrial employees in Edmonton and Calgary increased from approximately 25,000 in 1939 to 35,000 in 1943. Married women were the only relatively untapped source of industrial labour living in the two cities; consequently, care of their children became an issue. In 1941 there were 13,000 children under the age of five in Edmonton and Calgary, and another 13,000 aged five to nine years.[11]

Among the 10,000 employed in primary wartime manufacturing in Alberta, 2,000 were women. Even higher proportions of women worked in other wartime industries such as meat processing and garment manufacturing. For example, the Great Western Garment Company in Edmonton was the largest garment manufacturer in Canada during the war; in 1942, 425 of its 488 employees were women. Furthermore, in the first quarter of 1944 alone, the NSS in Calgary placed over 3,000 women in jobs.[12] Taking these figures into account, a conservative estimate would put female wartime industrial employment in Calgary and Edmonton at 40 percent of the total of 33,000 industrial employees in July 1944, or approximately 13,000. No statistics are available for how many of these women had young children, but because of the structure of the labour market at the time, we can assume that working mothers numbered in the low thousands. Many more young children now required day care than at any previous point in Alberta's short history.

STRUGGLES OVER WARTIME DAY NURSERIES

On 13 August 1943, Alberta's new premier, Ernest Manning, met with representatives of Edmonton's Committee on Day Care for Children of Working Parents and delighted them by announcing that the provincial government had entered into a cost-sharing agreement with the federal government to provide day nurseries "for the care of young children whose mothers are engaged in war industry." It looked at that moment, and for at least the next six months, as if Alberta would become the third province, after Ontario and Quebec, to partner with the federal government in funding wartime day nurseries. However, first the City of Edmonton and then the federal Department of Labour balked at the specifics of the province's funding schemes for day nurseries. This delayed the implementation of the agreement, signalled that the province would have to come up with more money than originally planned, and tempered the commitment of both Premier Manning and Dr. W.W. Cross, the provincial cabinet minister responsible for administering the cost-sharing agreement.[13]

In early May of 1944, Premier Manning and Minister Cross formally abandoned their plan to fund wartime day nurseries when they accepted the controversial and highly disputed conclusion of a provincial advisory committee that "there is not sufficient demand in either of the Cities of Edmonton or Calgary to warrant the establishment of day nurseries for the care of children of mothers employed in war industries."[14] A wide range of organizations in Edmonton and Calgary lobbied against this conclusion but to no avail. The possibility of reopening the matter greatly diminished once it appeared there would be a speedy end to the war in Europe after the successful Allied invasion of Normandy on 6 June 1944. The matter seems to have been definitely settled by the results of the Alberta election of 8 August 1944, when the Social Credit League easily returned to power. Ernest Manning had formulated a decidedly more conservative program than his predecessor, William Aberhart, and the 1944 election proved that Manning's conservatism offered electoral rewards, particularly in rural and small-town Alberta, where Social Credit won every seat (Finkel 1989, chap. 4).

Effective Research and Advocacy, 1942–43

A great deal of sophisticated research and advocacy work by citizen groups in Calgary and Edmonton preceded the Alberta government's decision of August 1943 to sign a dominion-provincial cost-sharing agreement. The first of such efforts occurred in Calgary in 1942. Preliminary investigations in the spring and summer of 1942 concluded that there were inadequate provisions for the care of the children of working mothers. Not only was there no charitable day nursery in Calgary, but the only kindergarten located in a city school offered only a half-day service[15] and "private kindergartens ... were very crowded and too expensive for many working mothers." The investigation also cited reports of children being left alone or in inadequate environments while their mothers went to work. This led to a study of the demand for day care by a joint committee of the Local Council of Women and the Council of Social Agencies (CSA) in the fall of 1942. It is significant that this effort in Calgary was initiated before the federal government's plan for wartime day nurseries was widely known, indicating that the groups were simply trying to get a day nursery going on their own. They failed, however, to find a suitable location for such a nursery.[16]

Research and advocacy did not begin in Edmonton until April 1943, when a broadly based committee was struck by the Edmonton CSA. From the outset, this group was in contact with federal government officials in charge of the wartime day nurseries program and geared their efforts toward trying to involve Alberta in the program. The immediate objectives of the Edmonton Day Care Committee (EDCC) were to survey "the need for day nursery care among women employees of the larger Edmonton industries" and to assess how the standards of care at the city's existing charitable day nursery, the Edmonton Creche, compared to what they believed should be the minimum standards for day nursery care. The committee also solicited support for its efforts from a number of women's organizations.

The group's needs study was very thorough. Discussions were held with experts such as plant managers, personnel managers, clergymen, and school nurses, as well as "large numbers of mothers." In addition, the committee studied newspaper advertisements seeking care for children of working mothers and distributed survey forms to women working in industrial plants and to other women through women's organizations. Most of the evidence pointed to the need for wartime day nurseries although the survey results were not nearly so conclusive. The committee argued that some forms were not returned because of a "language barrier" and that many women were unwilling "to commit themselves until they could see the nurseries in operation" or because they felt "the signing of a survey form would be an admission of neglect on their part." In the end, the committee concluded that both out-of-school care (OOSC) and preschool care were needed and should be established in Edmonton.[17]

The EDCC took a two-pronged approach to lobbying the provincial government. It first met with the deputy minister of Education "and had no difficulty in persuading him of the need for child care." However, the Department of Education was not willing to provide the funds required by the cost-sharing agreement. In late June, the EDCC met with the deputy minister of Health, who informed them that sponsorship from his department was only available through the Child Welfare Branch. In explaining why the EDCC favoured sponsorship by the Department of Education over the Child Welfare Branch, its secretary informed Fraudena Eaton, the associate director of the NSS, that "there is a definite lack of confidence in the Child Welfare Department among the members of the committee." One of the criticisms of the Child Welfare Branch was the low provincial standards for foster homes. In light of this, the EDCC did not believe that foster homes should be used for the day care of the infants of mothers engaged in wartime work, and inquired, "Are there any plans available for group care of the infant-two year old, with definite standards set by the Dominion?"[18]

All of this advocacy for wartime day nurseries occurred at an opportune political time—during the first weeks of the premiership of Ernest Manning, who took charge following William Aberhart's death on 23 May. Premier Manning's immediate political task was to rebuild the Social Credit League's electoral base prior to the next election, scheduled for 1944. In light of this, it is hardly surprising that he was open to representations from the Calgary Day Nursery Committee (CDNC) and EDCC, especially considering that they were supported by prominent women's and social services organizations in each city. In late July 1943, the Edmonton committee presented a report to the province that advised signing the Dominion-Provincial Agreement that specified a 50-50 split of the operating costs of wartime day nurseries. The provincial government accepted this advice, as announced by Premier Manning on 13 August, but only with an important condition.

Delays While Finances Are Negotiated

The provincial government was prepared to make a contribution toward the establishment of wartime day nurseries in Calgary and Edmonton, but only if each city made an equivalent contribution. On 31 August 1943, Minister of Health W.W. Cross sent a letter to the acting mayor of Edmonton proposing that "the Federal Government will pay fifty percent, the Province twenty-five percent and the municipality twenty-five percent."[19] After a meeting with Minister Cross in Edmonton in January 1944, Fraudena Eaton reported, "Honourable Dr. Cross has no illusions about being able to close down day nurseries once they are established and believes the province will have to continue the service in part at least after the war. For this reason he is insisting on the financial cooperation of municipalities at this stage."[20]

Minister Cross's letter of 31 August to the City of Edmonton indicated that he was prepared to establish an advisory committee that would have "almost full authority to decide whether the scheme is to be proceeded with or not." He also outlined a formula for choosing members of the advisory committee that would seemingly guarantee a favourable recommendation: "one recommended by each municipality willing to take advantage of this arrangement, one from the Department of Health and the one appointed by the [National] Selective Service." This demonstrates that the provincial government was enthusiastic to proceed with wartime day nurseries as long as its financial commitment could be limited.[21]

The City of Edmonton's administration responded to Minister Cross's proposal in haste without considering evidence on the need for wartime day nurseries in Edmonton and without any discussion with either the CSA or the EDCC. The city rejected participation because of the request to contribute toward the operating costs of day nurseries, and opined, "We feel that the present creche meets the local situation better than any organization which might be set up under the agreement."[22]

Despite lobbying from the EDCC, including a presentation to city council on 27 September 1943, the three city commissioners (two bureaucrats and Mayor John Fry) persisted in their hardline position. In a report on 6 October, they continued to reject municipal involvement in the wartime day nursery program and even called into question the province's involvement: "It is really an integral part of running the war and as such should be administered solely by the Dominion Government in conjunction with the employers concerned in war works." The commissioners also argued that any additional demand for day care could be accommodated by the Edmonton Creche and by the commercial centre, Edmonton College, which "is caring for 85 children of mothers employed in essential industries, and has accommodation for 50 more."[23]

If the provincial government had been lukewarm about wartime day nurseries, it could have used the City of Edmonton's intransigence in the fall of 1943 as an excuse to mothball the program. Instead, the province made a major funding concession that broke the impasse: it agreed to pay 25 percent of the gross operating costs of a day nursery, before parent fees. Since the federal government would pay 50 percent of the net costs, after parent fees, the municipality would only be responsible for the remaining operating deficit. At the 11 January 1944, meeting of city council, Alderman Ainlay estimated that the city would only have to pay $50 of the $1,000 monthly operating expenses of a day nursery filled to capacity. The commissioners were instructed to discuss the matter with the premier and minister of health and confirmed this estimate. However, they cautioned that there would be considerable start-up costs for a day nursery and concluded, "Your commissioners are still of the opinion that this is a matter entirely for the Dominion Government." This time, Edmonton City Council rejected the commissioners' position in total and passed the following motion on 24 January: "The establishment of a day nursery is desirable and that we authorize the commissioners to appoint a member of this [provincial advisory] committee with a report of the committee's conclusions to be brought back to council." Council made a fateful error at that meeting in delegating the choice of Edmonton's representative on the advisory committee to an administrative body that was unsympathetic to the project.[24]

Meanwhile, in Calgary, the CDNC had placed newspaper advertisements in September 1943 and again in November in order to establish that the demand went beyond the minimum of twenty children required under the terms of the

Dominion-Provincial Agreement. Working mothers were asked to call a telephone number to register their children. The September advertisement attracted forty-four applicants, while the November survey generated seventy-nine more, of whom forty-three had mothers who were working. Importantly, the City of Calgary did not express the same reservations about sharing in the funding of a day nursery, and the mayor informed Minister Cross that the CDNC was prepared to administer a wartime day nursery. Indeed, a Calgary Day Nursery Provisional Board appeared on the scene no later than January 1944.[25]

At the beginning of 1944, social agencies, women's organizations, and other community groups in Edmonton and Calgary continued to make a strong push for government-sponsored day nurseries. Calgary City Council was entirely behind this community effort, while Edmonton City Council had come around to a position of support despite significant opposition from the city commissioners. At the provincial level, the government was supportive but unwilling to take on primary financial responsibility for any aspect of new day nurseries. This was demonstrated in late 1943 when Minister Cross wrote to the federal minister of Labour, Humphrey Mitchell, to convince him to share the cost of purchasing and renovating a building that could house a day nursery in Calgary.[26] It is significant that in this letter, W.W. Cross demonstrated a pragmatic attitude toward which children would qualify for care under the cost-sharing agreement—he was not interested in applying his own definition of war industry to the list of mothers' occupations gathered in the CDNC survey, but rather in getting the NSS to apply its operational definition to occupations like teaching, nursing, and railway coach cleaner so that he could ensure sufficient demand to trigger federal participation in the cost-sharing agreement.[27]

For the federal Department of Labour, the wartime day nurseries program was strictly a means to increase the supply of married women at a time when there were widespread shortages of workers in industries deemed essential to the war effort. Fraudena Eaton was a consistent administrator of this policy: at no time did she promote the establishment of day nurseries for any other reason. Her observations on the labour market in Calgary in January 1944 are thus crucial to the eventual decision of the minister of Labour against purchasing property in Calgary for a day nursery. Eaton did not believe there was a serious shortage of women workers in Calgary. "The employment situation for women in Calgary is fairly easy," she wrote, "and will probably continue this way at least until the agricultural work opens up and some girls go back to the farms." On the question of purchasing the property, she concluded: "I do not believe the emergency is so great or would extend over a sufficiently long period of time to warrant agreement to share in the cost of purchasing property."[28]

This position was not formally conveyed to the Alberta government until a letter dated 10 March. Minister Cross would have received this letter just days before the membership of the provincial advisory committee was set by an executive council order on 17 March.[29] The federal government's unwillingness to assist with the purchase of a property in Calgary meant that the province was looking at a larger start-up cost than it had anticipated and also sent the clear message that the establishment of a day nursery in Calgary was not viewed by the Dominion as being crucial to the war effort.

Whether the federal government's decision on this matter affected the final composition of the advisory committee is not known. Back in August 1943, W.W. Cross had proposed a four-person advisory committee, with the provincial Health Department nominating one member, Calgary and Edmonton one each, and the NSS the fourth member. The committee appointed on 17 March had seven members, four of whom were nominated by the province. The key point is that three of Cross's nominees turned out to be unsympathetic toward the idea of establishing wartime day nurseries. Indeed, a letter to the *Calgary Herald* at the time noted that one of Minister Cross's nominees, "Mrs. Harold Riley, long associated with child welfare, is known to be opposed to Day Nurseries and had not attended any previous meeting on the subject." The federal government may have stacked the committee at the last minute in order to try to secure a negative recommendation.[30] It is also possible that the Social Credit government simply did not want to proceed unless the need for wartime day nurseries was vetted by a committee that included those who represented the socially conservative philosophy of the members of its core constituency. In either case, Minister Cross's nominations to the advisory committee ensured that its work would not be a routine exercise of endorsing the thorough research conducted by the Calgary and Edmonton advocacy committees and accepting their recommendations in favour of wartime day nurseries in each city.

Why the Provincial Advisory Committee Made a Negative Recommendation

Only three of the members of the advisory committee were not nominated by Minister Cross. The City of Calgary nominee was Alderman Hedley Chauncey, who represented city council's favourable view toward the establishment of a wartime day nursery. When Alderman Chauncey was unable to attend the second meeting of the committee, he was replaced by Mayor Andrew Davidson. Unfortunately, the elected council of the City of Edmonton did not demonstrate the same political acumen in nominating a representative. They had delegated the task to the city commissioners, who opposed council's position in favour of Edmonton's participation. The commissioners immediately nominated Frank Drayton, superintendent of the Children's Aid and Civic Relief departments for the city. The commissioners are bound to have known that this senior city employee was unsympathetic to the idea of day nurseries. Wartime day nurseries in Alberta would have been partially subsidized by the three levels of government and thus represented material support for working parents, many of whom were low income. Such a program of family support ran counter to the philosophy of the child welfare system that Drayton administered.[31]

Like the City of Edmonton, the NSS bungled their choice of a representative for the advisory committee. Marjorie Pardee was a member of the EDCC and the provincial commissioner of the Canadian Girl Guide Association. Even though she was firmly committed to the idea of wartime day nurseries, well versed in the research that had been done to establish the need for such nurseries in Edmonton, and extremely conscientious, she lacked the knowledge and status to definitively convey how the NSS administered the program.[32]

The question to which the NSS representative needed to respond authoritatively concerned which women worked in "wartime industries" according to the Dominion-Provincial Agreement. This matter was the subject of much discussion at the advisory committee's first meeting on 4 April 1944, with committee members offering conflicting interpretations. A fully informed NSS representative would have been able to rule this discussion out-of-order by pointing out that the operational definition of "wartime industries" had been established as priority A and B essential occupations and asserting that the authority to make this determination rested strictly with a local NSS office. Minister Cross's letter to Humphrey Mitchell dated 29 December 1943 had already accepted the federal government's authority on this crucial matter. Marjorie Pardee's lack of knowledge also made her unable to detail how an NSS office participated in determining which children qualified for care in a wartime day nursery; this would have allayed some committee members' fears that the nursery could be used by "mothers who merely wanted a place to park their children."[33]

The issue of eligibility was also debated at the advisory committee's second meeting on 26 April. The committee again treated eligibility as being open to subjective interpretation rather than as a technical question. Their *modus operandi* was to read out the name and occupation of women who had responded to a newspaper advertisement and have each committee member decide "whether or not the applicant was eligible to use Day Nurseries for her children! The results of this varying from 8 to 19 according to the individual member's opinion."[34] What should have been a bureaucratic determination based upon labour market data was turned into a normative debate.

In addition to Maude Riley, Minister Cross's nominees to the provincial advisory committee were the committee chair, Dr. Angus C. McGugan, superintendent of Edmonton's University Hospital; Harry Coombs, supervisor of the Child Welfare Department in Calgary; and David Sullivan, a high school inspector in Edmonton. The non-voting secretary of the committee was Alexander Miller, the secretary of the Bureau of Public Welfare in Edmonton and hence a close associate of Cross. One of these nominees, David Sullivan, turned out to be a consistent supporter of the establishment of wartime day nurseries. It is possible that his appointment was influenced by the Department of Education, which had signalled support for day nurseries in 1943. The other provincial nominees, however, were inclined against the idea. Marjorie Pardee took note of this at the first meeting of the advisory committee on 4 April and wrote to Fraudena Eaton that "the attitude of certain members of the committee did not encourage me in hoping to see day nurseries established, though Mr. Sullivan, Mr. Chauncey and myself feel the need does exist."[35]

The advisory committee made three telling decisions at its meeting in Edmonton on 4 April that suggested it was either inept or crudely looking for a way to justify a negative recommendation, or most likely something of both. First, it decided that the research completed by the EDCC and CDNC in the previous fall and winter was "not of much help" because it was out of date.[36] Second, instead of using that past research as a baseline and asking each advocacy group to take steps to update the baseline, the provincial advisory committee decided to embark on its own independent survey of the need for wartime day nurseries. An independent study is not in itself a bad idea although, if conducted properly, it would have been very time consuming. The provincial advisory committee, however, decided to do a minimal-effort, quick study of the current need for day nurseries using the single method that had proven most problematic in past research: getting working women to commit to a sight-unseen day nursery by returning a coupon advertisement through the mail. The survey coupon itself was biased since it requested responses from women employed in "war industries" without indicating that the federal government's definition of war industries was much broader than munitions and armaments. The method of distributing the survey coupon was equally suspect since it was simply printed in major newspapers for a number of days running.[37] Third, the committee instructed its secretary to write letters "to the provinces of Manitoba and British Columbia to secure information as to the reasons they had refused to participate in the agreement." This investigation fell outside of the committee's formal mandate, as established by order-in-council 355/44, and it is therefore peculiar that the committee pursued this course of action. It is likely that securing this information was a tactical move by the opponents of wartime day nurseries who were searching for ways to bolster their position.

A three-week gap separated the first meeting of the advisory committee in Edmonton and its second meeting in Calgary. In that time, both the EDCC and CDNC were very active. The Edmonton advocates did not try to mobilize working mothers to reply to the advisory committee's newspaper advertisement but instead initiated a major new systematic study. The study was conducted between 18 and 22 April 1944, and built upon the findings of a study carried out in December 1943 that had involved distributing a survey form to all elementary school children covered by the Edmonton Public School Board. Using the results of the December survey, the EDCC identified a ten-block area that had a high proportion of working mothers. Forty women volunteers from the Citizens' Volunteer Bureau conducted a new door-to-door survey in those ten blocks. This study effectively demonstrated the difficulties faced in any survey of working mothers. Despite repeated callbacks, some working mothers were never available for interviews. Others refused to be interviewed. The volunteer interviewers also found some children "who had no adult supervision" and "appalling conditions ... in some crowded houses where families with two or three children were living in one small room." These findings demonstrate the value of on-site investigations.

The survey results were probably not as convincing as the EDCC would have hoped. In the ten-block area, sixteen mothers of twenty-one children said they would use a day nursery if it were close to their home. To supplement these numbers, eight other working mothers known to the EDCC but living elsewhere in Edmonton were contacted. Representing ten children, they confirmed their desire for day nursery care. The EDCC then got the Edmonton NSS office to check the occupations of the twenty-four working mothers: "all but 3 fell in either A or B priorities and would be eligible for day nursery care." The EDCC also noted,

"This survey covered less than a quarter of the area which could conveniently be served by one day nursery."[38]

All this research effort in Edmonton went for naught. The advisory committee ignored the results of the systematic study and did not even invite representatives of the EDCC to appear before it. Instead the committee treated responses to the newspaper advertisement as the only relevant indicator of need. Since only eight Edmonton mothers had replied to the coupon advertisement, they concluded that there was insufficient demand to support a wartime day nursery in that city.[39]

Advocates in Calgary took a different approach. According to Marjorie Pardee, the CDNC phoned working mothers on their lists and encouraged them to respond to the newspaper advertisement. This elicited twenty-six replies from Calgary, more than triple the number from Edmonton but still not enough to secure a favourable recommendation from the provincial advisory committee.[40]

One of the interesting facets of the research on wartime day nurseries in Alberta is that nowhere in any archives have I found a document that opposes their establishment, whereas extant documents from dozens of different groups and individuals register support. However, a prominent opponent of the day nurseries program did address the advisory committee at its meeting in Calgary on 26 April: Rose Wilkinson, representing the Catholic Women's League (CWL) of Calgary, "waxed eloquent about the sanctity of the home" and made a submission that "was definitely unfavourable to the project." Wilkinson was also a prominent member of the Social Credit movement; indeed, she had just returned from Toronto, where she had been one of the Alberta delegates to the national Social Credit convention. She successfully ran as a Social Credit candidate in Calgary in the August 1944 provincial election and served continuously as a member of the legislature until her retirement in 1963. In 1944 Wilkinson was one of only two members of that caucus from Calgary and was one of the few female members of the legislature. She was, therefore, a very high-profile opponent of wartime day nurseries who undoubtedly had the ear of Premier Manning and Minister Cross, and who had a number of kindred spirits on the advisory committee itself. Her affiliation with the CWL was certainly less significant in this matter than her association with the inner circle of the Alberta Social Credit leadership. In fact, the position against day nurseries taken by the CWL of Calgary was contradicted by the support for wartime day nurseries expressed by the CWL of Edmonton, whose president had been a member of the EDCC.[41]

Separate votes on the need for wartime day nurseries in Edmonton and Calgary were taken at the advisory committee meeting on 26 April. "The result in both cases was the same," wrote Marjorie Pardee to Fraudena Eaton. "Mayor Davidson, Mr. Sullivan and myself being of the opinion that a need existed for the establishment of day nurseries. The other three members voting no and the chairman casting the deciding vote against."[42]

Why the Cabinet Accepted the Advisory Committee's Recommendation

The decision of the provincial advisory committee was immediately greeted by a flood of opposition. Within a week, the two daily newspapers in Edmonton had each published two editorials that disputed the conclusion of the advisory committee. The Edmonton Bulletin was particularly disparaging of the decision, noting the results of the systematic surveys conducted in December 1943 and April 1944 that were apparently ignored and criticizing the newspaper coupon questionnaire for being "vague and complicated and uninformative." The Bulletin expressed its contempt for the work of the committee when it prefaced its remarks with expressions like "anyone who knows anything at all" and "thinking people."

The Edmonton Journal took a more constructive tone in its editorials, at one point praising Minister Cross for showing "such a commendable desire to extend health and hospitalization services on a broad basis to the people of Alberta." Rather than belittle the advisory committee, the Journal simply argued that the CSA was the authoritative body on welfare matters and that the CSA's support for the establishment of wartime day nurseries in Edmonton carried more weight than the negative recommendation of the advisory committee.[43]

In contrast, the two Calgary daily newspapers did not editorialize on this subject in the days immediately after 27 April. Nevertheless, in the first ten days of May 1944, Premier Manning received messages of protest from the CDNC and the University Women's Club of Calgary to go along with similar messages from a number of Edmonton organizations: the Planning Board of the Citizens' Volunteer Bureau, the War Services Council, the Edmonton CSA, the Ladies Jay Cee Club, and the University Women's Club. Copies of the letters from the latter two groups were reprinted in the Bulletin, which also printed a letter from "a working mother" who testified as to the benefit her child received from attending a day nursery in Vancouver. The Journal published a story based upon the letters of the latter two groups.[44]

W.W. Cross at first indicated that the provincial cabinet would decide whether to accept the provincial advisory committee's recommendation at a meeting on 2

May. He was also quoted defending the recommendation in considerable detail, suggesting not only that he had been thoroughly briefed but also that he was in agreement with the logic of the committee's majority decision. One line of argument used by Minister Cross to defend the recommendation involved the low number of children of qualified working mothers who had signed up for the wartime day nurseries, specifically four in Edmonton and nineteen in Calgary. In addition, Cross emphasized that this decision to reject wartime day nurseries was consistent with the decisions in Manitoba, Saskatchewan, and British Columbia. He stated, "Vancouver turned down the plan flat, after making complete investigation."[45]

The provincial cabinet did not make a final decision on this matter on 2 May, presumably because of the storm of protest that had followed the release of the advisory committee's recommendation. Instead, the matter was put over to the following week for a decision by the Executive Council of senior cabinet ministers. On 9 May, Premier Manning issued a written statement that explained why the government had decided to accept the recommendation against establishing wartime day nurseries. The statement mainly reiterated the arguments that Minister Cross had offered previously in defence of the recommendation. Indeed, the only new element in the statement was the assertion that the advisory committee had decided to conduct its own survey of the need for day nurseries because "the evidence and the viewpoints" contained in the materials submitted to it "were so conflicting and contradictory." Since previous reports on the 4 April meeting of the provincial advisory committee had not mentioned this factor and since the archival record is devoid of documents expressing opposition to wartime day nurseries, it is doubtful whether this element of Premier Manning's statement is accurate. Perhaps he was confusing the sharp ideological conflict among committee members with what appeared in the submissions.[46]

The decision of the Executive Council sparked even more protest for the next several weeks. Both Edmonton papers editorialized against the decision on 10 May, as did the *Calgary Herald* on 26 May. The *Edmonton Journal* published its fourth editorial on the matter on 14 June. The *Journal* was particularly insistent that Frank Drayton be censured for his failure to represent city council's position on the matter. At about the same time, Edmonton City Council formally asked Minister Cross to reopen the question. Among the other groups who expressed support for wartime day nurseries were the Imperial Order Daughters of the Empire (Junior Branch) of Edmonton, Local No. 1 (Edmonton) of the Amalgamated Building Workers of Canada, the Council for Canadian Unity of

Edmonton, two different units of the Labour Progressive Party in Edmonton, the Stanley Jones Home and School Association in Calgary, the Edmonton Junior Chamber of Commerce, and the Soroptimist Club of Edmonton.[47]

Throughout the spring of 1944, there was a shortage of women workers for essential occupations in both Edmonton and Calgary. For example, for the week ending on 13 May 1944, there were 635 jobs available to women in Edmonton, more than double the number of women registered as out of work. At the end of June, the federal minister of Trade and Commerce described the shortage of workers in Edmonton as being worse than anywhere else in the country.[48]

The combination of an increasing number of married women in the paid labour force, a strong demand for even more married women, political pressure by prominent women's and social services organizations, and a looming provincial election led Premier Manning to announce on 17 July that wartime day nurseries would be reconsidered by the Executive Council "at the earliest possible date."

That same day, Calgary "clubwomen," in conjunction with the Calgary CSA, opened a demonstration day nursery for children between three and five and a half years of age. Their hope was that government funding would become available so that the day nursery could be kept open past September. Operated in the James Short school, the day nursery struggled to build an enrolment; only twenty-two children were in attendance by mid-August. Apparently parents were unwilling to discontinue other care arrangements for an experiment that might well be ended on 15 September. Their caution proved sensible, since the clubwomen were forced to close the day nursery when no government money was forthcoming.[49]

Indeed, the CSA of Edmonton never found out whether the Executive Council ever reconsidered the issue of wartime day nurseries and by the middle of October had concluded that "further agitation is probably useless."[50] The sweeping Social Credit electoral victory on 15 August, as well as successes on the European war front, had allowed the provincial government to quietly let the matter drop.

The Manning government of 1943–44 exhibited considerable pragmatism in its consideration of wartime day nurseries, even if at its philosophical heart was a social conservatism that celebrated the care of young children by mothers at home. That pragmatism covered gaining benefits from the Dominion government for Albertans and building sufficient popular support to ensure the election of the Social Credit League to a third consecutive term. This suggests that only compelling practical advantages would have prompted the Manning government to consider reopening the matter, and such advantages never materialized during the latter half of 1944.

Accommodating and Challenging the Gender Order

A number of arguments were put forward by advocates in Alberta to justify the establishment of wartime day nurseries, notably labour shortages, child neglect, juvenile delinquency, and child development. One argument that is noticeably missing from the historical record, however, is that day nurseries promote gender equality by giving women with young children greater opportunities to pursue paid work and education. This argument was anathema to Alberta society, where women's freedom from the homemaker role was widely feared. Despite advocates' efforts to dispel it, this fear was an important component of the belief system that rejected the establishment of wartime day nurseries.

Advocacy groups recognized that the care of young children in day nurseries contradicted the principle of mothers looking after their children at home. Some groups proclaimed allegiance to this principle but explained why they also supported wartime day nurseries. For instance, the CWL of Edmonton stated its belief "that women's proper sphere is her own home and that her work as the mother of a family is her noblest career." The CWL then argued that day nurseries are necessary when "the mother of young children is forced by circumstances to become the breadwinner of the family."[51] The EDCC implied support for this principle when it asserted, "This committee advocates the extension of day care of children only because our country is at war and women are called upon to meet a serious labour shortage."[52] And while an editorial in the *Edmonton Bulletin* proclaimed its adherence to the view that "for children there is no substitute for homes," it immediately added: "But pretty and high-minded as this view may be, it still merely dodges the facts. Whether mothers should work or not, they still do work. They still have children who need day nursery attention."[53]

Other advocates took an analytical approach to the contradiction. "We are aware that the greatest opposition to opening a Day Nursery here is the belief in the principle that mothers of preschool children should not be away from home," wrote the University Women's Club of Calgary. "The fact is that mothers of many children are already working. It is this existing condition rather than a theory with which we are concerned."[54] The CDNC offered a blunter dismissal of the relevance of normative principles to the current circumstances: "Whether you think a woman's place is in the home, that mothers of small children should not work, these principles do not enter this agreement at all. This is a Wartime Emergency measure."[55]

The analytical positions noted above highlighted how a normative view of women's role in raising children could not deal with important social and economic problems. Two problems in particular were emphasized by advocates: enabling women to produce goods needed for the war and ensuring that the children of those women would receive adequate care in their absence.

Advocates made many labour-market arguments to support the establishment of wartime day nurseries in Alberta, but these arguments never challenged the precepts of the existing gender order.[56] Nor did the arguments that day nursery care was needed to protect young children or that OOSC was needed to prevent juvenile delinquency. However, those advocates who promoted an educational form of day nursery care offered a partial criticism of the gender order. They did not directly critique women's inferior status but rather questioned the efficacy of women's child-rearing practices. According to these advocates, it was appropriate to liberate women from exclusive responsibility for young children not for their own benefit but to serve the developmental needs of children. Along this line, the Soroptimist Club of Edmonton wrote to Premier Manning, "We sincerely hope that the matter will be reopened, and that you will throw your influence on the side of 'supervised training and care' for small children, whether they be the children of mothers working in industrial plants, or in their own homes or offices." The *Calgary Herald* editorialized in favour of a preschool educational system and cast doubt on the quality of child care provided by many stay-at-home mothers.[57]

While this scientifically grounded critique had the potential to partially disrupt the gender order that tied mothers to the care of young children, it also had the potential to reinforce the class hierarchy: it divided stay-at-home mothers between the educated, who are familiar with and apply modern child psychology in their parenting, and the uneducated. Many in the latter category likely saw the experts' call for a preschool educational system as an affront to their competence as mothers.

As mentioned earlier, an important factor that promoted opposition to wartime day nurseries in Alberta was fear of women's freedom. It would seem that a belief in women's virtuousness was tied to their subservience as caregivers. Once free of that subservience, women's moral character was immediately suspect. Some members of the provincial advisory committee expressed this fear when they asked what controls would prevent "mothers who merely wanted a place to park their children from using the nurseries."[58] A wartime day nursery system, they worried, would be a temptation for some women to stray away from a life of virtuous domesticity.

The most widely read syndicated advice columnist of the day was Dorothy Dix. Her column of 3 May 1944 featured a discussion of young mothers who shirk their parenting duties when given the opportunity. Dorothy Dix responded to a letter from "Tired Neighbour," a middle-aged women who had been regularly looking after the children of a number of young mothers in her neighbourhood, apparently without compensation. "Every afternoon they dress themselves up, dump their young ones on me, and go shopping and to the movies," she wrote. "I am sick and tired of it." Dorothy Dix replied that "a woman's babies are her own individual responsibility," even if that meant "a 24-hour job at hard labour." She emphasized that a mother does not have "the right to wish them off on Grandma, or any kind neighbour, while she goes off to enjoy herself."

In this everyday moral drama, women appear hedonistic and self-centred once they are given any kind of personal latitude. But somehow when they are tied to the home, engaged in hard domestic labour for twenty-four hours of every day, they are the perfect caregivers for their children. Just as the fear of women is linked to their freedom, the idealization of women as caregivers is linked to their servitude.[59]

In the middle of June 1944, the National Council of Women met in Port Arthur, Ontario. The council called for the establishment of nursery schools under the education system and an end to discrimination in employment against married women. "Gone are the days when woman was content to accept a pattern of life laid down for her," stated Mrs. Frank Ritchie, a delegate from Manitoba, "and gone, too, are the days when whole aspects of life were accepted as closed to her." This was a clear demand for greater freedom for married women.[60]

Ritchie's comment was the focus of a strongly worded editorial in the *Calgary Herald* that predicted dire social consequences if married women pursued careers. Birth rates would fall and families would suffer. "The married woman who prefers to compete with her husband in the field of labour," stated the editorialist, "thus shirking or neglecting the vital responsibilities of her rightful sphere as a homemaker, definitely becomes a national liability."[61] The fear of freedom for women is unmistakable. The notion of a "rightful sphere" is invoked to justify married women's responsibility for the domestic milieu. It should be remembered that less than a month before this, the *Herald* had issued a strong editorial statement in favour of educational nursery schools. The coexistence of these two editorial positions demonstrates that the challenge to the patriarchal gender order coming from the proponents of scientific child study was indirect and very partial.

In conclusion, justifications for wartime day nurseries in Alberta largely accommodated rather than challenged the gender order. Advocates presented the nurseries as a necessary exception to a preferred state of child care by mothers in the home. It would take almost a quarter of a century before the demand for day care in Alberta would become more directly linked to feminist struggles for women's equality. But even then, with the Social Credit League of Ernest Manning still in power in the 1960s, advocates for public subsidization of quality day care downplayed the implications of day care for the gender order. Instead, they presented the same sorts of pragmatic arguments that had almost won support for wartime day nurseries in the 1940s.

3. The 1960s
Citizen Action, Civil Servants, and Municipal Initiatives Lead the Way

DEVELOPMENTS BETWEEN 1945 AND THE EARLY 1960S

The preceding chapter demonstrated that no significant challenge was mounted to the conservative gender order in Alberta society during World War II, despite the widespread employment of married women and the vigorous lobbying for day nurseries by groups in Edmonton and Calgary. In the years of "normality" immediately after the end of the war, women were expected to exit the paid labour force after marriage, and married women with young children were expected to be the primary caregivers for those children. In 1951 only 21,000 of the 63,000 females in Alberta's paid labour force were married. This group of 21,000 constituted merely 10 percent of all of the married women in Alberta (table 3.1).[1]

Among those who supported the establishment of wartime day nurseries in Alberta were proponents of a public system of education for preschool children. As noted in the last chapter, such a system received editorial support from the *Calgary Herald* in 1944. This high-profile endorsement reflected the strength of the movement for public kindergartens in Calgary in the mid-1940s. The Calgary Board of Education responded to this movement and expanded its kindergarten programs from one in the early 1940s to twelve in 1947 (LaGrange 1991, 109). Consequently, although the agitation for wartime day nurseries did not yield a day nursery in Calgary, it did contribute to the establishment of a significant public kindergarten system. The Calgary Board established relatively high standards for its kindergartens that were supported by grants from the province's Department of Education (LaGrange 1991, 109; Prochner 2000, 37).

The situation in Edmonton in the late 1940s and early 1950s was quite different. The Edmonton Creche and Day Nursery Society continued to operate

TABLE 3.1   Demographic and Labour Force Changes in Alberta, 1946 to 1971

	1946	1951	1956	1961	1966	1971
Population	803	940	1,123	1,332	1,463	1,628
% urbanized	44%	52%	57%	63%	69%	74%
Calgary[a]	101	133	191	276	331	403
Edmonton[b]	114	171	255	321	377	438
Together, as % of total Alberta population	27%	32%	40%	45%	48%	52%
Lethbridge	17	23	29	35	37	41
Medicine Hat	13	16	21	25	26	27
Red Deer	4	8	12	20	26	28
Grande Prairie	2	3	6	8	11	13
Together, as % of total Alberta population	4%	5%	6%	7%	7%	7%
Newborns to 4 year olds	85	117	150	180	174	152
% of total Alberta population	11%	12%	13%	14%	12%	9%
5 to 9 year olds	74	93	126	159	180	180
% of total Alberta population	9%	10%	11%	12%	12%	11%
Divorces per 100,000 people		63		78	107	225
Lone-parent families				23	27	34
% of all families				8%	9%	9%
Females in labour force		63		128		244
Participation rate		20%		31%		44%
% of total labour force		18%		26%		35%
Married women in labour force		21		77		157
% of married women		10%		26%		43%

SOURCES: Alberta Bureau of Statistics 1981; Alberta Bureau of Statistics, *Alberta Facts and Figures* (various years); Alberta Bureau of Statistics 1967; Canadian census tables for Alberta, various years (copies available from the author on request).

NOTE: All raw numbers are in thousands.

[a] Bowness, Forest Lawn, and Montgomery are included with Calgary for years prior to annexation.

[b] Beverly and Jasper Place are included with Edmonton for years prior to annexation.

the charitable day nursery it had first established in 1930, supported by the Edmonton Community Chest, the municipal government, and private donors. Yet no public kindergartens were established in Edmonton schools in the years after World War II. As a consequence, Edmonton parents looking for a kindergarten had to turn to unregulated, private programs. One such program, operated on a commercial basis, was offered at the Edmonton College Inc. This business had established day nursery and kindergarten divisions in 1935 and had argued in 1943 that a wartime day nursery in Edmonton was unnecessary because the Edmonton College could absorb the increased demand for day care from mothers employed in war industries. In 1951, when the building provided gratis to the Creche by the city government was condemned by the fire marshal and the Creche was looking for a new home, Edmonton College Inc. argued that there was no need for the Creche to continue since the Edmonton College could accommodate all of its children.[2]

After temporarily closing in 1951, the Edmonton Creche reopened in another city-owned building. However, the debate about the future of the Creche in 1951 demonstrated the strength of the conviction of those who opposed the use of public funds to extend the availability of day care. The suggestion that the Creche be relocated to the city's recreation building provoked a letter to city hall from the president of the Edmonton Table Tennis Club, which operated out of that building. He maintained that the Creche did not need a large space since it should be limited to serving children "who have an irresponsible parent." Furthermore, he argued that "many of the people" who had been using the Creche found it to be "a convenience but could make other adequate working arrangements if that convenience were not available."[3]

A second citizen wrote to a City of Edmonton commissioner after reading a letter to the editor of the *Edmonton Journal* by the president of the Association of Creche Parents, Anne Fairchild. At the time, the Creche was temporarily closed and the children were in new care situations. "Some of the arrangements are not too bad," wrote Fairchild, "but most of them are not very good, and the mothers are just about at the end of their rope." Her message was that "the need for a new Creche—a day nursery—is terrible and urgent and immediate." It was another section of Anne Fairchild's letter that raised the ire of Katherine Moar, who dashed off a letter to the commissioner that same day. In appealing for public support, Fairchild wrote, "Those of you who are parents, perhaps, can understand wives who work to help their husbands build a home, or to help them through university. These are the parents and these are the children who use the Creche." Katherine Moar underlined these sentences in the newspaper clipping she attached to the letter she wrote to the commissioner.

Moar maintained that it was a "grave misuse" of public funds if the city was providing day care subsidies to "parents buying a house or with a member of the family attending University." She also questioned the priorities of the mothers in such families: "Perhaps if the Creche remained closed for a time it might force a mother to put her child's welfare ahead of a personal financial gain." The city's commissioners replied that until recently, they too had held the "view that only those mothers who were widows or deserted wives should be accommodated, and not those cases where both parents were working." However, after further inquiry, they had determined "that many of the cases where both parents were working were even more in need of help than some of the others." They concluded by reassuring Kathleen Moar "that despite the words you have underlined ... each case that was cared for at the Creche was a proper one and worthy of support." This response continued to portray subsidized day care as a targeted welfare service but argued that some two-income families were so poor that they deserved the public subsidy along with lone-parent families.[4]

In Calgary, the movement for public preschool education suffered a significant reversal in 1954 when the Calgary Public School Board stopped offering kindergarten classes. This decision was made one year after the provincial government discontinued grants to support kindergartens (LaGrange 1991, 109) and has been attributed to "overcrowding in schools, a shortage of teachers, and a study by a local academic who concluded that the benefits of kindergarten do not last beyond grade 4" (Seguin 1977, 58, cited in Prochner 2000, 37). The population pressures on the school system in the 1950s were caused by the economic boom after the discovery of oil at Leduc in 1947 and the postwar baby boom. Overall, Calgary's population grew by 91 percent between 1946 and 1956 (table 3.1) while the number of junior elementary school children (five to nine years old) increased by an astounding 200 percent (from approximately 6,000 to 18,000).[5]

Even though they were closed in 1954, Calgary public school kindergartens had a long-term impact on the development of private kindergartens, nursery schools, and day cares in the city. This is because "there was a carry-over of standards from public school kindergartens to the private kindergartens that developed to take their place following their closure" (Olsen 1955, cited in Prochner 2000, 37). An important reason for the carry-over of standards was that the Public School Board assisted parents in establishing community-run kindergartens (Seguin 1977, 59, cited in Prochner 2000, 37). The high standards of the community-run programs put competitive and professional pressures on commercial operators of preschool programs to offer similar high standards. At this time, and carrying on into the 1960s, commercial operators would often combine half-day and full-day programs for older (four- and five-year-old) and younger (two- and three-year-old) children, and might call their service a nursery school, a day nursery, and/or a kindergarten.

Sheila Campbell confirmed the generally high standards of kindergarten/ preschool programming in Calgary in the late 1950s and early 1960s. She graduated with a Bachelor of Education degree from the University of Alberta in 1952. After teaching at the junior high and senior high levels in Edmonton, Campbell left the paid labour force in the mid-1950s to look after her young children. At that time, she joined a recent-graduates' study group organized by the University Women's Club. With the day care situation in Edmonton in the news in 1956 and 1957, this group selected day care as a study issue. This experience sparked Sheila Campbell's life-long involvement in early childhood education (ECE) and day care in Alberta. Campbell attributed the difference between the standards of private kindergartens in Edmonton and Calgary in the 1950s and 1960s to differences in the training of the operators:

> We always felt that there was a difference between Calgary and Edmonton in that Calgary had a more knowledgeable early childhood community because there were a number of kindergarten people from the United States in Calgary.... There were these private kindergartens and they were good kindergartens. They knew what kindergarten programming was, they came out of the kindergarten tradition in the States.... And I think when they started day care they had some idea of what kids needed. That was not true in Edmonton.[6]

Alberta changed in dramatic ways in the fifteen years after the end of World War II. Not only did the population increase by over half a million people, but it also shifted from being predominantly rural to predominantly urban (table 3.1). Indeed, by 1961 a majority of Albertans lived in the province's five largest cities. Furthermore, between 1951 and 1961, the participation rate of married women in the labour force jumped from 10 percent to 26 percent. Much of the increased demand for child care in the latter half of the 1950s came from married women with young children.

Beginning in the mid-1950s and carrying over into the early 1960s, a great deal of investigation took place into the need for governmental involvement in day care in Edmonton. One study was initiated in 1956 by Alderman Lorette Douglas, who reported to city council that she had received a number of requests for the establishment of a day nursery in the south of the city (the existing creche was located in the downtown area on the north side of the North Saskatchewan River). This led to a study conducted by a special committee struck by the Council of Community Services that included Alderman Douglas. This committee made three recommendations in the fall of 1957. First, the existing creche could accommodate the demand from lone-parent families and from two-parent families facing "drastic economic circumstances." Second, the growing demand for day care from other two-parent families "could be met by commercially operated day nurseries—provided these establishments meet adequate standards set for their operation." And, third, the City of Edmonton should begin licensing any premise where even one child was being looked after for a fee, and the licensing requirements should "incorporate the standards of day care as laid down by the Child Welfare League of America." This last recommendation was never acted upon since the province, not the city, had licensing and regulatory authority.[7]

One of the most distinctive features of this era of day care politics in Alberta was the intense involvement of a number of groups of professional women. In addition to the University Women's Club, which made its first submission on day care to the provincial government in June 1958, two other such groups were active in Edmonton at this time. The Study Group on Family Welfare Services—led by Marg Norquay, a minister's wife who held an MA degree in sociology from the University of Toronto—conducted a study on day care in 1960.[8] A third group was based at St. Paul's United Church and led by Anne Lightfoot; among its accomplishments was the creation of a study guide on day care for United Church women's groups.

During these years, Sheila Campbell participated in all three Edmonton groups and also began her association with the Canadian Committee on Early Childhood. She offered the following explanation for the involvement of professional women in day care advocacy at that time:

> I think we felt some obligation to do something in the community. I think
> we wanted some interest outside the home. We were all of us at that time
> stay-at-home moms. I think we just had to have something else in your life,
> especially professional women. We'd all been doing professional things,
> then all of a sudden you're not doing them. This is a way to do something that's
> rather meaningful. Like there were also book groups for reading, but this is
> more meaningful. I think the University Women's Club itself had had an
> orientation towards that kind of activity, more meaningful kind of activity than
> bridge playing and so on.[9]

The University Women's Club's submission to the provincial government in 1958 was based upon a study of child care offered through advertisements in the Edmonton Journal. Until this time, the province had not enforced its requirement that facilities caring for four or more children be licensed, and, as a consequence, only one of the fifty-four businesses surveyed in 1958 held a license.[10] In 1959, in response to continued lobbying by the University Women's Club, the province promised to license all day nurseries and to investigate those that advertised child care services (Campbell 2001, 86). This is the main reason that the number of licensed day cares jumped from five in 1960 to twenty-nine in 1961 (table A.1).

In the autumn of 1960, the study group led by Marg Norquay "noticed a large increase in the number of advertisements for child care" in the Edmonton Journal. In a one-month period, they identified 165 unduplicated advertisements. They visited seventeen of the advertisers, but only eight were caring for children. The study group reported the following observations:

Only one of these had adequate indoor and outdoor play equipment. One had twenty children in a room 12 x 14. Another ... had babies lying on a bare floor, unattended, in a small empty room. Yet another had babies, blue with cold, in cribs without blankets.

The study group was particularly concerned that babies were being "cared for in numbers too large to permit any individualized care." In 1960 the group members followed what was then the conventional interpretation of John Bowlby's research on children institutionalized during World War II: "that it is essential for young children and babies under three years of age to have the constant and consistent mothering of one person, that the child recognizes as belonging specifically to him." Consequently, they concluded in a somewhat alarmist fashion, "It is not too much to suggest that many of the day nurseries in Edmonton may be producing the Mental Hospital patients and juvenile delinquents of tomorrow."[11]

By 1961 day care advocates had at least succeeded in getting the provincial government to assume its responsibility to regulate and monitor day cares and other facilities for young children (albeit not as thoroughly or conscientiously as the advocates would have liked). In 1960 the province hired a civil servant, Frances Ferguson, to take charge of the area, and in 1961 the first set of standards for day care was issued (Campbell 2001, 86). That same year, a law was passed that gave the province the power to revoke licenses and steps were taken to return responsibility for kindergartens to the Department of Education.[12] In

1963 more substantial standards for day cares were issued (Campbell 2001, 86), and the Welfare Homes and Institutions Branch of the Department of Public Welfare was established. At this time, the only qualification for staff was that they be "sympathetic to the children's welfare." The minimum staff-to-child ratios were set at one to twenty for children between two and seven years of age, and one to ten for children less than two years old.[13]

By 1961 the populations of Edmonton and Calgary were 321,000 and 276,000, respectively. In the province as a whole, approximately one-quarter of the population was under the age of ten years (table 3.1). With 77,000 married women in the Alberta labour force in 1961, and 23,000 lone-parent families, the care of young children had become an important social issue. In 1960 the Study Group on Family Welfare Services reported, "It has been estimated that at least one thousand preschool children and babies, whose parents are resident in Edmonton, are daily being cared for outside their own homes."[14] At this point, neither the provincial government nor municipal governments took steps toward establishing new day care centres or family day home (FDH) projects. Consequently, the opportunity arose for commercial day care centres to fill the gap and become well established in Alberta's two major cities.

There were twenty-six licensed day cares in Alberta in 1962 (table A.1). Eight of these centres were located in Edmonton, thirteen in Calgary, and five in other locales. The combined capacity of the twenty-six day cares was 521, for an average of twenty per centre.[15] The small aggregate capacity of the licensed centres suggests that the vast majority of families that required preschool care for young children were relying upon family members, friends, neighbours, small FDHs, or unlicensed day cares. The average centre size of twenty suggests that, since some of the licensed centres were home based, a few of these early commercial centres were larger businesses run on a capitalistic basis.

One of the large day care businesses in Calgary in the early 1960s was owned by Kay Wedel and her husband. Their first centre was Happy Times Day Nursery, located in southwest Calgary. Irmtraud Walter immigrated to Canada in 1960 after completing a two-year course in household, young children, and infants in Germany. She started to work for Kay Wedel at Happy Times Day Nursery that fall. The demand for preschool care in Calgary in the early 1960s was so strong that the Wedels decided to open a second facility. They purchased an old United Church and moved the building to a new foundation. Irmtraud Walter worked at the new facility, also located in southwest Calgary, from its opening in 1963 and remembers it having a licensed capacity for 119 children. It was called Fairyland

Kindergarten and Nursery School when it opened (later renamed Fairyland Day Care), and Walter recalls this huge centre being largely full at the time. One reason for its popularity was that Fairyland operated two vans that picked up children from their homes and later returned them. Irmtraud Walter did not like this aspect of the day care, however, since it meant that she rarely got the opportunity to meet the children's parents. She described Fairyland as a "children's factory" and commented that it was "too impersonal." Nevertheless, it was very profitable. The Wedels would later sell Fairyland so that they could devote more attention to a jewellery business and a fast-food outlet.[16]

THE EDMONTON CRECHE CRISIS SPARKS GOVERNMENT ACTION ON DAY CARE

During the 1940s, proponents of ECE had cast a critical eye at the quality of care offered at Alberta's only charitable day nursery, the Edmonton Creche. The intense study of day care standards and needs by Edmonton organizations in the late 1950s and early 1960s meant that the practices of the Creche were once again critically scrutinized, apparently with good reason. At a meeting of the Council of Community Services Day Care Committee in 1961, the president of the Creche Board, Mrs. H.H. Stephens, reported that while "at one time they did have a kindergarten teacher ... they found that she was no longer needed." She stated further, "There is also a television set for those who wish to watch it." It would seem that the program in 1961 was little changed from that in 1955 when "the children's day consisted of long periods of unstructured play, and routines such as washing, eating, and sleeping" (Prochner 2000, 57). It is little wonder that Stephens was asked at that committee meeting in 1961 "whether attention was paid to the emotional needs as well as the physical needs of the children."[17]

The Day Care Committee subsequently raised concerns about "the administration and operation of the Creche" with the executive committee of the Council of Community Services, and in March 1962, the executive committee struck "an exploratory committee" to investigate the concerns. The criticisms voiced by an anonymous source included a single staff member looking after thirty-three children, lack of equipment, over-regimentation of the children, and the failure to employ a social worker to assess the social needs of new applicants. While the exploratory committee issued a report that was quite supportive of the Creche, undoubtedly the Creche's volunteer board members and its staff felt extremely beleaguered during the investigation.[18]

On 31 March 1964, the Board of the Edmonton Creche Society made the shocking announcement that it intended to close the Creche in one month's time. (The board was later convinced to keep running the facility until the end of May.) "Why the sudden antagonism of this 34th Board of the Society to its child, reared over 34 years by 33 previous doting executives and society members?" asked an astute letter writer in the Edmonton Journal.[19] There are two complementary explanations. First, while in previous decades the members of the Creche Board had been held in high esteem for their volunteer contributions to a worthy charity, in the 1960s they had begun to be stigmatized because the Creche did not meet the expectations of those familiar with the best practices in early childhood education and care. In 1968 the Creche president, Mrs. Stephens, looked back at the 1964 decision and stated, "We just got fed up. We had all worked very hard and were getting nothing but abuse for our troubles."[20]

In 1964 Alberta was at the cusp of redefining how governments should be involved in day care. Although minimal regulatory standards were in place, critics versed in the literature on early childhood programs were questioning whether those standards were adequate. Furthermore, two questions about funding were firmly on the public agenda: Is it a provincial responsibility to fund day care services? If yes, how wide a cross-section of the population should benefit from financial subsidization? The Edmonton Creche had been established in 1930 on a charitable basis to provide custodial care of young children so that female lone parents could take on paid work. In 1964 the members of the Board of the Edmonton Creche were unwilling to rethink this dated and extremely restrictive view of which families deserved help with day care. Their statement justifying the closure assumed that when a husband was fully employed, a wife worked out of choice rather than out of necessity. Consequently, they rejected the notion of subsidized day care for the family with two working parents on the ground that such a "family is maintaining a higher standard of living at public expense." As far as their traditional clientele was concerned, the Creche Board argued that times had changed and there were now enough commercial centres to look after these children, although the government would have to subsidize this commercial care. In fact, the supply of spaces in licensed commercial centres was very limited in 1964 (see below). Furthermore, the Creche Board ignored the issue of whether commercial centres provided a quality of care worthy of public subsidization. Overall, the main justification for closing the Creche was that "the cost to the general public would be very materially reduced."[21]

The decision to close the Creche had three effects. First, it put the opponents of publicly funded day care on the defensive because the decision appeared to be so retrograde and small minded. Second, it promoted activism by both working mothers (in the form of a Save the Creche Committee) and community agencies in favour of day care.[22] And, third, it forced the provincial government to decide once and for all whether to become involved in funding day care, even if on a very restricted basis.

In April 1964, the Edmonton Welfare Council (EWC) surveyed the parents of the children then enrolled at the Creche and determined that there was a need for the day nursery to remain open. At the time, Edmonton had only six licensed commercial centres with a total capacity of 130. Since these centres were operating at approximately 90 percent of capacity, they were incapable of absorbing any more than a handful of the more than 120 children who attended the Creche. In light of this information, the EWC, the United Community Fund (UCF), and the City of Edmonton decided to keep the day care going. The day after the Creche's closure on 31 May, the Community Day Nursery (CDN) opened in the same city-owned location. The Creche Board had been invited to participate in this new day care but refused. Indeed, the animus of the Creche Board was so strong that it refused to allow the reopened facility to use the Creche name, refused to turn over its assets for use in day care, and even promised to remove $4,000 in equipment from the building before turning over possession.[23]

A new building was needed for the CDN, since the existing building would soon be destroyed as part of a downtown redevelopment project. In March 1965, the City of Edmonton, supported by the UCF and the EWC, asked provincial officials to contribute to the capital costs of a new facility and to the ongoing operations of the day care. The discussions with the provincial civil servants in the Department of Public Welfare went very well. By April, tentative agreements with Deputy Minister Duncan Rogers had been reached on cost-sharing programs for a new CDN. The executive director of the EWC, Stewart Bishop, "indicated that Mr. Roger's reaction was most favourable to day care as it fell within his concept of preventive programs in the public welfare field."[24]

Day care continued to be viewed with considerable suspicion by members of the Social Credit caucus; even with the deputy minister's strong support, the matter was not settled. The next step was a meeting between the provincial minister of Public Welfare, L.C. Halmrast, and a delegation from Edmonton that included Mayor Vince Dantzer and the chairs of the boards of the UCF and EWC. Minister Halmrast then took the request to the provincial cabinet, which, in early

June, agreed to help fund the CDN starting in the 1966–67 budget year (a full ten months down the road). The province committed to covering up to $25,000 in renovation costs and one-third of the yearly deficit up to a maximum of $8,000 (with the city and the UCF sharing the remaining two-thirds). Minister Halmrast had to reassure his colleagues about who would receive subsidization before the matter received cabinet approval.[25]

This was a historic decision because it marked the very first time that the Province of Alberta had agreed to subsidize a day care. Two aspects of the decision are particularly significant. First, even though funds for the CDN were committed prior to the introduction of the Preventive Social Service (PSS) program, it was the idea of day care as a preventive measure that won support from both provincial civil servants and cabinet ministers.[26] Second, even though by 1965 a significant minority of married Albertan women were in the paid labour force, Alberta's political leaders (most of them male) continued to be reluctant to introduce any public policy that could be construed as supporting this development. Indeed, the provincial political elites' beliefs about gender roles seem to have changed very little during the twenty years since the end of World War II.

The CDN relocated in April 1966 to new premises (an old garage, of all places—the former maintenance shop for the city's Building Maintenance Department). However, prior to the move—and even for a short time after the move—the CDN continued to be the Edmonton Creche in everything but name due to continuity in staff and child care philosophy. Just prior to the relocation, two studies of day care in Edmonton levelled criticisms at the quality of care in the CDN. The Day Care Planning Committee of the EWC stated, "The number of children enrolled must be reduced, group care for youngsters under age three must be discontinued and staffing must be up-graded." The Family Service Association (FSA) also criticized the CDN. When the Edmonton Journal reported these criticisms on 23 March 1966, the director of the CDN, Jessie Holmes, immediately resigned. She was a registered nurse and had held the director's position for four years. Her resignation gave the CDN an opportunity for a fresh start.[27]

Sheila Campbell was a member of the personnel committee of the Board of the CDN in 1966 and was instrumental in hiring the new director, Mary Hull, who served continuously in this position from August 1966 to March 2001, when the centre closed.[28] In 1966 Mary Hull was working in Edmonton at a school for the mentally challenged. A co-worker knew she had trained in preschool teaching in England (after growing up in Scotland) and pointed out the CDN job advertisement. Her hiring turned child care at the CDN, and throughout Edmonton, in a new direction. Sheila Campbell explained:

> Full credit to Mary Hull. She is the person who introduced into this city the
> concept of a play-oriented program. Nobody knew what it was before.... Day
> nurseries had been under matrons. They were nurses, they ran them like
> hospitals, they were sanitary, spotless. They ground up all the food and gave it
> to the kids ... so nobody would choke.... They were sterile environments. So
> Mary brought in the play. We all learned from Mary.[29]

Mary Hull, supported by a sympathetic board, was able to quickly improve the quality of the program at the CDN. Less than a year after her appointment, the FSA wrote, "The conditions and standards at the downtown Community Day Nursery have improved considerably and we feel that this is an important step in the development of quality day care in the city."[30] The Creche era was truly over.

BUILDING THE ANTI-WELFARE-STATE WELFARE STATE

On 1 July 1966, the *Preventive Social Services Act* came into effect in Alberta. This innovative piece of legislation specified that municipal governments had the option (but not the statutory responsibility) to establish preventive social services in the municipality. The services could be run by the municipality or by a not-for-profit organization. If the province approved a particular program, then it would cover 80 percent of the costs, with the municipality responsible for the remaining 20 percent. For many PSS programs, however, the provincial cost would only be 30 percent of the total because on 15 July 1966, a new federal cost-sharing program, the Canada Assistance Plan (CAP), took effect. It transformed how welfare services were funded in the country, with the federal government now paying 50 percent of the cost of approved programs.[31]

The PSS program was the brainchild of Duncan Rogers, who had been appointed deputy minister of Public Welfare in 1959. It was designed to mute opposition from both municipalities and Social Credit politicians to the centralization of statutory social services in Alberta. Shifting statutory programs from municipalities to the province created efficiencies of scale and meant that welfare services in a province did not vary due to place of residence. "In Alberta," however, "the trend towards takeover of municipal welfare functions had proceeded more slowly than in the rest of Canada" (Bella 1978, 154). In the early 1960s, municipal welfare departments in Alberta still administered important aspects of the child welfare system as well as social assistance for employable citizens. Rogers wanted the province to have exclusive responsibility for these two statutory programs.

Internal discussions of preventive services began in 1963 and, in November 1964, Rogers formally asked his minister, L.C. Halmrast, "for permission to begin planning for a takeover of existing municipal welfare programs, and for a program of preventive services" (letter quoted in Bella 1978, 172). The provincial cabinet gave preliminary approval to the plan, and Rogers wrote on 3 March 1965 that "the Department is now committed by the Minister to some action aimed at preventing the dependence on welfare and the deterioration of family life" (173).

To ensure that municipal welfare departments would not organize against his plan, Duncan Rogers held discussions with municipal civil servants in early 1965 (Bella 1978, 59n13). Keith Wass, superintendent of Edmonton's Welfare Department at the time, recollected that the proposed new division of labour between municipalities and the province was justified by Rogers in these terms: "Now the municipalities are going to provide a preventive, meaningful role, and we'll pick up the pieces when things break up and so on at the provincial level."[32]

As a senior civil servant, Duncan Rogers was very familiar with the ideology of Social Credit politicians in Alberta and why they were uncomfortable with centralizing all child welfare and social assistance services in the province. "The Social Credit government's reluctance to take over municipal programs," writes Leslie Bella, "was due to their traditional concern for preventing the development of a welfare state, and their longstanding emphasis on municipal autonomy. Social Crediters considered big governments to be evil, and equated the growth and centralization of government with the welfare state, with socialism and with loss of freedom." The two main features of the PSS program were prevention and municipal responsibility, and both features appealed to the Social Credit world view. Prevention promised to lower the caseloads in statutory welfare programs over the long term, and municipal responsibility for preventive programs promised to counterbalance the increasing social welfare activities of the federal and provincial governments. The virtues of the new PSS program, however, were not enough to overcome reservations in the Social Credit cabinet about the growth of the provincial role in social welfare. As a consequence, to appease cabinet opponents, Rogers was forced to develop a revised proposal whereby the province would take over all child welfare functions but municipalities would retain responsibility for providing social assistance to employable residents (Bella 1978, 224, 239).

It was relatively easy for municipal governments and the provincial cabinet to support the new PSS program since so much new money was available to each level of government. The municipal windfall was due to municipalities' diminished financial responsibility for the social assistance program and the complete end of their responsibility for child welfare. "There were opportunities, within the municipal welfare budget," notes Leslie Bella, "for major program increases without increased burden to the municipal taxpayers" (1978, 112). The provincial windfall occurred because, during the negotiations concerning the terms of the CAP, the federal government agreed to share the costs of many existing programs like child welfare that were formerly funded solely by the provinces (103n124, 140).

It is indubitably the case that Social Credit politicians saw the PSS program as an antidote to the socialistic welfare state they so loathed. Al Hagan moved to Calgary from Saskatchewan in the spring of 1969 to become the city's first day care counsellor. He recollected that Social Credit cabinet ministers "were enthusiastic supporters of the PSS program. I couldn't say that they were particularly supportive of day care because there was that sort of old ethic, women should stay at home, and it was kind of wrong to encourage women to be out of the home working."[33] This hesitation toward day care existed even though Duncan Rogers had listed day care as an example of a possible PSS program as early as 1964 (Bella 1978, 214). Minister Halmrast came around to supporting public investment in day care because it would allow a single mother to get a paid job to support her children rather than be solely dependent on welfare (Bella 1978, 218). This indicates that Halmrast and other Social Credit political leaders in Alberta in the 1960s supported funding day care as a preventive service only to decrease welfare caseloads and costs. As Leslie Bella puts it, "Both day care and welfare were evils to many Social Creditors, but day care was a lesser evil" (1978, 147).

In trying to enforce this narrow view of provincially funded day care, however, Minister Halmrast and his colleagues faced two insurmountable problems inherent in the PSS program. First, "preventive" is a flexible concept with many different meanings. Consequently, the narrow definition of preventive day care preferred by the Social Credit cabinet in 1966 was open to challenge, particularly from social workers employed by municipal governments who were versed in the professional literature on preventive programs. For instance, the Social Service Department of the City of Edmonton chose to define preventive services in broad terms as "promoting sound general social health, and with the avoidance of specific social problems."[34]

John Lackey was hired as a social worker by the Province of Alberta in 1961. In 1974 he became the second provincial director of the PSS program. He offered the following insight into the variable definitions of prevention among those who supported the PSS program:

> The interesting thing about Preventive Social Services is that it fit most ideological viewpoints, or you could make it fit most ideological viewpoints. The conservative value that people need to be responsible for themselves and help themselves and pull themselves up by their bootstraps, that's what PSS was. It was local people making their own decision to help themselves, [make] them strong before they get into further trouble, be independent and all that, good fit. It just as easily fit the liberal or socialistic viewpoint because it's a capacity to provide services to people and support to people. So it cut right across the political spectrum.[35]

Second, by giving municipalities the responsibility for initiating PSS projects, the provincial government created a dynamic in which it was under constant pressure to improve existing preventive social services and introduce new ones, if not from one municipality, then from the next. In the mid-1960s, municipal welfare departments in Alberta employed a number of highly qualified social workers in key positions. As a result, municipal expertise in social work far exceeded provincial expertise. Furthermore, these municipal civil servants saw themselves as having a professional responsibility to advocate for the rights of citizens to high-quality social services. In this regard, Al Hagan observed: "PSS legislation carried with it a very strong mandate for and expectation about advocacy. And you didn't want to work for Sam Blakely [the director of Calgary's Social Service Department] if you weren't an advocate for, in this case, children and early intervention."[36]

An additional perspective on the significance of municipal initiative was provided by Howard Clifford, who became Edmonton's first day care director in February 1967. Clifford came to the job with a Master of Social Work degree and the conviction that social programs should be universally available to people. Nevertheless, over time he came to be a strong supporter of the way the PSS program allowed municipalities to take the lead in establishing high-quality day cares in Alberta. It is highly unlikely that Minister Halmrast and his Social Credit colleagues anticipated the way that demands for provincial government regulation of and spending on day care would be magnified by the powers given to municipalities by the PSS Act. "I saw the Preventive Social Service program as a really excellent one," stated Howard Clifford in 1996,

> but was probably not as thrilled about it as I would have been now looking back on it.... The problem with municipal involvement is that if you've got a good, progressive municipality you have really good things, if you have a poor one you have nothing. So the discrepancies across the board are really bothersome. And if you're a universalist ... then why would I argue for this kind of thing rather than a provincial program? But my problem with provincial programs, and this comes out of that experience actually, was that it usually becomes the lowest common denominator that is acceptable to the majority. Whereas if you get a progressive one then you're ahead of everyone else, and that puts leadership pressure on others to accomplish it. I don't think Calgary would have ever come up with what they did if Edmonton didn't have that first one, and Medicine Hat either, and Grande Prairie either.[37]

In passing the PSS Act in 1966, the Social Credit government thought it was on the road to building an alternative to the pernicious welfare state being created in other places in Canada. Ironically, those elements of the PSS Act that were supposed to be anti-welfare state (a preventive focus and municipal responsibility for program initiation) promoted the establishment of day cares throughout Alberta that were exemplars for the Canadian welfare state in the late 1960s and 1970s.

A STRONG MOVEMENT FOR QUALITY DAY CARE IN EDMONTON FORCES THE PROVINCE TO ACCEDE

The decision to close the Edmonton Creche in 1964 turned out to be a propitious turn of events for the development of quality day care in that city. It brought considerable public attention to day care and caused both the city government and social service organizations to undertake fresh assessments of the need for day care. As a consequence, when the PSS Act took effect in mid-1966, Edmonton already had a plan in place for how it wanted to use PSS funds to expand quality day care services.

The EWC took the lead in planning. It produced a position paper on day care in July 1964 and struck a Day Care Planning Committee in September 1964. The planning committee was not very active over the next eight months while the long-term future of the CDN was the focus of the efforts of the city, the EWC, and the UCF. However, in April 1965, the committee dedicated itself to studying "the need for day care services of employed mothers in Edmonton." Its report was presented to the Board of the EWC in December 1965.[38]

The conclusions of the report were based upon a survey of 512 employed women with children aged five years or less. Based upon the survey results, the planning committee estimated that there were 7,110 preschool children who required care while their mothers were at work. In May 1965, only 379 licensed spaces were available in day cares in Edmonton, meaning that "for every 20 preschool aged youngsters whose mothers work, licensed accommodation is available for one child." The committee concluded that more community day cares were needed in Edmonton and recommended that the first priority should be the establishment of "an experimental community group day care facility in the suburban ring of the City." It is noteworthy that, like the advocates for wartime day nurseries in Alberta, the planning committee felt compelled to address the dominant societal belief that mothers of young children should not work outside the home. The committee appealed to pragmatism and echoed the argument made by the University Women's Club of Calgary in 1943: "The over-riding question confronting Edmonton today is not whether mothers of young children *should* work—in fact they are, and in increasing numbers—but rather that child care arrangements are required to serve adequately the children of employed mothers."[39]

While significant in its own right, this report was doubly significant because it sparked an important series of investigative reports in the *Edmonton Journal* by Karen Harding. Harding and fellow reporter Catherine Carson interviewed the members of the Day Care Planning Committee on 20 December 1965. This led to a story by Harding in the paper's Family section that echoed the information and conclusions of the planning committee. A follow-up story the next day contrasted the "custodial care" that was the standard in commercial day care in Edmonton with the elements of a quality program of care. For these two articles, Karen Harding had visited a number of Edmonton's commercial day cares, and she reported that the treatment of the children in these centres was wanting. She concluded her second article by quoting Marjorie Bowker, an Edmonton lawyer who would soon thereafter be appointed as a juvenile and family court judge. In arguing for "much higher standards" in day cares, Bowker deployed the familiar pragmatic rationale to try and disarm opposition from those who objected to mothers working outside the home: "Whether we approve in principle of working mothers or not, the trend in this direction will not be reversed by ignoring the plight of the children involved."[40]

Harding's two stories were modest in scope and length, but they were noteworthy because they involved independent investigative reporting on commercial day cares and were written to support the push for more high-quality community day cares in the city. Indeed, the stories established the Edmonton Journal as one of the leading advocates for quality day care in the province. The paper continued to demonstrate its editorial commitment to the issue by flying Karen Harding to Toronto to observe what occurred in that city's subsidized day cares. Her subsequent report highlighted the superiority of the care in Toronto's subsidized centres compared to that in Edmonton's centres, including the CDN.[41]

One of the unusual features of the day care politics in Edmonton in 1966 was an intense rivalry between the FSA of Edmonton and the Welfare Department of the City of Edmonton (supported by the EWC) over who should take charge of the development of new community day cares in Edmonton. Since both organizations favoured high-quality day cares, the rivalry served to reinforce this position in public discourse. For instance, in March 1966, the FSA released its own study of the need for day care in Edmonton as a rejoinder to the EWC study released the previous December. The FSA study featured a survey of the child care arrangements and needs of the employees of the Great Western Garment Company, which then employed over twelve hundred women. The FSA study reported that the company had a turnover of 157 percent in 1965. "A large proportion" of the turnover was attributed to the employees not earning enough to pay for reliable babysitters and being forced to quit when an unreliable babysitter let them down. Disruptions in child care arrangements were also estimated to cause hundreds of hours of absenteeism every week. A survey of employees resulted in the conclusion that there was enough demand to locate a new day care centre near the plant.[42]

On 4 July 1966, the commissioners of the City of Edmonton (two civil servants and Mayor Vince Dantzer) recommended "the establishment of day care as a priority preventive social service to be developed at both the private and public levels." They further recommended that the initiative be led by the city, not the FSA, and that the city immediately hire a director of day care. Significantly, besides being responsible for policy, administration, planning, inspection, and staff training, the director was to engage in "public education on day care generally." As a concession to the opponents of public funding of day care, the commissioners added, "In part this would be aimed at encouraging mothers to stay home with preschool children."[43]

The movement for quality child care in Edmonton was relatively strong at this point, and a second not-for-profit day care, the O'Connell Institute, opened in August 1966. It was initially operated by the Sisters of Our Lady of Charity with the support of the UCF. The following summer, it was reorganized on a nonsectarian basis, renamed Primrose Place Day Care, and given funding through the PSS program. Primrose Place's director was Ellen Derksen, a social worker who at that time simultaneously served as the chair of the admissions committee at the CDN.[44]

In the fall of 1966, the city placed advertisements across Canada for a director of day care, but these advertisements "failed to bring suitable candidates" because of "the shortage of personnel in this field."[45] The position was only filled after Keith Wass convinced Howard Clifford, over a couple of lunch meetings, to take the job. Clifford, who like Wass held an MSW degree, was then the director of social services for the psychiatric hospital in Edmonton. While in this position, he had begun experimenting with the use of FDHs to ease the child care burden on mothers who were leaving the hospital and returning to their families. Nevertheless, he had reservations about accepting the job when first approached by Wass. "Even I was going through a transition in my thinking," Clifford observed. "It [day care] still seemed a bit like glorified babysitting, and did I really want to do that? And it was female-dominated ... and all those things." He went on to point out that such attitudes were "still with us somewhat today but not like it was then." Eventually he decided to accept the position, but only if he could use his first few months to learn more about day care by reading and visiting different jurisdictions. Wass agreed, and Clifford started as Edmonton's first day care director on 1 February 1967. He travelled as far afield as the United States to learn more about day care.[46]

In 1966 the commissioners had recommended that the Social Service Department (the renamed Welfare Department) establish an advisory committee to "work closely with the director of day care." Howard Clifford played an active role in recruiting the members of the advisory committee in the early part of 1967. Its members included Dr. Jean Nelson, a pediatrician who later served as

Alberta's deputy minister of Community Health. The advisory committee's first chair was Bruce Ryan, who had met Clifford when they both worked at the psychiatric hospital in Edmonton. "The committee gave Howard more confidence in his position," commented Ryan. "He could say there was an advisory committee recommending this course of action."[47]

Howard Clifford quickly became the public face of day care in Edmonton. "It's hard now to remember just how much pressure we were under all the time by the public that this was a bad thing somehow," he noted in 1996. "I used to say it as a joke, but there's a lot of truth to the joke, that when somebody came up to me and said, 'Mr. Day Care,' I didn't know whether to shake hands or duck. You hardly ever found neutral people.... Mainly it was either 'Right on' or 'You son-of-a-gun' sort of thing."[48]

One of Howard Clifford's first acts as director was to adopt the Child Welfare League of America's recommended day care standards as the City of Edmonton's minimum standards. They were much higher than the province's minimum standards for licensing. This had an unintended consequence in the spring of 1967 at the CDN, which had by then been officially designated as a PSS project (and hence made subject to the standards set by the city). The Board of the CDN determined that implementing the city's new minimum standards had raised the full cost of day care to $3.50 per day from its previous $2.50. It decided to start charging the full fee to unsubsidized parents in July 1967. The new fee was almost double the fee of commercial centres, and, if it had been implemented, it would have driven many of the children from full-fee-paying families out of the CDN. Most of these children came from two-parent families where both parents were working. Ellen Derksen commented at the time, "Except in the most exceptional circumstances, we do not feel that we can take children where both parents are working. We feel that most of these parents can afford to make other arrangements."

The stand of the CDN Board on this matter angered the parents who were confronted by the 40 percent increase in fees. At that time, expenses like mortgage costs or student loans were not deducted from income when calculating what a family could afford for day care. It is little wonder that one of the CDN parents complained to city council about the fee increase, and militantly commented, "We didn't fight for the Creche for this to happen." The matter was mediated by Keith Wass and Howard Clifford, who ensured that the actual fee that was charged was less than the cost of the service. They did so in order to ensure that the PSS day care program would have a universal character rather than serve only as a welfare service.[49]

On the provincial side of the PSS program, L.C. Halmrast remained the responsible minister until his retirement from provincial politics after the general election of 23 May 1967. Until then, the province had accepted all three of Edmonton's proposed PSS projects in the day care field: the hiring of a municipal day care director, the conversion of the CDN to a PSS project, and a flexible program that allowed for subsidizing care in FDHs for children under three and subsidizing care of children in not-for-profit day cares that were non-sectarian (such as Primrose Place).[50]

One of the central recommendations of the city commissioners in July 1966 had been to establish a pilot day care in a suburban neighbourhood with an accompanying FDH project. In 1967 the city had plans to build recreational centres in three different suburban neighbourhoods. Among the tasks of Howard Clifford and his advisory committee at that time was to determine in which of these recreational centres it would be best to incorporate the day care. On 26 June, city council accepted the recommendation of the Social Service Department that the day care be included in the Glengarry recreation centre in northeast Edmonton. A formal proposal to treat this new day care as a PSS project was then submitted to the province.[51]

At this point, an old-style Social Credit ideologue made a last stand against day care. After the 23 May election, Premier Manning appointed Alf Hooke, "the most rabid of all antisocialist Social Crediters," as the minister of Public Welfare. Leslie Bella argues that the premier himself had reservations about the PSS program, since he had cautioned L.C. Halmrast in 1966 against going "all out on it." Manning may therefore have appointed Hooke because there was no one better in his caucus to constrain the growth of the PSS program (1978, 227, 243).

In October 1967, the city received word that the province would not approve the pilot Glengarry day care as a PSS project—and would thus not share in its construction and operating costs. Minister Hooke told the *Edmonton Journal* that full-scale, government-supported day care programs "are for the birds," and the paper ran the story with an eye-catching headline. Demonstrating his ignorance of the philosophy of PSS day care, he remarked, "There are a lot better places the government can put its money than into babysitting services." The minister also indicated that he'd rather pay needy mothers to stay at home with their children than support day care centres, thus demonstrating that his opposition had a strong ideological element. Hooke added that day care for those who choose to work rather than stay at home with their children "can be left to private enterprise." He also echoed Ernest Manning's caution against going "all out on it" when he stated his opposition to a "gigantic wide-open" day care program.[52]

Howard Clifford thought that if Minister Hooke "had of played it smart, which wasn't his style," and used a financial argument in October 1967 to explain why he turned down Glengarry, "we would have been dead because the public didn't know what it was all about." Hooke's candid justification, however, "was of more assistance to us than anything we could have done."

Minister Hooke's decision and accompanying comments set off a storm of protest. *Edmonton Journal* reporter Catherine Carson published a series of articles that supported the movement for quality day care. Letters opposed to Minister Hooke's position flooded into the premier's office; the writers included eight women's organizations, three church groups, three non-profit social service agencies, two community groups, and thirty-four citizens, including six citizens I would classify as prominent (for example, Judge Marjorie Bowker). In contrast, only four submissions supported Mr. Hooke's stand, two of which came from Edmonton's Day Nursery Association (commercial operators) and its most outspoken member, Hilde Bloedow.

The letters to Ernest Manning that supported PSS funding for day care included a wide range of arguments. Some of these arguments were very well constructed but would not have received much sympathy from the premier because they contradicted his Social Credit ideology. For example, Catherine Sam wrote to support subsidized day care for children like her own: she had been a working mother over the past several years because her income was necessary while her husband completed medical school. Other arguments, however, would have drawn keen attention from the premier. Of particular note were powerful letters from two women, one separated from an alcoholic husband and the other from an abusive husband, and a very thorough statement by a Social Credit supporter, N. E. Olson, on why providing funds for the Glengarry day care was "consistent with the philosophy and the aims we want to support."[53]

Howard Clifford related the following story of how the Glengarry Day Care controversy was eventually resolved. After weeks of public commentary, Premier Manning called a meeting to discuss the matter. Keith Wass attended.

In Keith's recollection of that meeting ... it wasn't going really well, it's almost like a communist plot to break up the family, but he said what turned things around, and it was Keith that turned it around, and it was just a stroke of luck, actually of timing.... Keith made the statement, "Well, one of the things we don't want to do, Mr. Premier, is have kids sitting down all day long watching television." And apparently Manning had just been in some kind of a kerfuffle with the CBC.... That turned the conversation around.[54]

The meeting with Premier Manning resulted in the striking of two new committees. Until then, the minister of Public Welfare had had unchecked authority for approving or denying a PSS application. The two new committees diluted that authority. One comprised civil servants from four different provincial government departments; it was charged with reviewing all PSS proposals and making recommendations on their appropriateness. The second new committee, composed of two representatives from the Department of Public Welfare and two from the City of Edmonton (Wass and Clifford), was to review and make a recommendation on the Glengarry Day Care proposal. It had made a favourable recommendation by early March 1968.[55]

The official announcement that the Glengarry Day Care had been accepted as a PSS project was not made until May, but by that time approval was a foregone conclusion. The vigorous protest against Minister Hooke's original decision had convinced most Social Credit leaders, including Premier Manning, of the folly of trying to block municipal day care initiatives. While the movement for quality day care in Edmonton was relatively strong at that time, its efficacy was bolstered by the changing politics of the province. In the 23 May 1967 provincial election, the Social Credit share of the popular vote had fallen to 45 percent compared to 55 percent in 1963, and the Progressive Conservatives had emerged as the major opposition party with 26 percent of the vote and members elected in both Edmonton (three) and Calgary (three). In Edmonton, the Social Credit League had managed to win eight of the eleven constituencies but was badly out-polled by the combined opposition parties in all constituencies, except for the premier's own constituency (Chief Electoral Officer 1983, 92–97). Recognizing the seriousness of the Progressive Conservative challenge to its more than thirty years in power, the Social Credit government began to take urban social movements seriously in the late 1960s. Day care was a beneficiary of this renewed party competition in the province. The unusual political dynamics of this situation were demonstrated in the legislature in the fall of 1968, when the Progressive Conservatives put forward a resolution that called for more government assistance to day care centres. The Social Creditors voted in favour of the motion.[56]

TWO VISIONS FOR DAY CARE IN EDMONTON:
HOWARD CLIFFORD VS. HILDE BLOEDOW

In his first few months as Edmonton's day care director, Howard Clifford had to determine the role, if any, that commercial centres would have in the city's plans for subsidized day care. In Edmonton, the number of commercial centres increased from six in the spring of 1964 (with a licensed capacity for 130 children) to eighteen in the fall of 1967 (with a licensed capacity for 483). Among the new centres was Hilde's Day Nursery, opened in 1965 by Hilde Bloedow. When Howard Clifford began working for the city, Bloedow was the most outspoken member of the Edmonton Day Nursery Association. The association argued that governments should subsidize parents, not centres, and that parents with subsidies should be allowed to "send their children to any licensed Day Care Centre, or home, of their choice."[57]

Howard Clifford recalled that many people at the time liked this proposal, and he himself at first thought it "sounded really quite good." But his support for the proposal waned when he discovered that, contrary to Hilde Bloedow's contention, the quality of care in many of the commercial day cares in Edmonton was abysmal.

The *Edmonton Journal* published a piece by Hilde Bloedow in the summer of 1967 that defended the quality of care in commercial day nurseries. In material submitted to the premier a few months later, Bloedow specifically trumpeted the educational qualifications of the staff at her centre: "I myself have had kindergarten training in Germany, my helper has a teacher certificate, and so have many other day nursery operators a good education in business or otherwise."[58] These sorts of claims caused Howard Clifford, sometime during his first few months on the job, to ask Bruce Ryan (the advisory committee chair) to accompany him on a visit to Hilde's Day Nursery so that they could make first-hand observations of the quality of care. Clifford related his experience:

So we go out there and knock on the door and this old elderly lady, I think about seventy-two, answered the door, and we asked for Hilde, "Oh, she's out shopping." "Can we come in and wait for her?" There's a big hesitation before she allowed us to come in. In the basement there were a number of children sleeping on the floor with cots and these other older kids are all at a table, quiet as mice. And the only staff was this elderly person.

As Sheila Campbell later put it, Hilde Bloedow ran "a terrible day care.... But she was certainly a thorn in everybody's side because she thought she was so good."[59]

Within a short time of interacting with Edmonton's commercial operators, Howard Clifford came to reject the idea of subsidizing children to attend their centres. To illustrate how bad things were in these centres, he told the following story, which he had heard from Sheila Campbell. Clifford had asked Campbell and Ellen Derksen to attend the meetings of the Edmonton Day Nursery Association. The meeting in question featured a presentation on first aid. Campbell reported that the discussion soon moved to managing children, since commercial operators "didn't know how to manage, they had real problems with managing kids." One operator asked, "So what do you do with a really difficult kid?" Another operator replied, "Well, I know what you do. You hold their head in the toilet and you flush the toilet and you never have any more trouble." Sheila Campbell remembered that nobody in the room spoke up to challenge the appropriateness of this action. She and Ellen Derksen refused to attend the association's meetings after this episode.[60]

Hilde Bloedow is an interesting figure in the history of day care in Alberta because, although she ran a commercial day care, she had a very negative impression of many of the parents who put their children into day cares. With this view of her clientele, why did she go into the business? The answer seems to be that operating a day care was not her preferred line of work but was chosen when other lines of work were closed to her because she was a middle-aged woman. Hilde Bloedow accepted the male breadwinner norm and argued that subsidizing day care so that women could earn a second income for a family "is unjust ... toward the High School Graduates who can't find a job because they are taken by working mothers who want to have a second paycheck coming in." Furthermore, she argued that two-parent families should not be given a subsidy for day care because it encouraged irresponsible financial behaviour or at least rewarded such behaviour.[61]

In line with her negative view of the decision by mothers in two-parent families to place their children in day care, Bloedow blamed those same mothers for deficiencies in the quality of care. "There are a majority of working mothers who have a husband with a good paying job, a high percentage of them reluctant to pay more that $1.50 per day for one child for day care," she stated in 1967. "Those mothers have just the physical part of their children in mind, and it is very difficult to reach and convert their materialistic minds." In another passage, Hilde Bloedow's criticism of some of these working mothers with a working husband was even harsher. "Mothers who cannot stand their children are calling for public preventive child welfare," she averred, "so as to unload their own private responsibility."[62]

Given that "materialistic" mothers would have constituted a significant proportion of the clientele of Hilde's Day Nursery, one can only wonder how Bloedow's views affected her relations with such mothers and their children. As in Julia Wrigley's (1999) research on nannies in large U.S. cities, this example demonstrates that the values of a child care provider can be dramatically at odds with the values of the parents whose child is in care.

In Howard Clifford's view, the opponents of PSS day cares, such as Hilde Bloedow, had greater public support at this time than the proponents. "My belief was that if you'd asked the public to take a vote on day care," he commented in 1996, "we'd have lost every time. But it's just that fortunately we had a lot of good key citizens who believed in it and kept it going." The movement for quality day care was also helped by the fact that there were only eighteen commercial day cares in Edmonton in 1967, making the Edmonton Day Nursery Association a relatively weak pressure group, and by Hilde Bloedow's rhetorical excesses, which probably made some individuals hesitate to support her even when they agreed with her position.

Howard Clifford estimated that he put two-thirds of his working time into education and lobbying efforts. For example, in 1967 there were not yet any college-level courses in early childhood education (ECE) in Alberta, so that autumn, Clifford organized a series of ten weekly educational lectures on day care at the University of Alberta. The next year, he made eighty-four speeches to different groups. Many of his engagements were in Edmonton, but he also accepted invitations to speak throughout Alberta and, in this way, influenced the development of day care in other municipalities. He recalled that he would only turn down a speaking request if a bigger and more influential group wanted him to speak at the same time.[63]

EARLY DEVELOPMENTS IN OTHER CITIES

Other Alberta cities soon followed Edmonton in using the new PSS program to fund day cares. In the late 1960s, the baby boom was over and the number of preschoolers in the province was in sharp decline (table 3.1). At the same time, the participation of married women in the paid labour force continued to grow very rapidly. In 1961 there had been 77,000 married women in Alberta's labour force (a 26 percent participation rate) while in 1971 there were 157,000 (a 43 percent participation rate). Furthermore, changes in the law meant that the divorce rate more than doubled between 1966 and 1971, contributing to an increase by 7,000 in the number of lone-parent families (table 3.1). In light of these changes, new demands for public investments in day care were voiced for the first time in small Alberta cities as well as the two large metropolises.

Medicine Hat was the first of the other cities to establish a PSS day care. In 1961 the city's Council of Social Services had commissioned a survey to determine the need for day care. The survey did not reveal a very strong demand, and no action was taken toward establishing a publicly funded day care. Furthermore, although demand grew during the 1960s, it remained modest compared to Calgary and Edmonton, as evidenced by the fact that no licensed commercial centres were established in Medicine Hat prior to late 1968.

The City of Medicine Hat appointed John Millar as its PSS director in September 1966, and on 25 April 1967, he "detailed a proposal for the establishment of a day care project." The province approved the proposal in May 1968, the same month that Edmonton's controversial Glengarry Day Care was formally approved. In September 1969, the Medicine Hat Day Care, formally controlled by a volunteer board of directors, opened in five rooms of a public school. During its first four months of operation, the new day care enrolled 61 different children at one time or another. Significantly, the opening of this PSS project apparently forced the city's one and only commercial centre to close, and the city would not see another commercial day care for over a decade.[64]

In 1966 Lethbridge was the largest of Alberta's small cities with a population of 37,000. It was quick to take advantage of the new PSS program, and by 31 March 1968, Lethbridge had five projects approved by the province compared to three each for Red Deer and Medicine Hat (Bella 1978, 79). One of these projects was a day care study, and in 1969 the city submitted a proposal to the province to establish a PSS day care. Because Lethbridge was larger than Medicine Hat, there had been more demand for day care in the mid-1960s and at least two commercial day cares had opened by 1969. The owners of these centres vigorously objected to the prospect of government-subsidized day cares. Of course, the same objections were voiced by the more numerous commercial operators in Edmonton and Calgary at about the same time. However, unlike the two large cities, Lethbridge did not have municipal civil servants who would champion day care in the face of such opposition. Indeed, the city's first PSS director, Bill

Kergan, personally favoured commercial day care. Furthermore, religious conservatives were relatively numerous in Lethbridge—8.7 percent of the population of Lethbridge was Mormon in 1971, compared to only 1.9 percent of the entire population of Alberta (Bella and Bozak 1980, 6). Religious conservatives were among those who believed that mothers should stay home to look after their children, thus making day care superfluous. In combination, the opponents were sufficiently strong relative to the proponents that the Social Credit minister of Social Development, Ray Speaker, decided "to withhold the provincial approval until the conflict had been resolved" (Bella and Bozak 1980, 15, 32–33). Speaker was particularly attentive to the conservative opponents of day care since he himself was from southern Alberta and represented the large rural constituency of Little Bow, which started just north of Lethbridge. The numerous conservative voters in the south of the province were the heart of Social Credit support. Indeed, in losing the 1971 provincial election, the Social Credit League still won all eleven constituencies south of Calgary but only fourteen of the remaining sixty-four constituencies (Chief Electoral Officer 1983, 101–6).

Calgary was the other city where the PSS program instigated interesting developments in day care in the 1960s. Just prior to the PSS era, the first not-for-profit day care opened in Calgary, supported by the Catholic Church and the UCF. The Providence Day Care Centre was established in March 1966 as a new program in a complex of social services that had been operated by the Sisters of Charity of Providence since 1958. The Providence Day Care was committed to quality care of young children, which is why Karen Harding stated it "could be an example for all future Alberta day nurseries." The Sister Superior of the Order emphasized that "day care, to be effective, must have a training and educational basis—not just provide babysitting services." The Providence Day Care was reorganized on a non-sectarian basis in December 1967 and thereafter became the first PSS day care in Calgary, licensed for seventy children.[65]

Prior to this development, however, the province had approved PSS funding for a study of day care in Calgary. In the years prior to 1966, Calgary's Social Planning Council had been asked to study the need for day care "on numerous occasions." The group decided to initiate such a study in the wake of the new funding opportunities in the PSS Act (Brouwer and McDiarmid 1970, 5). The research was directed by Barbara Scott, who had previously worked for the EWC as the staff support person for its Day Care Planning Committee.[66] Once the research was underway, the city successfully applied to the province to fund it as a PSS project. Completed in June 1967, the study found "that there were about 9,000 preschool aged children in Calgary whose mothers work, while there were only licensed day nursery spaces available for approximately 732 preschool aged children."[67]

Based upon this research, in September 1967, the Day Care Committee of the Social Planning Council issued a set of recommendations. Most importantly, it advised the city to establish "a model day care service at standards approximating those of the Child Welfare League of America ... in a neighbourhood in need of, and demanding, day care services."[68]

The city itself was relatively slow in responding to the recommendations. It decided its first move would be to hire a day care counsellor, and in July 1968 it applied to the province for PSS funding for the position. Al Hagan did not take up his duties as the first counsellor until the following April, but, in the meantime, two very different sorts of community initiatives on day care sprung up.

The first was a grassroots initiative in the working-class communities of Bowness and Montgomery in northwest Calgary. It began in early 1968 when Barb Scott convinced Phil Lalonde, a community organizer with the Company of Young Canadians, to start "organizing the community around the issue of day care." When he accepted the challenge, she gave him the addresses of the fifty local residents who had been identified as interested in day care in the Social Planning Council survey of 1967.

The Company of Young Canadians had been created by the federal government in 1966. Its members were committed to organizing communities to pursue social change (Hamilton 1970). Bowness was one of the poorest areas of Calgary, and Lalonde was assigned to work there starting in the summer of 1967. During his first six months in Bowness, "he became pretty well known in the community" and helped to mobilize a group of immigrant parents to demand a kindergarten so that their children could better learn English before starting grade one. The demand was rejected by local school authorities, so Lalonde was looking for a new project when Scott convinced him to organize around day care. In keeping with the philosophy of the Company of Young Canadians, over the next year, Phil Lalonde talked "about day care as a community development project" (Brouwer and McDiarmid 1970, 8–9).

Phil Lalonde first gathered interested residents together at informal coffee parties. He also organized public meetings held on 13 and 28 March 1968, doing the "fancy leg work" such as ensuring that a number of invitations were delivered and posters were placed in schools and stores. The attendees at the 28 March meeting decided to develop a proposal for a day care using widespread community input: a number of subcommittees were struck, each charged with researching and writing a section of the proposal. Since this approach required the participation of more than the twenty residents in attendance, Lalonde, with the assistance of other members of the Company of Young Canadians, agreed to contact other interested residents and ask them to serve on the subcommittees. As the work proceeded in the spring of 1968, Phil Lalonde could be counted on to serve as a resource person for each subcommittee. For instance, he helped the admissions committee to get community feedback on its tentative ideas (Brouwer and McDiarmid 1970, 10–14). Later he assisted the whole group when it started holding regular meetings in May to discuss the work of the subcommittees. Evidently, a great deal of work was accomplished in a short time since a formal proposal "for a community day care centre in Bowness-Montgomery" was submitted to the city's Social Services Committee in June. The following month, an interim board of directors of the Bowness-Montgomery Day Care Association (B-MDCA) was appointed. Furthermore, in September 1968, a door-to-door canvas was organized to confirm community support for the day care and increase the membership of the B-MDCA.[69]

The association assumed responsibility for all aspects of the proposed day care, including finding a suitable location. After a couple of possibilities fell through, it secured the right to use the closed Bowness Public School, with the public school board agreeing to a rent of $1 per year (Brouwer and McDiarmid 1970, 16).

The second community initiative in 1968 involved the sorts of charitable women's organizations that had shown concern about day care for young children in Calgary as far back as World War II. On 24 May 1968, six such organizations held an inaugural meeting to begin organizing a proposal for a model day care. The organizations included the University Women's Club, the Local Council of Women, the National Council of Jewish Women, and the Junior League. They submitted a proposal for a Model Day Care (MDC) to the city in July; it was rejected "because their demands were too high" (Brouwer and McDiarmid 1970, 19), they lacked community support, and they did not have a building for a day care.

For the remainder of 1968, the Board of the Model Day Care resisted considering a merger with the B-MDCA even though this course of action had been suggested by Barb Scott of the Social Planning Council (Brouwer and McDiarmid 1970, 18–19). After discussions regarding the establishment of a Model Day Care at Mount Royal College proved fruitless in late 1968, the president of the B-MDCA, Catherine Martini (who was also an elected public school trustee), suggested to her counterpart with the Model Day Care, Jean Neve, that they work together. Within two months, the groups had amalgamated, with the official name remaining the Bowness-Montgomery Day Care Association. The merger brought significant benefits to the B-MDCA. The Junior League donated $15,000 and promised to provide volunteers to improve the quality of care in the centre. The National Council of Jewish Women donated $6,000.[70] Furthermore, the involvement of these prominent women's organizations increased the credibility of the proposal and meant that there was a strong push to make the project a model for quality child care.

The formal PSS submission for the Bowness-Montgomery Day Care Program was made in August 1969, and the province gave its approval in October. The program would be opened the following year. This was a trail-blazing initiative, not only because it linked day care to community development but also because it integrated a day care with a satellite FDH program and thus offered the potential for continuous care of children between the ages of a few months to twelve years. The PSS proposal called for the hiring of an assistant director, who would select FDHs, make placements in the homes, and provide follow-up supervision. The original idea was that the day care would accept preschool children aged three and older while younger children and school-aged children would be looked after in satellite FDHs.[71] More than forty years later, this type of integrated program is favoured by early childhood experts even though it is all too rarely found in reality.[72] This shows the extraordinary vision that guided the Bowness-Montgomery program.

The Bowness-Montgomery project was the first in a series of new initiatives in Calgary in 1969. This yielded a number of new PSS day cares in the early 1970s, which will be detailed in the next chapter. At the same time, commercial day care was flourishing in the city, even more so than in Edmonton. In November 1966, there had been twenty-five licensed commercial facilities in Calgary with a capacity for 663 children. Less than three years later, in July 1969, there were thirty-seven commercial facilities with a capacity for 1,166 children.[73] Furthermore, in 1967 commercial operators had founded the Day Care Association of Calgary (DCAC) to represent their interests.[74]

Commercial operators reacted with alarm to the initial organizing efforts in Bowness and Montgomery in 1968. At the first public meeting, organized by Phil Lalonde and community supporters and held on 13 March, "about twenty private daycare operators from across the city" attended and "took over almost immediately" with their self-serving arguments against PSS day cares. One participant commented that the commercial operators "were very determined not to let a local citizens group in favour of public day care to even exist." An owner of a centre in the area, described as "most hostile towards community development of day care," even volunteered to serve on a committee. Despite the owners' disruptive tactics, however, residents meeting in small discussion groups expressed a desire "for additional daycare resources to serve the needs of their community" (Brouwer and McDiarmid 1970, 10–11). At the time, there were two commercial day cares in Bowness-Montgomery, with a total capacity for at most fifty children, and the fees were well beyond the means of many residents.[75]

Over the next two weeks, the steering committee made plans to neutralize the influence of commercial operators on the process, and the operators responded by taking on an observational rather than a disruptive role at the second public meeting on 31 March 1968. This time only two commercial owners were in attendance, one being the secretary of the DCAC (Brouwer and McDiarmid 1970, 12–13). Over the next sixteen months leading up to the submission of the PSS proposal, commercial owners never again tried to disrupt the activities of the B-MDCA. Nevertheless, they were recognized as a significant interest group, and a short section of the proposal to the provincial government, titled "Opposition," argued against the notion that the proposed community day care would take business away from commercial centres.

The 1968 intervention of commercial owners in the organizing campaign for a PSS day care in Bowness foreshadowed how they would respond to the expansion of the PSS system in Calgary in the 1970s. Although there were only thirty-seven commercial centres in Calgary in 1969, this was a relatively large number since the entire province had merely seventy-eight licensed facilities (table A.1). Furthermore, as will be detailed in the next chapter, with minimal government regulations and a strong demand, commercial day care in the late 1960s and throughout the 1970s was very profitable. This meant that the owners, especially those who operated on a capitalistic basis with a large capacity, had a great deal to lose if preventive social service day cares became a template for a more extensive system of publicly funded, not-for-profit day cares.

PARALLELS BETWEEN DAY CARE POLITICS IN 1942–44 AND THE 1960s

For the most part, day care disappeared from the public agenda in Alberta between 1945 and the 1960s. Nevertheless, there are a great many similarities between the day care politics during World War II and the latter part of the 1960s:

ADVOCACY
Important role was played by middle-class women's organizations.
Prominent professionals were among the advocates.
Sophisticated studies of the need for day care were conducted by volunteers.

ADVOCATES' ARGUMENTS
Social needs, not normative principles, should guide policy.
Scientific research on children justifies demands.

QUALITY-OF-CARE DEBATES
Widely differing views were expressed on minimum and optimum
standards of care.
Advocates had a critical view of the quality of care at the Edmonton Creche and in
commercial centres.

ACCESSIBILITY DEBATE
Should publicly subsidized day care be a narrowly targeted welfare service
or a widely available service?

GENDER DEBATE
Should public policy support married women with young children who
wish to work outside the home?

INTER-GOVERNMENTAL DYNAMICS
A municipal-federal coalition took shape to pursue day care against the governmental
opposition of the province.
The province insisted that municipalities share some of the costs of day cares. The
initial proposal in 1943 was 50 percent federal, 25 percent provincial, and 25 percent
municipal. Actual cost sharing in the 1960s was 50-30-20.

PROVINCIAL POLITICAL DYNAMICS
Manning government was under political pressure from the Left
(CCF victory in Saskatchewan in 1944; medicare's introduction in 1966).
Socially progressive legislation was introduced in Alberta (Maternity Hospitalization in
1944; Preventive Social Services in 1966).
Manning government was hostile to the federal government but pragmatically
participated in programs that offered financial gain for Alberta. It modified federal
programs to better reflect its own orientation.

COMMON PERSONALITIES AND GROUPS
Premier Manning and fellow executive committee member Alf Hooke
Enid McCalla of the Edmonton Day Care Committee
Edmonton Creche
Women's groups such as the University Women's Club of Calgary

PARALLEL EVENTS
Province approved, then withdrew approval for, a program, followed by a storm of protest
(wartime day nurseries in 1943–44; Edmonton Glengarry Centre in 1967).

One of the primary reasons for these similarities is the continuity in Alberta's political elites. Indeed, Premier Ernest Manning dealt with a major controversy over provincial funding for day cares both at the beginning (1943–44) and at the end (1967–68) of his quarter of a century in office. In the first of these controversies (wartime day nurseries), the province refused funding while in the second (Edmonton's Glengarry Day Care), it granted funding. Nevertheless, despite the different funding decisions, the historical record suggests that the inner circle of the Social Credit government in 1965–67 had much the same reservations about funding day care as did their colleagues in the mid-1940s. The Social Credit political elite of the 1960s was stuck in the traditional conservatism that best characterizes the 1940s and 1950s, and was more rural than urban in sensibility. These are the major reasons for Social Credit's loss of the next provincial election and rapid disintegration as a serious political force.

The similarities listed above also exist because the struggle for quality child care that was fought and lost in the 1940s had to be re-fought in the 1960s. Since the advocacy for publicly funded day care in the 1940s was relatively strong, both in terms of argumentation and organization, it is not surprising that the advocates in the 1960s used some of the same arguments and engaged in similar campaigns. In fact, some of the important advocacy organizations, such as the University Women's Club of Calgary, were identical in the two periods.

Two other major factors help to account for the similarities. First, the government of Alberta was prodded into at least considering action on day care in each of the periods because of federal initiatives. At the same time, while the presence of a federal initiative accounts for some of the across-period similarities in day care politics, the different character of the initiatives goes a long way toward explaining the different outcomes in the two periods. During World War II, the federal initiative was limited by its single-minded focus on the progress of the war. In contrast, the federal initiative in the mid-1960s, in the form of the CAP, was very much part of a broader social welfare agenda that included the Canada Pension Plan and medicare.

Second, although the period from the mid-1940s to the mid-1960s saw considerable social change, particularly in the organization of the economy and the character of class relations, the patriarchal gender order remained relatively stable. Consequently, the normative belief that young children are best looked after during the day by their mothers at home was widely held in the mid-1960s, just as it had been two decades earlier. As the 1960s ended, this belief was increasingly viewed as irrelevant given the large number of young children who required care while their mothers engaged in paid labour. And, just as significantly, a new wave of feminists began questioning the desirability of mothers being primarily responsible for the care of young children. In this framework, day care became a component of the struggle for women's equality, just as it had become a component of the struggle for class equality in PSS initiatives like the Bowness-Montgomery Day Care Association.

4. The 1970s
Governments Fund High-Quality Day Cares
as Preventive Social Services

The participation of married women in the labour force continued to increase in Alberta in the 1970s, creating yet more demand for day care. By 1976 fully 48 percent of married women were in the paid labour force. Furthermore, there were 41,000 lone-parent families in Alberta in 1976, up by 21 percent from 1971 (Alberta Bureau of Statistics 1981). The demand for day care was felt most strongly in Edmonton and Calgary where, by 1976, 51 percent of Albertans lived. However, day care also became an important public issue in small cities and many towns during the 1970s, often because the market was too small or dispersed to entice commercial investment. Hence, of the sixty Preventive Social Service (PSS) day cares established between 1967 and 1977, 22 percent were located in Medicine Hat, Grande Prairie, Red Deer, or Lethbridge (line 7, table 4.1), and 30 percent were scattered across the province in communities such as High Level, Slave Lake, and Claresholm.

Until 1980–81, no provincial formula existed for how much of the PSS budget should be spent in each community. John Lackey, the second PSS director, noted that this ad hoc funding system encouraged "the most progressive communities [to come] in with well thought out projects [and] they tended to get the programming."[1] Therefore, the structure of Alberta's PSS program in the late 1960s and 1970s promoted important municipal variations in the extent and character of day care services. The first part of this chapter discusses the developments at the provincial level that at first resulted in the rapid expansion of the number of PSS day cares but eventually led to the removal of day care from the PSS system and the end to special funding for the existing PSS day cares. The second part profiles the development of PSS day care in each of the six largest cities as well as some smaller municipalities. My goals with these profiles are to highlight the

TABLE 4.1 Involvement of Six Alberta Municipalities in Day Care, 1966 to 1980s

	Edmonton	Calgary	Medicine Hat	Red Deer	Grande Prairie	Lethbridge
First day care director hired	1967	1969	1974	1979	1975	never
First PSS day care opened	1967	1968	1969	1972	1972	1974
Population (1976)	461,000	470,000	33,000	32,000	18,000	47,000
Population of newborns to 4 year olds (1976)	33,400	36,600	2,500	2,400	1,900	3,500
Number of lone-parent families (1976)	13,400	12,200	700	800	400	1,100
PSS spending per capita (1975–76 fiscal year)	$5.98	$4.96	$12.83	$4.42	$9.62	$4.94
Number of PSS day care centres (May 1977)	14	15	5	2	4	2
Number of municipally run centres	1	3	5	0	2[a]	0
Municipality opposed to the province's takeover of day care in 1978	Yes	No	Yes	Yes	Yes	No
Date the municipality joined the provincial system	Jan 1980	Oct 1978	Apr 1979	Apr 1979	Apr 1979	Dec 1978
Licensing responsibility, 1978–80	No	Yes	No	No	No	No
Support provided for preschool child care (start of the 1980s)	Subsidized quality care in thirteen approved not-for-profit centres	Subsidized quality care in three municipal centres	Subsidized quality care in five municipal centres; ran a satellite FDH project	Subsidized quality care in two not-for-profit centres	Ran a satellite FDH project; provided small grants to two day care societies	None

SOURCES: For rows 3 and 4: Statistics Canada Catalogue 92-823, table 15. For row 5: Statistics Canada Catalogue 93-822, table 10. For row 6: "PSS Per Capita Expenditures," memo from Dianne Anderson, research officer, Alberta Social Services and Community Health, 26 October 1976 (CA, Social Services, box 6290). Additional data from sources cited in the text.

[a] Two rural centres were partially run by Grande Prairie and District Preventive Social Services.

most important municipal initiatives and struggles, detail municipal responses to the provincial abandonment of the PSS day care system, and account for the differences among municipalities in both programming and political action.

SUPPORT AND THEN ABANDONMENT:
THE LOUGHEED GOVERNMENT AND PSS DAY CARES

Two developments in 1971 significantly changed the provincial landscape for municipal action on day care. The first was the formation of a province-wide lobby and education group committed to quality child care, the Alberta Association for Young Children (AAYC). The second was the election of a new provincial government, headed by Peter Lougheed from Calgary, that was more attuned to the social needs of urban residents. This part of the chapter analyzes the significance of these developments and then traces how the new government initially paid close attention to the AAYC's lobbying efforts for quality initiatives in the care of children but lost interest as the decade progressed. The process of abandonment culminated in the provincial government's unilateral 1978 decision to end the PSS model for funding high-quality day cares in favour of modest, income-tested subsidies that followed subsidized children to any licensed day care (commercial or not-for-profit) in which they were enrolled.

In late May of 1970, the Department of Social Development sponsored a "Day Care Seminar" in Olds, Alberta. The speakers at the seminar were a "Who's Who" of day care in Alberta at that time. They included three representatives of the Bowness-Montgomery Day Care Association (B-MDCA) in Calgary, including executive director Nancy Hall; Mary Hull of the Community Day Nursery (CDN) and Ellen Derksen of Primrose Place Day Care in Edmonton; Rita Wright of the Day Care Association of Calgary (DCAC); pediatrician Dr. Jean Nelson, who was then working as a provincial civil servant; Sheila Campbell, the only participant asked to make two presentations to the seminar; and both Al Hagan and Howard Clifford.[2]

Howard Clifford delivered the keynote address on the opening evening of the seminar. Many of the points made in his speech were later featured in his 1972 book, Let's Talk Day Care. In light of recent research that demonstrates the importance of quality child care for the brain development of young children (McCain and Mustard 1999; Heckman 2006), it is noteworthy that in 1970 Howard Clifford was already highlighting this issue: he summarized the work of researchers who "found that even rats who have been given a stimulating environment have an enlarged cortex over and beyond that of the rats who have not been so stimulated."[3]

Dr. Nelson's speech connected the imperative for quality day care to the World Health Organization charter. Five years later, she was appointed the deputy minister of Health Services in the Department of Social Services and Community Health (SSCH), becoming the first woman deputy minister in Alberta's history. This appointment meant that in the middle part of the 1970s, the Alberta government was being advised by a senior bureaucrat who had a superb knowledge of day care issues and an unquestioned commitment to quality day care.[4]

Participants left the Olds seminar thinking it would be a springboard for the establishment of a "province wide association of all groups and individuals catering to infants and young children." A committee led by Sheila Campbell organized the founding conference of the AAYC held in Edmonton in October 1971 and financially supported by the Clifford E. Lee Foundation (Campbell 1997, 7).

The AAYC's founding occurred just six weeks after the province's first change in government in thirty-six years. Between 1967 and 1971, the province's official opposition party, the Progressive Conservatives (PCs), had made improvements to day care an important public issue. Prior to the 1971 election, the leader of the Progressive Conservatives, Peter Lougheed, told Calgary's day care counsellor, Al Hagan, that his party "was going to push day care and that was part of their platform." Hagan also recalled that "prospective candidates for the Conservative Party ... wanted a lot of information about day care, and wanted to make that a major platform item."[5] Given this context, the Conservative victory on 30 August 1971 meant that the institutionalized political system was now open to much more innovation and change in the field of child care than it had been under the Social Credit government.

The AAYC conference managed to attract not one but two members of the new provincial cabinet as keynote speakers: Minister of Social Development Neil Crawford and Minister of Education Lou Hyndman, both of whom represented Edmonton constituencies (Campbell 1997, 7). Apparently, at the time of its founding, the AAYC was treated as a very important interest group by the new government.

There are different ways to categorize the nature of the relationships between interest groups and states. According to one such schema, interest groups that work with state institutions fall into three types: a core insider group is consulted on a broad range of issues in a particular policy area and has appreciable influence on state policies; a specialist insider group is consulted and influences policy on a narrow set of issues; and a peripheral insider group "has the insider form" (i.e., has access to state officials and is actively consulted) "but little, if any, influence" (Maloney, Jordan, and McLaughlin 1994, 27, 31). The AAYC undoubtedly began its existence with real influence on the provincial government, since the Progressive Conservatives had committed themselves to acting on day care. Furthermore, because the AAYC defined its mandate quite broadly (rather than restricting its attention to day care), it is better classified in the early 1970s as a core insider than as a specialist insider group.[6]

The primary public activity of the AAYC was its annual conferences that featured high-profile authors and researchers as keynote speakers. In the early 1970s, the conferences were intended to feed directly into provincial government policy. For instance, government ministers requested that the AAYC submit policy recommendations coming out of its 1972 conference, "The Child and His Family in the Context of Today"; these recommendations were voted on by conference participants and presented to the government in December of that year along with vote results.[7]

The core insider status of the AAYC is indicated by a number of its activities in 1973: a meeting with members of the legislature to explain its recommendations, the presentation of a brief to a legislative committee on regulations, the appointment of an AAYC representative to the province's Early Childhood Co-ordinating Council, the active involvement of provincial social service bureaucrats on AAYC committees, and the very public actions taken by the AAYC Board in opposition to a government initiative.[8] This protest fits the mode of action of a "high-profile" insider group that feels confident enough about its place in the policy-making process that it sometimes tries to mobilize the public to pressure government (Maloney, Jordan, and McLaughlin 1994, 28).

That same year, the AAYC presented to the provincial government a very detailed set of recommendations for standards in day cares and family day homes (FDHs). These recommendations were adapted from a document produced by the Day Care Centres Committee of the Canadian Pediatric Society. Nine pediatricians had served on that committee, including two members of the AAYC, Dr. Gerry Holman (the chair of the pediatricians' committee) and Dr. Jean Nelson. At this point, the AAYC was taking its core insider status so seriously that it was close to drafting legislation for the government.[9] In 1974 the organization actually produced an outline for a new "Child Day Care Act." It included regulatory language that could have been directly incorporated into a government bill. More importantly, however, the outline presented an idealistic vision of day care as a "total service." No statement better captures the tremendous optimism and communitarian philosophy of the advocates in the 1970s:

It is essential that the identity of day care services as specialized health and welfare services be recognized. Only under such circumstances will the services receive adequate attention and become available to all children and families. Day care is more than a social development service, it is more than a preventive welfare service, it is more than a health service, it is more than an educational service, it is more than a remedial service, it is more than an early childhood service, it is more than a family service; it is a total service providing for the needs of children, and the needs of parents, contributing to the prevention of family problems, and problem families, contributing to the growth and development of children, of parents, of families and of society.[10]

However, the Lougheed government was unwilling to adopt the AAYC's policy recommendations as its own. At the same time, with a provincial election on the horizon, the government had to be seen taking some action. Therefore, in the spring of 1974, a consultation process was launched, headed by Mel Finlay, who then held the position of program planner in the Department of Health and Social Development (HSD). The AAYC was invited to nominate a representative to help plan "a province-wide workshop to be held at Government House, Edmonton, sometime in September." Significantly, the DCAC received a similar invitation, indicating the Lougheed government had started to treat the AAYC and the DCAC as parallel interest groups. At this point, the AAYC's influence on the provincial government had definitely waned compared to 1971–72. Nevertheless, it is probably safe to say that the provincial government and civil servants still viewed the AAYC as a core insider group because of its expert knowledge in many policy areas, as well as its province-wide representation base. In contrast, the rising influence of Calgary's commercial operators was grounded in the increasing prominence of large and very profitable centres in the sector. as well as the sympathy for free enterprise rhetoric of many members of the Conservative caucus.[11]

The September 1974 workshop at Government House involved "representative parents, board members and staff from both publicly subsidized and privately operated day care centres across the province." The participants discussed documents prepared by the AAYC, DCAC, Canadian Council on Social Development, and Calgary Social Services (CSS), and came up with their own series of recommendations. In turn, Mel Finlay circulated these recommendations in November 1974 and welcomed further comments. In doing so, he indicated that the cost of raising standards was a concern and that no immediate action was forthcoming.[12]

Shortly thereafter, Premier Lougheed called a provincial election, which the governing Progressive Conservatives won handily. In comparison to the August 1971 election, in March 1975 the Conservative vote increased by 16 percent and the Social Credit vote decreased by 23 percent. As a consequence, in 1975 the Progressive Conservatives won most rural constituencies in addition to sweeping every constituency in Alberta's six largest municipalities (Chief Electoral Officer of Alberta 1983, 17, 109–14). The 1975 Conservative caucus of sixty-nine members had many more traditional conservative voices than the caucus of forty members that had been elected in 1971. This was far from a propitious turn of events for those who were advocating for quality day care. Indeed, the Tory sweep in the 1975 election meant that the governing party no longer needed to pay such close attention to urban social movements, since its base of power had extended well beyond urban Alberta. One sign of the changing composition and orientation of the governing party was the post-election appointment of Rocky Mountain House MLA Helen Hunley as the Minister of SSCH in place of Edmonton MLA Neil Crawford. In addition to being a highly successful municipal politician in Rocky Mountain House prior to her election to the legislature in 1971, Hunley was a member of the local business elite: she owned an insurance agency and in the 1960s had been the first woman in North America to own an International Harvester dealership.[13]

Following the 1975 provincial election, the Progressive Conservative Party did not turn to the AAYC for policy ideas on day care the way it had following the 1971 election. Indeed, the 1975 election constituted the beginning of a six-year period during which the AAYC rapidly moved from a core insider group to a specialist insider group to a peripheral insider group. During these years, the AAYC remained true to its convictions, while Premier Lougheed and his government abandoned their previous commitment to building a quality system of day care for Alberta's children.

The formal process of revising Alberta's licensing standards and funding for day care began when a "Proposal for Day Care Standards and Licensing," written by provincial civil servants, was released and widely circulated in July 1976. The proposal read like draft legislation; it combined existing Board of Health and Welfare Homes standards, advanced changes to some of the existing standards, and added some new standards. An example of a recommended change concerned staff-to-child ratios: a minimum ratio of one to twelve for children aged thirty months to six years was offered in place of the minimum ratio of one to twenty for children aged two to seven years. An example of an entirely new standard concerned staff training. The proposal recommended establishing a "Professional Day Care Workers Registry" where completion of a post-secondary course or a mix of training and work experience qualified a person for registration. A further recommendation was that upon adoption of the new standards, all day cares had to immediately employ at least one registered professional, and within seven years all staff members responsible for leading groups of children had to be duly registered (Alberta SSCH 1976, 14–16).

"Hundreds of letters, briefs and reports" were submitted in response to the proposal (ADCTF 1977, 1), including a twenty-four-page submission by the AAYC. Prior to the beginning of the entire process, however, Sheila Campbell had concluded that the AAYC had lost its status as a core insider group. In March 1976, she noted that the AAYC did not have access to the minister and senior departmental bureaucrats, and was not routinely consulted concerning social policy on young children; furthermore, department civil servants "are not making our position as clear to the minister as we would wish."[14]

By the end of 1976, day care was once again a highly politicized and polarized provincial issue, thanks in no small part to the government's own public consultation process. In an attempt to find a workable compromise between advocates for high-quality care and commercial operators who supported minimal standards, in January 1977 Minister Hunley appointed the Alberta Day Care Task Force (ADCTF) to quickly study and make recommendations on standards and subsidies. The composition of the task force demonstrated that the AAYC was still an important interest group in the eyes of the provincial government. Three of the seven members of the ADCTF, including chair Myer Horowitz, were prominent members of the AAYC. Therefore, even though the AAYC had lost its core insider status by 1977, it still had a prominent role as a specialist insider group.

The input of the AAYC leaders on the task force was countered by a leading member of the DCAC, Caroline Kiehlbauch (owner of Fairyland Day Care in Calgary, licensed for 119 children), a second commercial operator from Edmonton, and two "private citizens." The advocates for quality day care on the ADCTF took the approach of compromising with the others in order to come up with a set of recommendations that could be endorsed by all members. For instance, the task force recommended a minimum staff-to-child ratio for three and four year olds of one to twelve, whereas the AAYC's recommended minimum was one to eight. Furthermore, while the ADCTF called for half of all day care staff to be licensed within five years, it did not stipulate the minimum training requirement for licensing; in contrast, the AAYC unambiguously recommended that the minimum training requirement for a day care worker be "graduation from a two year training program in the field of child and family studies."[15]

Myer Horowitz, then the academic vice-president of the University of Alberta, did a masterful job of leading the task force and meeting the government's objective of fashioning a compromise. The final report, released on 30 April 1977, used language that would appeal to commercial operators and conservatives who harboured suspicions about more government involvement in day care (e.g., "Day care is not a substitute for the family unit" and "We do not think it is desirable to try to legislate detailed program requirements"). It also candidly discussed how its recommendations were far from ideal, thus appealing to advocates and the PSS community who would be unhappy with the compromises (e.g., "We want to emphasize that we are proposing a minimum standard for the immediate future and not the ideal for the next five years and clearly not the ideal for 1985 or for the year 2000"). All members of the task force endorsed the report (ADCTF 1977, 4, 8, 14).

The most important section of the report concerned "financial considerations." The task force recommended tripling government expenditures on day care so that every child who qualified for a subsidy received one: "Financial assistance for child care should be made available to families on an individual basis through the purchase of service within approved units, i.e., those which meet the specific standards of the province" (1977, 17). This sentence is ambiguous but seems to recommend that any provincially licensed facility should be paid a government subsidy for an eligible child. This is certainly how the provincial government subsequently acted.

The report recommended that the province and a municipality determine the maximum monthly subsidy they would pay to a day care centre. "In the event that the costs of a centre were above [the maximum subsidy] ... then it would be the responsibility of the unit to set fees above the municipal maximum or to acquire the extra funds from some other source" (1977, 19). Unfortunately, the members of the AAYC on the task force failed to consider the implications of this recommendation for the high-quality PSS centres. It was precisely these centres that had costs higher than the maximum subsidy because their current standards were well above the new licensing standards proposed by the ADCTF. Among those who picked up on this problem was the manager of neighbourhood services for the City of Calgary, Frank Hoebarth. On 8 August 1977, he wrote in a memo to Sam Blakely, "I am concerned about the effect the proposed purchase of service formula will have on subsidized centres." Hoebarth's fear was that, under the proposed system, "community based non-profit centres, such as Dover and Shaganappi, are likely to be priced out of the market."

The ADCTF had foreseen variability in the maximum allowable day care subsidy across the province. At a 10 August 1977, meeting, however, it was revealed that the province intended to impose "a uniform fee scale." The issue of the cost of higher standards in PSS centres was directly broached. The provincial civil servants indicated that the provincial government had not yet dealt with the issue but suggested that, at the very least, the PSS centres be given five years of grace before they would have to switch to the lower funding levels of the new provincial system. The following month, cabinet's Social Planning Committee accepted the Department of SSCH's recommendations that all deficit operating funding for PSS centres be phased out over five years and no new PSS centres be approved.

The Social Planning Committee also recommended "that the province set realistic minimum standards for day care operators"; this language indicates that quality of care was not of paramount importance and would be susceptible to downward lobbying pressure. Indeed, the documents discussed by the Social Planning Committee (followed within a week by discussions in Executive Council and cabinet) indicate that the cost of the new subsidy system was the overriding issue in government decision making.[16]

The Alberta cabinet gave final approval to the new provincial day care system on 13 December 1977; it was announced in March of the next year.[17] The new system proved very popular with commercial operators and the thousands of Albertans for whom day care subsidies became accessible for the first time. For the movement for quality day care, however, the new system was a disaster: not only did it fail to significantly raise the minimum licensing standards for day cares, but it signalled that provincial support for the innovative PSS day cares and FDH programs would be phased out. Significantly, the new standards were even weaker than the "compromises" recommended by the ADCTF. For instance, the staff-to-child ratio for babies in a day care centre was specified as one to six (Alberta 1978, 317), whereas the ADCTF had recommended a ratio of one to five (1977, 46), and FDHs were allowed to care for up to four children under two years of age in addition to any of the operator's own young children (Alberta 1978, 312), whereas the ADCTF had recommended that FDHs be allowed to care for a maximum of three children under two years of age, including any of the operator's young children (1977, 46).

The AAYC was highly critical of the province's new plans for day care. Indeed, the tone of its May 1978 submission to the provincial government was anything but conciliatory. The association believed the new provincial standards for day cares were "so nebulous and deficient that it is highly unlikely that any improvement in the quality of care for children in commercial day care centres will result." Furthermore, the organization feared for the future of PSS day cares.[18]

The members of the AAYC had thrown themselves into the job of reforming the entire day care system in the early 1970s and had willingly accepted the core insider role in policy discussions and development. An alternative would have been to concentrate exclusively on the development of exemplary or "lighthouse" PSS centres, thus eschewing the politicization of the quality of care in commercial centres. Among those who have argued in favour of this strategy is Howard Clifford.[19] The main advantage would have been a stronger PSS sector with advocates giving it more attention. In particular, advocates could have assisted in strengthening the links between communities and the centres in which they were located, perhaps by linking day care centres to a broader community development model of human services. Quebec provides an example of this type of communitarian model (Jenson 2001). In addition, given more time, advocates could have provided technical expertise to municipalities that were slow to join the PSS program, thus ensuring wider availability of PSS centres throughout the province. Nevertheless, Sheila Campbell and other AAYC leaders felt a strong moral duty to try to reform the entire day care system when given the opportunity by the Progressive Conservative government, knowing as they did the abysmal quality of care in some commercial centres. To their dismay, the Lougheed Conservatives not only did not strengthen day care regulations as thoroughly or quickly as they had hoped, but withdrew supplementary financial support from the network of high-quality day cares that had been created under the PSS system.

Changing the direction of day care in Alberta in 1978 was a challenging political process for the Lougheed government. The provincial system that had developed under the umbrella of the PSS Act was a series of partnerships between municipalities and the province, with municipalities holding the lead role in each partnership. Municipal governments therefore had to be won over to the province's new policy direction, or otherwise mollified or neutralized. Furthermore, the PSS system of day cares, which by 1978 involved hundreds of workers and thousands of families, had grown into a formidable interest group. The following section profiles the development of PSS day care programs around Alberta in the 1970s. It also traces how different municipal governments responded to the province's invitation to become a partner in the new system that featured portable subsidies for low-income families and a level of licensing standards that was merely custodial.

MUNICIPAL INITIATIVES IN DAY CARE

Edmonton

At the end of the 1960s, the City of Edmonton's PSS day care services far surpassed those of other Alberta municipalities. While Calgary and Medicine Hat each had only a single centre—and the first PSS centres would not be established in Red Deer, Grande Prairie, and Lethbridge until the 1970s—Edmonton had four PSS centres (line 2, table 4.1). Furthermore, Edmonton had initiated a PSS family day home program in 1968 and had started funding two out-of-school care (OOSC) programs in 1969.

New PSS centres were opened in Edmonton in each of 1970 and 1971. The six PSS centres in operation at the end of 1971 cared for slightly over three hundred preschoolers, with three of the centres also licensed to care for additional school-aged children. In addition, about eighty children received subsidized care in approved FDHs (Clifford n.d., 169).[20]

The mayor of Edmonton from 1968 to 1974 was Ivor Dent, a prominent member of the New Democratic Party (NDP). The steady growth of Edmonton's PSS system of day care in the early 1970s was facilitated by a sympathetic council led by Mayor Dent. As a consequence, the opponents of PSS day care in Edmonton were never able to utilize municipal political forums to air their arguments. This contrasts with what happened in Calgary, where in both 1971 and 1974–75, major public debates took place about the PSS approach to day care (see the next section).

Nevertheless, the commercial sector grew significantly in Edmonton at the same time as the PSS system was expanding. Between 1967 and 1971, the number of commercial centres doubled from eighteen to thirty-five. The city's fifth PSS centre, West End Day Care, opened in October 1970 just a few blocks away from Hilde's Day Nursery. A few months later, Hilde Bloedow protested to Mayor Dent and city council that she had lost two children to the PSS centre.[21]

The opposition from Edmonton's commercial operators to the PSS system of day care could be put down to narrow self-interest. However, as noted in chapter

3, Howard Clifford recognized that the majority of Albertans had considerable doubts about the wisdom of expanding the availability of publicly subsidized, high-quality ("Cadillac") day care. Therefore, into the 1970s, a major focus of his job as Edmonton's day care director was to counter those doubts through education. Of particular note in this regard is his small book *Let's Talk Day Care* (undated but apparently published in 1972). It was "directed to administrators, politicians and concerned citizens who are in a position to make or influence decisions which affect the implementation of day care programs" (8). Clifford believed that his educational efforts could at least give decision makers the information and arguments they needed to move ahead in the face of opposition.

Let's Talk Day Care opens with two chapters that cite an impressive list of studies defending the appropriateness of day care. Clifford's definitive conclusions include the following: "The overwhelming evidence is that as long as adequate substitute care of the children is arranged, our fears about maternal employment negatively affecting children are unfounded" (27) and "The conclusion that is evident from the existing body of knowledge is that the preschool years are the critical years for determining the child's future success" (39). In 1996 Howard Clifford remarked that, just as the opponents of day care had selectively emphasized research that supported their positions, he had selectively emphasized research that supported public investment in high-quality day cares.[22] Even after taking this admission into account, however, *Let's Talk Day Care* comes across as reasonably balanced.[23]

The municipally run Glengarry Day Care was one of a number of public recreational, social, and health services offered in the Glengarry area. One chapter of *Let's Talk Day Care* outlines with great enthusiasm the many ways that this day care tied into the other services offered by the city. For example, an OOSC program was operated in conjunction with the day care, mothers in the community could volunteer to work at the day care in order to improve their child care skills, and children in the day care were screened to identify those with developmental delays. The chapter demonstrates how seriously the City of Edmonton took the notion of day care as a preventive social service and how important a PSS day care could be to the quality of life in a working-class community.

Howard Clifford left his City of Edmonton position in the summer of 1972 to become the federal government's national advisor on day care. He had served as Edmonton's director of day care for over five years. In an interview conducted at the time of his departure, he opined that Edmonton had "by far the best day-care program in terms of quality" in the country. The strengths of the program, according to Clifford, were community involvement and the city's multidisciplinary approach involving health, recreation, education, and social services.[24]

One of Howard Clifford's last acts as the city's day care director was encouraging Edmonton Social Services (ESS) to hire Sheila Campbell to take his place. Campbell had just finished her master's degree at the University of Alberta (under the supervision of Dr. Myer Horowitz). She had spent the 1971–72 academic year as the first program head of the new early childhood education (ECE) program at Grant MacEwan College in Edmonton. (The program at Mount Royal College in Calgary had started the previous year.) Her duties at the college included designing and teaching all the courses. She decided to apply for the City of Edmonton position after she perceived that an all-male hiring committee had made fun of her candidacy for the position of chair of the community services department at the college.

Sheila Campbell lasted for only one year as the director of day care. "I ran into the old boys' club at the city," she remarked, recollecting that she was one of only two women employed by Edmonton at the director level and the only woman in ESS. When she got the notice for her first administrative staff meeting and mentioned her intention to attend, Keith Wass advised her not to go since the meetings involved male administrators playing poker and telling jokes. She was even excluded from the lunches that the other social services administrators regularly enjoyed together. "I heard about things that had happened that had obviously been discussed in the washroom, the beer parlour, someplace. I never had any input." She was also excluded from input on which day cares should receive grants from money donated to the city by the Edmonton Creche Society. In fact, she recollected that she only found out about the existence of this fund by accident.

Given this unsupportive work environment at the City of Edmonton, Campbell was pleased to accept a term teaching position at the University of Alberta starting in September 1973. Her decision to leave the city was also influenced by her desire for work that involved fewer meetings at night so she could spend more time with her children and by the unrealistic expectations of many members of the day care community who did not realize that it was inappropriate for the director of day care to give them special treatment. In retrospect, Sheila Campbell's difficult year as an employee of the City of Edmonton in 1972–73 suggests the extent of systemic gender bias in organizations at that time. Indeed, with its commitment to bettering people's lives, we could reasonably expect ESS to have been more hospitable to female administrators than most organizations.[25]

Mike Day, already an employee of ESS, became the director of day care in the fall of 1973. At that time, the PSS system of child care in the city consisted of eight day cares with a capacity for 431 preschool children, two OOSC programs that could look after forty-two children, and an FDH program that could accommodate 120 children. The city and United Way also subsidized fifty-eight OOSC spaces outside of the PSS program. However, this supply came nowhere close to meeting the demand for subsidized day care. In 1972 the city had surveyed 2,564 households and found that 29 percent of the families with preschoolers had mothers in the paid labour force. It was estimated, based upon the survey, that there were 10,500 preschoolers in Edmonton in 1973 whose mothers held paid work. In contrast, there were only 1,700 licensed spaces in the city. The gap between need and supply meant that there were long waiting lists at the PSS centres; information centres in Edmonton were fielding over one hundred calls per month from persons seeking child care.

The long waiting lists at PSS centres in 1973 brought together a number of organizations to lobby for an expansion of quality day care. The Community Task Force on Day Care included the Edmonton Day Care Council (EDCC, composed of representatives from each of the PSS centres), the Edmonton After-School Care Association, and the Community League After-School program. They were joined by a grassroots advocacy group, Parents for Day Care, and two advocacy organizations that had been initiated by Sheila Campbell and other professionals, the Edmonton branch of the Canadian Committee on Early Childhood and the AAYC. The movement in Edmonton benefited from the fact that although the AAYC was provincial in mandate, many of its key activists lived in Edmonton and made sure the organization was involved in the movement there. Furthermore, the Edmonton Social Planning Council not only participated in the Community Task Force but also published its report, "Information on Day Care." In contrast, the movement in Calgary was at a comparative disadvantage since the Social Planning Council in Calgary had been shut down by this time.[26]

In the run-up to the provincial election of 26 March 1975, the provincial government significantly increased the budget for PSS day cares. This allowed Edmonton to undertake a major expansion of its OOSC program: three centres were added in 1974 and two more in 1975. By September 1975, there were seven OOSC centres in the PSS system. Furthermore, the city added two more PSS day cares in 1974 and began subsidizing twelve spaces at the two day cares run by the Centre d'Expérience Préscolaire. In arriving at the count of twelve PSS centres in Edmonton in 1975 (table 4.2), I included the latter two centres in the total. Furthermore, the number of spaces in Edmonton's FDH program had grown to 220.[27]

Ivor Dent lost his bid for re-election in 1974, but the city council elected that year included three new aldermen who were strong supporters of publicly subsidized day care: Bettie Hewes, who had worked as the executive director of the Canadian Mental Health Association in Edmonton from 1964 to 1967 and as a planner and acting director for the Edmonton Social Planning Council between 1967 and her election to council; Ed Kennedy, a priest and educator who directed the Catholic Information Centre in Edmonton; and David Leadbeater, a left-wing economist with MA degrees from the University of Alberta and Oxford University who had been active in student politics while at the University of Alberta.[28] With a sympathetic council in place, in 1975 ESS presented an ambitious plan for the expansion of Edmonton's PSS day care services. It included two alternate expansion scenarios. The first assumed a growth rate in subsidized spaces of 25 percent per year over five years, and the second 50 percent per year. The 25 percent rate predicted a growth in the number of spaces in PSS day cares from 687 (table 4.2) to 1,675 in 1980: OOSC spaces would grow from 217 to 837 and FDH spaces from 220 to 837. The total cost for Edmonton's PSS day care system in 1980 was projected as $5.26 million, of which the province's share would be over $1.5 million (at 30 percent cost sharing). Given that the province spent only $1.23 million on PSS day cares in all of Alberta in 1976 (roughly three-eighths of $3,271,000: see table A.1), Edmonton's expansion plans undoubtedly seemed grandiose to provincial bureaucrats and politicians.

In September 1975, the provincial government had already agreed to fund three additional PSS day cares in Edmonton. In order to meet the objective of 25 percent growth per annum, ESS recommended establishing three new centres in 1976 and two centres per year from 1977 to 1980. The municipal department's plans, however, went far beyond a major expansion of the spaces in PSS services. It also proposed providing "consultation services to all child care programs regardless of sponsorship" and purchasing subsidized spaces in commercial centres that met "operating standards set near the level of the present subsidized centres." Under the scenario of 25 percent growth, ESS projected having 837 subsidized spaces in commercial centres by 1980.[29]

In developing this plan for expansion, the city confronted the difficult issue of how to fund the buildings for a large number of new centres. In the first five years of the Canada Assistance Plan (CAP), the federal government would only share the costs of staff salaries, staff training, and day care administration. This

TABLE 4.2 Licensed Day Care in Alberta, 1975, by Region and Auspice

Auspice	Edmonton			Calgary			Rest of Alberta		
	Number	Licensed capacity	Average size	Number	Licensed capacity	Average size	Number	Licensed capacity	Average size
Total commercial	46 (58%)	1,653 (53%)	36	65 (76%)	2,302 (69%)	35	15 (30%)	368 (25%)	25
PSS	12 (15%)	687 (22%)	57	13 (15%)	818 (25%)	63	21 (42%)	726 (50%)	35
Other not-for-profit	22 (28%)	762 (25%)	35	8 (9%)	200 (6%)	25	14 (28%)	362 (25%)	26
Total not-for-profit	34 (42%)	1,449 (47%)	43	21 (24%)	1,018 (31%)	48	35 (70%)	1,088 (75%)	31
All centres	80	3,102	39	86	3,320	39	50	1,456	29
Region as % of total for Alberta	37%	39%	n.a.	40%	42%	n.a.	23%	18%	n.a.

SOURCE: Calculated from Alberta Social Services and Community Health, Homes and Institutions Branch, "Day Care Centres Operating in the Province of Alberta as of July 1, 1975" (PAA, 83.386, file 12).

NOTE: Here and in other tables, "n.a." means "not applicable."

had not posed an insurmountable barrier to the establishment of PSS centres in Edmonton because community groups like churches had been willing to lease existing space to day cares at very reasonable rates and grants had been obtained to cover the costs of renovations and equipment. (The sources of grants included the Clifford E. Lee Foundation and the Creche donation controlled by ESS.) The situation improved in late 1972, when rent and equipment became eligible for cost sharing through CAP.[30]

The problem faced by Edmonton in 1975 was that the newer suburbs had no community buildings with excess floor space that could house a day care. Therefore, the city had to find ways to include day cares in new buildings constructed in those areas even though building costs were not directly shareable through CAP. ESS eventually decided upon two solutions to this problem. The first was to "borrow the money to cover the cost of constructing daycare facilities and in turn rent the facilities to community boards at a level which would cover the debenture payment." Of course, the rent paid by the day care would be eligible for PSS funding, of which the city's share was only 20 percent. "Thus the City in the final analysis has to cover only 20 percent of the costs of [a] facility which it will eventually own outright." The second solution was to "include the requirement for the inclusion of day care facilities in major new developments in which the developer has asked for concessions from the city (such as re-zoning to permit more intensive land use)."[31]

Edmonton did everything it could to orchestrate a major expansion of the PSS day care system in the mid-1970s. The city's plan, however, was thwarted by the province's unwillingness to provide operating funds for new PSS day cares. In the first part of 1976, Minister of Social Services Helen Hunley indicated that the province would limit the increase in its PSS day care budget to 8 percent in the 1976–77 budget year. Since inflation at this time was higher than 8 percent, this decision meant that the city would not have enough money to support its existing centres, let alone new ones. This point was made in June 1976, when council debated a bylaw authorizing the expenditure of $200,000 for a new day care facility. Bettie Hewes was among the aldermen who opposed constructing the facility since the city could not afford to operate it without PSS support. In contrast, Alderman Ed Kennedy "urged the city to spotlight the funding problem by building a new centre, not opening it and closing a couple of existing centres."[32]

Only two of the three PSS day cares planned for 1976 opened that year, bringing the total number of PSS day cares in the city to fourteen in the spring of 1977 (line 7, table 4.1). Furthermore, the plan for succeeding years was derailed by the province's funding curbs. Had the PSS operational funds been available in 1977–78, Edmonton would have been well on its way toward sustaining a 25 percent or higher growth rate in subsidized spaces between 1976 and 1980.[33]

Edmonton's model system of subsidized day care stagnated in the first half of 1977 due to lack of new funding. Recognizing the impasse in the spring of 1977, Alderman David Leadbeater proposed to city council "that the City open sixty new daycare spaces at fees equivalent to actual cost." The motion was referred to ESS. The department costed the idea based upon capital costs equivalent to building a new facility and estimated that parents would have to be charged $309 per month to recover the costs. The department concluded that such a fee would "render patronage improbable."

David Leadbeater rebuked the department for its action on his motion. First, he believed the cost of $309 per month was "highly misleading" because such a day care could be located in a facility built to specifications by a private developer as part of a development agreement and because "initiative [could] be taken to find means of scrounging, borrowing, building or gifting necessary furnishings." Second, he asserted that if the department had consulted with day care workers or supervisors, it would have discovered that "there are persons willing to pay full cost day care in sufficient numbers to make the proposal 'viable.'" Leadbeater's analysis suggests that if the department had wanted to make a full-cost-recovery centre seem attractive and worth pursuing, it could have easily done so. This is a case where an alderman was far more creative than municipal civil servants in responding to a crisis in provincial funding of PSS day cares.[34]

The politics of day care underwent an almost complete change in Edmonton between 1975 and 1978. In 1975 the City of Edmonton had taken the initiative on day care with its ambitious plan to expand the number of subsidized, high-quality spaces over five years from 1,124 to 4,186. By early 1978, the province had indubitably seized the initiative with its new plan to allow subsidized children to enrol in any licensed centre. David Gilbert took over from Mike Day as Edmonton's director of day care in the summer of 1977. Among his first duties was attending a meeting with provincial civil servants that sketched the provincial government's plans for policy change. Therefore, the city was well aware of the general direction of the new provincial policy on day care before it was announced in March 1978.

David Gilbert wrote a detailed memo on his meeting with provincial officials on 10 August 1977. (The meeting was also attended by Sam Blakely, representing Calgary.) The memo was circulated to the other senior managers in the department, including general manager Ande Dorosh, who had taken over earlier that year when Keith Wass moved into City Planning. Gilbert offered this assessment: "It is clear the Minister is scared of being unable to control the rising cost of day care. She has elected to choose a system of mediocrity, a 'levelling down' to a minimum standard, and a determination to de-escalate the process of better quality day care through the present municipal structure."[35] The city did manage to add two more day cares to its PSS system in the latter part of 1977, bringing its total to sixteen centres. Furthermore, the number of funded after-school programs grew to thirteen during the 1977–78 school year. Nevertheless, ESS informed newly elected Mayor Cec Purves in December 1977 that "continuing programmes of fiscal restraint will continue to weaken services which provide strength and support to the family."[36]

On 13 March 1978, Minister Helen Hunley revealed the new licensing standards that would accompany the portable subsidy system. The province's proposed new staff-to-child ratios, indoor/outdoor space requirements, and staff qualification requirements were lower than Edmonton's standards for PSS centres, and the Edmonton Day Care Council (EDCC) soon came out in opposition. Of particular concern to the EDCC was the indication that the maximum monthly subsidy in the new system would be $190 per month. Because the cost per child in Edmonton's PSS centres was in the $240–70 range, EDCC President Dorothy Keith predicted that "subsidized centres will have to lower standards, lower income parents will have to pay more when they are barely able to manage present fees, or charity drives will have to be held." The EDCC immediately began to mobilize parents with children in the PSS day cares. A leaflet unfavourably compared the proposed new provincial regulations to the existing city guidelines, and listed the following options:

- Close subsidized centres
- Lay off staff and lower salaries
- Do a lot of fund raising ($20,000 per year, which is impossible)
- Lower our standards to new provincial regulations
- Fight to keep our present standards

Parents were urged to write letters of protest, and the EDCC circulated a petition that asked city council to get the province to respect municipal autonomy over the subsidy system for PSS day cares. It was submitted in late March with 548 signatures.[37]

The city's Day Care Branch formally responded to the new licensing standards in April 1978. It echoed the criticisms of the EDCC and employed sarcasm to convey disdain for the province's approach:

It should be noted that the impact of the Day Care Regulation on the provision of Day Care services in Edmonton will be minimal. Parents may be assured that their children will be cared for not more than one level below ground, by someone who doesn't smoke, in a room that is not accessible only by ladder, folding stairs or trap door, and located within walking distance of a playground. The Regulation will not ensure adequate care for children in Day Care services, and may not provide the necessary protection for their custodial care.[38]

At its meeting on 23 May 1978, Edmonton City Council decided that it would not accept the province's new subsidy system and regulations as proposed but would negotiate "to develop a mutually acceptable system for subsidizing low income families." This quickly led to a series of meetings that culminated in Minister Hunley directly addressing city council on 26 June. The latter action shows how badly the provincial government wanted to strike a deal with Edmonton prior to the official starting date of the new day care system, 1 July. However, city council steadfastly supported the position of its bureaucrats and refused to accept the province's plan as it stood. The Day Care Branch prepared a document that "outlined desirable standards to day care services in Edmonton and spelled out the basis for negotiations with the province over day care." It was endorsed by council on 15 August 1978.[39]

. The document stated that "the City of Edmonton wishes to establish a distinctive program within provincial guidelines." It specified areas where the city would accept the provincial program and areas where the city was "not prepared to change." The six points on the latter list included (1) municipality to set standards to any day care that receives municipal funding and (2) not-for-profit programs to have priority for funding.[40]

At this point, however, negotiations between the province and city ground to a halt. Mayor Purves was not able to arrange another meeting with Minister Hunley until late January 1979.[41] By 1978 John Lackey was a director-general in the provincial Department of SSCH. He had worked behind the scenes to break the impasse between the province and the city, and on 18 December 1978, recommended to Chief Deputy Minister Mansbridge "that provincial policy explicitly grant municipalities the option to set municipal conditions on the operation of daycare centres." Lackey's proposal was to give municipalities the latitude to set conditions that fell outside the provincial regulation: "to request that operators establish parent boards, join a municipal Day Care Association, encourage staff to access available training sessions, etc."[42] The Policy and Planning Committee of SSCH agreed to Lackey's proposal on 5 January 1979. The specific language adopted was "The Province recognizes the municipal right to establish conditions as long as regulations and fee schedule guidelines, etc., are respected and as long as conditions don't render hardship on users." Edmonton's Day Care Branch interpreted the new language on municipal conditions as a "significant" modification of the province's position even though it recognized that "the implications of this change in policy are unclear."[43]

By the time Albertans were preparing to vote in the provincial election of 14 March 1979, the province and the city had declared a truce in their acrimonious fight over day care. Although Edmonton—unlike Medicine Hat, Red Deer, and Grande Prairie (line 10, table 4.1)—did not plan to join the new system on

1 April 1979, it had at least agreed to adopt the new provincial fee schedule (the maximum monthly fee was set at $210 for infants and $190 for preschoolers; see table A.6) and to accept provincial guidelines for determining who was eligible for subsidization. The Day Care Branch wrote on 6 March that "there remains an urgent need to define the specific operating conditions and ensure a meaningful role for the municipality."[44] Nevertheless, the accommodating approach taken by Lackey, Mansbridge, and Hunley in the winter of 1979 suggested that Edmonton's full participation in the new system could be negotiated without further confrontation. But the truce turned out to be temporary. Helen Hunley did not run in the 1979 election and was replaced by a new minister, Bob Bogle. As is detailed in chapter 5, Bogle was unwilling to pursue the conciliatory approach of his predecessor, and soon the City of Edmonton was once again at loggerheads with the province.

Calgary

Edmonton took the lead in establishing PSS day cares between 1967 and 1969. The response of CSS was to work to establish PSS day cares in Calgary that were even better than those in Edmonton. The first version of the City of Calgary's "Day Care Policy and Guidelines" was adopted by city council in October 1969. It specified standards for day cares and FDHs that were superior to the licensing standards of the province.[45]

Even before the Bowness-Montgomery project was approved (see chapter 3), Calgary proposed establishing a municipally run day care along with a social service unit in its first large-scale public housing project. The day care at the Shaganappi Village housing project was Calgary's answer to Edmonton's municipally run Glengarry Day Care. Then, in early 1970, the city supported proposals for a community day care at Pleasant Heights United Church and a day care at Mount Royal College. In fact, the college's day care, organized by the Students' Association, opened in February, before any government funding was in place. It was the first day care at a community college in Canada.[46]

Meanwhile, the innovative Bowness-Montgomery Day Care and FDH project opened on 1 May 1970 under the directorship of Nancy Hall. Like Mary Hull at Edmonton's CDN, Nancy Hall had trained as a nursery nurse in England. After emigrating to Canada in 1957 with her husband and young children, Hall had continued to work with children in various capacities. She moved to Calgary from Hay River, Northwest Territories, to take up her position at Bowness-Montgomery and would remain there until 1976.[47] The two programs at Bowness-Montgomery soon became well established. On 1 December 1970, there were forty-six children in the day care and another forty-three in satellite FDHs (Brouwer and McDiarmid 1970, 25).

Because it was a community-run project that was designed to serve as a model day care, Bowness-Montgomery played an important role in the development of day care in the early 1970s. For instance, the first cohort of ECE students from Mount Royal College commenced field placements at the Bowness-Montgomery Day Care in October 1970, and the project was visited during its first few months of operation by individuals involved in getting the Shaganappi and Pleasant Heights day cares up and running, by "a group from Toronto who were conducting a survey on day home projects," and by groups from Lethbridge and Drumheller who were looking at establishing day cares (Brouwer and McDiarmid 1970, 26). Two other factors enhanced the profile of the Bowness-Montgomery project at this time. The first was the involvement of women's organizations like the Junior League of Calgary. Nancy Hall cultivated that support by designating Friday afternoons, beginning at three o'clock, as an open house "for anyone who is interested in the centre and who would like to become familiar with this type of child development program."[48] The centre used volunteers from these groups to help organize conventional fundraising events such as the auction of donated items held in November 1970.[49] Second, both the members of the B-MDCA Board and Nancy Hall herself were committed to advocacy and education beyond the confines of their own project. The board was represented at the Poor People's Conference sponsored by the federal government in Toronto in January 1971, and Hall was regularly interviewed by the press, including, on a number of occasions, future premier Ralph Klein, then a reporter for CFCN-TV.[50]

By the end of 1970, five PSS day cares were operating in Calgary. However, the capacity of these centres came nowhere close to meeting the burgeoning need for day care in the city. Since subsidized care was only available in PSS programs, low-income families were forced to look for an inexpensive commercial alternative if they could not secure spaces in a PSS centre or day home. As a consequence, the number of licensed commercial day cares in Calgary grew from approximately forty in 1970 to sixty-five in 1975 (table 4.2). Most of these centres, however, did not accept children less than two years of age (since it was much more profitable to care for older children at a staff-to-child ratio of one to twenty than younger children at a ratio of one to ten). Because of this, many working parents with younger children were forced to arrange for care in small day homes and illegal day cares, such as the infamous Boutique Children's Hotel, where, in November 1971, provincial child welfare workers discovered thirteen children, including seven infants less than one year of age, being cared for in a garage without any running water (Langford 2003a, 16).

The growth of the PSS system of day cares in Calgary in the early 1970s was driven not only by a supportive municipal bureaucracy and government but also by a strong grassroots movement. One indication of the strength of the movement was the traffic into Al Hagan's office at city hall. In 1978 he recalled, "It used to be that I'd come to work and there'd be about six people in my office to bug me about some issue or other." A second indication was the militancy of an organizing group at the University of Calgary at the beginning of the school year in 1970. After the university failed to take the initiative in organizing child care on campus, the Women's Liberation Group threatened to occupy a dining room on campus for the purpose of co-operative child care. The tactic focussed media attention on the problem and even sparked an editorial in one of Calgary's daily newspapers, The Albertan, that was highly critical of the university administration.[51]

Support for government-subsidized PSS day cares in Calgary, however, was far from universal. The matter received a thorough public airing in 1971 after Louis Lebel, an oil industry executive who was an appointed member of the city's Social Service Committee, stated that the city-funded day care programs were "gold-plated" and "too blasted expensive."[52] An analysis of the written submissions made to the committee allows us to map who was supporting and who was opposing Calgary's approach to day care during the formative years of the PSS program.

Unqualified opposition to the city's involvement in provision of child care was restricted to four submissions from commercial operators and twenty-seven from parents and grandparents whose children were in commercial centres (some of them with multiple signatures). Only five commercial day cares were mentioned by name in these documents, indicating that the efforts to mobilize clients were restricted to a few activist owners.

Support for Calgary's day care policies came from a wider coalition of groups than did opposition. The critical submissions from commercial operators and their clients were almost evenly balanced by favourable submissions from the clients of PSS centres (twenty-two submissions) and the boards of those centres (four submissions). In addition, supportive submissions came from four other categories of advocates. The first was voluntary organizations such as the Calgary Local Council of Women and the Calgary United Fund. A second category comprised six scientific authorities offering expert opinion in areas such as medicine, psychology, economics, and social work. Third were individual citizens (eleven submissions), many of whom went out of their way to frame their arguments in a way that emphasized their public-mindedness rather than self-interest. Finally, CSS advocated for its existing approach to day care.

There is a great deal of overlap between the categories of supporters of quality day care in Calgary in 1971 and in Edmonton in 1967 at the time of the controversy over funding the Glengarry Day Care. The one exception is the greater prominence of scientific authorities in the Calgary debate. These authorities included Dr. Gerald Holman, then a professor and head of the division of pediatrics in the Faculty of Medicine at the University of Calgary, as well as the director of pediatrics at the Foothills Hospital. He argued, "Although it is recognized that quality day care requires significant funding, the expanded body of evidence which clearly indicates the first five years of a child's life is critical to its ultimate development as a future citizen, clearly shows the need for the provision of high quality programs for all those children who may need them." Like Dr. Holman, most of the scientific experts made general reference to research findings, and the submissions from the Alberta Guidance Clinic (a division of the provincial government's Mental Health Department) reported on four completed or current research projects in Calgary on topics such as the effects of day care on IQ scores.[53]

Given the polarization of views presented to the Social Services Committee, it is not surprising that its members were also polarized in their recommendations. The majority supported the city's standards, although they expressed a desire to cut public costs in the future by subsidizing commercial centres that met those standards rather than building new PSS centres. This majority recommendation was accepted by city council by a vote of seven to four on 20 September 1971.[54] The idea of subsidizing high-quality commercial day care would be regularly aired between 1971 and 1978 by Calgary's civil servants and politicians. It was never implemented, however: the province never latched onto the idea, presumably because, under the terms of CAP, the provincial government would have been forced to pay a much larger percentage of the costs of subsidized day care in commercial centres than in not-for-profit centres. Furthermore, the idea was never advocated by the associations representing commercial operators. This is understandable for two reasons: first, it would have divided the commercial sector between subsidized, higher-quality centres and unsubsidized, lower-quality centres; second, it would not have markedly improved the bottom line of newly subsidized commercial centres since the revenue they would have gained from accepting subsidized children would have been more than offset by the cost of meeting the higher city standards in areas such as staff-to-child ratios and staff training.

Many of the commercial day cares that existed in Calgary in the 1960s grew out of the movement for kindergarten education and thus offered good quality programs. As the number of commercial centres increased in the late 1960s and 1970s, however, so did the variability in the quality of care. In 1972 Irmtraud Walter decided to buy an existing commercial day care in Calgary. She had a strong background in the field, having completed a two-year training course in Germany and having worked at the Happy Times and Fairyland day cares in Calgary during the 1960s. Walter would eventually buy Charleswood Day Nursery and operate it continuously for thirty years. But before she purchased that centre, she looked at others, including one located in a residential area just south of downtown. Her visit to that centre remained vivid in her memory three decades later:

> When I walked in that day care I was just shocked. And I even phoned Social Services [and asked]: "How can you license a place like that?" It was extremely bad and I couldn't even see how parents could leave a child in a place like that. It had holes in the floor, curtains ripped down, the bathroom you smelled for miles away and dirty rings in the toilets and the potties in the corners. And the children had these army cots that you folded out and there was no sheets, no blankets, no nothing. And two children lying down on one cot, one with the head this way, one the other. And one staff in the kitchen.[55]

A second example of highly questionable care in a commercial day care in Calgary was documented by a mother in 1974. She informed the operator that her son was being withdrawn from the centre "due to your sadistical [sic] form of punishment (washing his mouth out with soap), which you told me you did, and a very noticeable swollen lip which you could not account for in our telephone conversation."[56] These two examples illustrate just how wide a gap in quality there was between the PSS centres and the worst (at least I hope these are examples of the worst) of the commercial centres.

Commercial day care in Calgary was a highly profitable business in the 1970s because demand far exceeded supply, very few staff members were needed to look after a large number of children, and there were no staff training requirements. Nancy Hall said that she employed seventeen staff to care for the sixty children at the Bowness-Montgomery Day Care. In contrast, Calgary's first day care chain, Mother Duck's Day Care, apparently employed four staff to look after the same number of children at one of its three licensed centres.[57] The profits made in commercial day care were so great in the early 1970s that Al Hagan remembers thinking to himself, "Why am I in this [the counsellor's job]? I should quit and open a few daycare centres now that I have the knowledge to do that."[58]

The 1970s brought a continuous expansion of PSS day cares in Calgary. Between 1970 and 1974, five new day cares opened, four of them administered by community boards and one by the city (like Shaganappi, the Bridgeland Day Care was connected to a municipal housing project). Two of the new day cares also served as hubs for satellite FDH programs. As a consequence, in November 1974, Calgary had ten PSS day cares with a capacity for 552 children and four FDH projects with a capacity for 215 children. The total cost of these projects was $826,000, with the city responsible for 20 percent. At the end of 1974, less than six months prior to a provincial election, the provincial government promised to share the costs of a $212,500 expansion for PSS day care in Calgary. This money was used to open two new day cares, bring an existing not-for-profit day care into the PSS system, and expand the capacity of some of the existing PSS projects.[59] As is recorded in table 4.2, there were thirteen PSS day cares in Calgary by the middle of 1975, with a capacity for 818 children. At that point, Calgary had 131 more PSS day care spaces than Edmonton and ninety-two more than in all of the rest of Alberta. Furthermore, the province had approved two additional day cares and two additional day home projects. Including these approved projects, Calgary's PSS system of child care consisted of fifteen centres with a capacity for 854 children and six FDH projects with a capacity for 365 children. The number of licensed commercial spaces in Calgary in 1975 was 2,302, 69 percent of all centre spaces in the city (table 4.2). When approved and FDH spaces are included in the calculation, the commercial sector still controlled 66 percent of the licensed capacity.[60]

The rapid expansion of PSS day care in Calgary in the early 1970s quickly led to the situation where spending on day care exceeded spending on all other PSS projects combined. In 1973 three Calgary representatives proposed to the minister of HSD, Neil Crawford, "that day care services be separated in some manner from the Preventive Social Service budget," and the minister committed to having his department study the proposal, "since the financial needs in day care presently consume over fifty percent of the total budget and there is no doubt that the day care needs will continue to increase substantially in the future."[61] The province eventually chose, in 1978, to not only separate the funding for day care from other PSS projects (as the city requested) but to remove day care from the PSS program entirely.

The city's efforts on day care in the mid-1970s were complemented by continuing community activism. For example, in 1974 a group called PLAY (People Looking After Youth) secured a Local Initiatives Project grant from the federal government to cover the start-up costs for a day care in the inner-city neighbourhood of Hillhurst-Sunnyside. The problem with these grants, however, was that they could not be used to cover the ongoing operating expenses of a day care. When the grant ended, the community group was forced to run the day care on a "shoestring budget," relying extensively on volunteer labour from parents. For a brief time, the PLAY day care was even held up by Alderman Barbara Scott as a low-cost alternative to the PSS system of day cares, but the community group willingly joined the PSS system in 1975.[62] A second example occurred in the same Calgary neighbourhood. In 1975 the Hillhurst-Sunnyside Community Association secured a grant of $2.25 million from the federal government's Urban Renewal Program. It was used to construct a multiservice centre and a social housing project, and to expand the community hall. The expanded hall included a not-for-profit day care that was never incorporated into the PSS system.[63]

In December 1974, after the municipal election, the City of Calgary's Community Services Committee held a public meeting on Calgary Social Service's proposals for increased standards in PSS day cares. Two groups of commercial operators used the meeting to express their displeasure with the PSS system: the DCAC and the Mother Duck's and Panda commercial chains, represented by Dennis Sorensen, owner of Mother Duck's. This was one of the meetings where Nancy Hall of the B-MDCA and Dennis Sorensen went head to head. Although a few of the speakers at the meeting, including a spokesperson for the Coordinating Child Development Council, supported the draft guidelines, Sam Blakely stated that "he was disappointed the people who seemed to be interested in establishing standards did not attend."[64]

A decision on the matter of raising or lowering standards was made at the Children's Services Committee meeting in January. Just prior to that meeting, Alderman Barbara Scott presented a list of points that she hoped would "provide a useful framework" for making the decision. When Scott had been elected to city council in 1971, she had been a proponent of developing "Calgary's child services to a level that has been shown through research and experimentation across North America, to contribute most effectively to children's sound physical, social and personal growth and well-being." During her first term in office, however, she turned into a meddlesome opponent of css's development of pss day cares.[65] In 1975 she called for the city to "cease operation forthwith of City-operated daycare centres" and to turn those centres (Shaganappi and Bridgeland) over to community groups. This recommendation was consistent with her philosophy that less government was better. "She always had a thing about the department being involved where others could do it," noted Al Hagan. Interestingly, however, Alderman Scott did not merely want the department to cease operating day cares; she wanted it to close "its day care division as a special project."

Barb Scott also opposed, in principle, the city specifying its own standards for pss day cares (although she favoured the retention of reduced city standards until the province's standards were upgraded to meet them). In her view, the city should end its policy of higher standards because it "should not discriminate" against children who did not attend the pss centres. In making this argument, Scott turned her back on her own history as an advocate for pss day cares: she rejected the notion that governments should fund high-quality day care as a preventive social service for low-income Calgarians.

Alderman Barb Scott's approach proved to be very influential, as did the lobbying of commercial operators. The Albertan reported that the Children's Services Committee "abandoned most of the Social Services Department's recommendations for standards" and asked the department to find "ways to make the regulations even more acceptable." The committee also "rejected any position that would imply they think the private day care operators are not doing an adequate job." However, Alderman Scott failed to convince her colleagues to get rid of the municipally run centres or the department's day care division.[66]

In the summer of 1975, the Children's Services Committee, and then city council, voted to reduce the staff-to-child ratios in the city's pss centres (for instance, the ratio for three to six year olds was reduced to one to twelve from one to ten) and to give a greater role to both volunteers and employees without formal training. It is noteworthy that the new ratio for three to six year olds was still closer to the guidelines of the Canadian Council on Social Development (one to nine for children between thirty months and four years, and one to twelve for five year olds) than to the Alberta licensing requirement of one to twenty. Nevertheless, advocates for quality care were unhappy with the change and attacked Alderman Scott for leading the campaign to reduce standards.[67] Interestingly, the reduction in staff-to-child ratios did not mean that each of the city's PSS centres was able to immediately increase its capacity. Other standards, such as the requirement that there be one wash basin for every ten children, meant that capacity could not be increased until "more capital funding from the province became available for alterations" (Bella 1980, 9). It is noteworthy that municipal civil servants failed to mention at any time during the policy discussions in 1974–75 that immediate increases in the capacity of PSS centres required changes in facility standards to accompany changes in staff-to-child ratios.[68]

Overall, the policy debates in 1974–75 were quite different from those in 1971. First, the later debates dragged out for almost two years rather than being concluded in less than a year, thus allowing opposition to build. Second, not nearly as many community organizations and ordinary citizens advocated on behalf of the city's system of PSS day cares and day homes. And, third, the opponents of PSS day care commanded considerable support on city council. Given these factors, the best that municipal civil servants could do was to minimize the damage by fashioning compromises between Scott's proposals and the existing standards, and by being somewhat less than forthcoming about the ways that facility standards would prevent the immediate enrolment of more children in some day cares even after staff-to-child ratios were decreased.

In 1976 and 1977, the provincial government slowly moved toward raising its licensing standards and changing the way it funded day cares. The expertise of Calgary's civil servants was recognized when Eric Haffenden, Calgary's day care consultant and the chair of the AAYC's board of directors, was appointed by the province to be a member of the Day Care Task Force that reported in April 1977. He was the only municipal bureaucrat on the task force.

By 1977 Calgary was sponsoring fifteen day cares (line 7, table 4.1) and six FDH projects through PSS. Furthermore, planning for another PSS day care (Connaught) was relatively advanced and four OOSC centres were receiving limited PSS funding.[69] Despite its commitment to the PSS system of child care, however, CSS knew that the provincial government intended to follow the task force's recommendation that commercial centres be eligible to accept subsidized children (ADCTF 1977, 17). In anticipation of provincial action, and perhaps in the hope of influencing the final form of the province's new system, CSS put forward a new plan to increase the number of subsidized day care spaces in Calgary from 900 to 1,600. The 700 new spaces would be purchased from commercial day cares or FDH agencies that met the province's new standards (the city expected these standards to follow the recommendations of the task force, and thus be quite a bit higher than the licensing standards then in existence). City council approved the plan in January 1978. However, the city had no intention of proceeding with this initiative until it secured the province's commitment to cover 80 percent of the $1.5 million cost.[70]

When the province's new day care standards were announced in March 1978, Calgary's civil servants were as dismayed as their counterparts in Edmonton. On 12 May 1978, Sam Blakely wrote a long letter to John Lackey. One paragraph dealt with staff-to-child ratios:

> The child-staff ratios in the new regulations are absolutely distressing. The report of the Day Care Task Force represented a compromise position to the City of Calgary standards. We were prepared to accept such compromise on condition that the principle of encouraging better care in accordance with children's needs was understood. The new regulations not only go below the minimum recommended by the Task Force, but neglect the direction that parents and caregivers should strive for and be given incentive to exceed the standards. This places our department in the position where we have serious reservations about supporting or enforcing such a set of standards.[71]

CSS attacked the new regulations at a special meeting of the Community Services Committee in early June. Sam Blakely argued that the new regulations were aimed at getting women off welfare and not at giving good child care. Despite their reservations about the proposed standards, however, Calgary's municipal bureaucrats anticipated that the city would soon agree to participate in the new day care program. At the next meeting of the Community Services Committee, they recommended that money be set aside so that the city could take over the licensing of day cares. Calgary's civil servants were evidently far more pragmatic in their opposition than were their counterparts in Edmonton.

On 13 June 1978, the Community Services Committee voted to recommend that city council reject the provincial standards and negotiate with the province for improvements. The dynamics of this meeting were influenced by a protest organized by PSS day cares. Approximately four hundred people, many of them mothers with young children, rallied at city hall and attended the meeting to support the position of CSS. Among the messages on placards carried by the young children were "Where's All the Oil Money Pete??" and "Must Alberta Always Have Lowest Day-Care Standards?" On the other hand, a number of Calgary's commercial operators publicly supported the new regulations and condemned the opposition of the PSS sector. Among these operators was Caroline Kiehlbauch of the DCAC, who had been a member of the ADCTF along with Eric Haffenden. A former president of the DCAC, Kurt Darmohray of Marlborough Day Nursery, wrote that it would be a good thing if the PSS centres had to lower their staff-to-child ratio since "they have too many on the staff anyway."[72]

City council considered the matter on 26 June 1978. Prior to that meeting, Mayor Ross Alger accompanied a provincial cabinet minister on a visit to three (presumably commercial) day cares. The mayor cast the deciding vote when council decided to join the new provincial day care system, thereby rejecting the recommendation of the Community Services Committee that participation be subject to further negotiation. Calgary thus became the first municipality to agree to participate in the new day care program and in September 1978, the city was allocated provincial funds to establish a new municipally administered system of portable day care subsidies. Later that month, over Alderman Scott's objections, city council decided that CSS should take on the task of licensing day cares; Calgary was the first—and ultimately the only—municipality to do so (line 11, table 4.1).[73]

The day care policies and politics in Calgary during the 1970s had several distinctive features. First, there was a stronger emphasis in Calgary than anywhere else in Alberta on day care as a focus for community development. Second, Calgary led the way in linking FDH programs to day cares so that children could obtain continuous care from one agency between birth and twelve years of age. Third, although Calgary developed more PSS day cares than Edmonton, it was well behind Edmonton in the number of other not-for-profit day cares (see table 4.2), so the not-for-profit sector was considerably smaller in Calgary than in Edmonton. Fourth, partly as a result of the third feature, the commercial sector was larger and more politically active in Calgary than anywhere else in the province and exercised increasing influence on public debates and policy decisions as the decade progressed.

Medicine Hat

Between 1970 and 1973, Medicine Hat had only one PSS day care, the community-run Medicine Hat Day Care (MHDC). At the beginning of 1970, four months after it opened, forty-two children attended this facility, which was licensed for fifty. Since the only licensed commercial day care in the city had recently closed, parents had to turn to the new MHDC for licensed care. Fortunately,

MHDC was located in an old school building that could be licensed for many more children. The capacity was increased to sixty in November 1970, but by the following October, this number of spaces was inadequate. To ensure that high-priority children could be enrolled in the centre, some unsubsidized children even lost their places. In June 1972, the facility's license was increased again, this time to 101. For the time being, this soaked up the demand for day care in Medicine Hat and discouraged any would-be entrepreneurs from establishing a commercial centre.[74]

Two other events in 1972 caused day care in Medicine Hat to move in a unique direction. First, the city's original PSS director, John Millar, retired and was replaced by Bob Wanner, who had recently completed a master's degree in social policy at McMaster University. Whereas Millar had established the city's first PSS day care in 1969 as community run, Wanner saw considerable advantages to the municipal administration of PSS day cares. Second, the city conducted a large survey of the need for day care in Medicine Hat: over five thousand interviews were conducted. The interest in and support for day care evidenced in this survey, while not overwhelming, was sufficient to support expansion of the PSS system.

What is particularly interesting about the survey is that it did not generate very many general comments about the controversial nature of day care. While a few negative opinions were recorded (e.g., "Day Care not necessary—mother should stay at home" and "Taxpayers should not have to pay for this"), they were balanced by some highly positive opinions (e.g., "Best thing started in this city").[75] In 1972–73, opposition to Medicine Hat's involvement in day care was not a significant political force. Unlike the situations in Edmonton and Calgary at that time, there were no commercial day cares in Medicine Hat and hence no owners who were motivated by their investments to fight city bureaucrats at every turn.

The forty-one extra spaces added to the MHDC in June 1972 quickly filled up, and by January of the next year, the day care had a waiting list. In response, the board of directors recommended to the city "that the day care program be expanded into neighbourhood areas." City council approved a plan to establish four small centres (with an aggregate capacity of one hundred children) in different parts of the city.[76]

In preparation for the establishment of the new centres, the city assumed administration of the MHDC at the beginning of 1974. Susan Costea, formerly the executive director of the MHDC, was appointed the coordinator of Medicine Hat Day Care Services and took on the many tasks associated with opening four new centres. Two of the new centres opened at about the same time in December

1974 and January 1975; the other two opened in September 1975 and February 1976. Altogether the four new centres were licensed for 130 children. The expansion allowed the city to reduce enrolment at the original MHDC to a more manageable 71 children. According to Bob Wanner, Medicine Hat went the route of direct administration of day cares in order to make it easier to coordinate child care with other community services and to further the cause of pay equity for day care workers.[77]

The city was certainly fortunate that it conceived and began implementing its plan for the decentralized expansion of day care services in the run-up to the March 1975 provincial election. For one thing, the Lougheed government sharply increased its spending on PSS day cares at this time (table A.1). Furthermore, given that the Medicine Hat-Redcliff constituency had been handily won by the Social Credit candidate in 1971, the Lougheed government showed no aversion to new PSS spending in Medicine Hat in late 1974 and early 1975 in order to bolster the chances of the Progressive Conservative candidate, Jim Horsman. As it turned out, every dollar of extra spending seemed to be necessary, since Horsman won the constituency by only 130 votes in 1975. The key change in the voting patterns between the two elections was the sharp decline in the NDP's share of the popular vote from a healthy 16 percent in 1971 to an inconsequential 3 percent in 1975 (Chief Electoral Officer of Alberta 1983, 104, 112). New provincial spending on day cares in Medicine Hat would have appealed to a significant proportion of the voters who switched from the NDP to the Tories in that election.[78]

By the mid-1970s, day care in Medicine Hat looked nothing like day care in any other city in the province. For one thing, the doubling of licensed capacity in the PSS system meant that the municipal program could begin serving "all families who wished to use the facilities rather than just low income or single parent families." Consequently, middle- and upper-income families could enroll their children in the PSS day cares in Medicine Hat without worrying that their children would get bumped by subsidized children. Indeed, in the spring of 1977, the city formalized a policy of reserving 10 to 15 percent of spaces for children of full-fee parents "in order to ensure a cross section of clientele."[79]

Day care in Medicine Hat in the mid- to late 1970s was also unique because it was closely associated with early childhood services (ECS) programs for children between four-and-a-half and five-and-a-half years of age. ECS, or kindergarten, was a voluntary program, but the provincial government was committed to funding enough ECS spaces to serve all those children who were enrolled by their parents. In late 1973 the city hired a "temporary ECS coordinator" to study the need for ECS programs and "work with various groups of parents in the city wanting services for preschoolers, etc."[80] When, in 1975, the Medicine Hat School District decided against sponsoring ECS programs because it feared that the cost to local taxpayers would be too great, the city was a logical choice to fill the gap, becoming the only Alberta municipality to take on this role. By 1977 Medicine Hat operated ten ECS programs, six in schools, two in churches, one in a day care, and one in a senior citizens' complex. Bob Wanner estimated in the spring of 1977 that 85 to 90 percent of all children in Medicine Hat between four-and-a-half and five-and-a-half years of age were enrolled in a city-run ECS or day care, and municipal civil servants had big plans to integrate the two programs. Their idea was to build neighbourhood community centres that would include recreation facilities, a day care, and a kindergarten.

But while the plan may have been visionary in terms of community services planning, it was hatched with little consultation with staff and parents, particularly in the ECS programs. Consequently, it provoked vigorous opposition from the members of the ECS Co-ordinating Council, whose chair stated, "The city bureaucracy is not prepared yet to accept parent involvement in decision making. That's a hell of a conception of democracy." This episode shows the political dangers inherent in the municipal administration of services for young children. Parents are intensely involved in the lives of their preschool children. When parents run a day care or kindergarten directly, civil servants must necessarily consult and collaborate with those parents when changes are being contemplated. In contrast, when civil servants run the show and parents are restricted to an advisory role, it is quite possible for civil servants to miss some of the necessary stages of consultation and hence alienate those parents.[81]

In 1978 Medicine Hat hired Al Hagan from Calgary to run its community services division. With Hagan's commitment to community development and his expertise in day care, the city was in a position to repair its relations with staff and parents, and to get its ambitious plan back on track. However, the province's decision that year to end PSS sponsorship of day cares meant that the plan to integrate educational and recreational services became financially unfeasible. The city continued to administer the ECS programs until 1983, when they were turned over to the Medicine Hat School District.[82]

One important area where PSS day care in Medicine Hat in the 1970s lagged behind Edmonton and Calgary was that of quality standards. For its first few years, the MHDC operated with staff-to-child ratios equivalent to the province's licensing requirement: one to ten for babies and toddlers, and one to twenty for older children. Looking back on this situation in 1994, Susan Costea reported, "These ratios were highly ineffective and little besides basic feeding and toilet training was accomplished."

In her 1973 report as MHDC executive director, Costea recognized the limitations in the quality of care offered at the day care: "The MHDC has had a high child-staff ratio and low salaries which has accounted for the tremendous turnover in staff in the past year, " she wrote. "Due to the large turnover of staff we have encountered much difficulty operating with untrained and inexperienced staff." The ratios were improved for the first time in 1973–74, when the MHDC was able to hire five additional staff members using a six-month Local Initiatives Program grant. Costea reported, "We have noticed a remarkable change in the children with two staff in a room and are able to catch problems before they become habits."[83]

While Susan Costea did not have advanced training in ECE, her successor in the position of co-ordinator of day care services, Karen Charlton, believed that "[Susan] had the vision. The kids should have good care and they had that care." Beginning in the early 1970s, Costea encouraged the staff to take continuing education courses through Medicine Hat College and to attend workshops. She also provided in-service training. Nevertheless, the first two employees with an early childhood development (ECD) or ECE certificate (awarded upon completion of a one-year course) were not hired until 1975, and the first employee with a ECE diploma (awarded upon completion of a two-year course) was not hired until 1977. Therefore, right through the 1970s, the vast majority of the employees in Medicine Hat's PSS day cares had not completed a college course in the field.[84]

Karen Charlton was that first employee with a college diploma. She had moved to Calgary to get her college education from Mount Royal College, since Medicine Hat College at that time did not offer a one-year certificate, let alone a two-year diploma, in ECE. She started working as a child development worker for the City of Medicine Hat in June 1977. Two decades later she noted that "there wasn't a person in the system who didn't care about kids, but there were lots of people in the system that didn't understand child development and how to foster that." In 1978, when Medicine Hat College started offering its one-year certificate course in ECD, eighteen of the twenty-three full-time child care workers in Medicine Hat's five day cares did not hold a certificate or diploma in the field. The city adopted a new salary schedule in August 1978 that provided considerable financial incentive for these eighteen staff members to pursue the certificate. That year, five staff took leaves and enrolled in the course on a full-time basis, funded by Canada Manpower. Some others continued with their employment and took night courses, while others again quit their jobs rather than take the course (even though taking the course was not mandatory—when the city made a ECD/ECE certificate a requirement for employment in its day cares in 1986, long-time employees were protected by a "grandfather" clause).[85]

Satellite FDHs and OOSC were two other areas where Medicine Hat lagged behind Edmonton and Calgary for most of the 1970s. In May 1977, the city's day care advisory committee began a study of the need for OOSC, particularly among the children of lone parents. The city decided to organize OOSC through FDHs, and the first supervisor for this service was hired at the end of 1978. By the end of 1979, Medicine Hat had plans to add ten spaces in day homes for children under two years of age to the thirty spaces for school-aged children.[86]

All told, Medicine Hat offered a comprehensive package of publicly administered child care services at the end of the 1970s, including day cares, satellite FDHs for both young children and school-aged children, and kindergartens. The movement in Medicine Hat had the good fortune of operating in a small city where it was possible for the city government to keep ahead of commercial interests. Nonetheless, child care advocates deserve full credit for taking advantage of that opportunity and building a unique experiment. Consequently, it came as no surprise that Medicine Hat was one of the municipalities in 1978 that strongly opposed the province's new method of funding day care with portable subsidies.

Medicine Hat joined with Edmonton to sponsor a resolution at the 1978 annual convention of the Alberta Urban Municipalities Association that called for negotiations to ensure that municipalities secured a larger role in the new day care system. The city had no choice but to implement the financial terms of the portable subsidy system on 1 April 1979 since funding for PSS day cares would otherwise be discontinued. Nevertheless, it held off approving the details of its participation until 6 March 1979.[87]

At the end of the 1970s, all licensed child care in Medicine Hat continued to be run by the municipality, and a concerted effort was underway to upgrade the average level of training of the workers in the municipal day cares. Medicine Hat's unique approach to day care was a source of considerable civic pride and meant that the city remained committed to its program even after the province abandoned the PSS model in favour of a funding formula that promoted commercial investment. However, the changes made by the province meant that, beginning in the early 1980s, Medicine Hat's own services would face competition from commercial operators that would grow over time. The history of the city's involvement in day care after 1979 is recorded in chapter 8.

Lethbridge, Red Deer, and Grande Prairie

In both Lethbridge and Red Deer, the initial attempts to establish PSS day cares were unsuccessful because of significant community opposition. As described in chapter 3, after Lethbridge proposed a PSS day care in 1969, opponents mobilized to such an extent that the provincial government refused to approve the project. In January 1971, Red Deer City Council voted against the Red Deer Day Care Society's proposal for a PSS day care despite a favourable recommendation from the alderman who chaired the city's Social Service Board. Opponents of the PSS day care submitted a petition with 431 signatures and argued that the day care would amount to "an unnecessary tax load" since there were vacancies in lower-cost commercial centres. Rather than give up, though, the society proceeded later that year to open a day care in Parkland Christian Church that was staffed entirely by volunteers. It was designed "to demonstrate the need and feasibility of the project." This strategy was successful: city council soon reversed its earlier decision and accepted the day care as a PSS project. The Red Deer Day Care was officially opened in January 1972 with a license to care for fifty children.[88]

Opposition to publicly subsidized day care in Lethbridge, however, proved to be more stubborn, and, as a consequence, a PSS day care did not open there until 1974. Even relatively tiny Grande Prairie (only about one-third the size of Lethbridge) had a PSS day care before then (line 2, table 4.1). The failure to establish a PSS day care in Lethbridge before 1974 was not because of lack of trying. Indeed, in the early 1970s, there were a number of advocates for quality, non-profit day care in Lethbridge. The most prominent was Dr. Barbara Lacey, a pediatrician who was elected as the founding secretary of the AAYC in 1971 and who served a term as the chair of the AAYC in the mid-1970s.[89]

One of the earliest PSS projects in Lethbridge was a preschool designed to prepare children from disadvantaged backgrounds for school. This project became very well accepted in the city, and in 1973 a second preschool opened. The following year, Lethbridge Preschool Services project opened a third preschool and quietly expanded its services to include a small day care in the north part of the city, licensed for twenty children. Barbara Lacey said that this approach was taken in order to try to avoid negative community reactions to the day care (Bella and Bozak 1980, 33–36).

Lethbridge finally took some initiative on day care in 1975 when it struck an ad hoc committee to examine the supply and demand for day care in the city and to make "recommendations about the financing of increases in the supply, if it felt such increases were warranted." Barbara Lacey was one of the seven members of the committee, as was the owner of the Kradle Koop Day Care Centre.

The committee organized a small door-to-door random survey to estimate the demand for day care. Forty-four of one hundred households reported having children of preschool age. The parents of the children in these forty-four households were asked about their preferences for child care, and their answers were then used to extrapolate the demand for day care in all of Lethbridge. The committee estimated that there was an unmet demand for about five hundred day care spaces over and above the 205 licensed spaces that existed in October 1975. The strong demand for day care in Lethbridge at this time was also evidenced by the licensing of fifty new spaces between July and October 1975, and by "the fact that, for some years, the private operators of daycare centres in Lethbridge have been attempting rather substantial expansion of their operations."[90]

Not a word of criticism of commercial day care can be found in the ad hoc committee's report, but the committee did criticize the municipal planning commission and other unnamed municipal departments for obstructing the establishment of commercial day cares in residential neighbourhoods and called for city council to remove the obstructions. Furthermore, the committee argued that in an ideal world, commercial operators could meet all of the unmet demand for day care. It ended up recommending the expansion of the PSS system of child care in Lethbridge only because of the "rigidities" in the way that the provincial and federal governments funded day care.[91]

This argument was as conciliatory toward commercial operators as it could possibly have been, short of abandoning the PSS model for day care entirely. At the time, Lethbridge had only three commercial day cares, so the size of this interest group does not explain the conciliatory character of the report. Rather, it would seem that the influence of commercial operators was magnified by the belief that for public policy to be acceptable, it had to cater to the city's conservative ethos. That ethos had been demonstrated in the 1971 provincial election when Social Credit candidates won both Lethbridge-East and Lethbridge-West

(Chief Electoral Officer 1983, 103), and again in 1974 when community opposition caused city council to remove PSS funding from a birth control centre that had been established in 1972 (Bella and Bozak 1980, 52).

Beginning in the mid-1970s, however, there were signs that Lethbridge's political ethos was changing. In the 1975 provincial election, both sitting Social Credit members for the Lethbridge constituencies ran for re-election, and both were handily defeated. Furthermore, the percentage of the vote for Social Credit in Lethbridge was relatively low in the 1979 provincial election compared to the party's percentage in Red Deer and many rural constituencies in southern and central Alberta. Indeed, the percentage of the vote gained by the defeated Social Credit candidate in Lethbridge-West in 1979 (18.5 percent) was far closer to the percentage gained by the Social Credit candidate in Medicine Hat (13.6 percent) than the Social Credit candidate in Red Deer (40.7 percent; Chief Electoral Officer 1983). This certainly calls into question whether by the end of the 1970s, Lethbridge remained Alberta's most conservative city. As will be described later in this section, civil servants in Red Deer were relatively successful in overcoming the initial opposition to PSS day care led by commercial operators and slowly expanded their involvement in day care, eventually getting approval for the hiring of a day care director in 1979. This suggests, contrary to the argument of Bella and Bozak (1980, 57–58), that municipal civil servants in Lethbridge could have likewise become successful advocates for PSS day care in the 1970s if they had been so inclined. The belief that the city's conservatism would have squelched such advocacy became, by the later part of the decade, a convenient excuse for inaction.

Lethbridge had been the last of Alberta's six major cities to support day care through the PSS program and the only one of these cities to never hire a day care director (lines 1 and 2, table 4.1). With the province's removal of day care from the PSS program, Lethbridge was the first of these cities to end all financial support for preschool day care (line 12, table 4.1). Deficit funding for the two PSS centres in the city was discontinued in April 1979.[92] Calgary ended deficit funding on the same date but instituted a new subsidy program for its three municipal centres. Lethbridge did not commit any municipal tax dollars to the care of preschool children after that date, even after it learned that Children's House would close its day home project because of a lack of finances (Bella and Bozak 1980, 38).

The development of PSS day care in the City of Red Deer followed an entirely different course in the 1970s than in Lethbridge, despite the fact that commercial operators in each city were able to block the initial attempts to establish PSS day cares. In Red Deer, municipal civil servants were committed to providing publicly subsidized child care as a preventive service, and, as a consequence, the program grew in a step-by-step fashion throughout the decade. In the mid-1970s, there seemed to be little difference between the PSS day care programs available in Red Deer and Lethbridge. Each city had two PSS day cares in May 1977 compared to the five in Medicine Hat and four in Grande Prairie (line 7, table 4.1). Each city also had a single FDH program supported by PSS. Partly as a consequence of the weak development of day care, in 1975–76 Red Deer and Lethbridge expended far less per capita on PSS programs than did Medicine Hat and Grande Prairie. Indeed, even though Red Deer and Medicine Hat had almost the same population in 1976, overall PSS expenditures in Medicine Hat were almost three times those in Red Deer (line 6, table 4.1).

Appearances, however, were deceiving since behind the scenes there was far greater commitment to PSS day care in Red Deer than in Lethbridge. For instance, in 1976 the PSS staff in Red Deer initiated a meeting of the directors of day cares in the central region of the province "to give them an opportunity to talk over common concerns" (Red Deer and District PSS 1976, 13). The regional character of this meeting reflected the fact that Red Deer had eschewed organizing a PSS program just for itself but had instead organized PSS for "Red Deer and District." Neither Medicine Hat nor Lethbridge took a similar leadership approach in their regions.

In 1977 Red Deer hired a new PSS director, Rick Assinger, who most recently had been the director of ECS for the City of Medicine Hat. Knowing first-hand how successful PSS day care was in Medicine Hat, Assinger prodded his new hometown toward doing more for quality child care. In 1978 the Red Deer Day Care Society and the advisory committee of the day care at Red Deer College proposed that a day care coordinator be hired for the first time in the area. The coordinator's duties would include helping to plan the expansion of the PSS system in the region, supporting the existing PSS programs, and consulting with commercial day cares. The project was approved and Judy Wong was promoted into the position effective 1 January 1979.[93]

After the province announced its intention to fund day care through portable subsidies, Red Deer was one of the cities that expressed concern about the provincial proposal and delayed joining the new system.[94] However, on 27 November 1978, Red Deer City Council voted to join the provincial system effective 1 April 1979. But the council resolution specified four municipal expectations before day cares (commercial or not-for-profit) would be approved to enroll subsidized children: (1) parent advisory boards must be established, and they must hold regular meetings; (2) operators must encourage their staff to participate in training programs organized by the city's PSS department; (3) operators must participate in a day care association; and (4) operators must submit financial reports to the PSS department. The city presented these conditions as steps "to promote the improvement in the quality of day care operations and involve parents more directly in the daycare operations." One of the new day care coordinator's first priorities was to get commercial operators to agree to these conditions and enter into formal agreements with the city. By August 1979, three of the five commercial centres in Red Deer, in addition to the two PSS centres, had accepted the conditions and were eligible to receive subsidized children.[95]

Compared to Medicine Hat, where there were no commercial day cares, and Grande Prairie, where commercial day care did not seem to be particularly viable, in 1979 Red Deer had a number of successful commercial day cares. In this regard, the situation in Red Deer was very much like that in Lethbridge, but the two cities' responses to the provincial system could not have been more different. Lethbridge agreed to administer the province's system without any supplementary conditions on centres while Red Deer insisted that day cares agree to supplementary conditions before they were eligible to receive subsidized children. Red Deer's approach, proven viable when the majority of the city's commercial centres had signed on by the summer of 1979, became a model of renewed provincial-municipal partnership that encouraged Edmonton to finally join the new system.

By the end of the PSS period, therefore, civil servants and local political leaders were strongly committed to the promotion of quality child care in Red Deer. This commitment carried over into the 1980s and 1990s as the city continued to use municipal tax dollars to improve the quality of care in the Red Deer Day Care and Normandeau Day Care (line 12, table 4.1). Red Deer is evidence that consistent advocacy and organizing by municipal civil servants could gradually diffuse opposition to day care during the 1970s. In achieving this success, Rick Assinger and other municipal bureaucrats had the advantage that Red Deer's commercial sector was relatively weak compared to that of Calgary and Edmonton, and there were as yet no large capitalist owners in the city. As a consequence, civil servants had the upper hand in framing the debates about day care in Red Deer and in pushing for greater city involvement in quality initiatives.

The last city to be discussed in this section, Grande Prairie, was considerably smaller than the other mid-sized cities discussed to this point. Its population in

1976 was only 18,000 (line 3, table 4.1), and it did not always register on the radar screens of provincial bureaucrats and politicians. Nevertheless, Grande Prairie played a very important role in the history of PSS day care, both because of the relatively high per capita level of PSS spending in the city (line 6, table 4.1) and because Grande Prairie's civil servants actively promoted the establishment of day cares and FDHs in smaller municipalities throughout northwestern Alberta.

The first PSS day care in Grande Prairie was run by the Grande Prairie Children's Society out of the basement of a church. It served children between three and five years of age. The centre also organized FDHs to look after children under three years. In the year that this project was established, 1972, Grande Prairie had three commercial day cares. The city's PSS director, Jean Lowe, reported that there were "negative feelings about the government moving into day care and forcing private people out of business. In order to prevent this negative feeling and forcing private centres out of business (which did not happen) the publicity has been very low-key."

The new PSS day care in Grande Prairie attracted the attention of some families in the village of Hythe who were interested in better child care. On 1 January 1973, the Grande Prairie Children's Society opened a small day care in Hythe, which had a mere five hundred residents. Jean Lowe wrote, "I feel that none of us really expected it to work or that there would be such a need in the small community." But the pilot project was so successful that the day care was continued as its own PSS project; it operated at full capacity of fourteen children for most of the fall of 1973.[96]

Quality day care in northwestern Alberta received a boost the next year when Grande Prairie Regional College began its early childhood education and development program. Before the end of its second year of operation, the program had satellite classrooms in Spirit River, Slave Lake, and Peace River in addition to its main location in Grande Prairie, and eighty students were enrolled.[97]

Until 1975, the Grande Prairie and area PSS day cares received budget advances that were unconnected to the number of children served. In order to control costs, Jean Lowe instituted a per diem funding system in 1975. That same year, Grande Prairie hired a day care coordinator, whose duties included helping community groups develop proposals for new day cares, organizing in-service training for staff, and encouraging parental involvement in the centres. In July 1975, a new PSS day care started operating in another nearby village, Beaverlodge.

A fourth PSS day care was established later in 1975. Earlier that year PSS had helped cover the costs of a commercial centre in Grande Prairie, Pat's Day

Care, which was in danger of going out of business.[98] Even with this assistance, Pat's Day Care was unprofitable and PSS chose to discontinue the subsidy. This spurred some parents with children in the day care to pursue the idea of buying the business from the owner and running it as a non-profit society that would qualify for full PSS support. Stepping Stones Day Care started operating in November 1975.[99]

The development of the PSS day care system in the Grande Prairie region was not without internal problems. The day care coordinator position, held by Norma Harper, was terminated in early 1977 at about the same time the Volunteer Services Bureau was closed. A provincial civil servant suggested that the actions were taken because Harper and the director of the Volunteer Services Bureau were "bright and articulate" young women and "seem to have threatened a few of the PSS Board—including the chairman." If this analysis is correct, then these actions are further evidence of the gendered character of municipal bureaucracies in the 1970s.[100]

The bigger problem, however, was finances. One indication of this problem was a report that the director of Alberta's Day Care Unit, Catarina Versaevel, wrote in November 1979 on "the various methods municipalities are using to phase-out their deficit method of funding and make the transition to the Family Subsidy method of funding." She wrote, "We anticipate that Grande Prairie will experience difficulty in phasing out the deficit." A large reason for this difficulty was that, unique among Alberta's six major cities, Grande Prairie had taken the initiative to establish PSS day cares in nearby rural centres (Hythe and Beaverlodge). Rural PSS day cares were faced with the dilemma that although their costs were significantly higher than the maximum subsidy provided by the province ($190 for a preschooler), many of their clients did not have the means to pay those extra costs out of their own pockets. The only solution to this dilemma was to cut costs by lowering quality. It appears that the two former PSS day cares in Grande Prairie itself, Awasis and Stepping Stones, also ran into financial difficulty at this time because of an unwillingness to charge parents anything beyond the minimum required by the province.[101]

Grande Prairie, like Red Deer and Medicine Hat, protested the terms of the new provincial system for day care but then joined the new system effective 1 April 1979. Municipal civil servants and politicians, however, remained very committed to quality child care. The city facilitated both the Awasis and Stepping Stones day cares in owning their own properties by providing municipal debentures for which interest did not have to be paid until the principal was retired. Furthermore, small annual grants were made to the day cares to cover the cost of children's bus fares and the use of municipal recreational facilities. More significantly, when Awasis moved to its new location in order to cut costs and no longer had the room to run an FDH program, the city agreed to begin administering that program. The municipal government felt obliged to remain as a direct service provider because its FDH program was the only one in the city that accepted babies and had higher standards than the program operated by Stepping Stones.

The biggest contribution that Grande Prairie made to quality child care at the end of the 1970s and beginning of the 1980s, however, was an extension of its trail-blazing work in Hythe and Beaverlodge. Many groups and individuals in northwestern Alberta contacted the city for advice on setting up FDHs. Municipal civil servants provided that advice and invited people to come to Grande Prairie for a week to observe how the city ran its own FDH program. Grande Prairie's FDH program was so well regarded at the time that the province itself utilized Grande Prairie's standards as a model when it finally developed provincial standards for satellite FDH programs.[102]

Of the three cities discussed in this section, therefore, Grande Prairie was the most innovative in its involvement in child care. Indeed, in the 1970s, no other Alberta municipal government established day cares in neighbouring rural centres (although Red Deer tried to do so) and no other municipal government helped to convert a commercial centre into a community-run PSS centre. With the end of the PSS program, Grande Prairie joined Medicine Hat as the only two of the six major cities that directly administered a satellite FDH program. Overall, while Grande Prairie's level of spending on and commitment to quality initiatives fell somewhat short of Medicine Hat's, this small city made an impact on the development of day care in Alberta that went far beyond its size. This demonstrates one of the greatest virtues of the PSS program: it facilitated exciting developments in day care wherever municipal bureaucrats and politicians took the initiative. The next section briefly surveys the establishment of PSS day cares in centres smaller than Grande Prairie.

Smaller Municipalities

In the 1970s, many local governments in Alberta did not use the PSS program to establish a day care. Among the municipalities in this category were the towns of Leduc and Fort Saskatchewan near Edmonton and the town of Airdrie near Calgary. In the case of Airdrie, in 1978 a provincial civil servant reported that the "mayor and one or two councillors are very much anti-day care." He concluded, "Day care developments in Airdrie are unlikely to take place soon." Without doubt, elected officials in some other centres shared this aversion to day care. But even without ideological opposition to publicly subsidized day care, cost to the municipality was a strong deterrent. The PSS program required municipalities to cover 20 percent of the cost of programs, and 20 percent of the cost of a day care was a heavy burden for a municipality with a small tax base.[103]

The cost issue was documented in a 1975 brief to the provincial government by the Lesser Slave Lake Preventive Social Services Advisory Board. The brief was written "on behalf of small rural-urban municipalities who are finding it financially impossible to provide proper and quality Day Care services as well as continuing the funding of existing [PSS] projects." The town of High Prairie in northwestern Alberta had entered the PSS program in 1969 and thereafter convinced smaller communities near Lesser Slave Lake (notably, the towns of Slave Lake and Kinuso, as well as three Metis settlements) to undertake preventive services as a district project. The brief noted that to open PSS day cares in Slave Lake and High River, the municipalities would have to increase their contributions to PSS by 140 percent. It went on to assert that "a quality Day Care service is essential to a community" and noted that there is considerable "citizen pressure for Day Care services." Nevertheless, covering 20 percent of the cost for PSS day care was creating a "grave situation for municipal finances." It suggested an alternative funding mechanism whereby the province would cover 100 percent of a subsidy up to a particular ceiling, with the municipality covering any subsidy beyond the ceiling.[104]

In 1975 there were twenty-one PSS day cares outside of Calgary and Edmonton (table 4.2). Of these, thirteen were located in towns and villages (excluding the Hythe day care run by the Grande Prairie and District PSS). By 1977 the number of PSS centres in towns and villages had risen to eighteen (excluding both the Hythe and Beaverlodge day cares). Although PSS day cares could be found in rural areas in all regions, they were definitely over-represented in the northwest (seven of the eighteen centres), in part because Grande Prairie served as a model and resource for developing day cares in small communities in the region. In addition, day cares in the northwest qualified for capital grants (to cover renovations or equipment purchases) from the Edmonton-based Clifford E. Lee Foundation. These grants were not available to day cares south of Red Deer.[105]

The province stopped accepting proposals for new PSS day cares in March 1978 but honoured commitments to PSS funding that had already been made.

As a result, new PSS day cares were established in Canmore, Coaldale, and Fort McMurray in 1978 and 1979, bringing the total number of PSS day cares in small centres to twenty-one.[106] At this time, two other small centres—Jasper and Beaumont—had publicly supported day cares.[107] Significantly, these latter two day cares were local initiatives (in Jasper by a school board and in Beaumont by a municipal government) independent of the PSS framework. They demonstrated that local governments in small Alberta communities had the option of making licensed day care a funding priority for their communities. It is noteworthy that both of these publicly administered centres continue to operate in 2010 and, at the time of writing, are the only licensed day cares in their respective communities. With a modicum of financial support, the provincial government could have encouraged many more small municipalities across Alberta to open similar day cares. However, as was described in the first part of this chapter, at the end of the 1970s, the provincial government turned its back on special grants for high-quality, not-for-profit day cares in favour of a portable subsidy funding system. This made it much more difficult to establish not-for-profit centres after 1978, especially in small communities where alternative sources of community funding were limited.

As the province moved toward an election in March 1979, it finally looked as if the provincial government and civil servants were listening to the municipalities and advocates who had so strenuously opposed the 1978 reforms to the day care system. Municipalities still had an important role in day care, and the province had seemingly accepted that municipalities' legitimate role was to promote standards of care that exceeded the province's licensing standards. This offered the hope that although special provincial funding for the PSS day cares was being phased out, new versions of higher-quality day care would emerge under the guidance of municipal civil servants and politicians. What lay ahead, however, was the sudden and unilateral termination of municipal involvement in the provincial day care system.

5. Years of Turmoil, 1979–82

A New System for Day Care Is Born

The events between 1979 and 1982 are more closely scrutinized in this book than events in any other period. This is partly because the political struggles are so compelling but mainly because the policy decisions were so momentous. Bob Bogle, a southern Alberta teacher who had first been elected to the provincial legislature in 1975, was appointed the new minister of Social Services and Community Health (SSCH) shortly after the government of Peter Lougheed crushed the opposition in the provincial election of 14 March 1979. Although in the previous cabinet, Bogle had been a minister without portfolio responsible for Native Affairs, his new assignment in 1979 did not impress the leader of the Alberta New Democratic Party (NDP), Grant Notley, who stated, "It's obvious that Social Services are being downgraded." Notley probably did not know that at least a few Tory insiders were touting the young and energetic Bogle as a rising star in the cabinet, perhaps even the heir apparent of Premier Peter Lougheed himself.[1]

Bob Bogle was an active minister who set a fundamentally new course for day care in Alberta. Specifically, he ended the provincial-municipal partnership in day care for preschool children, introduced and then substantially improved a system of operating allowances that promoted the rapid expansion of commercial day care spaces in urban areas, and cancelled the government's commitment to require training for day care workers. The main legacy of the Bogle years is the infrastructure of aging commercial day cares in urban areas, particularly Calgary and Edmonton. Many of these centres were built to take advantage of the high rates of return on investment that were virtually guaranteed by the provincial government's generous operating allowances. Chapter 6 will analyze the expansion of commercial day care in Alberta in the 1980s and 1990s: how it happened, what profits were made, how the provincial government reacted to the emergence of day care chains in Calgary, and the consequences of commercial expansion for the overall day care system.

This chapter is concerned with the policy initiatives between 1979 and 1982 that laid the groundwork for day care in Alberta in the 1980s and beyond. My goals are to explain why certain policy initiatives were taken while others were abandoned and to analyze how the advocates for quality child care in Alberta were largely marginalized during these years. The chapter concludes by comparing the day care system that took shape in Alberta between 1979 and 1982 with the systems found in Sweden and Texas at about the same time. Alberta's new approach to day care had a number of unique elements. Nevertheless, in terms of its essential features, Alberta's new system was like that found in Texas, just as Alberta's old system of PSS day cares was similar to that of Sweden. This reflected an important shift in the type of liberal welfare regime pursued by the provincial government.

BOB BOGLE'S STYLE AND SYMPATHIES

The new minister of SSCH quickly proved himself to be confrontational and headlong in style, and eager to chart a new policy direction in day care that emanated from commercial operators and their supporters on the backbenches of the Tory caucus.

Right from the start of his term, Bogle seemed to harbour a disdain for the intricacies of day care policy issues and a certain disrespect for the civil servants working in the area. Two of the bureaucrats who worked on day care in SSCH at that time have argued that the minister was unable to work with civil servants in a collegial and respectful fashion. Apparently he interpreted critical comments by civil servants as having an ulterior political motive rather than as an attempt to improve policy and programs. This was seen during the 1980 review of the Preventive Social Service (PSS) program that preceded its replacement by the Family and Community Support Services (FCSS) program in June 1981. Bogle's political assistant, Catharine Arthur, issued an "edict" that only supportive/constructive advice and commentary were welcome from civil servants. The expectation was that any reservations or negative opinions would not be communicated. In this context, when reservations or negative opinions were expressed, they were judged as an attempt to undermine the government and as lacking good professional intent. At least one mid-level manager who defied the edict during the PSS review was summarily transferred from his position in the department.[2]

Given his distrust of civil servants, it is not surprising to learn that Minister Bogle's political assistants, Catharine Arthur and Gordon Thomas, played very important roles inside the department. In fact, both were moved into senior civil service jobs. Arthur became an associate deputy minister and the chair of the department's executive council in early 1983 and Thomas became the director of FCSS. When the department was reorganized on a regional basis in 1981, some of the regional manager positions were likewise filled by political insiders rather than career civil servants. One of the unintended consequences of these political appointments was that the appointees tended to stay in the same job for an inordinate length of time, simply because they were judged as unqualified for other positions at the same or higher levels. For example, Gordon Thomas remained as director of FCSS for approximately a decade.

Provincial civil servants had been working to incrementally improve day care standards over time throughout the 1970s and had enjoyed professional working relationships with the two ministers who had preceded Bob Bogle, Neil Crawford and Helen Hunley.[3] Long-time civil servant John Lackey immediately recognized the threat to the incremental approach posed by Bogle's intention to let backbench Tory MLAs play a leading role in reviewing and initiating changes to the day care program. A memo from early May 1979 analyzed the role of the Saskatchewan day care advisory board (established in 1975) and offered arguments in favour of establishing such an advisory board in Alberta. The memo envisioned an advisory board "with representatives with day care expertise from the varying sectors" along the same lines as the Day Care Task Force of 1977. It also systematically outlined how such an advisory board would be superior to the proposed MLA Review Committee. The memo concluded with strong support for the establishment of an advisory board, "possibly as an alternative to the proposed MLA Committee." This was an audacious bureaucratic initiative to try and abort Bob Bogle's plan for a one-sided, backbenchers' review of day care.

More memos followed in June. One analyzed the history of the Ontario advisory council on day care that existed between 1974 and 1976. A second indicated strong support for the establishment of an Alberta advisory committee even if the MLA Review Committee did proceed. John Lackey wrote:

I think an independent—but relating to government—Committee could do much to defuse the current situation in Day Care. It could be an excellent neutral sounding board for all parts of the daycare system, assist with better information distribution and generally act as a knowledgeable catalyst for the incremental change that is inevitable in the daycare system during the next five years.[4]

The last sentence clearly presented the bureaucratic vision of incremental change, a vision that civil servants justifiably feared might be rejected by the new minister if he listened too closely to backbench Tory MLAs and the commercial operators who were strongly lobbying those MLAs. The advisory committee was eventually established in 1980 and survived until 1986. However, it did not even start its work until after the committee of Tory backbenchers had completed its review and Minister Bogle had decided to make fundamental changes to day care in Alberta. Bureaucratic resistance proved futile to this strong-willed minister, who dreamt that reform of day care could be one of his springboards to the premier's office.

Among opponents of the Lougheed government, Bob Bogle became a favourite target of criticism. By the spring of 1980, his name had become synonymous, at least in the letters pages of the *Edmonton Journal*, with mismanagement. Following the 2 November 1982 provincial election, the *Calgary Herald* editorialized that Bogle was one of two members of the old cabinet who "should not find places in the new."[5] Yet it does a disservice to the complex day care politics of 1979–82 to explain what happened solely as the consequence of the force and faults of the minister's personality. It was Bob Bogle's ideological affinities with commercial day care owners that played a more important role during these years than the dogmatism, suspicion, anti-intellectualism, and confrontation that marked his management style. The Lougheed government had come to power in 1971 with the strong support of urban voters in Edmonton and Calgary who were supportive of progressive action on day care. The minister from 1971 to 1975, Neil Crawford, was elected from Edmonton and was thus very aware of the political importance of the urban new middle class, along with urban workers. Bogle had run in the 1971 election but had been defeated by a Social Credit candidate. In the 1979 election, Social Credit won only 19.9 percent of the popular vote across the province and elected but four members. A large proportion of the free enterprise conservatives who had formerly supported Social Credit had switched their allegiance to the Tories by 1979. Bogle aligned himself with the free enterprise lobby in day care and put his considerable energies and ambitions to work for them. He undoubtedly believed in their cause, but he would have also seen them as a significant group of potential supporters in any run he might make for the leadership of the Tory party.

Bob Bogle became minister of SSCH approximately one year after his predecessor, Helen Hunley, announced that the province would partner with willing
municipalities to subsidize the day care costs of low-income Albertans through
a portable subsidy program. She predicted that 40 percent of the families with
children in commercial centres would qualify for subsidization. A year later,
Edmonton, unlike other major municipalities, had still not agreed to become a
partner in the new subsidy program. This was the first pressing day care issue
that the new minister had to address.

Two groups who were unhappy with the situation were commercial operators
and their clients. The Edmonton Independent Day Care Operators Association
launched a petition drive in April 1979 and organized a rally on 16 May. The petition protested the possibility that the City of Edmonton would be allowed to
impose supplementary quality-of-care standards on commercial centres before
parents in those centres could receive subsidization. It was posted in twenty-two
commercial centres and concluded, "We are happy with the respective centres
we now use." At the time of the rally, Bogle's assistant, Catharine Arthur, stated
that "parents are understandably angry because they haven't received day-care
fee subsidies promised to them a year ago."[6]

Those involved with Edmonton's fifteen PSS day care centres also mobilized
at the time. They sought to win funding concessions from the province that
would allow the centres to maintain the high standard of care they had offered
under the PSS system of deficit funding. In late May, the Edmonton Day Care
Council, composed of the directors and non-profit operators of the PSS centres,
lobbied the eighteen MLAs elected for Edmonton.[7]

David Gilbert remained the director of Edmonton's Day Care Branch in
1979–80. He remembered the commercial operators in Edmonton having the
provincial government's ear although they were not as well organized as those
in Calgary. They certainly had much better access to MLAs than advocates from
the not-for-profit sector. Gilbert recalled that Edmonton's not-for-profit directors were told that cabinet ministers did not want to talk with them, but those
same ministers continued to meet with commercial day care owners. This was
certainly bad for the Lougheed government's political image since, as Gilbert
noted, "it would have appeared more open if they had at least met with both
sides." The fact that Bogle and other cabinet ministers were, at one point, not
even willing to talk to non-profit advocates left no doubt that their ideological

loyalties lay firmly in the camp of the business owners who ran day cares on a commercial basis.[8]

In the early spring of 1979, the Day Care Branch raised the possibility of the city ending all involvement in day care rather than accepting the terms of the new provincial program. It argued, "The provincial proposal essentially changes the status of day care from that of a preventive social service developed by a municipality in response to local needs to a provincial program, with provincially determined standards and under provincial control, but with the *option* of municipal administration." To exercise that option, the city would have to pay 20 percent of the costs of the provincial program. In justifying the withdrawal option, the Day Care Branch drew "a parallel ... with child welfare and social assistance services": in the past, these had been "areas of considerable municipal responsibility," but the province had assumed full responsibility for the former in the mid-1960s and the latter in the mid-1970s, and now regarded them as "statutory services." "Day care, except for expectation of municipal cost-sharing, appears now to be considered by provincial authorities in the same light."[9] This would seem to be a very prescient analysis given the Lougheed government's decision to end all municipal involvement in preschool day care in 1980. Nevertheless, I will argue later in this section that the end of municipal participation in Alberta's day care programs was far from inevitable; rather, it was the result of the conjunction of a small number of determining factors.

The question of refusing to participate in the provincial day care program was debated by Edmonton City Council in April 1979. By a narrow margin of two votes, council decided to continue negotiating with the province "after several aldermen, including Lois Campbell and Ron Hayter, warned the City would be foolish to abandon its day-care involvement and allow children to face the consequences."[10] Senior bureaucrats for the province and city met in early June to look for common ground. Shortly before this, however, Minister Bogle stated that he would not negotiate provincial day care standards with Edmonton and "criticized Edmonton's publicly-funded Glengarry day-care centre, saying it had the highest per capita costs in the province." When Bogle met with Mayor Cec Purves on 12 June, it came as no surprise that he was unwilling "to allow the City special concessions with respect to conditions or criteria that would amend or contravene the Day Care Regulation." Nevertheless, the city's representatives left the meeting with the understanding that for the next four years, the province would continue to cover 80 percent of the deficits for all aspects of the city's PSS day care program. It was on this basis that city council voted on 15 August 1979 to join the provincial day care system effective 1 January 1980, although the city declined the opportunity to assume responsibility for licensing day cares. This left Calgary as the only municipality that had taken over licensing.[11]

Any goodwill created by Edmonton's reluctant decision to join the new day care system was very short lived. Between August and October, Bob Bogle and Mayor Cec Purves engaged in a correspondence that ended on a very acrimonious note. Purves' notification of Edmonton's decision to join the provincial program had stated his "understanding ... that the cost of quality day care will be shared 80 percent by the Government of Alberta during the transition period [until 1983]" and had listed a number of outstanding issues, resolution of which "is urgent." The most surprising issue on the list was "Municipal requirements for commercial Day Care Centres," since this issue had not been minuted in Purves' 12 June meeting with Bogle. It was as if the mayor thought that by joining the new day care system, he could immediately win further concessions from the minister. Given that Minister Bogle was, if nothing else, dogmatic, this proved to be a colossal miscalculation: the city's attempt to continue negotiating the non-negotiable backfired.[12]

Bob Bogle replied to Purves on 17 September 1979, stating, "There still seems to be some misunderstanding about the terms of the Provincial Day Care Program." His first clarification was that the province would not continue to cover 80 percent of the deficit in Edmonton's community day care program until 1983 but would step down its contribution in each of the next three years. The minutes of the 12 June meeting are ambiguous on this question, but both Mayor Purves and Edmonton's commissioner of public affairs, A.H. Savage, were convinced that Bogle had agreed to the 80 percent deal. The mayor's language on this issue was very blunt and inflammatory. In his first reply, he stated, "I don't understand how Commissioner Savage and myself could have misinterpreted the content of our discussions together" and indicated that Bogle's position was "of grave concern." His second reply accused the minister of misleading him on the matter and threatened to re-examine the city's involvement in the day care program.[13]

I have no way of knowing whether this dispute occurred simply because the province and city misunderstood each other at the 12 June meeting. A second possibility is that Bogle was purposefully vague about the deficit funding phase-out as part of his negotiating strategy. There is also a possibility that, given Minister Bogle's confrontational style, he decided to "stick" Edmonton with a larger share of the deficit as a "reward" for continuing to dispute issues that the province had clearly indicated were not open for discussion. In support of the last of these three possibilities, we know that in November 1979, Catarina Versaevel wrote to PSS directors and indicated that each PSS program could come up with its own plan to phase out deficit funding of day cares up to 1983, and in February 1980, the department policy was recorded thus: "PSS centres have until March 31, 1983 to phase-out existent deficit with no explicit formula and/or imposed provincial procedures." There is no doubt, therefore, that in September 1979, Minister Bogle was imposing a unique condition on Edmonton rather than applying an established department policy on the phase-out of deficits in PSS day cares. As a consequence, the partnership between the provincial government and Edmonton on the new subsidy system got off to a decidedly rocky start.[14]

As mentioned at the beginning of this section, commercial operators and their clientele were worried that the City of Edmonton would somehow limit their access to the province's subsidy money. This fear seems justified by Mayor Purves' mention of "Municipal requirements for Commercial Day Care Centres." Bob Bogle's reply on this question was unambiguous:

I would like to reaffirm that under the terms of the Family Subsidy Program the issuing of a provincial license automatically qualifies a private centre for participation in the program. There can be no phase-in for private centres. All centres licensed, publicly funded and private, can expect to receive the family subsidy effective January 1, 1980.[15]

This kind of language would have been music to the ears of commercial operators. It is important to note that Minister Bogle's uncompromising line on this matter was a departure from the position taken by the department at the very end of Helen Hunley's tenure as minister. Prior to Bogle's appointment, provincial bureaucrats had encouraged and expected municipalities to play an important role in pressuring poor-quality commercial centres to improve the quality of care, lest those centres be denied subsidized children.[16]

When it came to the issue of standards, the City of Edmonton proved to be just as uncompromising as Bob Bogle. In the fall of 1979, Edmonton Social Services (ESS) prepared a set of policy guidelines for the family subsidy program. Among those guidelines was a requirement that "the Operator or staff shall not discipline a child through the use of corporal punishment." ESS felt it necessary to include this guideline since the 1978 Alberta Day Care Regulation ignored the issue of child discipline. On 17 January 1980 and again on 11 February 1980, the province requested that the city delete the requirement. In doing so, it implicitly defended the right of day care staff to use corporal punishment. The city refused to delete the requirement and creatively defended its position by quoting from a 1975 memo written by Duncan Rogers, then the acting deputy minister of Alberta Social Services, stating that corporal punishment "is not condoned by this Department."[17]

The Day Care Branch circulated the draft guidelines to commercial operators on 9 November 1979. In a covering letter, David Gilbert wrote, "I know day care has been a controversial subject in this city for quite some time. However, we must now work together in the best interest of the children and families in this community." A total of ninety-five commercial operators were invited to participate in the family subsidy program. By the middle of January, however, only twenty-one of these operators had signed participation agreements, presumably because the majority of operators found one or more of the city's requirements to be onerous. This meant that the vast majority of families whose children qualified for day care subsidies were still not collecting those subsidies in the middle of January, even though the new system was officially up and running in Edmonton from 1 January 1980.[18]

This was a crucial moment in the history of day care since the committee of backbench Conservative MLAs was completing its comprehensive review of all aspects of the day care system, and Bob Bogle was considering his options on how to proceed with regulatory, administrative, and funding changes. At exactly the same time, many commercial operators in Edmonton were complaining about the conditions to which they had to agree in order to participate in the subsidy program. Furthermore, numerous low-income parents were undoubtedly displeased that they had not yet received the subsidy that had been promised.[19]

Minister Bogle demonstrated his concern with the situation in Edmonton in late January, when he indicated that the provincial government might have to "move unilaterally to provide assistance to Edmonton residents who are entitled to day care subsidies."[20] The City of Edmonton's principled opposition to the province's new day care system had caused it to raise policy issues like corporal punishment in the midst of establishing administrative procedures and had led it to be content with involving only a minority of commercial operators at the onset of the system. By the middle of February 1980, only about a third of the commercial operators in the city had joined. From the standpoint of day care programming, these were sensible positions, but from a political standpoint, they merely strengthened the hand of those who saw day care as a custodial service best run by commercial interests.

Even after the problem of Edmonton's non-participation in the family subsidy system was solved, ESS continued to be a thorn in Bogle's side. My contention is that Edmonton provoked a reaction from the provincial government by constantly placing political and administrative roadblocks in the way of the timely implementation of the family subsidy plan. If the city had joined the plan earlier and/or if the city had taken steps to ensure that low-income families received subsidies as soon as the plan began, there is a reasonable chance that the province would have continued to treat day care as a joint responsibility with municipalities.

Provincial civil servants learned that Bogle was contemplating a major change in the day care system when, on February 11, 1980, he raised "tentative directions" that emanated from the MLA Review Committee chaired by Charles Anderson. At a meeting on February 18, Anderson listed the five principles recommended by his committee:

1. The province should provide 100% funding.
2. The [province] should license day care facilities.
3. If municipalities wish to provide care beyond the basic regulation level, they should provide the necessary extra funding.
4. Stop deficit PSS funded centres as quickly as possible.
5. Reduce and simplify the subsidy application procedures and simplify and streamline the wording in the Regulation.[21]

This information makes it clear that the Government of Alberta ended its partnerships with municipalities in the administration of day care on the recommendation of the MLA Review Committee. Minister Bogle was completely in tune with the thinking of his Tory colleagues on the committee, so he not only accepted this recommendation but almost immediately began implementing it. The province announced the end of municipal involvement in the provincial day care system on 29 April and began the new system on 1 August 1980. It is also noteworthy that the government announced its new direction before it had made plans for the future of satellite family day home (FDH) programs and out-of-school care (OOSC) programs, thus creating considerable problems for itself in subsequent months.[22]

In analyzing this dramatic shift in the direction of day care in Alberta, a shift that reversed fifteen years of joint municipal-provincial responsibility, the key question is this: what is the underlying reason for the review committee's recommendation and Bob Bogle's hasty implementation of that recommendation?

One possible explanation is that the MLA Review Committee was simply bringing day care into line with a general program shift away from municipal involvement in the funding and administration of social services. A proponent of this explanation is a former day care director for Edmonton, David Gilbert, who argued in an interview: "I think that what happened was that the province had a much larger social services agenda at the time. I think that if they'd shared it with us, we would have understood where it was they were going." In Gilbert's view, the trend toward provincial control of social services, which dated back to the 1960s, was supported by two specific factors in 1979–80. First, the Lougheed government had decided, after being in power for two terms, "that it was easier to run the province ... based upon the corporate management style than it was to have local community involvement." Second, the chief deputy minister of SSCH, Stanley Mansbridge, had come to Edmonton from Ottawa and had a broad provincial perspective on programs.

This is an interesting and plausible explanation for why the province decided to arbitrarily end its partnership with municipalities in preschool day care, but it is unsupported by documented evidence. Prior to 1980, neither the political nor administrative branches of the provincial state had formulated plans for day care that would exclude municipalities. Indeed, there was no discussion whatsoever of this policy shift prior to Minister Bogle's "tentative directions" of 11 February 1980. Consequently, I am certain that this policy initiative did not originate with Mansbridge or any other provincial civil servant. Furthermore, the cabinet never discussed the change, either prior to or after 11 February, indicating that this was likely not a top-down initiative of the Lougheed government.[23]

A second possible explanation for the decision to end municipal responsibilities in the provincial day care system is citizen complaints. Specifically, it is possible that citizens in many parts of the province were complaining to the provincial government because their local governments were unwilling to join the subsidy system and hence they could not obtain a day care subsidy. Ray Petrowitsch, co-owner of Happy Day Care in Calgary and past president of the Private Day Care Society of Alberta (PDCS), offered this rationale in early May 1980, and so did the minister. While this also seems plausible, the facts suggest otherwise. Thirty-two municipalities had signed subsidy agreements by 1980, including all of Alberta's major cities. Furthermore, by the middle of 1979, the new portable day care subsidy system had provoked "increased municipal involvement in day care services," with many small municipalities having contacted the provincial Day Care Unit about possible involvement, including municipalities that had not set up day care services under the PSS program.[24] It is reasonable to conclude that within a couple of years, access to day care subsidies would have been almost province-wide and that special arrangements could have been made to assist those relatively few citizens who lived in communities that decided against joining the system. On this latter point, it is noteworthy that in 1979 municipalities and the province were discussing whether a municipality that had joined the provincial plan could make arrangements to subsidize the day care costs of families who lived in an adjacent municipality.[25]

In my view, the problem of access to day care subsidies in rural parts of Alberta was a convenient justification for ending municipal involvement in day care rather than a determinant of policy change. If the problem had been generating a great deal of dissatisfaction in the province, civil servants would have highlighted it in their internal communications in 1979. It is significant that this problem was not listed among the "contentious day care issues" in the briefing notes prepared for Minister Bogle prior to the fall 1979 session of the provincial legislature.[26]

While the preceding two explanations are suspect, a third explanation for the ending of municipal involvement has a great deal of support: Bogle and the MLA Review Committee were simply reforming the day care system along the lines suggested by commercial day care operators in Calgary and Edmonton. The idea that a single interest group had captured a democratic government's policy agenda should be treated with considerable suspicion, especially on an issue like day care where competing interest groups are well defined and have considerable public support. But for three reasons, this is precisely what happened in Alberta in 1979–80. First, the Lougheed government decimated the opposition parties in the election of March 1979, repeating its previous election success in 1975. This made ministers like Bob Bogle less likely to pay attention to interest groups that usually aligned themselves with opposition parties. Second, whereas civil servants often act to ensure that the ideas and concerns of prominent interest groups are fairly presented in policy discussions, in this case an MLA Review Committee was allowed to formulate a plan without the checks and balances of bureaucratic input. And, third, the minister shared the free enterprise zeal of commercial day care operators to make major changes to the day care system. As a consequence, while advocacy groups like the AAYC enjoyed less influence during the Lougheed government's second term (1975–79) than in its first term (1971–75), during Bob Bogle's tenure, their influence became almost negligible.[27]

There is a great deal of evidence that commercial operators had unprecedented access to and influence on Bob Bogle from 1979 to 1982. Some of this evidence is relatively innocuous, such as a reporter's observations in May 1980 that "private operators, who run most day-care centres in the province, seem to have caught the minister's ear with the arguments for change" and that they gave "Bogle nothing but praise" after he announced the end of municipal involvement in the day care system on 29 April.[28] Earlier in this chapter, I provided evidence that Bogle favoured commercial operators over non-profit advocates in the 1979 struggle over the terms of Edmonton's participation in the new subsidy system. Further proof of the cozy relationship between Bogle and commercial operators will be outlined in my discussions of operating allowances and staff training programs later in this chapter. At this point, I will examine a day care licensing appeal that occurred at exactly the same time as Bogle accepted the recommendations of the MLA Review Committee. This incident again suggests that the minister had very strong sympathies for the commercial sector.

The dispute involved an Edmonton commercial day care that had recently been sold. Under the previous ownership, this day care had been operating according to the standards in place prior to the 1978 Regulation. Upon the change in ownership, however, it was legally required to adhere to the new standards. Furthermore, the new owner applied for an increase in the licensed capacity. Routine inspections were carried out and reported to the director of licensing, Pieter de Groot. He decided that he could not approve a license since day care consultants had concerns about the quality of the program, licensing inspectors advised that the day care did not meet the new standards, and the fire inspector would not approve the proposed increase in capacity.

Pieter de Groot's decision was quickly appealed and Minister Bogle established a three-person appeal committee, the chair of which was none other than Jacqui Kallal, head of the Edmonton branch of the PDCS. The appointment of a commercial operator as the chair was referred to by the president of the Alberta Association for Young Children (AAYC), Michael Phair, as a "conflict of interest." Indeed, at the time, Kallal was herself disputing a decision by Pieter de Groot concerning the size of her operation.[29]

Kallal's appointment to the appeal board is further confirmation of the very close relations between Minister Bogle and the PDCS. It also calls into question the judgement of the minister, since he failed to recognize that the appeal board's finding would be tainted by the perception that its chair could not render an impartial judgement. Bogle could have diffused this criticism by ensuring that the other two appointees to the appeal board had professional expertise in early childhood education (ECE) or day care, but he failed to do so.[30]

I have already detailed the frustration that both commercial operators and Minister Bogle felt at the slow implementation of the family subsidy program in Edmonton. In general, commercial operators in Edmonton and Calgary were apprehensive about municipal involvement in the day care system. Because both cities had long supported quality care, they could be counted on to continue to do so within the limited roles they had in the new system. For instance, Edmonton linked its day care subsidy program to a ban on corporal punishment despite repeated requests from the province not to do so. Furthermore, the provincial Day Care Unit suggested that Calgary's licensing inspectors were monitoring the Day Care Regulation more closely than were provincial inspectors.[31] For commercial operators, eliminating municipal involvement in day care administration was the next best thing to lowering standards or even deregulation.

Indeed, the relaxation of government oversight and regulatory standards was the fifth recommendation of the MLA Review Committee, which read, "reduce and simplify the subsidy application procedures and simplify and streamline the wording in the Regulation." The perspective of commercial operators is unmistakable in this recommendation given the general tendency of business owners, day care owners included, to treat reasonable regulatory distinctions and expectations as red tape.

My conclusion, then, is that municipalities were phased out of preschool day care in 1980 not because of any long-term reorientation of social services in Alberta, not because of a centralized directive from the inner cabinet, and not because of a public relations crisis caused by the failure of some small municipalities to join the provincial system, but rather because commercial operators found a minister who shared their free enterprise ideology and who, over the course of his first year on the job, developed a personal antipathy toward the municipal day care program run by the City of Edmonton. It might very well be the case that there was nothing Edmonton could have done to change the outcome, given the highly ideological cast of Bob Bogle's actions. But it seems likely that had the portable subsidy system been working efficiently in Edmonton during the time of the MLA Review, there would not have been the same level of criticism of municipal involvement in the system. And if, at the same time, Edmonton had toned down its policy criticisms of the province, it is at least conceivable that Minister Bogle might have decided to leave well enough alone and maintain the provincial-municipal partnerships in preschool day care.

The province took over complete administrative control of the day care system on 1 August 1980. Barely one month later, Bob Bogle announced a breathtaking improvement in the minimum required staff-to-child ratios in day care. The improved ratios meant that day cares would have to hire many more workers to care for the same number of children. Whereas the 1978 Day Care Regulation had stipulated a ratio of one staff person for every six babies (eighteen months of age and younger), the new regulation required a ratio of one to three. For toddlers (nineteen to thirty-five months), a doubling of staff was also mandated: a new ratio of one to five supplanted the old ratio of one to ten. And for children aged three and four years, a 50 percent increase in staff was necessitated by the introduction of a one to eight ratio, replacing the old ratio of one to twelve.

All things being equal, the new staff-to-child ratios would have resulted in a sharp increase in the cost of day care to pay for the extra staff. To limit such increases and to speed the adoption of the new ratios, the province introduced a new universal funding program. Known as "operating allowances," it involved financially subsidizing every child in a licensed day care. Day cares that operated with the new ratios would immediately qualify for an operating allowance of $50 per child per month, even though the new minimum standards would not become mandatory until 1 August 1982. By meeting a new indoor space requirement of three square metres per child (up from 2.5 square metres), a centre could qualify for an additional allowance of $5 per child per month.[32]

Advocates for quality child care praised the minister's announcement. Alderman Barbara Scott of Calgary opined, "They're the first forward steps in day care in years." The president of the AAYC, Michael Phair, endorsed the improvements in ratios and group size, and commented, "We are pleased and convinced that these significant changes will help Alberta's children receive the kind of care that they deserve." Support for the new standards and operating allowances also came from Jacqui Kallal, president of the PDCS. The minister knew that some commercial operators might object to the initiatives on philosophical grounds, so he made a point of holding a meeting with day care operators in Calgary within hours of announcing the program. He explained that the operating and space allowances were necessary so that "full fee-paying parents wouldn't be driven away from day care." As will be discussed in the next chapter, not all commercial operators were convinced by Bogle's argument. Nevertheless, the influential capitalist operators supported the initiative since they recognized that a dramatic improvement in staff-to-child ratios at no additional cost to the consumer would make it easier to market their service. The government's initiative had created new investment opportunities in day care.[33]

A number of factors contributed to the timing of Minister Bogle's announcement, its exact content, and the subsequent increases in the value of operating allowances between 1980 and 1982 (see table A.6). But a single group deserves credit for putting the notion of operating allowances on the policy agenda: the MLA Review Committee of 1979–80.

At the same time as it called for ending the provincial-municipal partnerships in the day care system, the MLA Review Committee recommended improving the nutritional and staff-to-child requirements in the Day Care Regulation. Furthermore, the committee recommended "a grant on a per child/space to pay for increased child/staff ratio, nutrition, etc." The committee termed this "an overhead cost." This was a novel idea for provincial civil servants since a hand-written addition to a memo explained the proposal as "above subsidy to family."[34]

Minister Bogle and Charles Anderson immediately requested that the director of the day care unit estimate the cost of improved staff-to-child ratios at five different centres so that they could get an idea of the required size of the operating allowance. Three of the centres were from the not-for-profit sector, and the other two were owned by leaders of the PDCS: Marlborough Day Care Centre in Calgary, owned by Kurt Darmohray and his wife Gertrude, and Northeast Day Care Centre in Edmonton, owned by Jacqui Kallal. At that time (February 1980), the MLA Review Committee proposed two possible schedules of staff-to-child ratios. The first mirrored the ratios in the 1978 regulation except for slight improvements in the ratios for babies and mixed age groups above two years in age. The second improved the ratios in all age groups but fell decidedly short of the improvements that were eventually introduced in September.

While Minister Bogle almost mechanically implemented the proposals of the MLA Review Committee when it came to ending municipal involvement in the day care system, this was not the case for the new staff-to-child ratios and operating allowances. In this section, I will identify the factors that pushed the government toward requiring such high minimum staffing levels in day care, supported by an innovative universal financing program.

Legislated minimum standards for day care was an important public issue in Alberta in 1980. In 1978 the Day Care Unit had studied how Alberta's new and improved Day Care Regulation compared to the regulations in other provinces. It concluded that on a number of measures, including staff-to-child ratios, staff qualifications and training, space per child (indoor and outdoor), and washroom facilities, "Alberta regulations and requirements are clearly below the requirements of most other provinces." In regard to staff-to-child ratios in Alberta, the report stated, "The requirement of one staff person to six children 0-18 mos. of age is clearly the lowest in Canada as is the 1:10 ratio for children 2-3 yrs. of age."[35] This report was not released to the public, although advocates for quality day care were well aware that many of the standards in Alberta's 1978 Day Care Regulation did not measure up in comparison to other provinces or to the recommendations of child care professionals.

There was greater public scrutiny of Alberta's day care standards in 1979 after the Edmonton Journal surveyed day care facilities across Canada and "found that Alberta ranks at the bottom end of the scale in the care provided." The survey concluded "that Alberta ranks last in one crucial area, the ratio of staff to children, which determines the amount of personal attention a child receives." A report on the survey was featured in the Calgary Herald. It included the views of the secretary of the Joint Committee for Quality Child Care, Connie Conway, who stated, "The regulations are terrible." At around the same time, the province's Day Care Unit updated the interprovincial comparisons it had completed the previous year.[36] Consequently, provincial civil servants and politicians were well aware that day care standards, particularly staff-to-child ratios, would have to be improved or else Alberta would continue to be portrayed as a laggard on the national stage. It is hardly surprising that the MLA Review Committee in February 1980 recommended improving the ratios.

Nevertheless, Minister Bogle did not proceed with immediate ratio improvements. When he announced on 29 April 1980, that the province would fully fund and administer day care, he indicated that the MLA Review Committee would continue to "consider" the issues of ratios and staff qualifications into 1981. Alberta NDP leader Grant Notley immediately criticized the government for failing to improve staff-to-child ratios. He called on Alberta to meet the ratios in effect in Ontario and Saskatchewan, and a reporter noted that "average staff-child ratios are one to five in Ontario and one to 11 in Alberta." Comparing Alberta unfavourably to other provinces had become a favourite tactic of those advocating higher day care standards. A leaflet distributed by activists compared Alberta to other provinces on four criteria: staff-to-child ratios, maximum centre size, nutritional requirements for lunch, and indoor space. It concluded: "WHY DOES ALBERTA HAVE THE WORST STANDARDS IN CANADA????" This is the type of argument that was impossible for the government to refute and that just would not go away.[37]

Until the summer of 1980, commercial operators had generally argued against making any improvements to the staff-to-child ratios specified in the 1978 Regulation. Calgary's pre-eminent day care entrepreneur, Dennis Sorensen, warned against "overstaffing" in day care and argued that critics needed to "respect the phase-in period [to 1983] for both standards and staff qualifications." The president of the PDCS, Jacqui Kallal, defended Minister Bogle's decision to delay improvements in standards. "She said higher standards will result in higher fees" and also argued that criticism of the care in commercial centres "insults parents who are the best judges of standards for their children."[38]

However, two events in the spring of 1980 increased the pressure on the government to make immediate improvements in staff-to-child ratios. The first involved one of the centres in the Panda chain in Calgary. This centre had continued to operate according to the day care standards that were in effect prior to 1978, which meant that the required staff-to-child ratio for children aged two years and above was one to twenty. (Day cares that were in existence prior to the 1978 regulation had the legal right to operate according to the old standards until 1983, although they were not eligible to receive subsidized children.) Dissatisfied with the quality of care, about twenty-five parents pulled their children out of the centre at the end of April and formed an informal committee to lobby for better day care. Such coordinated parental action in itself is noteworthy. but the incident took a strange twist when the group was joined by one parent whose child remained enrolled in the Panda centre. When she learned of this father's involvement in the group, the centre's manager, May Grieg, expelled his daughter. The manager also incorrectly declared the parents' group to be illegal and threatened lawsuits against parents who had made critical remarks about the quality of care in the centre, accusing them of trying to "discredit private day care."

The press coverage of this event highlighted how controversial it was to have any day cares operating on the pre-1978 standards. The former day care licensing supervisor for the City of Calgary reported that the Panda centre in question did not always meet the one-to-twenty ratio. He stated, "There have been occasions when the staff-child ratio has crept up on one to 25 and the operator has been cautioned." Even casual observers would have been shocked at these ratios: this type of minimal custodial care might have been acceptable in the early 1900s, but it certainly fell outside of community expectations three-quarters of a century later.

The press coverage also eroded the credibility of the owners of Panda and their supporters in the PDCS. Commenting on the expulsion of the child, the president of the Day Care Association of Calgary (DCAC), Caroline Kiehlbauch, said, "We would never take this approach." About half of the commercial centres in Calgary, but not the Panda chain, belonged to the DCAC. In contrast, the president of the PDCS, Jacqui Kallal, stated that the Panda centre was justified in its decision because the parents' group was "trying to discredit private day care."[39] In this incident, prominent commercial operators reacted very defensively to criticism, and did not seem capable of putting children's interests ahead of their business interests.

Second, if the Progressive Conservatives (PCs) had not yet realized that inaction on day care was a political liability, they would have come to this understanding when Social Credit issued a major policy statement on day care in late May 1980. The statement called for up to $5 million per year in new spending in order to improve day care standards; this meant that both opposition parties with seats in the legislature (the NDP and Social Credit) were now criticizing the Lougheed government from a leftist perspective. The Social Credit leader, Bob Clark, argued that since Alberta had a budget surplus of more than $1 billion, it could easily afford $5 million more per year for developing a comprehensive day care program. Clark's specific proposals included hiring more civil servants for day care consultation, setting a maximum size for a day care at sixty-five children, and improving staff-to-child ratios to a level slightly better than the best of the MLA Review Committee proposals.[40]

The first indication that the government might act quickly to improve day care standards came in early July 1980. Two Tory MLAs from Calgary stated that they and other caucus members favoured immediate improvements in staff-to-child ratios. Dennis Anderson, MLA for Calgary-Currie, reported that he'd received "a fair number of calls" on the subject. The callers were concerned "with standards and the level of care in Alberta in comparison to that in other provinces." The MLA for Calgary-Forest Lawn, John Zaozirny, stated that he'd received sixty to seventy letters and phone calls on day care over the preceding two months. "It's been a concerted but sincere lobby effort by daycare operators and parents," he said. The next day Minister Bogle demonstrated that this was more than wishful thinking on the part of the MLAs: he indicated that some day care standards "may be dealt with in the near future." However, he left the impression that a day care advisory committee would first be appointed and that he would act after he had received its recommendation on appropriate staff-to-child ratios.[41]

At about this time, Minister Bogle would have learned the results of a new study conducted by Price Waterhouse Associates for his department. It addressed exactly the same question that internal department studies had addressed in 1978 and 1979: how did day care in Alberta measure up to day care in other provinces? Price Waterhouse concluded, to no one's surprise, that Alberta's staff-to-child ratios were at "the low end of the range." The fact that this study was even commissioned shows the provincial government's sensitivity to criticism.[42]

The staff-to-child ratios announced by the minister in early September 1980 and included in the 1981 Day Care Regulation far exceeded the ratios initially considered in February 1980; they moved Alberta from worst to first in the national rankings. The new standards on group size and indoor space also moved Alberta to the top of the national rankings. As a consequence of these three improvements in standards, Calgary Social Services (CSS) reported a significant improvement in the overall ranking of day care standards in Alberta relative to other provinces. Whereas prior to the reforms Alberta had been ranked dead last in the country, CSS now ranked Alberta as being tied for the fourth-best day care standards in Canada, and not very far behind the second- and third-ranked provinces.[43]

The influence of provincial civil servants can be seen both in the high level of standards introduced by Minister Bogle and in a number of his concurrent announcements. First, the government established the Alberta Day Care Advisory Committee (ADCAC), something bureaucrats had been promoting since the spring of 1979. Second, the government committed itself to financially supporting the development of a satellite FDH program, especially for the care of babies and toddlers. Satellite FDHs had been one of the innovative features of municipal day care programs, something provincial bureaucrats well understood. Until this time, however, Bogle's reforms in day care had ignored this option for care. Third, the government returned OOSC to the PSS program, where it would be planned and administered by municipalities and cost-shared by the province and municipalities on a 80 percent/20 percent basis, respectively. This corrected another mistake that the minister had made when he acted so quickly in ending municipal involvement in the day care system. Finally, the government promised to expand its day care consultation services. This had been recommended by the Day Care Unit in February 1980 but opposed at the same time by Charles Anderson of the MLA Review Committee, who "cautioned that the staff of the Day Care Unit should not increase." A few months later, the bureaucratic position had won out over that of the Review Committee.[44]

One other development confirms that, in the later part of 1980, provincial civil servants were successful in influencing the direction of governmental policy. The MLA Review Committee had explicitly recommended that the government not set a size limit on day care centres. This would have been a very popular position with day care developers in Calgary, since they had recently built and were planning to build centres that served as many as 156 children. No announcement on this issue was made by Bob Bogle on 4 September, but the government soon decided to limit the size of centres to eighty, as indiçated by an instruction sent to licensing inspectors on 17 September 1980.[45]

My argument is that the provincial government rushed into offering operating allowances as a result of mounting political pressure in the spring and early summer of 1980. An unusual aspect of this policy initiative is that it was announced well before cabinet had agreed to fund it. On 27 November 1980, Bogle submitted a formal request to cabinet for funds to cover the payment of operating allowances (retroactive to 1 September) as well as administrative fees for FDH agencies and expenses associated with the planned regionalization of service delivery. Cabinet approved the request on 16 December 1980. Given that Bob Bogle was a junior minister, he would not have fast-tracked the introduction of operating allowances in this way without first receiving high-level approval.[46]

Another indication that this was a rushed policy initiative is the flat $55 offered for every licensed space in a day care. The flat fee ran counter to the reason that operating allowances were introduced in the first place—to cover the increased staffing costs associated with improved staff-to-child ratios. Since the new regulation called for a doubling of the staff looking after babies and toddlers, but only a 50 percent increase in the staff looking after three to four year olds, it made sense that the operating allowances for the former two groups should have been much higher than for the latter group. This problem would be corrected in 1981.

In the end, operating allowances were introduced to quell the mounting concerns about day care standards among advocates, parents, and the press while simultaneously enhancing the profitability of commercial day care. At this point, the investment of a few more millions of dollars in day care did not appear to faze the Alberta cabinet in the least. The funding, approved on 16 December 1980, meant that the operating budget for day care would increase from about $7 million in 1980–81 to an estimated $16.5 million in 1981–82. Furthermore, there is no indication of the government discussing the fact that the allowances given to commercial centres for day care would be entirely ineligible for cost-sharing under the terms of the Canada Assistance Plan, while allowances given to not-for-profit centres would likely be ruled eligible for federal funding. As will be discussed in chapter 7, this would soon become an important issue. However, in 1980 the provincial government was literally awash in oil royalties so could afford to spend a considerable amount of money on the problem of day care standards. For the fiscal year 1979–80, Alberta had a surplus of over $1 billion for the third consecutive year, and non-renewable resource revenue alone almost matched government expenditures of $4.7 billion. The provincial budget tabled in April 1980 projected a surplus of $1.7 billion in 1980–81, with an additional $1.7 billion to be added to the Heritage Savings Trust Fund. Expenditures were budgeted at $5.4 billion. Furthermore, the government began the year with an accumulated cash surplus of about $2.8 billion.[47] This was a unique moment in Alberta's history, a time when it was fiscally possible to introduce any number of innovative programs for the care and education of young children and for the support of families with young children. The policy direction chosen by Minister Bogle and his backbench colleagues showed a strong commitment to a free market conservative blueprint for day care.

The provincial cabinet approved substantial increases in operating allowances on 14 April 1981. The size of the increases had been recommended by the ADCAC established in the fall of 1980. An across-the-board increase in operating allowances was to compensate for the high rate of inflation in 1980–81. In addition, there were substantial increases in the operating allowances for infants and toddlers "to reflect ... actual cost to operators in salaries for additional staff required to meet higher improvement levels." The allowances for infants and toddlers were raised to $180 and $110, respectively, while the allowance for three to four year olds was only raised to $70.[48]

At the same time as the government increased its financial support for very young children in day cares, it did not add any money to the FDH program. Therefore, the care of a baby in an FDH was supported only by a $40 monthly administrative fee paid to the day home agency while care of the same baby in a day care was supported by the $180 monthly allowance. The Tory caucus expressed some reservations about the size of the new operating allowance for infants since "it may make it more difficult to implement Caucus' intent to focus family day homes services on infants up to 18 months of age." The new funding arrangement was also criticized by a commercial operator and leader of the DCAC, Caroline Kiehlbauch, who "said it makes more sense to have women care for babies in their homes than to have them in centres where staff levels must be one for every three infants." Furthermore, the director of Little People's Day Care in Calgary, Kitty Fenske, noted that most non-profit centres used FDHs to care for infants rather than group care centres. Fenske, who was also a leader of the Calgary Joint Committee for Quality Day Care, expressed disappointment that no new funding was committed to day homes.[49]

Despite these criticisms, the operating allowance for infants increased by another $60 in 1982 (to $240 per month; see table A.6). Throughout his term as minister of SSCH, Bob Bogle remained committed to ensuring that day cares could continue to profitably care for infants while meeting the one staff to three children ratio. This is evidence of the continuing influence of large commercial operators on government day care policy. It also reflects an imbalance in the composition of the ADCAC, which did not include a single representative from the FDH sector.[50]

STRUGGLES OVER STAFF TRAINING PROGRAMS
AND QUALIFICATION REQUIREMENTS

The 1978 Day Care Regulation had promised the establishment of a registry of qualified staff as a basis for requiring 50 percent of the child care workers of a day care to be registered by 1 April 1983. By the middle of 1980, no progress had been made toward this goal, but when Minister Bogle announced the establishment of the ADCAC on 4 September 1980, it looked like the government would finally get around to fulfilling the promise. The members of the ADCAC "were charged with being 'the eyes and ears of the Minister' to inform him of the reception of the new regulations and funding and to explore the question of establishing a Registry of trained Day Care workers." Indeed, a press release indicated that the minister expected the committee to help design an "on-the-job training program" that would complement the existing post-secondary education programs in ECE. The PDCS would later argue that this promised training program was exactly what they had proposed earlier that year.[51]

In May 1980, the PDCS had publicly criticized ECE programs at colleges like Mount Royal in Calgary and Grant MacEwan in Edmonton, and had expressed a desire to establish its own self-regulated staff education program. PDCS president Jacqui Kallal admitted that commercial operators did not want to fill 50 percent of their staff positions with college graduates and hoped that completion of the PDCS education program would qualify a worker for inclusion on the proposed staff registry. This was a creative attempt by the PDCS both to deskill the notion of a qualified day care worker and to directly control the credentialing process.

Kallal made very disparaging comments about ECE graduates from community colleges, claiming that they did not know how "to love and cuddle children," were unwilling to change diapers, and used their study of psychology in college to "psych out our children." When hiring for her own day care, Kallal said she looked for workers with nurturing, motherhood instincts who enjoyed children. She claimed that within three to six months, such women were usually much more accomplished employees than college graduates. Reading between the lines, however, the PDCS seemed to have two interrelated concerns. First, if only college graduates were eligible for the staff registry, wages would likely be driven up because of a shortage of registered workers. Second, if a commercial operator was forced to employ college graduates in half of the staff positions, that group of employees might well challenge work patterns that shortchanged children in favour of increasing profit.

Both ECE educators and students at Mount Royal College contested Kallal's arguments. Some students were aware of instances where college-educated staff refused to follow the instructions of commercial operators because they were expected to perform kitchen or janitorial duties in addition to caring for children and this went against their professional responsibilities to the children. One student also challenged Kallal's assertion that loving children is an adequate foundation for becoming a qualified day care worker. "Loving children isn't enough," stated Cathy Lane. "It's important to understand the best ways of caring for children."[52]

From 1980 to 1982, responses to the PDCS proposal were mainly negative. It was opposed by civil servants in the Department of Advanced Education and Manpower; by Minister Jim Horsman, who followed his bureaucrats' advice; by advocates for quality child care; and by those associated with the post-secondary programs in ECE. But the PDCS proposal did have a key supporter: SSCH Minister Bob Bogle. Indeed, Bogle's consistent efforts to promote the establishment of a PDCS training program, despite opposition from most quarters, are the best evidence we have of the depth of his commitment to the commercial day care sector. With the help of three separate grants approved by Minister Bogle, the PDCS eventually established the Early Childhood Academy (ECA) of Calgary. It began operating in 1983 and held a graduation ceremony for its first class of twenty-six students in early 1984.[53] Such was Bogle's support for the academy that the PDCS could have easily justified naming it in his honour.

Bob Bogle had the PDCS's staff training proposal in mind when he named the members of the advisory committee. Five appointments were made to the ADCAC in September 1980, and none of these individuals was employed as an ECE professional (such as a college instructor or day care consultant). In a letter to the minister, the president of the AAYC termed this "a serious oversight," but the minister chose to ignore this criticism when he made two additional appointments in early 1981. The ADCAC in 1981–82 comprised two commercial operators, one of whom was a past president of the PDCS; two parents with children in commercial centres; two parents with children in non-profit centres; and the chair, Dr. Audrey Griffiths, a family practitioner who had served as Alberta's representative on the Federal Commission for the International Year of the Child. Minister Bogle was astute enough to realize that ECE professionals would have been very critical of the PDCS plan for staff training, and keeping them off of the advisory committee would at least make it possible for the committee to accept the PDCS plan. The AAYC again complained in May 1981 about the absence of an ECE professional on the committee, and the organization also called for the appointment of a day care worker and a representative from northern Alberta.[54]

While the composition of the ADCAC was fairly one-sided, tilted in favour of commercial interests, the chair, Dr. Griffiths, was every bit as much an advocate for children's rights and quality day care as an ECE professional. She took her appointment very seriously and was highly regarded throughout the province, and it was primarily through her efforts that the ADCAC accomplished a great deal of work and developed a stance that was quite independent of the government. Also promoting an advocacy role for the committee until she resigned in the fall of 1982 was Ann Moritz, one of the parents with a child in a non-profit centre. She was an education student who had previous training in early childhood development.[55]

It was at this time that the PDCS established itself as the dominant lobby group for commercial operators in the province, with the DCAC and the Edmonton Independent Day Care Operators Association fading from public view. In the early 1980s, the PDCS's members owned more than one hundred centres across Alberta.[56] Most importantly, its members included the entrepreneurs who were building day care chains in Calgary. Because of the major investments they were making in day care, and because of the substantial profits that were at stake, these day care capitalists actively supported and generously funded PDCS initiatives.

The PDCS formed an education committee and submitted its first staff training proposal to Minister Bogle in the fall of 1980. At about this time, the organization received a feasibility grant from the Department of SSCH, although the grant does not seem to have been publicized.[57] Even though the PDCS proceeded with its attempt to redefine the notion of staff training in day care, it did not give up on the possibility that it could get the government to abandon the plan for mandatory staff qualifications. In 1981 Mel Finlay had the job of coordinating the licensing, consultation, and subsidy units of day care. On 26 January 1981, he reported that "the first 200 letters received by the Day Care Advisory Committee were against changes to the regulations and against the requirement for trained staff in day care centres." The following month, Minister Bogle spoke at a meeting of day care operators and parents in Lethbridge, where a number of parents complained to him that the staff-to-child ratios introduced the previous year were unnecessary and should not have been introduced. Noting the "raging debate" over standards that had occurred in previous years, Bogle asked these parents, "Where were you?"[58]

In March 1981, Bob Bogle approved a $25,000 pilot grant to the PDCS so that it could further develop its proposal for an apprenticeship training program. When the ADCAC asked Bogle about it at their meeting on 12 June 1981, he indicated that this was a one-time grant meant to develop one of the possible options for training day care staff. He also reported that the Department of Advanced Education and Manpower had indicated it could not gear up for this type of apprenticeship program. Since there was "a need to do something during the next year for day care," he suggested that the PDCS apprenticeship program may not go through advanced education. This grant allowed the PDCS to complete, in October 1981, a proposal for the Day Care Assistant Certificate Program.[59]

In the meantime, ADCAC had received a number of submissions on mandatory staff qualifications from groups such as Alberta community colleges, the AAYC, and CSS.[60] The advisory committee submitted a staff registry plan to Bogle in the fall of 1981. The minister was very active in getting the committee to revise its plan to include the proposed PDCS certificate program and address other matters. At a meeting on 8 December 1981, Dr. Griffiths advised her ADCAC colleagues "that what she felt was needed was a statement which would be acceptable to the Minister but in the same spirit as the committee's original recommendations, and which would include the assistantship grade of training of the PDCS."

The ADCAC's new plan for a staff registry included four categories of workers: (1) those with a two-year college diploma in ECE and "directors grandfathered into the Registry on the recommendation of an Evaluation Committee," (2) those with a one-year college certificate in ECE, (3) those who had completed a certified day care assistant program, and (4) those who were enrolled in one of the aforementioned courses. The ADCAC recommended a gradual phasing in of requirements for qualified staff, such that by 1 January 1988 "every day care centre shall have 50% of its workers in category 1 and all other workers in category 2, 3 and 4, but no more than 25% shall be in category 4." This proposal accommodated the PDCS by giving its training program equivalent standing to a one-year college certificate in ECE. However, it was unacceptable to commercial operators since it would require them to hire many college graduates with ECE diplomas over the coming years. For example, with the staff-to-child ratios announced in 1980, a centre that looked after sixty-one children (six babies, fifteen toddlers, and forty preschoolers) needed to have a minimum of ten primary staff on duty just to look after the children. Under the advisory committee's proposal, by 1988 at least five of those ten staff would need to have a two-year college diploma in ECE.[61]

At the end of 1981, it looked like the government was prepared to establish the staff registry and enact mandatory staff qualifications. Minister Bogle apparently discussed this matter with the cabinet on 16 December, although there is no documented record of that discussion. In preparation for that cabinet meeting, the minister scheduled a working meeting with the ADCAC on the evening of 15 December in his office.[62]

At exactly the same time, the education committee of the PDCS was engaging in discussions with both Mount Royal College and the Department of Advanced Education and Manpower over its proposal for a day care assistant certificate program. The committee was composed of four individuals, all of whom held post-secondary educational credentials of some sort. Three of the committee members were commercial day care operators while the fourth member, Colleen White, was the director of another commercial centre.[63]

The PDCS had criticized the ECE programs at community colleges in 1980 and continued these criticisms into 1981. In the fall of 1981, the chair of the Department of Social Sciences at Mount Royal College initiated a meeting with Colleen White to investigate these criticisms. He reported "that the Private Day Care Society of Alberta had no criticism to make of our programs, but were simply attempting to get more money from the government to fund training programs for daycare workers." After meeting with the director of college programs for the Alberta government, Neil Clarke, the college decided to have further discussions with the PDCS. The dean of Community and Health Studies at Mount Royal met with Colleen White and two other members of the PDCS education committee on 22 December 1981. The dean learned that the members of the education committee were not even aware that Mount Royal's certificate program in ECE was offered in the evenings for individuals currently employed in day cares. In reference to the proposed certificate program for day care assistants, the committee emphasized that it would "not be overly academic" and that it would be designed to engage the interest of an individual who "often lacks the necessary motivation to pursue an educational program." Furthermore, they indicated that the PDCS wanted to maintain control over "their program" since they felt that "employers provide valuable input to any academic program." These observations made it clear that the PDCS wanted an educational program that would help it maintain a large pool of low-wage labour and would be generally sympathetic to the commercial operator's perspective.[64]

In the fall of 1981, the PDCS submitted three separate drafts of its education proposal to the College Programs Division of the Advanced Education and Manpower Department. Civil servants had reservations about the "prescriptive" curriculum in the proposal that "appears to respond to the needs of owner-operators of day care centres rather than children placed in these centres."[65] After the PDCS submitted a budget for the proposed program in February 1982, Deputy Minister Henry Kolesar informed Minister Jim Horsman that "the Society's budget is more than 50 percent overhead, and represents a per student cost of approximately $1,300. A similar program at Grant MacEwan Community College or Mount Royal College would cost between $900 and $1,000." He added that "the type of training apparently being proposed by the Society does not live up to the standards of the program in the Public Colleges. Hence, it is difficult for us to advocate approval of the Society's proposal."[66]

Advanced Education took the approach of putting off making a final decision, presumably hoping that the matter would be otherwise resolved. In June an internal memo noted, "We are checking on a rumour afield in Calgary that the Kallal proposal has been funded (probably by Mr. Bogle's office)." Formal approval for funding from SSCH was given by Minister Bogle on 28 July 1982, and Advanced Education never had to communicate a final decision on the PDCS proposal.[67]

This sequence of events convincingly demonstrates Bob Bogle's affinity for commercial day care operators and in particular the PDCS. His strong support for the day care assistant certificate program stands in sharp contrast to the minister of Advanced Education and Manpower, who was inclined to follow the advice of civil servants in his department on the matter.

No sooner did Bob Bogle approve funding for the ECA than he abandoned the idea of required staff qualifications in day care. On 13 September 1982, the

ADCAC "was informed by Hon. Bob Bogle ... that cost of implementing regulations and the registry would be too high due to apparent lack of trained staff in many centres (especially private), low rate of hiring from college programs, possibly due to low wages compared with other occupations, high turnover of staff in centres, and apparent low cost benefit from requesting Advanced Education and Manpower to expand diploma programs." Bogle arrived at this conclusion based upon the results of an internal government study of day care workers in Alberta. The study showed that 68 percent of commercial centres did not have even a single staff member with an ECE diploma and that only 13 percent of all day care workers had this credential. Of the workers with an ECE diploma, slightly more than half were concentrated in a mere 10 percent of the province's centres. Furthermore, the turnover of workers with ECE diplomas was estimated to be "at least 40 percent per year."[68]

Minister Bogle's decision coincided with an economic recession. The unemployment rate in Alberta in September 1982 was 9.4 percent, up sharply from 3.4 percent in September 1981, and there was a marked change in the finances of the provincial government: a budget surplus of $41 million in 1981–82 turned into a budget deficit of $2.1 billion in 1982–83 (these figures do not include royalty revenues transferred to the Alberta Heritage and Savings Trust fund). The recession had a significant impact on the demand for day care. The not-for-profit Dover Day Care in Calgary reported a vacancy rate of 30 percent in September 1982 even though it had been filled to capacity in the Septembers of the previous few years. The overall vacancy rate in Calgary was estimated at 20 percent, and more than half of the 121 centres in the city were now running OOSC programs. Such programs were far less profitable than day care, partly because they involved only a portion of the day and partly because the government did not provide operating allowances for the care of six- to twelve-year-old children. Nevertheless, many day care centres were in financial difficulty due to the high vacancy rate and turned to OOSC programs to weather the economic recession.[69]

With demand for day care falling, and with the government no longer rolling in cash from petroleum royalties, the opportunity for further advances in day care standards had suddenly closed. It would not be until the beginning of the 1990s that the provincial government would introduce a staff qualifications regulation in day care (albeit not as strong a regulation as the ADCAC had recommended in 1981). And it would not be until 2002 that the high annual turnover rate of qualified workers was finally addressed when the government introduced wage enhancements for qualified staff. In walking away from the staff qualifications issue in 1982, Minister Bogle followed an economic logic that defined the Lougheed Tories; as a result, a unique historical opportunity to improve the quality of licensed day care was lost.

DAY CARE ADVOCATES ON THE PERIPHERY OF POLICY DEVELOPMENT

An important consequence of the end of municipal participation in Alberta's system of preschool day care in 1980 and of Bob Bogle's relentless promotion of the interests of commercial operators from 1979 to 1982 was the marginalization of advocates for quality child care. Groups like the AAYC and the social services departments of urban municipalities desperately sought to influence the direction of day care policy in Alberta in the early 1980s. As they had all along, they rejected the role of "outsider" and attempted to work as "insiders" with the provincial government.

As described in chapter 4, groups advocating for quality day care in Alberta went from being core insiders in the early 1970s to specialist insiders in the mid- to late 1970s. During Bob Bogle's tenure as the minister of SSCH, these groups became peripheral insiders—groups with "the insider form ... but little, if any, influence" (Maloney, Jordan, and McLaughlin 1994, 27, 31). Although the minister and his department continued to formally treat groups like the AAYC as insiders, they became increasingly marginal to important policy discussions and decisions. Indeed, the provincial government and bureaucracy came to see important advocacy groups as opponents, and those groups acted in kind. Earlier in this chapter, I outlined the adversarial relations that developed between the province and the City of Edmonton in 1979–80. By 1982 relations between the AAYC and the provincial government had a similar oppositional character. Given Minister Bogle's ideological sympathies for the commercial sector, it is difficult to see how things could have been otherwise.

The plan for mandatory staff qualifications was withdrawn just prior to the campaign for the 1982 provincial election, held 2 November. It had the potential to be an election issue, especially after a member of the ADCAC, Ann Moritz, resigned in mid-October to protest government inaction on the staff registry. Civil servants in SSCH panicked about the potential for political fallout after attending the annual conference of the AAYC, held on 16 October. One of the sessions at the conference was titled "Who Makes Day Care Policy in Alberta?" Speaker Sheila Campbell identified the "determinants of policy in hierarchical order." A provincial civil servant attended and made notes on her presentation. I reproduce these notes verbatim both to set the stage for the government reaction to the remarks and to record Campbell's considerable insights into the politics of day care in Alberta at that time.

ORDER OF INFLUENCE	FACTORS OF INFLUENCE
Political philosophy of significant members of Cabinet	"laissez-faire—a no accountability policy" "a caveat emptor policy—let the parent beware"
Cabinet and Legal Branch	"quality sacrificed to cost factors" "concerns about legal hassles impede the closing of poor centres"
Minister	"heavily influenced by private operators and media and masked from reality" "Day Care lost in huge department"
Caucus	"if no input from constituency they are influenced by their own biases"
Bureaucrats	"implementation of policy varies, best intention but subjective. No status." "appears MLAs distancing themselves from bureaucrats in favour of non-professional advisors"
Municipal governments	"Bureaucratic commitment to quality has impact"
Programs	"Cost/quality decisions have impact"
Interest groups/ individuals/ associations/ community colleges	"limited impact"
Parents	"impact only if they exercise the power of the dollar"
Children's needs	"no impact on policy"[70]

After the AAYC conference and the receipt of Ann Moritz's letter of resignation, the director of the Day Care Branch prepared and hand delivered a "sensitive alert" to Minister Bogle, with the notes on Sheila Campbell's presentation attached. Melane Hotz observed that Moritz's statements were similar to Campbell's remarks and speculated that "the two incidents in one week, at this time, may be related, as I have been told that there was some informal questioning from outsiders at the Conference about 'trouble on the Committee' and the 'cancellation' of the Registry." She advised Minister Bogle "that there may be media enquiries on the issues of the Advisory Committee role, the two Committee vacancies, and the Registry, in an effort to obtain some commitment from you prior to the election." This was a "sensitive alert" because the minister had not made public his decision to abandon the staff registry plan.[71]

Melane Hotz prepared a further warning on 5 November (just after the election) when she learned that Ann Moritz had released to the *Edmonton Journal* the internal government study of day care workers and had been interviewed by the paper. A reporter for the *Journal* was prepared "to do an exposé of day care," although the reporter had honoured Ann Moritz's request that all the information she provided not be made public until after the election.[72]

This episode is perhaps a fitting end to Bogle's tumultuous years in charge of day care in Alberta. The exposé was published on 13, 15, and 16 November. Despite his apparent desire to remain as minister of SSCH, Bob Bogle became the minister of Utilities and Telecommunications on 19 November, when the new cabinet was sworn in. He left his post under a dark cloud, having been accused by Ann Moritz "of blocking desperately needed daycare improvements, and of being unconcerned about daycare quality." "I've toured daycare centres across Alberta," stated Moritz, "and most private centres are a complete and utter disgrace. I'm afraid of what happens to kids who come out of those." To support her argument that the government needed to legislate a requirement for trained staff, Moritz noted, "I felt the few private centres I saw which were anywhere near good had trained workers."

Ann Moritz also said she had witnessed the physical abuse of children in day cares, including a severe spanking, and complained that government inspectors were "terrified of losing their jobs" if they tried to close a bad centre. Referring to the former director of day care licensing, Pieter de Groot, Moritz noted, "The last time someone tried to do something about a [bad] centre, he was fired."[73]

These events demonstrate that in the early 1980s, advocates for quality day care could still find an audience for their concerns through the mass media, and the provincial government was still very sensitive to their criticisms. While they had become peripheral insiders in the provincial policy process, advocates continued to indirectly influence the direction of Alberta's day care system through their capacity to critique and politically embarrass the provincial government. Consequently, the unique configuration of standards and funding that developed in Alberta at this time was not a pure market model, despite the free enterprise proclivities of Minister Bogle and many of his colleagues in the Tory caucus.

UNIQUE FEATURES OF ALBERTA'S NEW DAY CARE SYSTEM

Between 1966 and 1978, the provincial government had partnered with municipalities to establish and maintain a network of high-quality, not-for-profit day cares throughout Alberta. The provincial government then decided to turn its back on this model and struck out in an entirely new direction. This new direction was determined by three main factors. First, key provincial politicians, and in particular the minister of SSCH from 1979 to 1982, supported free enterprise ideology and looked to the commercial sector to meet the growing needs for day care. Second, a strong movement for quality day care had developed alongside the not-for-profit PSS day cares. This movement was provincial in scope and included municipal bureaucrats and politicians, ECE professionals, trained day care workers, and the thousands of parents whose children had benefited from high-quality day care. An important source of strength for this movement was that it could point to the day cares developed with PSS support as practical alternatives to what the commercial sector had to offer. Third, the change from one system to another coincided with an economic boom in Alberta that saw the provincial government awash with royalties due to high oil prices.

The unusual configuration of Alberta's new system is shown in interprovincial comparisons of day care for 1982 and 1983. The commercial sector was stronger in Alberta than in any other province, controlling 70 percent of all preschool spaces.[74] At the same time, the Government of Alberta spent more on day care per capita than any other government ($98.36 per person per year). Alberta also led the other provinces in supply of licensed spaces, with 8.1 spaces for every one hundred preschool-aged children, well ahead of second-place Manitoba (6.8 spaces) and third-place Ontario (6.0 spaces). Alberta's record on day care standards was mixed: while its staff-to-child ratios were among the best in the country, it was among the provinces that had no training requirements for day care directors or workers. Finally, the average cost of day care was considerably less than the cost in Ontario and approximately the same as in the other large Canadian provinces, despite Alberta's requirement of relatively high staff-to-child ratios (Price Waterhouse Associates 1982).

Another way to identify the unique features of the Alberta day care system in the early 1980s is to make comparisons with two jurisdictions outside Canada where day care was developing in two very different ways. The first comparator is Texas. As in Alberta, Texas had a strong demand for day care because of the economic boom caused by high oil prices. And as in Alberta, the number of licensed day cares in Texas increased rapidly at this time, especially in the commercial sector. But the growth of licensed day care in Texas occurred without significant public investment and consequently was driven by market forces. Nevertheless, the Government of Texas did play an important role in the expansion because it left in place very low staff-to-child ratios, allowing the owners of licensed day cares to keep their prices low and compete for market share with unlicensed babysitters.[75]

For four year olds, Texas required a ratio of either one to eighteen or one to twenty (depending upon the age structure of the group). The latter ratio tied Texas with five other states for the lowest required ratio in the United States and was equal to the ratio that existed in Alberta prior to the 1978 Day Care Regulation. For two year olds, Texas required a ratio of either one to eleven or one to thirteen; the latter ratio was the lowest in the entire United States (Morgan 1992, 15–16).

Low staff-to-child ratios facilitate the expansion of the licensed day care sector since the fees charged to middle-class parents can be kept very low. Therefore, Texas was a magnet for capitalist investment in day care in the 1980s, as were other states with low ratios and strong economies, such as Florida and Georgia.

A state-subsidized sector similar to that in Alberta developed in Texas at the same time, offering care for children from low-income families. However, this sector was proportionally much smaller in Texas than in Alberta because of limited government funding and had a hard time maintaining a high quality of service. In 1984 it represented merely 2 percent of the total number of day care and nursery spaces in Dallas. In comparison, the PSS sector represented 28 percent of all licensed spaces in Alberta in 1975 (calculated from data in table 4.2).

The second comparator is Sweden. A mid-1990s study of services for young children in the European Union noted that "Sweden is known for having a well developed public system of services for young children, highly subsidised and with a high level of availability and affordability. It is internationally recognised as having a high level of quality" (European Commission Network on Childcare 1996, 113). Indeed, public day care and parental leave have become defining characteristics of the Swedish social-democratic welfare state. This was not always the case, however. In 1965 only 3 percent of preschool children in Sweden were cared for in state-supported day cares and FDHs (Broberg and Hwang 1991, 92; Gunnarsson 1993, 500–501).

In response to an ongoing economic boom and a strong demand for female labour in the 1960s and 1970s, as well as strong pressure from the feminist movement, the governing Social Democratic Party, supported by the Liberal and Communist parties, greatly expanded the availability of publicly funded and administered day care until its defeat in the election of 1976. The centre-right coalition government from 1976 to 1982 included the Liberal Party and also supported the public day care system, although it did extend arrangements for parental leave to make it more likely that women would take leaves than men. By 1980 there was 0.31 of a public space per preschool-aged child; this was almost four times the total availability ratio found in Alberta in 1982 (Broberg and Hwang 1991, 92; Esbensen 1983; Gunnarsson 1993, 495–500; Mahon 1997).

The Social Democratic Party returned to power in 1982, and in 1985 the Swedish parliament resolved that all children had the right to receive munici-pal day care from the age of eighteen months (the end of the period of paren-tal leave). That year there was 0.45 of a public space per preschool-aged child (Broberg and Hwang 1991, 92; Mahon 1997, 10).

The day care system that developed in Sweden between the mid-1960s and mid-1980s was somewhat like the PSS system of day cares in Alberta in the 1970s. This reflects the social liberal content of the PSS system and supports Mahon's observation that there is a "fine boundary between social liberalism and social democracy" (2008, 344). One key difference, however, is that Sweden's system was more or less universal in design while Alberta's system merely incorporated universalistic elements (such as reserving spaces for children from middle- and upper-income parents) into a welfare-program design. A second key difference is that Sweden's system was much better funded and hence able to serve a much larger proportion of the population of young children. For an average day care space in 1987, the central government covered 47 percent of the cost using a payroll tax on employers, and municipalities met 43 percent of the cost with tax revenue. The remaining 10 percent was born by parents. Most municipalities charged parents on a sliding fee scale, dependent upon income (Broberg and Hwang 1991, 80).

Nevertheless, a similar commitment to quality characterized both Alberta's PSS day care system and the public system developed in Sweden. In Sweden, the staff-to-child ratios were low and all staff were required to have a two- or three-year educational course. In the early 1980s, the required staff-to-child ratios ranged from one to three for children less than three years of age to one to six for older groups of children (Esbensen 1983, 10; Hwang and Broberg 1992, 41).

One characteristic shared by all three day care systems in the early 1980s was affordability, at least for middle- and upper-income families. In Sweden, afford-ability was made possible by large universal state subsidies. In Alberta, afford-ability resulted from a combination of universal operating allowances and the absence of training standards for day care workers. In Texas, affordability was a consequence of low staff-to-child ratios along with no training standards. A second similarity of all three systems was the exclusion of low- to middle-income families who made too much to qualify for subsidization based upon income but too little to find the regular fees affordable. For these families, the only option was the unregulated private day home. It is surprising that this problem existed in the heavily subsidized Swedish system (Gunnarsson 1993, 512). The lesson is that any parent fees create problems of accessibility for a segment of clients unless the threshold for paying fees is well above the middle of the income range.

In building its ambitious day care system, Sweden faced many of the problems that bedevilled the old PSS day care system in Alberta, only on a much larger scale. Due to municipal administration, there was geographical variability in the availability and cost of services (Broberg and Hwang 1991, 78–81). Furthermore, demand consistently exceeded supply (Gunnarsson 1993, 509–10). The problem of excess demand had a different character in Sweden, however, since the state promoted demand by declaring quality, not-for-profit day care to be a right. In comparison, the PSS day cares in Alberta were, in the main, an advanced social welfare initiative for lower-income families. Sweden responded to the excess demand by committing itself to expanding supply and in the meantime ignoring the private child care arrangements that families made because a place in the public system was unavailable. Not only did such private services receive no public funding, but they were unregulated (Broberg and Hwang 1991, 82).

In conclusion, the new day care system established in Alberta in the early 1980s was quite distinct from that found in either Texas or Sweden. Public money fuelled the rapid expansion of commercial day care in Alberta, and the government legislated high minimum staff-to-child ratios in order to promote custodial care that guarded the well-being of young children. Given that a significant proportion of provincial spending was on business subsidies to commercial owners, this appears to be a distinctive variety of the liberal welfare regime. Nevertheless, it was clearly liberal in orientation, and Alberta's new system was therefore more like that found in Texas, just as Alberta's old system of PSS day cares was more like that found in Sweden. The prototypical day care in Alberta's new system was the commercial chain centre, the most important advocacy voice was the day care entrepreneur, day care workers were horribly underpaid with many leaving the field every year for other employment, and day care's potential to promote widespread early learning was unrealized.

6. From Corporatized Chains to "Mom and Pop" Centres
Diversity in Commercial Day Care

Until 1978, commercial day cares in Alberta received no funding assistance from the provincial government. The introduction of the portable subsidy program that year and the subsequent introduction of operating allowances in 1980 encouraged significant commercial investments in day care centres in Alberta in the following decade, particularly in Calgary and Edmonton. In both of these cities, the commercial sector not only expanded in absolute terms but increased its market share relative to the not-for-profit sector. Furthermore, the promise of an excellent return on investment attracted a number of capitalist investors. Several local day care chains grew quite rapidly in these years, and the largest day care chain in the United States, KinderCare Learning Centers, built a day care in Calgary in 1982.

Needless to say, the politics of day care in the province were transformed as large investors used their financial might to political advantage. The main proponents of quality child care were relegated to the margins of policy decisions in those years, but the political influence of day care capitalists would gradually wane as successive years of relatively high unemployment and the growing popularity of family day homes (FDHs) and nannies eroded the demand for group day care, and persistent government deficits precluded any new spending initiatives. Furthermore, the "back-to-the family," or "pro-family," movement became a political force in Alberta in the 1980s, and this movement soon exercised an influence on Tory politicians that exceeded that of day care capitalists.

A former director of the provincial Day Care Branch, Dennis Maier, noted that "there was an expression, and I only present it as an expression, that operating a day care centre in the 1980s was a license to print money. It was very, very lucrative."[1] By the mid-1990s, however, the economics of day care were fundamentally changed. One indication of this change was that the Kindercare chain in Calgary (no organizational connection to the U.S.-based KinderCare Learning Centers: thus the difference in spelling) was put into receivership in 1994, followed two years later by the Educentres chain. In politics, the old animosity between the commercial and not-for-profit sectors gave way to an uneasy alliance as the very survival of licensed day care became the overriding policy question. Their common opponent was the pro-family movement, proponents of which called on the province to redirect government monies toward the care of young children at home.

A FLURRY OF CAPITALIST INVESTMENT, 1975–82

Between 1975 and 1982, the number of licensed day cares in Alberta increased by 75 percent while the number of licensed spaces increased by 122 percent (calculated from data in tables 4.2 and 6.1). The greater increase in licensed spaces was accommodated by an increase in the average capacity of a day care from thirty-six to forty-six children. In addition, the commercial sector's share of day care spaces increased from 55 percent in 1975 to 69 percent in 1982. In all three regions reported in these tables, the commercial sector's share of day care spaces grew between 1975 and 1982, with the percentage increase being smallest in Calgary (10 percent) and largest in Alberta excluding Calgary and Edmonton (29 percent). The size of the latter increase reflects the fact that there were relatively few commercial day cares outside of Calgary and Edmonton in 1975 (a mere fifteen in total), and thus many opportunities arose to establish commercial day cares in the late 1970s and early 1980s as Preventive Social Service (PSS) funding was discontinued, particularly in small cities where the demand for day care was growing. In Calgary, the 10 percent increase raised the commercial sector's share of licensed spaces to 79 percent in 1982 (table 6.1).

I have defined a day care chain as two or more centres under the same ownership with an aggregate capacity of eighty children or more. In 1982 chain day cares numbered twenty-three in each of Edmonton and Calgary. However, there was a significant difference between cities in the character of these chain centres: while their average capacity was seventy-nine children in Calgary, it was only fifty in Edmonton (table 6.1). A breakdown of the twenty-three chain centres in Calgary is found in table 6.3. Thirteen of the centres were part of either the Kindercare or Panda chains, the two chains that meet my definition of larger

TABLE 6.1 Licensed Day Care in Alberta, 1982, by Region and Auspice

Auspice	Edmonton			Calgary			Rest of Alberta		
	Number	Licensed capacity	Average size	Number	Licensed capacity	Average size	Number	Licensed capacity	Average size
All chains[a]	23 (17%)	1,154 (21%)	50	23 (18%)	1,834 (25%)	79	4 (4%)	224 (5%)	56
Independent commercial	69 (51%)	2,705 (48%)	39	79 (61%)	3,906 (54%)	49	54 (48%)	2,299 (50%)	43
Total commercial	92 (68%)	3,859 (69%)	42	102 (78%)	5,740 (79%)	56	58 (51%)	2,523 (54%)	44
Total not-for-profit	43 (32%)	1,752 (31%)	41	28 (22%)	1,518 (21%)	54	55 (49%)	2,116 (46%)	38
All centres	135	5,611	42	130	7,258	56	113	4,639	41
Region as % of total for Alberta	36%	32%	n.a.	34%	41%	n.a.	30%	26%	n.a.

SOURCE: Alberta Social Services and Community Health, Day Care Branch, "Day Care Centres Operating in the City of Calgary [likewise "in the City of Edmonton" and "in the Province of Alberta"], Updated January 1, 1982" (PAA, 92.150, box 2). The data for Calgary include day cares that started operating in the early part of 1982.

[a] A "chain" consists of two or more centres, under the same ownership, with an aggregate capacity of at least 80 children.

chains (those that consist of a minimum of four centres with a minimum aggregate capacity of two hundred children). These thirteen centres had an average capacity of ninety children, with Abbeydale Kindercare being licensed for 156 children in a building with over five thousand square feet of floor space. The largest centre in the Panda chain was licensed for 120 children. At this time, both the Kindercare and Panda chains were building centres that were larger than the industry standards in the United States. They were at the forefront of a trend to introduce significant economies of scale into commercial day care, thus reducing per-unit costs. With a favourable cost structure and a strong demand for day care, these centres could squeeze competitors by offering lower prices for day care; even when offering comparable prices, they could generate a higher return on investment.

It is important to note that both the Kindercare and Panda chains made investments in large day cares prior to the introduction of operating allowances in 1980. Their investments were made on the basis of Alberta's relatively lax regulatory standards at the time (which meant that licensed day care could effectively compete with unlicensed day homes for middle-class business) and the booming economy. These favourable market conditions also attracted the interest of the largest American day care chain, KinderCare Learning.

KINDERCARE LEARNING (BRIEFLY) COMES TO ALBERTA

Until 1968, commercial day care in the United States was offered solely in "mom and pop" centres, just as it was in Alberta. The following year, the first KinderCare centre opened in Montgomery, Alabama, the brainchild of a real estate entrepreneur, Perry Mendel.[2] KinderCare centres were each topped by a red roof and steeple with a decorative black bell, and in American cities such as Atlanta, soon became as much a feature of the urban commercial landscape as McDonald's and other fast food restaurants. "Kentucky fried children" and "Kentucky fried day care" were the caustic terms coined by KinderCare's early critics, as much for the firm's slick mass marketing as for the fact that its red roof tiles were virtually indistinguishable from those of KFC restaurants (Goyette 1981; Lelvveld 1977; see also Englade 1988, 44, and Neugebauer 1988, 29). But while the critics despaired at the thought of children being cared for in cookie-cutter chain outlets, Mendel himself revelled in the comparison and treated McDonald's as a business model (Lynn 1978, 20).

KinderCare expanded rapidly in the 1970s by forming partnerships with real estate developers in different cities. By 1978 there were two hundred and fifty centres in the chain, spread across twenty-four states. The company only owned about 20 percent of these centres, however. The other 80 percent were owned by developers and their investment partners, who purchased land and built a centre to KinderCare specifications and then leased the centre to KinderCare on a long-term basis (Lynn 1978, 18). It is this latter business model that was to be the basis for KinderCare's arrested expansion into Alberta in the early 1980s, with Great-West Life serving as the developer.

During the 1970s, KinderCare Learning lagged behind La Petite Academy as the day care chain with the most centres in the United States, but in 1979, KinderCare purchased one of its main rivals, Mini-Skool Ltd., and unambiguously established itself as the leading American day care chain. Mini-Skool had begun in Winnipeg in 1969, but at the time of its acquisition by KinderCare, Mini-Skool had many more centres in the United States (seventy-one) than in

Canada (seventeen) (Cowern 1986). Significantly, in 1977 Mini-Skool Ltd. had a larger revenue than either La Petite Academy or KinderCare (Lynn 1978, 18), thus making it an attractive target for a takeover.

In the late 1970s, KinderCare Learning was generally building centres to hold seventy or one hundred children (Lynn 1978, 18). For instance, the Beamer Road KinderCare in Houston opened in 1977 and accommodated a maximum of one hundred children in 2003. However, the company found that larger centres were much more profitable because of economies of scale and consequently chose to increase the size of the new centres it opened in the 1980s and 1990s. A 1988 investment analysis reported, "In the past two years, KinderCare Learning Centers has enlarged its prototype unit from an average capacity of 110 children to 135" (Alex, Brown & Sons 1988). By the mid-1990s, KinderCare was designing centres to hold 150 to 200 children. A 1998 investment report noted that the prototype for new KinderCare centres accommodated 180 children, although the company had opened centres with a capacity as high as 280 (Moody's Investors Service 1999).

When KinderCare Learning and Great-West Life officials met with Alberta civil servants in early 1981, they were informed of the government's intention to set the maximum day care size at eighty. But this did not discourage KinderCare from proceeding with plans to expand into Alberta, undoubtedly because the company had recent experience with building centres with capacities as small as seventy and because provincial operating allowances enhanced the profitability of smaller centres. It is unlikely the company would have made the same business decision in the later 1980s or the 1990s, both because it had decided that much larger centres were a better investment and because Alberta stopped increasing operating allowances, thus allowing the value of the allowances to be slowly eroded by inflation from 1984 onwards (table A.6).

KinderCare Learning Centers had bought Mini-Skool Ltd. from its third owner, Great-West Life of Winnipeg. Thereafter, Great-West Life purchased 1.5 percent of the common shares of KinderCare Learning (for $1 million), and the two companies began talking about a joint venture in day care in Canada.[3] Given the oil boom and the business-friendly policies of the provincial government, Edmonton and Calgary were identified by KinderCare as prime places to build day care centres in Canada. When the company indicated its interest in expanding to Alberta, there was an immediate negative reaction from the president of the Day Care Association of Calgary (DCAC), Caroline Kiehlbauch, operator of Fairyland Day Care. "We have enough daycare centres as it is," stated Kiehlbauch. "A chain would take away the personal touch of each community centre."[4]

TABLE 6.2   Licensed Day Care in Alberta, 1995, by Region and Auspice

Auspice	Edmonton Number	Edmonton Licensed capacity	Edmonton Average size	Calgary Number	Calgary Licensed capacity	Calgary Average size	Rest of Alberta Number	Rest of Alberta Licensed capacity	Rest of Alberta Average size
Larger chains [a]	9 (4%)	580 (5%)	64	50 (29%)	3,441 (32%)	69	2 (1%)	96 (1%)	48
Smaller chains [a]	34 (14%)	1,923 (17%)	57	36 (21%)	2,102 (20%)	58	12 (6%)	685 (7%)	57
All chains	43 (17%)	2,503 (22%)	58	86 (49%)	5,543 (52%)	64	14 (7%)	781 (9%)	56
Independent commercial	148 (60%)	6,562 (59%)	44	51 (29%)	2,889 (27%)	57	99 (51%)	4,568 (50%)	46
Total commercial	191 (77%)	9,065 (81%)	47	137 (78%)	8,432 (79%)	62	113 (58%)	5,349 (58%)	47
Total not-for-profit	56 (23%)	2,152 (19%)	38	38 (22%)	2,181 (21%)	57	82 (42%)	3,873 (42%)	47
All centres	247	11,217	45	175	10,613	61	195	9,222	47
Region as % of total for Alberta	40%	36%	n.a.	28%	34%	n.a.	32%	30%	n.a.

SOURCE: Alberta Social Services, Day Care Information System, *Listing of Facilities: Day Care Centres*, 7 June 1995.

[a] A "larger chain" consists of a minimum of four centres, all under the same ownership, with a minimum aggregate capacity of 200 children. A "smaller chain" consists of two or three centres with an aggregate capacity of at least 80 children or four or more centres with an aggregate capacity greater than 79 children but less than 200 children.

It is significant that from 1975 to 1982, independent commercial operators maintained their share of licensed day care spaces in Calgary at approximately 55 percent (compare tables 4.2 and 6.1). However, they knew they would have difficulty withstanding competition from chains over time. This concern was born out in subsequent years, since by 1995 independent commercial operators would control only 27 percent of licensed spaces in Calgary (table 6.2).

Provincial day care bureaucrats, however, had a broader view of the potential negative repercussions of a KinderCare Learning expansion into Alberta. On 22 January 1981, three senior day care bureaucrats met with six individuals involved in planning the expansion, including the Ontario-based director of Mini-Skool, a KinderCare Learning public relations executive from the United States, and three representatives of the real estate division of Great-West Life. Great-West had agreed to spend up to $50 million to bankroll KinderCare Learning Centers' expansion in Canada. The plan was for Great-West Life to build approximately one hundred new day care centres on sites selected by KinderCare Learning and then lease the facilities to KinderCare, which would operate the day cares.[5]

Although the meeting "was amiable and friendly," the KinderCare Learning and Great-West Life representatives proved to be singularly inept lobbyists. The corporate officials "outlined the history of Mini-Skool, showed a film and gave indication of their plans to build many centres in Urban Alberta where they feel the market is good."[6] However, a follow-up letter by a Great-West Life real estate representative set alarm bells ringing for the civil servants.[7] Larry Taggart suggested that Mini-Skool would soon be a dominant player in Alberta day care. He portrayed this as a good thing for civil servants since "your department will be able to effect changes and suggestions in a significant sector of the child care community by simply contacting the Mini-Skool Director in Alberta."[8]

Taggart had hoped that the civil servants would see government's role in day care being made easier when Mini-Skool assumed a pre-eminent position in the urban marketplace and government could work hand in hand with the company. This was precisely the wrong argument to make. For one thing, the civil servants dealt with the owners of homegrown day care chains and had learned that these capitalists were more likely to oppose government initiatives than co-operatively fall in line after a phone call. In situations of policy or administrative conflict, day care chains were difficult adversaries because their economic position gave them considerable political resources, particularly access to a large body of parents for mobilization and the economic power to mount concerted lobbying campaigns.

KinderCare Learning and Great-West Life anticipated opening a number of Mini-Skool centres in Alberta in the early 1980s. In the middle of 1980, a KinderCare Learning vice-president estimated that "a maximum of five or six centres" would be built in each of Edmonton and Calgary, and as the corporate plan developed in 1981–82, Alberta was apparently slated for ten centres. In 1982 Great-West Life made an initial investment of $5 million to construct four new Mini-Skool centres in Canada, one of which was actually constructed in Calgary. However, it was never opened as a Mini-Skool centre because of a highly successful boycott threat levelled by the Canadian Union of Public Employees (CUPE). CUPE believed that "the profit motive in day care poses a serious threat to the quality of care provided to children."[9]

The initial announcement of the partnership between Manitoba-based Great-West Life and KinderCare Learning Centers led to the Manitoba Child Care Association withdrawing its business from a Great-West Life insurance and benefits plan effective 1 July 1981. The child care association expressed concerns that the quality of care in KinderCare Learning centres would be inferior to that found in not-for-profit centres. Great-West Life lost 204 customers but indicated that the plans to build day cares for KinderCare Learning would proceed.[10] But the boycott of the insurance firm went from small potatoes to the big time when it was joined by CUPE. At its May 1982 national convention, the union passed a resolution calling on locals to cancel insurance policies with Great-West Life if it continued its business association with KinderCare Learning. Within weeks, Great-West Life announced it would "divest itself of all interest in a chain of daycare centres as soon as it is financially possible." A Great-West Life official credited the CUPE boycott with forcing the decision: "When enough of your policy holders express concern about what you're doing, you have to be attentive to them."[11]

KinderCare Learning was highly contemptuous of the threatened union boycott and critical of Great-West Life for withdrawing from the business deal. The company's vice-president of real estate referred to CUPE members as "idiots," "socialists," "communists," and "lunatics." In regard to Great-West Life, he said, "They allowed a bunch of union people, who don't know what they're talking about, to spew garbage and force them to dump us." Despite all of this tough talk, however, KinderCare Learning was beaten: it cancelled its planned expansion into Canada.

It is noteworthy that the president of the Day Care Society of Alberta (DCSA), Jacqui Kallal, spoke against CUPE's threatened boycott of Great-West Life because it undermined the "open market" in day care. This indicates that the existing commercial operators in Alberta were split over the possibility of KinderCare Learning coming to Alberta. While the president of the DCSA (which represented 120, or about 45 percent, of the commercial centres in Alberta, a large number of which were part of chains) favoured allowing KinderCare to compete for Alberta business, the president of the DCAC was firmly opposed. U.S.-based KinderCare Learning's planned expansion into Alberta between 1980 and 1982, therefore, did not serve to unite the Alberta-based commercial sector against the Yankee invader. Instead, it served to highlight and reinforce the deep division between the two main camps of commercial operators. At the same time, however, the episode created an interesting coalition of opposition that included advocates for not-for-profit care, government bureaucrats, and smaller commercial operators.[12]

The issue of foreign control of day cares had seemingly been addressed in the Day Care Regulation of 1978. It specified that day care licenses would only be issued to a corporation if it "is incorporated by or under an Act of the Legislature" and "is controlled by residents of Alberta" (Alberta 1978). However, KinderCare Learning planned to skirt the regulation by setting up a subsidiary corporation that listed Alberta residents as directors and then having this subsidiary hold the day care licenses.[13]

Shortly after the collapse of the Great-West Life/KinderCare Learning partnership, the Alberta Day Care Advisory Committee (ADCAC) tried to close the loophole that would have allowed KinderCare Learning to use a subsidiary to secure day care licenses in Alberta. As part of its recommendations for a new day care act, the ADCAC proposed that the regulatory wording "a corporation ... controlled by residents of Alberta" be changed to "a corporation ... in which a majority of the issued shares are held by residents of Alberta." The department of Social Services and Community Health (SSCH) officially endorsed this proposal a few months later, recognizing that it would "prevent foreign companies, e.g., American Mini-Skool, from establishing themselves in Alberta."[14]

The plans for a new day care act were abandoned in 1983, and the social planning committee and cabinet rejected "the recommendation to eliminate possibility of foreign ownership ... as it is not viewed to be a necessary step at this time."[15] This is a good example of cabinet disregarding the advice of civil servants and proceeding on its own distinctive policy path. The failure to close the foreign ownership loophole is a sign of the Lougheed cabinet's fundamental aversion to limiting the rights of business owners.

The regulatory wording in question remained in place between 1978 and 1995, seemingly preventing American corporate day care giants from expanding into Alberta but in fact doing no such thing. In 1995 the neo-liberal government of Ralph Klein abandoned the charade by removing all mention of Alberta residency as a precondition for day care licensing (Alberta 1995).

With KinderCare Learning exiting from Alberta in mid-1982, the field was left wide open for homegrown day care capitalists to take advantage of the generous provincial operating allowances to expand their own chains of centres. The next section profiles Alberta's premier day care capitalist for two decades, Dennis Sorensen, whose day cares were known by the Kindercare brand name even though he had no organizational tie to the U.S.-based KinderCare Learning chain. Nevertheless, there are some important parallels between how Sorensen's modest local chain developed in the 1980s and early 1990s and what happened with Perry Mendel's large U.S.-wide chain. These parallels point to the limitations of a corporatized approach to day care.

ALBERTA'S PREMIER DAY CARE CAPITALIST

In 1975, 13 percent of the licensed day care spaces in Calgary were controlled by the owners of small chains, with each of these three chains including two or three centres (table 6.3). Dennis Sorensen and his first wife, Darlene, owned the three centres in the Mother Duck's chain. These were modest-sized day cares with an average capacity of forty-five children. Like many commercial operators in the 1960s and early 1970s, the Sorensens had started out in the business by establishing a day care in the basement of their own home. In the late 1960s and early 1970s, Dennis Sorensen took a leading role among Calgary's commercial operators in opposing the city's system of PSS day cares.[16]

Sorensen saw the potential to take a corporate approach to day care in Calgary and moved decisively in this direction in the late 1970s. All three Mother Duck's centres had been sold by 1978 and Mr. Sorensen began to build large centres with capacities for one hundred or more children.[17] He also abandoned the Mother Duck's brand name in favour of Kindercare.

In the early 1980s, some of the Kindercare centres were owned solely by Dennis Sorensen through stand-alone corporations (e.g., Abbeydale Kindercare Centre Ltd.). Many of the centres, however, were owned by Canadian Kindercare Ltd., Sorensen being one of the four partners in this company and holding a 25 percent ownership stake.[18]

Sorensen's corporate approach to day care was quickly opposed by the same coalition of interests that had objected to U.S.-based KinderCare Learning establishing a presence in Alberta. At its meeting on 14 August 1982, the ADCAC unanimously recommended that no operator be allowed to control more than four hundred licensed spaces.[19] The fact that the commercial operators on the committee, including a past president of the Private Day Care Society of Alberta (PDCS), did not object to the recommendation suggests the widespread concern generated by Sorensen's dynamic entrepreneurship. Indeed, in the mid-1980s, Dennis Sorensen was publicly critical of the leadership of the DCSA, asserting that they were "a bunch of broads afraid of the competition."[20] As is detailed in the next section, in 1983 the provincial government amended the Day Care Regulation to restrict the ownership rights of Dennis Sorensen and the other

TABLE 6.3   Ownership Status of Day Care Centres in Calgary, 1975, 1982, 1995, and 2002

Ownership type	1975		1982		1995		2002	
	Number of centres (average size)	% of total capacity	Number of centres (average size)	% of total capacity	Number of centres (average size)	% of total capacity	Number of centres (average size)	% of total capacity
Larger chains[a]	0	0%	13 (90)	16%	50 (69)	32%	32 (68)	24%
Smaller chains[a]	8 (53)	13%	10 (66)	9%	36 (58)	20%	23 (65)	17%
All chains	8 (53)	13%	23 (79)	25%	86 (64)	52%	55 (67)	40%
Independent commercial	57 (33)	56%	79 (49)	54%	51 (57)	27%	60 (52)	34%
Total commercial	65 (35)	69%	102 (56)	79%	137 (62)	79%	115 (59)	75%
Total not-for-profit	21 (48)	31%	28 (54)	21%	38 (57)	21%	39 (59)	25%
All centres	86 (39)	100%	130 (56)	100%	175 (61)	100%	154 (59)	100%
Total licensed capacity	3,320	n.a.	7,258	n.a.	10,613	n.a.	9,068	n.a.

SOURCES: For 1975: Alberta Social Services and Community Health, Homes and Institutions Branch, "Day Care Centres
Operating in the City of Calgary [likewise "in the City of Edmonton" and "in the Province of Alberta"] as of July 1, 1975"
(PAA, 83.385, file 12). The list for Calgary omitted day cares whose names began with the letters D, E, and F.
Supplementary information was used to correct this error.
For 1982: Alberta Social Services and Community Health, Day Care Branch, "Day Care Centres Operating in the City of
Calgary" [likewise "in the City of Edmonton" and "in the Province of Alberta"], Updated January 1, 1982" (PAA, 92.150,
box 2). The data for Calgary include day cares that started operating in the early part of 1982.
For 1995: Alberta Social Services, Day Care Information System, Listing of Facilities: Day Care Centres, 7 June 1995.
For 2002: Spreadsheet provided by Alberta Children's Services, Child Care Information System.

[a] For definitions, see table 6.2.

owners of large day care chains. However, Sorensen and the other day care capitalists soon found ways around the restriction, and the government lacked the
conviction to force the matter.

In the mid-1980s, Dennis Sorensen was the outspoken and flamboyant
face of corporate day care in Calgary. A 1985 newspaper story portrayed him as
ostentatiously wealthy, driving a $52,000 Jaguar owned by his day care com-
pany and boasting that he had been able to pay cash in a recent takeover of a
Calgary microelectronics company. Sorensen's wealth was fuelled by the hundreds of thousands of dollars in government-issued operating allowances that
his day cares received each year.[21] In the mid-1980s, Sorensen had diversified his

business holdings. In doing so, he was simply following a basic rule of capitalism: shift capital to where the potential return on investment is highest. The pitfall of this strategy, however, is that when speculative investments go sour and/or the economy slows, there will be insufficient financial resources to maintain the integrity of the original business—in this case, day care. In such an eventuality, young children suffer the consequences of entrepreneurial failures. For those Albertans who believe that child care is too important to be subject to the vagaries of the capitalist marketplace, this scenario points to the fatal deficiency of corporatized day care. Their alternative blueprint requires any surplus generated by a day care to be directly reinvested in quality care or preserved in a contingency fund to be used to cover emergency capital expenditures or the deficits in difficult years.

Dennis Sorensen's business affairs became complicated in 1984 when he and his three partners in Canadian Kindercare Ltd. had "a falling out."[22] They split into two businesses, which were formally separated in the 1986 Yellow Pages. Sorensen's former partners adopted the new brand name of Playcare and listed eleven centres in their chain, while Kindercare listed nine centres. During the next few years, the Playcare chain slowly declined: by 1991 it had shrunk to two centres. Meanwhile, Kindercare listed eighteen centres in both 1989 and 1990, and in 1990, for the first time, took out a display advertisement for the entire chain.

With eighteen centres and over fifteen hundred spaces in Calgary in the late 1980s, Dennis Sorensen was by far the largest day care operator in Alberta. Compared to the nationwide commercial chains found in the United States, however, his business was tiny. The largest of those chains, KinderCare Learning, had grown from 250 centres in 1978 to 1,290 in 1989 (Neugebauer 1988, 31; 1989, 20). Despite the differences in the size of their businesses, however, Dennis Sorensen was every bit as much an entrepreneurial capitalist as Perry Mendel, and he undermined the financial integrity of his day care chain just as Mendel did his.

The early 1990s was a very difficult time for Kindercare and numerous other day care operators in both the commercial and not-for-profit sectors. The government had last increased operating allowances in 1984, so inflation had gradually reduced the real value of those allowances (see table A.6). Then, in June 1990, the provincial government announced a plan to reduce operating allowances (see details in chapter 7). By 1995 the monthly operating allowance for an infant was only 48 percent of its real value a decade earlier ($226 versus $469 [in

2006 dollars]; see table A.6). For toddlers and preschoolers, the allowances paid in 1995 were 50 percent and 65 percent, respectively, of the real value of allowances paid in 1985.

The reductions to operating allowances in the first half of the 1990s created financial problems for many day cares, since demand was weak due to an economic recession. This meant that if they increased fees to compensate for the reduction in operating allowances, they ran the risk of losing price-sensitive customers who were ineligible for a low-income subsidy. In early 1994, Pierette Sorensen, Dennis Sorensen's second wife and then-president of the DSCA, cited "underground babysitting" as the main reason that licensed day cares were having problems filling their centres.[23]

In the economic recession of the early 1990s, the unemployment rate for Alberta women twenty-five years and older peaked in August 1993 at 10.6 percent.[24] In January 1994, Kindercare, with the blessing of its mortgagors, announced its desire to sell four or five of its seventeen day cares and apply the proceeds to paying down the mortgage at the other centres. At the time, the vacancy rate at some Kindercare centres was 50 percent or more. Abbeydale Kindercare, for example, had an enrolment of around forty-five children in the spring of 1994 even though it had a combined day care/out-of-school care (OOSC) license for 160.[25]

The attempt to sell some centres was unsuccessful, however, and in April 1994, the mortgagors put three of Dennis Sorensen's companies into receivership. Sorensen saw his day care chain shrink from seventeen to five centres as a result of the bankruptcy. In the case of one of the centres he held onto, Dover Kindercare, Sorensen seems to have gotten a very favourable deal from the receiver, likely because there were no other interested parties. He repurchased the day care, licensed for eighty children, for only $110,000 on 7 July 1994 and was able to mortgage the property for $108,750 with CIBC Mortgage Corporation. A conservative estimate would put the purchase price at approximately 25 percent of the replacement cost of the day care.[26]

In the years leading up to bankruptcy, Dennis Sorensen's Kindercare chain had no financial reserves, since profits had been invested in other businesses in the 1980s. This had very telling consequences for the quality of care at the Kindercare centres. Nizar Daya, whose Kidsland chain bought six of the former Kindercare centres from the receiver in 1994, noted that although the buildings were fairly new, Kindercare had not invested in their upkeep and maintenance. Consequently, although they remained attractive from the curb, they needed new interior paint and carpeting, "equipment was fairly sparse," and "playgrounds were in very bad shape." Daya noted, "I virtually had to put new playgrounds in all the centres when I took over." He also asked, rhetorically, "How can you run a day care without equipment?"[27]

On a very small scale, Dennis Sorensen's business problems mirrored those of Perry Mendel in the United States. KinderCare Learning's growth in the 1980s was financed with money raised on bond markets rather than through deals with developers like Great-West Life. Perry Mendel and his close business associate, Richard Grassgreen (appointed company president in 1985), not only expanded their day care company with money raised by issuing bonds, but they also purchased a range of diverse companies. These included a potash company, a shoe retailer, and the American Savings & Loan Association of Florida. Mendel and Grassgreen had close working relations with the 1980s master of junk bonds and leveraged takeovers, Michael Milken of Drexel Burnham Lambert, whose advertisements featured KinderCare, "touting how innovative financing can provide capital for a new industry" (Lewin 1989, 89). The KinderCare executives even went so far as to commit their firm to buying $200 million of junk bonds of other companies through Drexel. For one of these transactions (involving $125 million in junk bonds), Drexel paid a $965,000 commitment fee (kickback), which Mendel and Grassgreen pocketed. Eventually the two executives were charged and convicted with insider trading (securities fraud) on their takeover deals and with tax evasion on the $965,000 kickback. Grassgreen was a prominent witness for the prosecution in the trial of Michael Milken.[28]

As part of their diversification schemes, Mendel and Grassgreen had severed the day care business (still called KinderCare Learning) from the parent company in 1987, although the former remained a wholly owned subsidiary of the parent (Shearson Lehman Hutton Inc. 1989). Nevertheless, the day care business continued to serve its owners' diversification scheme. For instance, in late 1987 and early 1988, KinderCare Learning raised $150 million by selling fifteen-year subordinated notes; it then loaned the money to its parent company for the purchase of American Savings & Loan (Alex, Brown, and Sons 1988). By the late 1980s, the parent company had "$620 million worth of Milken junk versus $278 million in tangible net worth." Facing a severe financial squeeze, Mendel and Grassgreen sold KinderCare Learning in 1989 (Dubashi 1993, 32). This did not put the day care business back on its feet, however. For one thing, the operational side of the company had suffered since 1986, when senior management started funnelling profits from day care into the other businesses and neglecting the day care business. As a consequence, buildings were not properly maintained and day care programming stagnated (Neugebauer 1994). A second and more severe problem was the terms of the takeover deal. The new owners purchased KinderCare Learning for only $200 million but agreed to assume $350 million in debt. The huge debt load inhibited growth in the early 1990s since it entailed $45 million in annual interest payments, and it eventually forced the company to seek bankruptcy protection in 1993; the debt load was relieved by convincing creditors to accept equity in exchange for debt (Neugebauer 1994).

The owners of KinderCare Learning had used profits from their day care business as a springboard for entry into the 1980s world of junk bond financing and corporate diversification. The speculative activities of Mendel and Grassgreen compromised the quality of the care offered at KinderCare Learning Centers in the late 1980s and early 1990s, and the firm was eventually forced into receivership. Greed, excess, corruption, and failure—one might argue that these are merely the negative consequences that one must be prepared to tolerate in a dynamic economic system that rewards risk taking and innovation, and values profit above all else. But when the integrity of a day care business is put in doubt by speculation and when the quality of children's care is compromised because financial resources have been squandered on other investments, the appropriateness of corporatized day care is certainly called into question.

When Dennis Sorensen's Kindercare chain in Calgary collapsed in 1994, a number of investors competed against each other to pick up the pieces. In addition to the six centres purchased by the Kidsland chain, three centres were purchased by the Magic Mountain chain based in Airdrie, two by the Panda chain, and one by Playcare. For the best of the Kindercare centres, these companies bid against each other.[29] Nevertheless, one thing this receivership sale did was put a lie to the notion that one's principal is safe in a commercial investment in a day care in Alberta. Day care buildings have very specific design features and are not easily converted to other uses, so the market for a day care property is fairly small, especially when the day care vacancy rate is high and the property itself is in poor condition.

Dennis Sorensen survived bankruptcy and the dismantling of his day care chain in 1994, and he persevered to remain in the day care business. After his tragic death from a heart attack, Pierette Sorensen continued to operate the downsized Kindercare chain for a few years: a Yellow Pages advertisement featuring all five Kindercare centres ran until 2004–5.

Responding to pressure from both commercial and non-profit groups, and to the recommendation of the ADCAC, in 1983 the government moved to formally limit the power of Dennis Sorensen and other entrepreneurs with ambitions of building large day care chains. A regulatory amendment (Alberta 1983) was intended to prevent a single operator from controlling more than five hundred day care spaces.[30] Five reasons for the amendment were subsequently listed by a civil servant:

a) to ensure a continued variety of auspices and parent choice,
b) to reduce the risk of unions entering the industry, as they have with Mini-Skools in Ontario, and the passing on of increased costs to parents,
c) to prevent a large single lobby of operators and parents, when government funding or program standards are being amended,
d) to reduce the possibility that as programs of chain operations tend to become institutionalized, staff may become less responsive to needs of individual children and families,
e) to prevent unfair competition with small, family operated centres.[31]

Of particular note are (b) and (c). Point (b) reveals the willingness of the provincial government to take the unusual step of restricting the ownership rights of day care owners in order to reduce the likelihood of the unionization of commercial day care workers. Point (c) indicates that the government not only favoured a fragmented day care lobby but enacted policy to sustain that fragmentation.

At the time of the 1983 amendment, Dennis Sorensen already controlled in excess of five hundred licensed spaces. The good news for him was that the five hundred limit did not apply to the ownership of existing centres or centres under construction. Furthermore, in an interpretation that appears to contradict the wording of the 1983 amendment, "both *Dennis Sorensen Day Care* and *Canadian Kindercare Ltd.* were viewed as separate business entities" with independent aggregate capacities of five hundred when the amendment took effect.[32]

It must be remembered that this amendment was introduced at the exact moment when there were huge profits to be made in commercial day care (due to the size of the public subsidy available through operating allowances and the low wage costs associated with an unskilled workforce). As a consequence, Dennis Sorensen and his partners in Canadian Kindercare first tried to prevent the introduction of the amendment and then, after it was implemented, actively circumvented it.

The new minister of SSCH, Neil Webber, received a letter from Canadian Kindercare on this matter in late December 1982. It argued that the proposed restriction "would be an unwarranted intrusion by government into the private sector" and that its intent "seems to be an attempt to limit the growth of a very successful company." It also complained that the ADCAC had not given them early notice of its proposed amendment and had "declined to meet with us on other issues." Minister Webber met with the Canadian Kindercare president on 9 February 1983.

The Kindercare partners were unsuccessful in blocking the ownership limit from becoming law. Nevertheless, they did not let the new regulation slow down their planned corporate expansion. They circumvented the regulation through leasing arrangements by having an employee or a family member hold the license for a particular day care and by splitting the ownership of the day cares in their chain among different registered companies. By 1985 two other Calgary day care chains—Panda and Educentres—were butting up against the five hundred limit. They also chose creative ownership arrangements to bypass the regulations.[33] Provincial civil servants favoured closing the loopholes being used by day care capitalists to create large chains in Calgary, but their recommendations to this effect in July 1985 and July 1986 were not acted upon.[34]

The regulation capping day care ownership at five hundred spaces had been approved at a sensitive point in provincial day care politics. On 25 May 1983, the executive committee of SSCH recommended against the ADCAC's proposal for a special act for day care. This negative recommendation was based upon the Executive Committee's opposition to mandating a developmental focus for day care in Alberta, partly because it would require increased regulations and "the infusion of a substantial amount of new funds" and partly because "as yet, there does not appear to be a very strong demand for such focus from parents using day care centres."[35] This negative decision was followed within weeks by the decision to proceed with a regulatory limit on the size of day care chains. The five hundred-space limit can thus be seen as a concession to the ADCAC and the broader movement for quality day care at a time when most of its agenda had been swept aside.

In the years immediately after the proclamation of the regulation, however, there was a substantial change in the political dynamics of the day care issue in Alberta. The ADCAC was disbanded in 1986, removing a constant thorn in the government's side. Furthermore, advocates for early childhood education and care (such as the Alberta Association for Young Children and municipal social services bureaucrats) had less and less influence on provincial policy. Not coincidentally, the influence of the DCSA grew in this period in step with the rapid expansion of commercial day care, especially the chains. Civil servants captured this change in political climate with their 1986 observation, "Of particular note is the fact that while Kindercare has continued over the past year to grow through leasing arrangements, there appears to have been no public concern expressed on the part of day care operators or the community at large."[36] By 1986 there remained very little political pressure on the government to rein in the growth of Calgary's expanding day care chains.

GOVERNMENT AND COMMERCIAL OPERATORS UNITED AGAINST LABOUR UNIONS

The difficulties that labour unions have had in trying to organize workers at bank branches, fast food restaurants, and even department store outlets are well documented. The unity of a small group of workers can easily be disrupted by the employer, and a large employer can spend large sums of money in fighting unionization. As a last resort, a pretext can be found to close a unionized branch, restaurant, or store since any one outlet is relatively insignificant to the overall business.[37]

A drive to unionize the workers at one of the centres owned by a large American day care chain like KinderCare Learning or La Petite Academy would run into exactly the same difficulties. Indeed, apparently not a single centre owned by a major American chain was unionized in 1998.[38] In the early 1980s, however, a number of Mini-Skool centres in Ontario were successfully unionized, and a lengthy strike ensued. This development was closely monitored in Alberta by both provincial bureaucrats and commercial operators who feared the same thing might happen in their province.

Three Mini-Skool centres in Ontario were organized by the Ontario Public Service Employees Union. When contract negotiations broke down between the union and Mini-Skool Ltd., workers at the three centres went on strike in early October 1982. The major issue in the Ontario strike was wages. In 1982 the minimum wage in Ontario was $3.50 per hour while unionized workers in municipally run centres in Toronto earned around $10 per hour. The largest category of worker at the Mini-Skool centres, assistant room supervisors, earned just $4.08 per hour before the strike. A contract agreement between the

Ontario Public Service Employees Union and Mini-Skool Ltd. was finally reached in late May 1983 to cover two centres (a third centre was closed). The wage rate of assistant room supervisors was raised to $5.16 per hour as of 1 September 1983, an increase of 26 percent compared to October 1982.[39]

While the Ontario strike was ongoing, the DCSA held its first meeting with Minister Neil Webber.[40] Although the previous minister, Bob Bogle, had abandoned the government's promise to establish a registry of day care workers, the DCSA was concerned that the idea might make a comeback. President Jacqui Kallal wrote, "The Registry of the type being proposed by some people in your department is in our opinion a stepping stone for the unionization of day care workers in Alberta." After this meeting, Minister Webber asked the civil service to comment on the issues raised by the DCSA. In regard to the proposed registry, Webber asked a number of questions, including "Would it facilitate unionization?"[41]

The director of the day care program, Melane Hotz, prepared a twenty-one-page document that systematically addressed the issues raised by the DCSA with Minister Webber. The section "Potential for Unionization" began with the observation: "The registry of workers proposed will, in the first place, lead to higher salary demands, rather than unionization." Hotz stated that if day care workers were legally required to hold college credentials, they would soon be demanding salaries on a par with individuals holding similar college credentials in other fields. This eventuality would put pressure on both commercial operators' profits and parent fees. In turn, increased fees would increase the vacancy rate in day care.

It must be remembered that when Hotz wrote this document, the Mini-Skool strike in Ontario was ongoing and the Ontario Public Service Employees Union was using the wage levels in municipally run centres as a reference point for its contract demands. Hotz apparently had this situation in mind when she made the following prediction for Alberta: "Unionization is likely to spread to the private sector, using the union salary levels in municipally operated centres as the benchmark, if a registry of workers is put in place. This has been the pattern elsewhere."

Melane Hotz's prediction had the effect of legitimating the DCSA's strident opposition to a provincial system of staff qualifications. This likely had a significant effect on the new minister, who was just learning about key policy issues. When Neil Webber replied to Jacqui Kallal, he made it clear that his department had no intention of proceeding with a mandatory registry of day care workers.[42]

Nevertheless, even in the absence of a staff qualifications regulation, CUPE had fleeting successes in unionizing commercial day care workers in Calgary in the late 1980s. Although these successes did not involve any of the large day care chains in the city, the owners of those chains played a crucial role in the eventual defeat of this drive. A number of them, along with other commercial operators who belonged to the DCSA, made financial contributions to cover the cost of the negotiator and lawyers who worked against the union.

In the middle of 1988, employees at five day cares in Calgary were members of labour unions: Calgary's three municipal day cares, the day care on the grounds of the Calgary Forces Base in Calgary, and the day care run by the Providence Child Development Society. Significantly, none of the unionized centres were in the commercial sector.[43]

In 1988 a majority of the forty-two employees at the two Children's Creative Learning Centres in downtown Calgary signed CUPE membership cards. The owners of the Children's Creative Learning chain, Tanya Bobbitt and Kory Smith, opposed the certification of CUPE as the collective bargaining agent of the workers. This union drive was also opposed by many of the other commercial day care owners in Calgary, who were concerned that if CUPE gained a foothold in the industry, their employees could be the next to unionize. The analysis of CUPE business agent Susan Keeley would not have reassured those owners. "If this one goes ahead," she stated, "it will show other daycare workers it can be done without much pain and anguish." The response of Calgary's day care capitalists was to cause the Children's Creative Learning workers as much pain and anguish as possible in order to discourage other commercial day care workers from pursuing unionization.

As would be expected, the president of the DCSA, John Samaska, spoke against unionization of commercial day cares. He predicted that unions would drive commercial day cares out of business, leaving only "socialized day cares." Surprisingly, the chair of the Calgary Association for Quality Child Care also strongly opposed this development. It just so happened that the chair at the time, Patti Penner, was the owner of one of the very few commercial centres that belonged to the association. "With unions," she inaccurately argued, "owners no longer will make decisions on what they can financially and reasonably do."[44]

The Alberta Labour Relations Board certified CUPE as the collective bargaining agent for the workers at the Children's Creative Learning centres on 15 December 1988. It also ruled that an employee, Brenda Ames, had been unjustly fired for union activity and ordered her reinstatement with full back pay. This success sparked another unionization drive that culminated in a representation election at the Lynnwood Child Care Centre, an independent commercial centre. CUPE won that election in early 1989 by a narrow ten-to-nine count.[45]

CUPE alleged that in early 1989 a number of commercial operators had started a "war chest" so that the owners of the Children's Creative Learning and Lynnwood centres would not have to carry the high costs of fighting the union. Co-owner Kory Smith refused to comment on the allegation, and his lawyer, David Laird, said he did not "intend to reply to unsubstantiated allegations made mainly to get press attention." But DCSA president John Samaska more or less confirmed the allegations when he said that while he had heard talk about starting a war chest, the DCSA had not organized contributions. If there is a war chest, stated Samaska, "private operators are doing it on their own."

Both Children's Creative Learning Centres and Lynnwood Day Care Centre hired Ken Barrass to negotiate on their behalf—further evidence of coordinated action to oppose the unionization of commercial day care in Calgary. Barrass, in conjunction with company lawyers, engaged in prolonged negotiations with CUPE over the Children's Creative Learning contract, apparently without any intention of coming to an agreement. Unlike a number of other provinces, there is no arbitration mechanism in Alberta's Labour Relations Code to force a first contract when negotiations are unsuccessful. Furthermore, the code gives a certified union only a ten-month window to sign a first contract before allowing disgruntled employees to file a decertification petition. Therefore, Ken Barrass's instructions would have been to drag out negotiations until the ten months had elapsed—the middle of October 1989. Shortly thereafter, the Alberta Labour Relations Board received a petition, signed by eighteen of the company's thirty-six employees, calling for the decertification of CUPE. By this time, all of the original union organizers among the staff had quit. "Life was made pure hell for them until they gave up," remarked Susan Keeley. The union was decertified by a vote of twenty to eleven on 17 November 1989.

One of the workers who voted for decertification, Patricia McAuley, had only been with the company for three months. She was hired without any training or experience in day care, and was being paid $6 an hour, $1.50 above the minimum wage. This elevated wage rate (at least, elevated for entry-level workers in commercial day care at that time) suggests that the owners were trying to buy the loyalty of at least some of their employees during this crucial time. In the case of McAuley, the relatively high wage worked as intended, since she stated, "I feel I'm well paid for what I'm qualified for."[46]

An identical scenario played out at Lynnwood Child Care Centre, where the union was decertified in the first part of 1990.[47] Thus ended CUPE's campaign to organize the commercial day care sector in Calgary. The campaign had cost tens of thousands of dollars (mainly in staff labour costs), costs that would have only been recouped if hundreds of day care workers had eventually joined the union, following the lead of their colleagues at the Children's Creative and Lynnwood centres. It was the union's hope that being able to negotiate first contracts at an initial group of day cares would spark widespread interest in unionization across Calgary and the entire province. Commercial operators were among those who saw this as a plausible scenario, so they did everything in their power to stop CUPE from gaining a toehold in the sector. It is even reasonable to presume that if the attempts to decertify the union had failed, commercial operators might well have employed a Plan B that involved closing the centres in question.

IMMIGRANT OWNERSHIP OF DAY CARES

Until 1990 Alberta had no minimum educational requirements for day care directors. For many years, critics condemned the provincial government's failure to act on this issue. Nevertheless, as so often happens in public policy, there was a positive effect mixed in with the negative consequences of government inaction: immigrants with strong backgrounds in child care and education could become directors of their own day cares without having to worry about whether their foreign educational credentials would be recognized by Canadian authorities. Foreign-trained educators such as Gertrude Darmohray of Marlborough Day Nursery and Gulshan Daya of Kidsland Daycare were blocked from becoming teachers in Canada because their training was not recognized by Canadian authorities. They turned to self-employment in day care because not only did it allow them to work with children and utilize their education, but it promised to yield larger earnings than they would have received as employees in day care or some other industry.

Since the 1970s, major Western cities had seen a boom in immigrant entrepreneurship. Robert Kloosterman (2000) theorizes the institutional context for this development. He argues that "ideal-typical immigrants, lacking appropriate education qualifications and financial capital ... are channelled towards economic activities that require relatively small capital outlays, no specific educational qualifications and where technical barriers are low" (94). Kloosterman

TABLE 6.4 Asian-Canadian-owned Commercial Day Cares in Calgary and Edmonton, 1975, 1982, and 1995

	Edmonton	Calgary
1975	2 (4%)	1 (2%)
1982	19 (21%)	11 (11%)
1995	91 (47%)	44 (32%)

NOTE: Asian-Canadian owners are defined as those having a Middle Eastern, South Asian, or East Asian surname. Some names may have been misclassified, however, and the data in this table should be viewed only as a rough approximation.

notes that a number of economic activities in post-industrial advanced economies fit this profile, including a range of personal and producer services (95). In some circumstances (such as in the mid-1980s in Alberta when operating allowances made day care very profitable), immigrants might choose to invest in day care over other businesses on strictly business grounds. Most of the time, however, immigrants will choose to invest in day care because of expertise in the area and a desire to apply that expertise in one's working life.

Another important aspect of immigrant entrepreneurship in day care is that it typically involves a married couple. The wife uses her expertise to direct the day care program and the husband provides supplementary support in the form of outside employment income for continuing investments in the business, construction and repairs, and/or business management.

Robert Kloosterman notes that immigrants often invest in a business sector that is in decline. An example is small-scale retailing, where immigrants have largely replaced indigenous entrepreneurs in recent years (2000, 96). A declining sector attracts investments from immigrants because of relatively low business prices.

Table 6.4 compares the number of commercial day cares in Edmonton and Calgary whose owners had Asian surnames in 1975, 1982, and 1995. My interest is in the ownership of day cares by immigrants, but, unfortunately, no systematic data on the immigration status of owners are available. For the purposes of this study, I have assumed that all of the owners with Asian surnames are first-generation immigrants, although I recognize that this overestimates the extent of immigrant ownership.

In Edmonton, only 4 percent of commercial centres were owned by Asian Canadians in 1975, compared to 21 percent in 1982 and 47 percent in 1995. In the latter year, ninety-one commercial centres in Edmonton had Asian-Canadian ownership. The trend is the same in Calgary, although the number of Asian-

Canadian owners is decidedly smaller. In 1975, 2 percent of commercial centres in Calgary were owned by Asian Canadians, compared to 11 percent in 1982 and 32 percent in 1995. In the latter year, forty-four commercial centres in Calgary were owned by Asian Canadians, with twelve of these centres being owned by Nizar and Gulshan Daya of the Kidsland chain.

By 1995 day care chains had come to dominate the commercial sector in Calgary (table 6.2). This meant that in the 1980s and early 1990s, there were fewer independent commercial centres in Calgary than in Edmonton that immigrant investors could buy. Furthermore, the dominance of large chain centres meant that independent commercial centres in Calgary tended to be larger than in Edmonton, and hence more expensive. For instance, in 1995 the average size of independent commercial centres in Edmonton was only forty-four children compared to fifty-seven in Calgary (table 6.2). Other factors being equal, the larger the capacity of a centre the more it is worth, so price-sensitive immigrant investors would find more day cares in Calgary outside of their price range than in Edmonton.

Not all of the immigrant investors in Alberta day cares in the 1980s were the ideal-typical immigrant entrepreneur with limited financial resources. At least one business-class immigrant invested in Alberta day cares. Under the business-class program, immigration is conditional on the new immigrant making a modest to large capital investment in Canada. (The size of the investment depended upon the part of the country where the immigrant settled.) Prem Singhmar came to Alberta in 1985 under this program. His initial investment of $250,000 was in a chicken and egg farm, but he soon sold the farm and invested in day cares. At one point, he owned three day cares in the Edmonton area before selling out and becoming a property developer. Singhmar is an example of an investor without any long-term or professional commitment to day care.[48]

More typical of the immigrant day care owners in the Edmonton area in the late 1980s and 1990s was Niwatra Klainatorn, a native of Thailand. In 1988 she purchased Merry Mermaid, a small commercial day care located in the basement of the Sherwood Park United Church. The owner in 1982 had been Colleen Bird. Klainatorn has a PhD in early childhood education (ECE) and represents an example of a highly educated immigrant woman who turned to commercial day care ownership because her occupational mobility in Canadian society was otherwise limited. She operated Merry Mermaid for over a decade until an unfavourable public health inspection reduced enrolment and made the day care uneconomical.[49]

In the 1960s and 1970s, immigrants from Europe had a very important place in commercial day care in Alberta. Many of these immigrants continued to operate day cares in the 1980s and 1990s, and they were joined by a new wave of immigrant owners. The major sources for immigrants to Canada had changed, however, so there were now many day care owners who had come to Canada from the Middle East, South Asia, and East Asia. Alberta's commercial day care sector varied, therefore, not only according to the class of ownership (large chain, small chain, and independents) but also according to the ethnic background and immigrant history of the owners. The next section illustrates the diversity of the commercial sector through four distinctive profiles.

THE DIVERSE WORLDS OF COMMERCIAL DAY CARE

Conny Hippe, owner-operator of Rainbow Day Cares in Edmonton, graduated from a small German university with a degree in education and then travelled to Canada in May 1976 to join her fiancé, a millwright-machinist who had emigrated from Germany in January of that year. In 1978 Hippe purchased a day care in Millwoods, a working-class neighbourhood in Edmonton. She attended several meetings of the PDCS in 1979 and 1980, but then dropped out. She explained:

I could not agree with the policy. The emphasis was, in all discussions, always the business aspect. And I really have a problem with that. So for a while there I felt like an island unto myself until I started working with people such as Ellen Derksen and Sheila Campbell, and they steered me, knowingly or unknowingly, more towards the non-profit sector.[50]

Conny Hippe expanded the Rainbow Day Care business from one to six locations in the 1980s. She contended that her expansion was not the product of overriding entrepreneurial ambitions but a response to what people in the community asked her to do. Indeed, every one of the centres in the Rainbow chain was located in the Millwoods area, all within a short drive of Hippe's business office.

Conny Hippe did not corporatize her business affairs in the 1980s by investing profits made in her day cares in other businesses or opening day cares that were spread over a wide geographical area. In this regard, she stands in sharp contrast to Dennis Sorensen. Hippe's approach allowed her to offer a relatively high standard of day care (for instance, by hiring trained staff and paying higher wages to ensure a low turnover of staff) and also meant that her business did not collapse in the difficult economic conditions of the 1990s. Indeed, during that decade, she closed two centres because of excess capacity but successfully operated her other centres. This planned reduction in capacity was certainly better for children, families, workers, and creditors than the turmoil created by the bankruptcy of the Kindercare and Educentres chains in Calgary.[51]

Conny Hippe ran her chain with the personal touch of a small business owner. Although in 1995 her business fit my definition of a "large chain," it was being run more like a small chain where the philosophy of the owner has a strong influence throughout the business. Hippe's commitment to quality is best seen through her support for college-based training programs. When staff training requirements were finally stipulated in 1990, Conny Hippe proposed a "Daytime/Part-time Early Childhood Program" to Grant MacEwan College. The college accepted the proposal and had the program in place within three months. The new program allowed some staff to take courses in the mornings and then go to work between 11:30 a.m. and 6:00 p.m. while a second group of staff members would study in the afternoons after working the morning/lunch shift. At its outset, Hippe had twenty of the Rainbow Day Care staff enrolled in the program, split between the two shifts.

A second example of an Alberta-based chain is Kidsland Daycare Centres. With the bankruptcies of Kindercare in 1994 and Educentres in 1996, Kidsland became Calgary's largest day care chain. The owners of Kidsland, Nizar and Gulshan Daya, moved to Calgary in 1980.[52] Because Gulshan Daya's teaching credential was not recognized in Canada, the couple decided to open a day care so that she could work with children. They looked at day cares that were for sale at the time but found they were too expensive, so they built their own for around $250,000, opening it in 1983. From the outset, Kidsland had a corporatized approach to building a chain of centres, looking for the best possible investments across the greater Calgary region. By the end of the 1980s, Kidsland operated six day cares stretching from Airdrie to Okotoks. A building opened by the Dayas in 1985 was the first in Calgary to receive an OOSC license (for twenty-eight children) on top of the maximum license for eighty preschoolers.[53] The economies of scale that came with a larger building were crucial to the continuing expansion of day care chains in the 1980s.

The Kindercare chain's bankruptcy in the spring of 1994 occurred when the vacancy rate of day cares in Calgary was fairly high. As a consequence, the twelve Kindercare centres sold by the receiver represented very good value, and Kidsland bought six of them. The rapid growth of the Dayas' chain in the mid-1990s was therefore an opportunistic response to the availability of undervalued day cares. The chain's expansion did not reflect an improved business environment for commercial day care but rather occurred precisely because the business fundamentals were so poor. As shown in table A.3, the number of day cares and the licensed day care capacity in Alberta had peaked in 1991. Between 1991 and 1995, the licensed capacity declined by approximately three thousand spaces, or 6 percent. The shrinkage of day care capacity in Alberta would continue over the next decade, with a decline of another 6,942 spaces (22 percent) between 1995 and 2005. The business challenge for Kidsland Daycare over this period was how to downsize their chain while preserving capital investment.

Despite the growth of day care chains like Kindercare, Rainbow, and Kidsland in the 1980s and early 1990s, independent commercial centres continued to hold an important share of licensed spaces in 1995, albeit much larger in Edmonton (59 percent) and Alberta outside of Calgary and Edmonton (51 percent) than in Calgary (27 percent) (table 6.3). The remaining business profiles involve two independent commercial centres in Calgary that were operated by the same owners throughout the entire period of chain ascendancy. Both Marlborough Day Nursery and Charleswood Day Nursery successfully withstood competition from chains and the ups and downs of the economy even though they operated according to very different business models.

Kurt Darmohray designed Marlborough Day Nursery so that his family could live in a second-floor apartment in the building. It opened in 1972 and by the end of the 1970s, the day care's capacity was ninety children. In contrast, the average capacity of independent commercial centres in Calgary in 1982 was forty-nine while the average capacity of large chain centres was ninety (table 6.3). Because of its size, Marlborough Day Nursery was an independent commercial operation that shared many of the concerns of chain operators. This partially helps to explain the active involvement of Kurt Darmohray and his daughter, Traudi Kelm, in the DCSA over the years.

Nevertheless, the family never expanded beyond its single centre. I wondered why this was the case. "Quality of care" was Traudi Kelm's short reply in 2002. She explained:

You know it's really easy to lose control over the quality of service you provide if you're not a hands-on type of an operator, and we're very hands on. I think we can do well in one. We know what's happening in one. We can maintain a high standard in one and when you start diversifying and moving out into the community and having more than one facility I believe that you lose a little bit of that control.[54]

Traudi Kelm indicated that she had never been tempted to expand the business although her father might have been. "He was more of the businessman in the family and we [her mother, Gertrude, and herself] were looking at what was in the best interests of the children." Kelm's aversion to expanding her own business beyond one facility, however, did not stop her from identifying with and even representing the interests of large day care chains. Over the years, she became the public face of the DCSA. More recently, she agreed to become a director of Edleun, a venture capitalist firm that announced its intentions in late 2009 to buy the 123 Busy Beavers chain of eleven day cares in Alberta and then to build a Canada-wide chain of day cares.[55] Traudi Kelm failed to see the many pitfalls of child care organized as the source of profit for speculative investors. Her record in this regard compares poorly with commercial operators like Conny Hippe, who consciously distanced herself from corporatized day care despite the fact that she was the owner-operator of the Rainbow Day Cares chain.

Central to the longevity of Marlborough Day Nursery has been its willingness to diversify the range of its services. An out-of-school program was added in the 1990s and a teacher was hired to teach in a kindergarten program based at the day care. Furthermore, many services were added for the 30 percent or more of the children who, in later years, had special needs. Traudi Kelm reported: "We have speech language, occupational physical therapists that come in on a weekly basis, we're connected with mental health." In 2002 there were five full-time resource people at the centre to work with these children. Funding for children with high needs was provided through Alberta Learning. Funding for children with mild to moderate needs was provided by the Child and Family Services Authority. Therefore, a key component of the success of Marlborough Day Nursery was that it took advantage of the availability of dedicated funding for specialized programs and thereby better served the needs of families in the area. In an important sense, it transformed itself into a commercial version of a Preventive Social Services (PSS) day care, combining child care with education, health, and social services. It is hard to imagine a corporate day care chain taking on this sort of responsibility.

The second independent commercial centre featured here is a small day care in a modified private home. Irmtraud Walter bought Charleswood Day Nursery in Calgary in 1972 and since the early 1980s, it has been licensed for twenty-six children.[56]

In her early years in business, Walter's clientele came from the young families in surrounding neighbourhoods. As those communities aged, the clientele expanded to the many new suburban neighbourhoods to the west and north. Because all of these communities have a predominantly middle-income or upper-middle-income population, Charleswood Day Nursery has enrolled relatively few children whose families qualified for a low-income subsidy. Irmtraud Walter estimated that on average only six of the twenty-six children would have qualified for a government subsidy. In contrast, Traudi Kelm estimated that 85 percent of the children at Marlborough Day Nursery qualified for a low-income subsidy in 2002.

Irmtraud Walter's capacity to offer a quality service was grounded upon her post-secondary training in early childhood development, obtained before she emigrated from Germany in 1960. "Why is there no training for any of the day care staff?" was the question she asked government inspectors from her first years as the owner-operator of Charleswood Day Nursery. Walter supported the staff qualification requirements that were introduced in 1990, which specified that directors of day care centres must hold a Level 3 qualification certificate, issued to those with a two-year college diploma in ECE or equivalent formal education. She gained partial credit for her courses in Germany but was required to complete five courses through Mount Royal College before being eligible for a Level 3 certificate. She was pleased to take these courses and she responded to the new staff qualification requirements by hiring another Level 3 staff as well as a Level 2 (granted for a one-year certificate in ECE). To keep these staff, she had to pay them more than they would have received from most commercial day cares.

A low staff turnover was one of the features of the Charleswood Day Nursery that parents appreciated. They also liked the way Walter treated children like part of her family—in this sense, the day care was like a very large FDH. In keeping with the family atmosphere of the day care, children called her Auntie Irma.

Irmtraud Walter's political views on day care were consistent with her class position as a small, independent owner-operator. She had been a member of the DCAC and later had joined the PDCS, but only for a short time. She said she didn't like meetings and didn't have time to attend. But despite her political inactivity, she had strong opinions on arrangements that appeared to threaten the family-like relationships of her business. Her view of Dennis Sorensen was this: "Children are not a business. Children need that personalized care and the

love and the attention and the hugs that they might not get in bigger day care."
She was even more adamant in her opposition to unions in day care:

> There was a time when the unions were pushing to get into day care. And I would
> have closed the day care right then and there. I would have never gone for
> unionized day care because I felt it would get too impersonal, it would be just
> business, and I didn't want a business.... Day cares can't afford to carry a union
> on top of the other expenses they have.

Finally, Walter also objected to the introduction of operating allowances.
At the time, she was making a comfortable living running a centre that had no
vacancies. Her preference was for the government not to become involved in the
commercial relationship between herself and parents who could fully pay for day
care. Her concern in 1980 was that the government would eventually take away
the allowances, causing a sharp jump in fees that might hurt enrolments.

It is difficult to dismiss Alberta's entire commercial day care sector out of
hand after considering the preceding four profiles and the earlier analysis of
the rise and fall of the Kindercare chain. While corporatized day care commodi-
fies the care and education of young children and presents an unacceptable risk
to the long-term integrity of the service, other sorts of commercial operations
need not follow this business model. Indeed, some of the commercial day cares
encountered in this study appear to confirm Colin Williams' contention that
private businesses need not be driven primarily by the profit motive (2009, 72).
It thus seems apparent that in commercial child care in Alberta, processes of
decommodification co-exist with processes of commodification. When commercial operators are committed to children's interests, have a strong background in ECE, and do not have overriding entrepreneurial ambitions, outcomes
for young children may well be exceptional. It is my contention that a not-for-
profit centre will necessarily be superior to a decommodified commercial centre
only because of its capacity to be the hub for family involvement and community development.

The single unambiguous conclusion of this chapter is that when day care is
treated as a centre of profit to fuel corporate expansion, sooner or later children
and their families will suffer. Since corporatized day care has been shown to
have a fatal deficiency, it is reasonable to ask whether this deficiency is shared by
corporatized health care, elder care, and educational services. One need not be
an ideological foe of corporate capitalism to recognize that in certain essential

fields of human life, the pursuit of an entrepreneurial logic has public policy risks that may well be intolerable.

Day care had been established as a core responsibility of the provincial government for less than two decades before critics—both inside and outside the government—began to question that responsibility. This questioning resulted from the conjunction of two factors: the strong desire of the provincial government to limit its spending on day care and the rise of a pro-family movement that challenged the notion that day care was good provincial social policy. This mix of fiscal and social conservatism proved to be a heady brew for Tory politicians. By 1988 it looked like it was only a matter of time before the government would eliminate operating allowances and redefine day care in Alberta as either a private responsibility or a welfare service for low-income families. Nevertheless, the DCSA, along with other advocates for publicly supported day care, managed to dissuade the province from eliminating operating allowances for over a decade. This demonstrates that large commercial operators still had some political clout with the government into the 1990s, even if their influence had diminished. It also indicates that once social policy has developed in a particular direction over a period of time, there are many institutional and political impediments to changing the direction of that policy. In the case of Alberta in the early 1990s, at the same time as politicians toyed with cutbacks, privatization, and deregulation in day care, civil servants managed to keep a long-standing promise and introduce requirements for staff qualifications.

7. Day Care in Question, 1984–99

Compared to the mid-1980s, the profit margins for commercial day cares were much lower in the 1990s. Furthermore, over this period of time the political influence of commercial owners diminished. Four issues were central to the political economy of day care in Alberta between 1984 and 1999: federal/provincial cost sharing, the rise of a pro-family movement that called for the province to direct resources away from day care toward stay-at-home parents of young children, the persistence but eventual end of operating allowance payments, and the move toward government policies that promoted greater private responsibility for child care, either in the form of families or markets.

This chapter contains much discussion about money, particularly the amount that the provincial government was willing to spend on day care at different points of time. More fundamental than the money the province was willing or unwilling to spend, however, are the beliefs about gender and young children that underlie policy discussions on day care. Alberta's day care controversy "seems to continue endlessly"[1] because beliefs about child rearing, families, and gender have continued to be both highly salient and polarized over time. Indeed, between 1984 and 1999, these beliefs became even more polarized in Alberta society, largely because of the successes of conservative movements and politicians.

Nevertheless, once staff qualification standards are in place, they are a constant reminder of the need to maintain a stable, trained workforce in day care, and they can thus serve as a focal point for further demands to improve quality. It was the inability of day cares to find trained workers to meet staff qualification requirements, particularly after operating allowances were eliminated in 1999, that convinced the provincial government that it had to enhance the wages of trained workers. Although the size of the wage enhancements introduced in

2002 was trivial, the policy itself was highly significant since it ran counter to the deregulation and privatization philosophy that had defined Alberta's provincial government for the preceding decade; it also provided a template for large increases in wage enhancements in succeeding years. These important developments are considered in more detail in chapter 9.

COMMERCIAL DAY CARE AND THE LOSS OF FEDERAL COST SHARING

Until 1978, all of the Alberta government's spending on day care was through the subsidization of not-for-profit Preventive Social Services (PSS) centres. Under the policy guidelines of the Canada Assistance Plan (CAP), fully 50 percent of the deficit incurred by each PSS centre was recoverable from the federal government, so long as families with an income above the provincial average were charged the full cost of day care.[2]

CAP guidelines also allowed for the sharing of the costs of subsidizing children's care in commercial centres, but only when a family's ability to pay was assessed through an investigation of their assets and liabilities. This was known as needs (or means) testing. Ontario, which like Alberta had a large commercial sector in day care, employed needs testing in order to secure CAP funds for subsidized children enrolled in commercial centres. This option was available to Alberta when it established the new portable day care subsidy program in 1978, and it certainly could have been implemented in 1980 when municipal participation in the system ended and the province assumed administrative responsibility for day care subsidies. However, Alberta chose to stay with the income-testing method. In 1980 Alberta was awash in petroleum royalties and day care was still a relatively small budget item, so the loss of a few million dollars a year in federal transfer payments "was not an issue" for provincial political and bureaucratic elites at that time. Furthermore, "needs testing was seen as expensive to administer, with a welfare connotation that would have added to public protest about the changes."[3]

Alberta's finances were so favourable in 1980–81 that the province was slow in claiming CAP cost sharing for the day care subsidies of children enrolled in not-for-profit centres.[4] However, with the downturn in the provincial economy that began in 1982, Alberta's lackadaisical approach toward CAP funding for day care quickly ended. In 1983 a meeting of federal and provincial deputy ministers of social services discussed Alberta's proposal for CAP sharing of income-tested subsidies in commercial day care.[5]

In 1984–85 spending on child care in Alberta was $134 per capita. This ranked Alberta second only to Quebec (at $142 per capita) and well above the national average of $116 per capita. But on another financial statistic, Alberta ranked first although it was unhappy with this ranking: the provincial share of the money spent on child care was higher in Alberta (at 73 percent) than in any other province. In Canada as a whole, provinces and territories contributed 60 percent of the money for child care while the federal government contributed 40 percent. The ineligibility of low-income subsidies in commercial centres for any CAP reimbursement was one reason for the Alberta government's funding burden. The more important reason, however, was the fact that the province's major funding program, operating allowances, was largely ineligible for cost sharing (Blain 1985, 178). As a consequence, in federal-provincial discussions, Alberta had the broader objective of securing federal cost sharing for operating allowances and, by extension, for any program an individual province decided to initiate.

By 1985 Alberta seemed to have won full support for this idea from the federal government and from all provincial governments except Manitoba. The Federal/Provincial/Territorial Working Group on Child Care argued that "there is a need for a more flexible funding arrangement for child care services authorizing a federal contribution of 50% of all the costs incurred by provinces in the field of child care services." The first principle articulated by the working group was a dramatic assertion of provincial/territorial rights over child care. This assertion implied the end of federal conditions on funding since a province was to have full responsibility for establishing and regulating programs.[6]

By this time, Alberta was doing exact calculations of the amount of CAP money it was losing because income-tested children in commercial centres were ineligible for cost sharing. In 1983–84 the federal government had not yet agreed to any cost sharing on Alberta's operating allowances. On the subsidy program, the province received only $4.1 million from the federal government instead of the $8.6 million it would have received if the full amount spent on subsidies had been eligible for cost sharing.[7] In a similar accounting for the 1985–86 budget year, Alberta received about $5.1 through CAP for the low-income subsidy program, far less than the $11.8 million it would have received if all its expenditures had been cost shareable. Furthermore, by this time the federal government had agreed to cost share the operating allowances paid on behalf of subsidized children but only if they were enrolled in not-for-profit centres (Health and Welfare Canada 1985, 15). The Alberta government received $1.6 million from CAP for operating allowances in 1985–86 compared to the $6.3 million that constituted half of its expenditures. The bottom line for the 1985–86 budget year was that the federal government's refusal to recognize income testing for subsidized spaces in commercial centres cost Alberta $11.4 million in transfer payments ($6.7 million on the subsidy program and $4.7 million on operating allowances).[8]

As noted above, by the mid-1980s, it looked as if Canada was on the verge of changing the rules for federal funding of day care so that all of a province's expenditures would qualify for 50 percent cost sharing. In 1985–86 Alberta spent about $58 million on day care but received only $6.75 million in reimbursement under the rules of CAP. The new rules proposed by the Federal/ Provincial/Territorial Working Group on Child Care would have yielded $29 million in reimbursement, an increase of 330 percent over that provided by CAP. But intergovernmental negotiations for virtually any change in the Canadian federation are notoriously slow, doubly so for changes in a key funding formula. Therefore, Alberta began to look at other ways of recovering more of the money it was spending on day care. This was a pressing issue since commercial centres were increasing in number much more quickly than not-for-profit centres.[9]

In early 1986 Connie Osterman replaced Neil Webber as the minister of Social Services. While Webber had seemed uninterested in day care during his three years in office, Osterman was soon talking about major changes in the government's approach to day care and was engaged in active dialogue with advocates throughout the province.[10] One of the first ideas broached by Osterman was switching from an income to a needs test so that subsidies paid for children in commercial centres would qualify for CAP cost sharing. In early 1987, she estimated that this would net the province an extra $17 million in CAP transfer payments. (Even after taking into account increased spending on day care in 1986–87 compared to the previous year, the $17 million figure still seems inflated compared to the $11.4 million exact calculation for 1985–86 shown above.) The department's draft business plan, dated 10 March 1987, listed the switch to needs testing as a key strategy for day care.[11]

It looked as if a major change in federal-provincial funding of child care was imminent, however, so Alberta never acted on the cumbersome plan to introduce needs testing. The federal government of Brian Mulroney outlined its "National Strategy on Child Care" in December 1987 (Health and Welfare Canada 1987). The plan initially called for $3 billion in federal money to be available for cost sharing on provincial initiatives on child care between 1988 and 1995. "The cost-sharing mechanism approved by the federal cabinet will enable the federal government to share 50% of eligible operating costs and 75% of eligible capital expenditures incurred by the provinces and territories." The exact cost-sharing ratio would vary from jurisdiction to jurisdiction, with Alberta predicted to receive reimbursement at the rate of 51.1 percent. A key element of the federal proposal was that commercial services would qualify for cost sharing.[12]

The Alberta government fully expected the new cost-sharing mechanism to be implemented in 1988. An internal departmental report drafted in January 1988 projected that of the budgeted total of $81.2 million for day care in 1988–89, $40.6 million would be recoverable from the federal government.[13] But Bill C-144, the *Canada Childcare Act*, was not passed by the federal parliament until the fall of 1988. Many advocates for quality child care saw the new act as inferior to the provisions of CAP; their lobbying delayed passage of Bill C-144 in the Senate, and the bill died when parliament was dissolved for the election of 22 November 1988. It was never reintroduced (Prentice 1999, 144).

Because of these events, CAP lived on beyond 1988. Had she retained full control of day care, Minister Osterman might well have returned to her original plan to introduce needs testing in order to maximize the federal transfer payments available through CAP. But in September 1988, some of the responsibility for day care was shifted to the new minister of Families, Jim Dinning, who was also the minister of Education.[14] This broke the continuity in policy development on day care. After the provincial election in early 1989, yet another new minister, John Oldring, took charge and the issue of switching from income to needs testing for day care subsidies does not seem to have ever again been identified as a policy priority. When CAP was terminated in 1996, the federal government rolled child care funding into a block grant known as the Canada Health and Social Transfer. The preference for not-for-profit over commercial day care disappeared with the end of CAP. The Canada Health and Social Transfer provided no incentive for the provinces to spend money on day care, let alone on day care of a particular type. The federal government recognized this policy vacuum and looked at new ways to encourage provincial spending on the care and education of young children. Chapter 8 summarizes Alberta's participation in the "early intervention" programs developed in the 1990s, and chapter 9 details Alberta's response to the "early learning and child care" initiative of the federal Liberal government in 2004–5.

The Government of Alberta's political commitment to commercial day care had important financial repercussions for the citizens of Alberta between 1979 and 1996. Detailed calculations of the amount of CAP money lost by Alberta are only available for 1985–86 (see above). In that year, Alberta forfeited $11.4 million on a total spending of $58.3 million (see table A.4), or 19.6 percent of the total spending. Assuming that this percentage holds for the other years in the series, the total amount forfeited by Alberta between 1979 and 1996, converted to 2006 dollars (see table A.5), was approximately $255 million.[15] If Alberta had received this CAP money, it could have used the provincial dollars saved to enhance day care, invest in other programs, or simply decrease the size of the provincial debt of more than $15 billion that accumulated between 1985 and 1994 (Mansell 1997, 31). Evidently, the government's commitment to free enterprise in day care came at a surprisingly high cost for the citizens of the province.

THE PRO-FAMILY MOVEMENT CHALLENGES DAY CARE

The first of Canada's pro-family (or family values) groups was formed in Alberta in 1981 to mount opposition to the pro-choice stance of the Alberta Status of Women Action Committee. Originally named Alberta Women of Worth, this group soon became known as the Alberta Federation of Women United for Families (AFWUF) and has been a fixture on the political scene in the province ever since. AFWUF is the provincial affiliate of a national organization of a similar nature that formed in 1983—Realistic, Equal and Active for Life (REAL) Women (Anderson and Langford 2001, 38). AFWUF and REAL Women had their roots in hardline anti-abortion activism that portrayed the growing societal acceptance of abortion as symptomatic of a deep social malaise. According to Lorna Erwin, these groups saw "the rising toll of abortions ... [as] the most visible evidence of a widespread rejection of the values associated with the breadwinner ethic and the traditional family—a rejection that was rooted in the movement of women into paid employment, in the social derogation of housewives, and especially the increasing legitimacy of feminism and feminists" (1993, 405–6). Christian fundamentalism underlies the pro-family advocacy of these groups. Other prominent pro-family groups, such as the U.S.-based Focus on the Family and the Calgary-based Canada Family Action Coalition, likewise hold a conservative Christian world view and express alarm at the weakening of the hegemony of the traditional patriarchal family (Anderson and Langford 2001, 46–47).

The pro-family movement in Alberta took an interesting turn in 1987 with the formation of the Kids First Parents Association. Like AFWUF, Kids First was organized to counter significant changes in the gender order in Canadian society. But while women's reproductive rights was the trigger issue for AFWUF, publicly funded day care prompted the emergence of Kids First.

Kids First grew out of the groundswell of opposition that greeted the release of the report of the federal Task Force on Child Care in March 1986. The report had "recommended the development of a publicly funded, comprehensive, high quality non-profit childcare system, accompanied by extended parental and maternity leaves" (Prentice 1999, 142). This task force had been established by a federal Liberal government, but in the meantime, a Progressive Conservative government had been elected. The new federal government established a special parliamentary committee to further study child care policy. That committee held hearings in Alberta during the week of 2 to 6 June 1986.[16]

Two Calgary women, Brenda Ringdahl and Teresa Del Frari, made a presentation to the committee in Calgary, arguing that the tax system discriminates against single-income, two-parent families. Ringdahl and Del Frari founded Kids First the following year. Like the members of conservative, Christian pro-family groups, they believed that "child care is the responsibility of the family and that a willing and caring parent does the best job of raising a child." However, they did not embed this argument in a religious vision and were not particularly strident in their opposition to day care. They merely argued that governments should "give equal child-care tax credits to all parents to use as they wish ... in day care or at home." This argument for tax fairness and equal treatment resonated with many single-income, two-parent families. By 1990 Kids First represented five thousand stay-at-home parents.[17]

The anti-day care arguments of pro-family advocates soon found a sympathetic audience among the members of the provincial Conservative caucus, including the cabinet (Harder 1996, 53). "The government always struggled with child care," explained former civil servant Dennis Maier in 1998. "I had many discussions at the ministerial level where people would share anecdotes about how they were raised by aunts or other relatives, [and ask] why that wasn't happening today. The 'back-to-the-family' movement was seen as something whereby the family should take on more responsibility for things like child care so why should government provide child care—you're interfering with the functioning of families." Dennis Maier stated that pro-family groups like AFWUF "lobbied very, very hard," making the following complaint: "If we neglect our children and go out to work you will pay us money for somebody else to look after our kids, but if we stay at home and look after our children and sacrifice the extra income that we're giving up we don't get really hardly anything." Maier commented that this argument was hard for Alberta's Tory government to ignore since it invoked basic tenets of conservative philosophy.[18]

The Alberta government signalled that it was paying attention to pro-family arguments in the 1986 speech from the throne (Harder 1996, 53). Shortly thereafter, it replaced the Alberta Day Care Advisory Committee (ADCAC) with a new Advisory Committee on the Family.[19] Behind the scenes, Minister Connie Osterman and her staff were reading papers criticizing day care that had been presented in Calgary to the special committee on child care. One was by Ringdahl and Del Frari and the other was by Dr. Philip Ney, then a professor in the Department of Psychiatry at the University of Calgary. Ney's paper, unimaginatively titled "Day Care or Nightmare," was a philosophical treatise defending the heterosexual nuclear family as "the most effective, efficient core group upon which any society can develop and grow."[20]

There is no recorded evidence that Ney's views guided policy discussions in Alberta. Nevertheless, they helped to contribute to a policy environment in the late 1980s and 1990s that was increasingly skeptical of the efficacy of day care. It is noteworthy that Philip Ney was listed as a member of the professional advisory board of Kids First in 1996, indicating that despite its relatively tame rhetoric, Kids First was happy to associate with those who offered sweeping and intemperate denunciations of day care. By 1996 Ney was a clinical professor at the University of British Columbia. He is best known for his research on the "connection between an abortion and later difficulty bonding to a child," which in turn is hypothesized to lead to child abuse and neglect. Ney's research on "post-abortion syndrome" is cited as justification by anti-abortion groups.[21] Philip Ney is thus an example of an academic whose research and writing helped to maintain some links between the hardline anti-abortion and anti-day care camps.

Another pro-family advocate who came to the attention of Minister Connie Osterman around this time was Beverley Smith of Calgary. Smith offered a pro-family argument that was at least superficially respectful of the women's movement. In a 1987 interview, she stated that "the women's movement has gotten rid of the chains that forced us to be in the home, but it has also—possibly inadvertently—gotten rid of the dignity for being in the home." Like Kids First, Beverley Smith called for changes in the tax system to benefit the stay-at-home parent.[22] But unlike most others in the pro-family movement, she acknowledged that care of young children outside the home could be equivalent in quality to that provided by parents so long as the caregiving relationship was stable and personal (Anderson and Langford 2001, 46–47).

In 1987 Smith sent Minister Osterman a copy of a research report titled "Watch Me, Mama! Watch Me Dad!" Smith called for "more money to parents for child-rearing regardless of labour force participation" and recommended "present expenditures on day care to be abolished or matched by grants to all moms." The report was twice acknowledged by Osterman and summarized by social services staff in late 1987.[23]

In the mid-1980s, Beverley Smith's rhetoric on day care was relatively tame. At the same time, however, she was an implacable foe of any public policy that encouraged day care over parental care or even regulated day care over informal child care arrangements. Like many outside of the pro-family movement, Smith called for public initiatives to assist parents with the difficult job of parenting. But instead of combining these initiatives with support for accessible, high-quality, regulated day care, Beverley Smith promoted public funding for informal child care arrangements so that there would be no financial incentives for parents to use regulated over unregulated services. Her antipathy to day care caused her to advocate that all child care services should receive equal public funding regardless of the quality of those services.[24]

By this time, both Osterman and Premier Don Getty were enamoured with pro-family ideas. The federal government of Brian Mulroney released its "National Child Care Strategy" in December 1987. In reply, the premier stated that while he supported the federal strategy, it did not "address those who stay at home with their children." He indicated that "the province might add to the federal initiatives, which include tax relief, or grants to families might be considered." A few weeks prior to making this public comment, the premier had "requested that government financial support for parents who stay at home to care for their preschool children be reviewed, and that options for ensuring that those families receive additional support be developed." A Working Group on Child Care Support for Women in the Home had been struck in November 1987. It included representatives from the Women's Secretariat and three provincial government departments (Treasury, Social Services, and Community and Occupational Health). Nevertheless, the working group was very much the premier's creation.

By December 1987 the working group had concluded that the "simplest and fairest" way to support child care by women in the home was to supplement the child care benefits available through the tax system even though the premier had indicated he did not favour this approach. Before proceeding any further, the working group wanted to know "the total amount likely to be available for the initiative, and the desired annual per child benefit which is being contemplated."[25] Planning for this initiative continued throughout 1988.

In the spring of that year, Connie Osterman demonstrated her ongoing sympathies for the position of the Kids First Parents Association by addressing a rally organized by the group in Calgary. Attended by 250 people, the rally protested the federal government's intention to invest in day care through the Canada Childcare Act.[26]

The appointment of a minister of Families in September 1988 seemed to indicate that stay-at-home parents would soon be rewarded by the provincial government. However, shortly after his appointment, Minister Jim Dinning expressed concern at the potential cost. He stated that "subsidizing stay-at-home parents at the same rate as parents who use day care could cost the province an estimated $260 million." This amount was of concern because although the government had budgeted for a deficit of around $500 million in the 1988–89 fiscal year, it was headed for a deficit of just less than $2 billion (Mansell 1997, 31).

Just prior to the 1989 provincial election, the government contemplated a much more modest subsidy for stay-at-home parents. An internal report proposed providing a tax credit of $100 per month if total family income was $40,000 or less, and a smaller credit if family income exceeded $40,000. The estimated cost of the program was $20 million. But even though support for families was a key theme of the provincial throne speech on 17 February 1989, the government made no immediate commitment to subsidizing stay-at-home parents. Furthermore, after details of the internal report were released, even the pro-family movement was unimpressed: Diane Klein of Kids First called the proposed tax credit "meagre."[27]

The campaign leading to the provincial election of 20 March 1989 started poorly for the Tories, and by early March, the premier was looking for a dramatic initiative that would reverse his party's fortunes. The proposal to subsidize stay-at-home parents was shelved, presumably because it would likely either be ignored or, even worse, attract criticism for inadequate benefit levels. The premier instead aggressively criticized federal policies on interest rates and offered to help Alberta homeowners and small businesses pay for the high cost of borrowing money. The "interest-shielding programs" included relief for homeowners who were paying more than 12 percent on a first mortgage of up to $75,000; the programs were projected to cost $70 million in 1989–90.[28] The fact that expensive interest-rate subsidies were instituted at this time while a modest tax credit for stay-at-home parenting was abandoned shows that the Getty government was largely driven by pragmatic rather than ideological concerns.

Nonetheless, even if the pro-family movement could not get the Alberta government to implement its central demand, it definitely changed how that government viewed day care and responded to key interest groups in the day care community. From the early 1970s to the mid-1980s, the main political cleavage in Alberta's policy debates on day care had been between those who supported commercial day care and those who supported not-for-profit day care. By the end of the 1980s, the main division was between the supporters of day care and their pro-family opponents. The 1990s witnessed a return to the day care politics of the 1960s and even the 1940s, when day care itself was questioned as appropriate public policy for Alberta. At the same time, the terrain for those politics had changed. The need for day care was much higher in the 1990s than in the 1940s and 1960s. Furthermore, the large day care system in place in the 1990s proved to be very difficult to change, let alone dismantle.

Connie Osterman's work on day care was highly regarded by a number of the activists in the Alberta Child Care Network (ACCN) who met with her. Among those who would later praise the former minister were Conny Hippe, owner of the Rainbow day care chain in Edmonton; the first facilitator of the network, Noreen Murphy; and the founder of Choices in Childcare, Wendy Reid, who served as the ACCN facilitator in 1993–94.[29] One reason for Connie Osterman's popularity was that she did not favour the Day Care Society of Alberta (DCSA) over other interest groups; indeed, at one network meeting, she upbraided a DCSA representative for expecting too large an influence on government policy.[30] A second reason was her accessibility. For example, between 25 May 1987 and 12 May 1988, she met with the ACCN at least three times.[31] The Department of Social Services paid the travel expenses for everyone who attended these meetings. Furthermore, Minister Osterman seemed to genuinely listen and learn in these meetings, and she cultivated warm personal relations with network leaders. Wendy Reid commented that Connie Osterman "participated as a member of [the network], rather than coming in as a guest." This contrasted favourably to the approach taken by John Oldring, minister of Social Services from 1989 to 1992.[32]

Nevertheless, those advocates for quality child care who enjoyed working with the minister so much seemed to have misjudged Connie Osterman's politics. Her support for the parental information service in Calgary, Choices in Childcare, was consistent with her conservative emphasis on parents assuming more responsibility for monitoring day cares. Her coolness toward the DCSA grew out of her sympathies toward the pro-family movement rather than a commitment to quality day care. Although the network meetings undoubtedly helped the minister to better understand some day care issues, they were also an effective way for her to freeze large day care capitalists out of the policy development process. Whereas under Ministers Bogle and Webber, the DCSA had enjoyed the status of special-ized insiders in policy development, under Minister Osterman, they joined not-for-profit advocates as peripheral insiders. Osterman's refusal to meet with interest groups on a one-to-one basis, in combination with her meetings with the network, was a way to make this political transition.[33] The quality advocates mis-takenly assumed that the diminished status of the DCSA meant that things were looking up for them, but what it really meant was that the pro-family movement's arguments against day care had gained considerable ground among provincial Conservative politicians. This set the stage for the gradual dismantling of the sig-nature Alberta funding program for day care—operating allowances.[34]

One advocate for quality day care who quickly recognized the importance of the pro-family movement was Eva Roche. Somewhat of a maverick in day care circles in Edmonton, Roche had been working as an instructor in early childhood education (ECE) at Grant MacEwan Community College since 1973. In 1983 she published an article that articulated a number of the arguments that would later be widely disseminated by Kids First and Beverley Smith. Eva Roche wrote:

> As we look realistically at the cost of good day care, with government subsidizing up to $400 per month per child in some cases, the question arises; should this subsidy be available to enable one of the child's parents to care for the child at home if they so choose. For those parents who have careers from which it is difficult to opt out for a long period of time, or for single parents, should we be lobbying for shared jobs, flexible hours, comparative benefits and chance for advancement for part time workers....
>
> As day care becomes institutionalized, will problems develop similar to the educational system, such as lack of parental input and decision making, runaway costs, lack of individual attention? ...
>
> There has always been a need for alternative child care. Years ago the alternative care giver was frequently a maiden aunt in the home, or a grandparent. There will continue to be a need for quality day care, perhaps used more on a part time basis, as one of a number of options open to young Canadian families. (1983, 2–3)

In the late 1980s, Eva Roche was elected as the president of the Alberta Association for Young Children (AAYC). One of the initiatives she undertook was to get pro-family organizations to dialogue with organizations that promoted quality day care. Both AFWUF and Kids First were invited to the two-day liaison meeting held in Edmonton in late January 1989, although only Kids First attended. The other groups in attendance included Parents for Quality Child Care, Citizens for Public Justice, the AAYC, and the Alberta Status of Women Action Committee.

Christine Macken was a member of the AAYC Board of Directors at the time, although she represented Parents for Quality Child Care at the liaison meeting. She later described the meeting as an "emotional roller coaster," commenting that the two Kids First representatives "offended [at] first because [they] could be ill informed," but they proved to be "open to new ideas and information." Macken also noted that at a New Democratic Party meeting held subsequent to the liaison meeting, the Kids First representatives were "much more accommodating." She saw this as evidence that Kids First had learned from the liaison meeting.[35]

Eva Roche continued to pursue this dialogue after her term as the AAYC president ended in 1989. At the 1990 AAYC conference, she organized a session titled "Mommy Wars," which featured a representative of Kids First and a mother from a two-career family. Roche later commented, "The premise is we don't want to be fighting each other, we want to fight for more resources for young children and families."[36]

Despite Eva Roche's efforts, the attempt to bridge the divide between the pro-family and quality day care movements in Alberta never amounted to much.[37] It is especially significant that the dialogue never extended to Calgary, where pro-family groups were headquartered. A study of pro-family organizations in Calgary in 1998 revealed no ongoing liaison of the kind envisioned by Eva Roche (Anderson 1998). My assessment is that the ideological gap between the two movements was simply too great to allow for meaningful joint work. Furthermore, by the early 1990s, it was clear that the pro-family movement's arguments were winning the day inside the provincial government, while both the commercial and not-for-profit day care sectors were on the defensive. In this political context, pro-family organizations had little incentive to pursue dialogue. By the end of the 1990s, they were cheering the end of operating allowances for spaces in licensed day cares.

THE SLOW DEATH OF OPERATING ALLOWANCES

Almost as soon as the system of operating allowances for day care spaces was fully established, the Alberta government expressed concern about the rising costs of the system. Between 1982 and 1984, the cost of operating allowances increased by 78 percent (from $11.3 million to $20.1 million; see table A.4). The minister projected that the Day Care Program would face a shortfall of $9 million in the 1984–85 fiscal year if service levels were not changed. This is because for the second consecutive year, the government was planning a "hold-the-line" budget in order to control the rising cost of expenditures (Mansell 1997, 29–30).[38] In light of this, Webber requested that the ADCAC provide recommendations for how "to bring costs into line during this period of fiscal restraint." Provincial civil servants and Canadian Kindercare Ltd., the day care holding company established by Dennis Sorensen and his partners in Calgary, also took on this task. Kindercare clearly had a specialist insider role in the policy process in the mid-1980s.

The ADCAC recommended an across-the-board cut of $15 per space in operating allowances, a cut of $5 per child in the administrative fee paid to satellite family day home (FDH) agencies, and a one-year freeze in the number of spaces that qualified for operating allowances. This would have resulted in savings of $3.3 million. Canadian Kindercare Ltd. and provincial government staff members each recommended modest decreases in staff-to-child ratios and large cuts in the operating allowances for infants. Provincial staff also recommended a freeze on the number of infants who qualified for operating allowances and a short-term freeze on the number of other children who were eligible. Kindercare's proposal would have resulted in less savings than that of the ADCAC (by $0.3 million), and the staff's proposal would have resulted in the most savings ($1.1 million more than the ADCAC).[39]

None of the proposals for cutbacks in operating allowances were ever implemented by Minister Neil Webber. Provincial revenue from non-renewable resources increased by 47 percent between 1982–83 and 1983–84, and remained at approximately that level the following year.[40] As a consequence, the province had a small net surplus in 1983–84 and a surplus of $1.6 billion in 1984–85 (Mansell 1997, 30). In this fiscal context, cost control was no longer a pressing issue.

By the end of the 1985–86 budget year, the combined cost of operating allowances and FDH agency administrative fees was $33.8 million. In four years, the cost of operating allowances/administrative fees had increased by 200 percent in current dollars (table A.4) or 161 percent after correcting for inflation (table A.5). Indeed, by 1985–86 the spending on operating allowances and administrative fees was 43 percent higher than spending on the low-income subsidy ($33.8

million vs. $23.7 million). This helped to make day care very affordable for middle-income Albertans and encouraged commercial operators to establish new day cares to profit from serving the middle-income market. The number of licensed day care spaces in Alberta grew by approximately ten thousand between 1982 and 1986, an increase of 60 percent (table A.3).

Because of budgetary restraint in 1983 and 1984, the provincial government never proceeded with a proposal to extend operating allowances to the FDHs that were administered by an approved agency. This plan had originated with the provincial civil servants working in day care. In June 1982 they recommended that an operating allowance of $100 be paid for infants in satellite FDHs (with $40 for the agency and $60 for the provider) and an allowance of $50 be paid for toddlers nineteen to thirty-five months of age (with $20 for the agency and $30 for the provider). These allowances were intended to supplement the $50-per-child agency fee that was paid regardless of the age of a child. The main rationale for this proposal was the difficulty in securing care for young children in FDHs. The Day Care Branch wrote: "Both caregivers and agencies have little incentive to offer superior care in a family setting, as the rewards are the same as for pre-school care, while the risk and effort is much greater. In the meantime, unsupervised, unlicensed baby farms exist in the side streets, charging high fees (up to $300 per month) for crowded babysitting arrangements."[41]

It is noteworthy that this proposal originated with civil servants and not the ADCAC. At the time, the latter did not have a representative from the FDH sector and consequently provided little leadership in this policy area. Nevertheless, the director of the Day Care Branch, Melane Hotz, did get the ADCAC to review and approve the proposal at its meeting on 1 June 1982.[42]

The government made a modest increase in the agency fee for children less than thirty-six months ($84 in early 1985) while leaving the fee for three to five year olds virtually unchanged ($52.50).[43] However, an operating allowance for satellite FDH providers was never introduced. This was an important omission because such an allowance would have encouraged many unregulated FDH providers to join the satellite system, thus extending the reach of regulated child care in Alberta.

The collapse of oil and grain prices in 1986 (see Mansell 1997, 27) sparked renewed concerns about the cost of operating allowances. Just prior to the provincial general election of 8 May 1986, the government announced a 14 percent increase in the amount it was budgeting for day care subsidies and operating allowances because of an expected increase in caseload. The new premier, Don

Getty, handily won the election, but he had little time to enjoy his victory because of the precipitous drop in government revenue from non-renewable resources. The province netted only $1.4 billion in 1986–87, a decrease of 61 percent over the previous year.[44] The provincial deficit for the year ballooned to almost $3.5 billion (Mansell 1997, 30–31). In October 1986 the minister of Social Services directed her staff "to prepare a five to ten percent budget reduction" that included "recommendations ... to reduce/eliminate specific program components."[45]

In early November 1986, Connie Osterman first indicated that she was considering abolishing the operating allowance for every day care space so that her department's money could be directed toward those in financial need. "Where will the dollars go?" she asked. "Will they go in operating allowance to people who have a reasonably high income, or will they go to support people to buy groceries and clothing and shelter?" She added, "I think you know what my answer is." Osterman also mentioned that if the province ended the across-the-board operating allowance, it could raise the income level under which a family qualified for a day care subsidy.[46]

At this point, the minister was already strongly committed to ending the system of operating allowances. Deputy Minister Mike Ozerkevich met with the social planning committee of the Conservative caucus on 24 November and gained their support for a number of changes, including "needs testing of day care operating allowance, with the existing allowance phased out gradually."[47]

Two days later, the minister unilaterally implemented "a freeze on the provision of operating allowances to all new daycare spaces in Alberta." Exemptions for new spaces were issued in regions where "the demand for spaces exceeds the supply," or where, as of 26 November, finances had already been invested toward establishing new day care spaces. Significantly, eligibility for operating allowances was not affected by the sale of a day care, so the freeze immediately increased the value of any day cares that were on the market.

Minister Osterman expected that the freeze would be the beginning of the end for operating allowances. She warned, "Both existing and prospective operators must know that there is no guarantee operating allowance will be provided when the freeze is removed."[48]

The minister's comments and actions in late 1986 sparked concern and action by both commercial and not-for-profit operators. Almost immediately, at least two commercial operators in Calgary sent letters to their clients "informing them daycare fees will soar if operating grants are cut" and asking them to write protest letters to Connie Osterman.[49] More concerted opposition was led by Conny Hippe and six other commercial operators in Edmonton who came together to form the United Child Care Association of Alberta (UCCA) in early 1987. The UCCA spent thousands of dollars to develop and mail out a package of information to all licensed centres in the province. The objective of the mailing was to get thousands of parents to contact the premier and their MLAs to protest the plan to eliminate operating allowances. Consequently, in each package, the UCCA included enough fact sheets for all parents in a centre, along with enough copies of form letters addressed to the premier and the local MLA. The fact sheet, titled "Daycare Fees Could Double," listed the current value of operating allowances (see table A.6 for 1987) and asked, "Can you afford these increases or any increases which will result from cutbacks in government funding?" The fact sheet predicted that many day cares would have to close if operating allowances were eliminated. The package mailed to day cares also included a poster, titled "Good-Bye Operating Allowances, Good-Bye Day Cares," that could be posted inside a day care to attract the attention of the parents.[50]

Information on the lobbying efforts of the UCCA was disseminated at a conference of early childhood administrators held in early May 1987 at Grant MacEwan College in Edmonton. That conference included a workshop on group networking led by Sandra Griffin of the School of Child and Youth Care, University of Victoria, who would shortly thereafter serve a term as the president of the Canadian Child Day Care Federation.[51] This workshop immediately sparked action. The following Friday, a "meeting was held in Calgary to explore the possibilities of a child care network." It was attended by two representatives of the DCSA, two representatives of the AAYC, and six other people, including Conny Hippe of the UCCA, Avril Pike of the Edmonton Coalition for Quality Child Care, and Noreen Murphy, director of the day care at the Alberta Vocational College in Calgary. Paddi Solem, one of the AAYC representatives, noted, "Yes we were strange bedfellows, but surprisingly enough, and through the careful tutelage of Noreen Murphy ... acting as facilitator, we did good."

The group's plan was to wait until the government started to receive the form letters circulated by the UCCA and then have Noreen Murphy contact Minister Osterman to request an "audience." Although it succeeded in coming up with a common plan of action, the first meeting of the ACCN did not eliminate the deep divisions between the not-for-profit and commercial sectors. Afterwards, the board of the Early Childhood Professional Association of Alberta decided it would not be "comfortable" including the advocacy letter written by the UCCA in its newsletter, instead deciding to make its own appeal for action. And at this point, the largest organization of commercial operators, the DCSA, withdrew from participating in the ACCN, thus missing the meetings with the minister held on 25 June and 19 August.[52]

At her first meeting with the network, Minister Osterman did not reveal that she had long ago sought the approval of her caucus colleagues to gradually eliminate operating allowances and that this was the plan of her department. However, she did predict that as the day care system evolved, there would likely be "a redirection of funds away from high income families, to serve those who need it most." At her second meeting with the ACCN, she again did not reveal her full thinking on operating allowances, stating only that there was "no assurance that operating allowances will continue in their present form."[53] These could hardly have been reassuring words for the advocates who attended the meetings, although at least they learned that any cutbacks were not imminent.

The full scope of Minister Osterman's thinking on funding for day care was revealed in a background paper prepared by civil servants in January 1988. It began by listing three criticisms of the funding approach then in place:

- it allocates approximately 30% of the total budget to the support of families which do not have low incomes (through operating allowance, day home administrative fees and integrated day care funding for families not qualifying for the family subsidy);
- the existence of operating allowance has led to the rapid growth of day care centre spaces, 18% of which are currently vacant;
- high operating allowance rates for infants have made infant care in day care centres very accessible and affordable, and there is increasing evidence that other types of care for infants (e.g., family day homes) are more appropriate than centre-based care.

The paper then listed a number of principles that would be used to guide future policy decisions. They included directing funds to lower-income families; shifting the care of infants to FDHs; controlling government expenditures; allowing market forces to determine the number of licensed spaces; and enhancing "parental responsibility and involvement in selecting and monitoring their child's care." This was a recipe to return Alberta's day care system to its roots as an employment aid for low-income families, to loosen regulatory standards in favour of "parental responsibility," and to reprivatize a significant part of the system by withdrawing universal public subsidies for regulated care.[54]

There is no indication that the letter-writing campaign mounted by the UCCA in 1987 caused Connie Osterman to rethink her plan to eliminate operating allowances. When she met with the network on 12 May 1988, she reiterated her intention to redistribute dollars to lower-income families but reassured the group by saying, "Change will not be abrupt, it will occur over time." The delay at that point was the ongoing negotiations with the federal government associated with the proposed *Canada Childcare Act*.[55] That delay, followed by the assignment of day care to the new minister of Families in September 1988, resulted in a reprieve for operating allowances (although the freeze on allowances for new spaces remained in effect). After the provincial election of May 1989, the new minister of Family and Social Services, John Oldring, inherited the problem. He met with the ACCN on 25 July 1989 and confirmed that his department had held back from making any changes in day care funding because it had expected the federal government to act on day care. It was now apparent, however, that the government of Brian Mulroney would not reintroduce the proposed *Canada Childcare Act* that had died in the Senate when the 1988 federal election was called (Prentice 1999, 144). As a consequence, Oldring's department was reviewing both the subsidy and operating allowance programs.[56]

The 1989–90 review of day care was a major undertaking. Although it was mainly concerned with funding, the review also examined the issues of staff qualifications and staff-to-child ratios. This sophisticated exercise, much different than the haphazard approach to reform in the Osterman years, involved two noteworthy features. First, the government presented its new directions for day care as the application of principles that the Getty cabinet had approved in 1988 to guide the development and reform of all social policy in the province. Second, an elaborate communication and consultation strategy was implemented in order to dissipate opposition to the policy path chosen by the government.

The review occurred shortly after the Alberta civil service had lost its complete management line in day care, from the assistant deputy minister down to the director of day care programs. Furthermore, the department had just introduced a new system for determining eligibility for subsidies and a new computerized information system, and was "trying to bring more uniformity and consistency in the application of provincial standards and funding across the province." Fortunately for the government, the new day care program director, Dennis Maier, had considerable familiarity with day care issues and was willing to take on the "horrendous" workload. In his first three years as the director, starting in 1989, Maier did not take any holidays.[57]

John Oldring came to the Family and Social Services (FSS) portfolio with some background knowledge on day care stemming from his involvement in PSS planning in Red Deer in the 1970s. Nevertheless, like Connie Osterman, he was sympathetic to the pro-family movement. He demonstrated this bias when he addressed the annual meeting of AFWUF in November 1989 and stated that he did not support universal day care (Harder 1996, 53).

Not all civil servants shared Minister Oldring's distaste for universal operating allowances. Dennis Maier stated that he and others made the following argument in favour of keeping "day care inclusive of a broader sector of the population": "If you remove [operating allowances] it will become so costly that basically only people who apply for subsidy will be able to afford it, and it will be seen as a poor family's service. It will be seen as for people who are considered marginal in society." Whether Minister Oldring was persuaded by this argument or not, he decided against entirely eliminating operating allowances. The White Paper released in March 1990, partway through the review process, proposed to reduce operating allowances to a uniform $50 per space over a three-year period.[58] This represented a substantial decrease in the allowance for very young children but only a modest decrease for children aged three to five years.

The 1989–90 review of day care proceeded in the context of the Getty government's new framework for social policy. This framework was first and foremost a response to the difficult economic conditions in 1987. It was written by Neil Crawford, who had served as minister of Health and Social Development in the early 1970s.

Neil Crawford produced a relatively short statement on social policy in March 1988. One of his arguments stressed the growing need for quality care: "Our family and social lives are very different from what they were in previous generations. Increasing numbers of women participate in the labour force by necessity to support themselves and their families, or by choice to fulfill their career aspirations. The matter of quality child care is an ongoing issue."[59] Yet the White Paper on day care released two years later did not highlight this point on quality child care. Instead, other statements were extracted from the Crawford document in order to justify the redirecting of most provincial monies to low-income families and the off-loading of some of the government's responsibilities in day care onto individuals and their families. In sum, the White Paper presented a selective pro-family reading of the Crawford blueprint for social policy and used that reading to portray its proposed changes to day care in the most unproblematic light possible.

In practice, it appears that provincial civil servants were able to partially fend off the pro-family inclinations of the government during the review process. As a consequence, the rhetoric of family and individual responsibility in the White Paper went far beyond the actual content of the reforms. This was demonstrated in the decision to reduce rather than eliminate operating allowances. It was also seen in the decision to improve the quality in licensed day cares by finally introducing requirements for staff qualifications. Dennis Maier reported that civil servants pushed very hard for qualification requirements in the internal discussions that preceded the release of the White Paper. "We went through the usual kind of massaging process," he explained, "where you tend to shoot for the ideal, and then whatever resources allow and the political agenda of the day allows, you have to retreat into something that the policy leaders can approve, so what was approved was not what we put together, what was approved was the best we could do for the day." This explains why, under the regulations introduced at that point and carried over into the new Child Care Licensing Regulation (Alberta 2008, 15), up to three-quarters of the front-line staff in a day care require only a fifty-hour orientation course. Nevertheless, the other parts of the new regulation did substantially improve the minimum staff training standards in Alberta day cares: directors were now required to hold a two-year college diploma in ECE or equivalent, and at least one-quarter of the front-line staff were now required to hold a one-year college certificate. Until these reforms were introduced, Alberta and New Brunswick were the only provinces that did not require special training for day care workers.[60]

In 1990 commercial day care was still a reasonably profitable business, especially for the day care chains that had flourished in Calgary and Edmonton in the 1980s. Day care capitalists aggressively defended their investments during Minister Oldring's review process. This involved the mobilization of parents to protest the proposed cutbacks to operating allowances and the persistent lobbying of government MLAs. The protests included a mass meeting in Calgary in early February 1990 (prior to the release of the White Paper) that was attended by "700 outraged parents," along with the submission of hundreds of form letters. Unlike Connie Osterman, Minister Oldring agreed to private meetings with the DCSA.[61]

In the end, the government proved to be flexible on some of the details of the reforms, although it did not alter any of the basic principles. For instance, the original proposal had suggested changing the staff-to-child ratio for infants (birth to eighteen months) from one-to-three to one-to-four in order to compensate for some of the increased cost of caring for infants due to the sharp reduction in the operating allowance for this age group (Alberta FSS 1990a, 26). This idea was widely criticized.[62]

In light of safety and quality-of-care concerns, the government left the ratio for infants (birth to twelve months) at one to three but decreased other ratios in order to realize the same cost savings. For infants between thirteen and eighteen months of age, the staff-to-child ratio decreased from one-to-three to one-to-four and for toddlers between nineteen and thirty-five months, the ratio decreased from one-to-five to one-to-six (Alberta FSS 1990b, 16).

There were also two elements of the reforms that were meant to assuage commercial operators. The first was a promise to "carefully monitor the impact [of the reductions to operating allowances] on groups and organizations which may be sensitive to the proposed changes" (Alberta FSS 1990a, 31). Spreading the reductions over three years would allow the government to do so in a meaningful way. Second, the government not only lifted the freeze on operating allowances but allowed centres that had come into existence between 1986 and 1990 to apply for the same operating allowances that older centres were receiving (Alberta FSS 1990b, 10).

The public consultation on the White Paper was a very significant exercise even though it did not yield major changes to the government's plans. Alongside the more than 2,400 letters and the numerous calls received on the matter, some 5,000 people attended meetings. Minister Oldring himself claimed to have "personally reviewed 2,400 letters that revealed a broad spectrum of responses."[63] (Given how many of the submissions were form letters, this feat is not as impressive as it at first sounds.) The involvement of so many people was a massive, albeit superficial, communication exercise. It marked a sharp departure from previous consultations on day care (such as the 1977 Task Force and the ADCAC of 1980–86) that had involved intensive, in-depth work by a select group of individuals, many of whom had pre-existing expertise in the area. From the standpoint of the governing party, the advantage of the 1990 exercise was that it diffused rather than concentrated opposition, allowing the government to pick and choose from among the avalanche of opinions without being compelled to identify either the most considered or most prevalent response. It is true, as the government claimed, that the White Paper "began a province-wide examination of the role of day care in our society" (Alberta FSS 1990b, 4), but this was a stage-managed examination that had no chance of deflecting the government off its chosen path. It is an example of using the trappings of mass participation to legitimate what had already been decided rather than allowing democratic participation to shape policy directions.

The new staff-to-child ratios for children aged thirteen to thirty-five months took effect on 1 November 1990 and were accompanied by the first of five planned reductions in operating allowances. The reductions as projected in July 1990 (Alberta FSS 1990b, 9) are recorded in table 7.1 along with the reductions that were actually made between 1990 and 1995.

The first deviation from the 1990 plan occurred in 1992. In February of that year, the unemployment rate in Edmonton was almost 11 percent. This meant that fewer parents were looking for day care, and there was an increased supply of low-cost babysitters competing against licensed facilities to care for children. As a result, the vacancy rate in day cares, especially commercial centres, was very high, and the president of the DCSA, John Samaska, stated that some day cares were in danger of going out of business. After the 1991 cuts, the government "received letters and input from individual operators and parents that further reductions would put their survival at risk." Of particular note was a large letter-writing campaign mounted in the northwest region of the province that had a strong influence on the government.[64]

Additional cuts in operating allowances were scheduled for 1 July 1992, but these did not occur. Later that month, Minister John Oldring announced that reductions to operating allowances for infants and toddlers would occur on 1 October, although the cuts for infant spaces would be less than half the amount projected in the 1990 plan (table 7.1). The revised plan at that point was to make the same total cuts to operating allowances as planned in 1990 but to stretch those cuts over five years instead of four. The government also remained committed to its promise that "all funding re-directed from the Operating Allowance Program will be allocated directly to the Child Care Subsidy Program" (Alberta FSS 1990b, 11).

The Edmonton leader of the DCSA, Carolyn Lister, immediately praised the move, stating, "It incorporates the middle-income earners into the equation." By this point, however, some not-for-profit professionals no longer supported operating allowances and objected to Minister Oldring's revised timetable. They did so because in order to compensate for the higher-than-planned operating allowances, the coverage of the low-income subsidy program would not be expanded by as much as had been expected. This meant that low-income families then receiving a partial subsidy would not receive as large an increase in their subsidy as had been planned, and other low-income families who had expected

TABLE 7.1 Monthly Operating Allowances for Alberta Day Cares (Actual Versus 1990 Projections)

Child's age	1984– 1990	Nov 1990	July 1991	July 1992	July 1993	July 1994	Dec 1995 [a]	1996 [a]
0–12 months	$257	$257	$200	$180 ($150)	$180 ($100)	$170 ($50)	$165	$160
13–18 months	$257	$190	$160	$140 ($110)	$140 ($80)	$130 ($50)	$125	$120
19–35 months	. $131	$110	$110	$100	$100 ($70)	$90 ($50)	$85	$80
3–4.5 years	$78.50	$78.50	$78.50	$78.50	$78.50 ($60)	$70 ($50)	$65	$60
Over 4.5 years	$65	$65	$65	$65	$65 ($55)	$58 ($50)	$53	$48

SOURCES: For the allowances projected in the 1990 plan, see Alberta FSS 1990b, 9. The allowances in December 1995 are from "Day Care Staff Make a Difference, but Not Much Money," *Edmonton Journal*, 3 December 1995, B1. The history of allowances in the mid- to late-1990s was recorded in a handout given to parents at Mill Creek's Finest Child Care Centre, Edmonton, 1999 (in possession of author). The history of allowances between 1991 and 1994 was provided by Tom Rosettis, administrator of Day Care Licensing, Calgary, early 1994.

NOTE: Allowances projected in the 1990 plan, if different from the actual, are in parentheses.

[a] The 1990 plan projected that, after 1 July 1994, operating allowances would remain stable at $50.

to qualify for subsidization for the first time would not do so. The main results of the revised timetable were to encourage middle- to upper-income families with infants and toddlers to continue to use regulated centres (since, because of the payment of operating allowances, the cost of day care was below the market cost and hence well within their means) and to force low- to middle-income families with infants and toddlers to continue to use unlicensed babysitters (since the cost of day care remained beyond their means without additional subsidization).[65]

The governing Progressive Conservative Party elected a new leader at the end of 1992: Ralph Klein took office just as the provincial government was headed for its eighth consecutive annual deficit. Indeed, in the two years ending 31 March 1993, the province added over $6 billion to its accumulated debt, which was growing at a much faster rate than that of any other province (Mansell 1997, 31, 42). In the provincial election campaign of May–June 1993, the premier promised to balance the provincial budget within four years. His plans for doing so were largely borrowed from the Alberta-based Reform Party of Canada and included "a smaller more open government" and "responsible social programs that help people to help themselves." The Progressive Conservative Party won its seventh consecutive majority government that year in a tight race with the Liberal Party, which had also promised to eliminate the deficit through expenditure cuts. After the election, a former social worker, Mike Cardinal, was Klein's surprise choice as the new minister of FSS, and the government soon embarked on "deep and quick reductions in expenditures" (Mansell 1997, 57).[66]

As part of its cuts to FSS, the Klein government chose to abandon John Oldring's 1990 plan to raise the low-income subsidy in step with reductions to operating allowances. The overall budget, announced in January 1994, called for an 18.3 percent cut in FSS expenditures spread over two years (Mansell 1997, 58). In day care, the plan was to reduce operating allowances by $20 per space while leaving the low-income subsidy unchanged.[67] Reductions were made in three stages between 1994 and 1996, as shown in table 7.1. The agency fee for satellite FDHs was also reduced: for instance, in 1993 an agency would have received $2,060 per month for the enrolment of twenty infants and toddlers (less than three years of age) while in 1995 it only received $1,660 for enrolling the same number of young children (CRRU 1994, 59; 1997, 56). Between 1994–95 and 1997–98, the Government of Alberta reduced spending on operating allowances by 19 percent and on satellite FDH agency fees by 27 percent (table A.4).

The cuts in operating allowances between 1994 and 1996 coincided with and exacerbated a severe financial crisis in commercial day care caused by high vacancy rates. The fact that operating allowances were only cut by $20 in these years is an indication of the severity of the crisis and the lingering influence that the DCSA and other commercial operators had on Tory politicians. Nevertheless, two of Calgary's large day care chains were put into receivership in the mid-1990s. Across the province, the number of day cares declined from 644 to 572 between 1994 and 1997, and the number of licensed spaces declined by 14 percent (table A.3). Even the exemplary satellite FDH system contracted, with the number of children falling by 18 percent between 1995 and 1997 (table A.6).

The Klein government chose to make sudden and dramatic cuts in expenditures instead of gradually cutting expenditures and/or increasing taxes (Mansell 1997, 52–58). This approach had the potential to cause a recession in the provincial economy, a possibility that was averted because of a fortuitous rise in the market prices for oil and natural gas. With considerable luck, Klein's reputation as the hard-nosed slayer of government deficits was cemented in Albertan and Canadian political culture. Yet as in most matters, the devil is in the details. In the case of day care, the first stage of the Klein revolution amounted to indiscriminate budget cutting with remarkably little attention to principles and fairness.

One might be critical of the gradualist reforms envisioned by Connie Osterman in the late 1980s and John Oldring in the early 1990s for a number of reasons, but at least their plans were marked by careful thought and serious engagement with the realities of care for preschool children in Alberta. The same cannot be said for the reforms instituted by Mike Cardinal between 1993 and 1996.

Minister Cardinal's main priority was to quickly reduce the welfare rolls in Alberta, which he did in a big way: the number of welfare recipients fell from 94,087 in March 1993 to 49,001 in December 1995. A significant component of this reduction was due to a change in the eligibility rules governing transitional assistance for lone mothers who had recently given birth. In the past, a lone mother could collect welfare until her child was two years of age, but this was changed such that she had to seek paid employment once the child was six months old. As a result, the number of cases of transitional support fell by an astounding sixteen thousand over this period (Shedd 1997, 257–60).

In light of this change in the eligibility for temporary social assistance, it is noteworthy that the government did not enhance its day care subsidy program. Lone mothers earning very low salaries continued to receive social assistance as a supplement to earnings and thus were not faced with covering day care fees beyond the amount of subsidy. But lone mothers who earned even a modest salary did not qualify for a social assistance supplement, and a net income of $25,765 or more made them ineligible for even a partial day care subsidy (CRRU 1997, 56). By cutting operating allowances without improving the low-income subsidy, the Klein government forced many low- to middle-income families to look for low-cost babysitting as an alternative to a regulated day care or a satellite FDH. "Each time we give an increase because of an operating allowance cutback or their subsidized amount doesn't go up," noted the director of a not-for-profit centre in Edmonton, "it's really hard because some families drop out. Not because they want to but because they have to. They're forced to."[68] The shift of children from regulated to unregulated care is the reason that the total amount paid in subsidies also significantly decreased between 1995 and 1998 (by $7.5 million, or 19 percent; see table A.4) even though there was no decrease in the subsidy level. By 1997–98 the province's spending on day care had fallen to $60.3 million, down from $73.5 million four years earlier (table A.4). In constant dollars, the decrease amounted to 23 percent (table A.5). Much of the money saved by corporate and individual taxpayers had been at the expense of hard-working, economically independent parents who simply could not afford regulated day care without help from the government. In the absence of subsidization, they placed their children in care arrangements that were sometimes substandard, and they were burdened with the responsibility of worrying about and trying to monitor the adequacy of those arrangements themselves.

The final chapter in the history of operating allowances in Alberta was written in the weeks following the re-election of the Klein government on 11 March 1997. Mike Cardinal was replaced by Lyle Oberg as the minister of FSS. Like Stockwell Day, who had briefly served as the minister in 1993, the new minister was a former chair of the premier's council in support of children and families. Without any public or private consultation, Lyle Oberg decided to abolish operating allowances by 1 April 1999; the decision was announced in July 1997. The minister indicated that low-income subsidies would increase as the operating allowances were phased out, and Premier Klein claimed that all money removed from operating allowances would be reallocated to low-income families.[69] The premier thus renewed the promise of the Oldring plan of 1990, but there were two important differences between Lyle Oberg's reform of 1997 and what John Oldring had earlier proposed. First, a large proportion of the operating allowance budget had already been cut by 1997 without any corresponding reinvestment in subsidies (see table A.4). In 1997 neither Oberg nor Klein promised to improve the subsidy system to compensate for this significant loss of resources in the mid-1990s. Second, whereas an across-the-board operating allowance of $50 would have been retained under the Oldring plan, operating allowances were entirely eliminated by Minister Oberg.

Within a few months, the government appeared to renege on Premier Klein's promise to maintain the overall level of funding in day care. Over the same two-year period that operating allowances were to be eliminated, the government made plans to reduce its overall day care budget by 9 percent. This meant that of the $15.5 million in operating allowances paid in 1997–98, only 71 percent was to be transferred to low-income subsidies, with the rest eliminated from the budget. This information was conveyed in a fact sheet distributed by FSS in November 1997.[70]

The last major protest rally in defence of operating allowances was organized in Edmonton on 29 January 1998. It was attended by five hundred people but not by Minister Oberg or any other members of the government. The director of day care programs, Lynn Groves-Hautmann, was sent to defend the decision to cut $15 million from operating allowances and only reinvest $11.5 million in low-income subsidies, and she was jeered for her trouble. The key organizers of the rally were the AAYC, the Early Childhood Professional Association of Alberta, and the Child and Family Resource Association (CAFRA), and the rally was supported by both not-for-profit and commercial centres in the Edmonton area. CAFRA, formed in the mid-1990s, was like the Calgary Association for Quality Child Care in that it was made up of centres that were accredited by meeting a predefined set of quality standards. In the 1990s, almost all of CAFRA's members were not-for-profit centres.

The rally coincided with the release of a CAFRA-commissioned survey of non-subsidized Alberta families using day care in the fall of 1997. The survey was returned by 1,048 families, representing 1,525 children enrolled in day cares. Based upon the income data reported in the survey, Sylvia Church estimated that only "14% of presently unsubsidized parents will qualify for some sort of subsidy (either full or partial) under the new proposed Income Qualification Table for Subsidy" (1998, 7). One of the survey questions asked what parents would do if they were faced with a 15 to 25 percent increase of fees due to the elimination of operating allowances. Of the parents who responded to this question, 35 percent stated they would consider switching from a day care to some sort of informal care, and an additional 20 percent said they would look for less expensive day care (7–8).[71]

The Edmonton rally was only one part of the movement in opposition to the funding cuts. In addition, there was an organized letter-writing campaign, media coverage that was generally favourable to those opposing the government's action, and attempts to directly lobby the minister. A form letter, along the same lines as that distributed in 1987 by the UCCA, was distributed to parents by some day cares. It had a space at the bottom for a parent's own comments. In her letter, a mother from Patricia, Alberta, asked, "Why give day cares another reason to raise prices and make it harder for the honest, hardworking parent to make it, or worse yet, why let in the chance that they may reduce the quality of food, shelter and care for our children?"[72]

For two reasons, this protest movement against cuts to operating allowances did not have the same impact on the government as the earlier protest movements in the Connie Osterman and John Oldring years. Most importantly, Minister Oberg had made up his mind on cutting operating allowances and was uninterested in building a consensus for government reforms through consultation.[73] Advocates were faced with an ideologically driven minister who believed that the government's sweeping electoral victory in March 1997 was all the endorsement he needed for major changes in day care.

The second reason for the ineffectiveness of the 1998 protest was that the major lobby groups were simply not as powerful as they had once been. The AAYC was on a downward spiral and ceased to function in 1999. Dennis Maier's assessment at the time was that the not-for profit sector had "by and large been extinguished. They're just tired, they've just run out of breath." Maier also saw commercial operators as being in a weakened position when it came to fighting the government's plans. When asked to assess the nature of commercial lobbying in 1998 compared to 1990, he stated: "A lot of the big players have gotten out of the business. They were in it because it was a business, because it was lucrative, and with some of the changes that were brought in under John Oldring there was a large turnover of operators and a lot of the big players simply got of the business because they saw the handwriting on the wall."[74]

Operating allowances were slashed on 1 April 1998 and eliminated entirely on 1 April 1999 (table A.6). But before the first decrease occurred, the provincial government backed away from its unpopular plan to further cut the overall day care budget. It promised instead to use all the money eliminated from operating allowances to enhance the low-income subsidy program.[75] This indeed seems to have occurred, since overall spending on day care increased in each of the 1998–99 and 1999–2000 budget years despite the phasing out of operating allowances (table A.4).

Part of the credit for the increase in Alberta's day care spending in the late 1990s goes to the federal government and the National Child Benefit (NCB), introduced on 1 July 1998. The NCB increased federal tax benefits for all low-income families but then allowed the provinces to claw back the increased benefits from families on welfare. The NCB was thus designed to increase the financial incentive for families to get off of welfare. Provinces were given the freedom to spend the money they saved through the clawback as they saw fit, as long as it was on programs for children.[76]

Alberta's initial reinvestments of the clawback included a $1.9 million addition to the day care subsidy program, effective 1 July 1998. On 1 April of that year, the province had increased the amount of the low-income subsidy and raised the income qualification levels (turning and break-even points) by an average of $3,000 after sharply reducing operating allowances. The NCB money allowed it to further increase the qualification levels by an average of $1,000. This infusion of federal money into the subsidy program came at an opportune time for the Alberta government since it took some of the sting out of opponents' criticisms of the cuts to operating allowances.[77]

Modest improvement to the subsidy system also accompanied the end of operating allowances in 1999. At that time, the province eliminated the requirement that all subsidized parents pay at least $40 per month, effectively increasing the size of subsidies by that amount. Furthermore, it increased the break-even points for partial subsidization although the turning points for full subsidization remained unchanged (table A.6).

At this point, the funding for day care in Alberta appeared to have reached its nadir in 1998 and would now consistently rise due to regular infusions of NCB money. But although the federal government did continue to increase funding for the NCB, between 1999 and 2004 the Alberta government decided against using any more of its share of the money to improve the low-income day care subsidy program (table A.6). This amounted to abandonment of those low-income families who made too much money to qualify for a substantial subsidy but who did not make enough money to afford regulated child care. Their only option was to cobble together an affordable child care alternative, invariably involving relatives or an unregulated babysitter. The Alberta government's failure to improve the low-income day care subsidy program between 1999 and 2004 demonstrated a major problem with federal funding for children's programs through the NCB. Provinces were given great latitude in determining priorities for funding and had no financial incentives to invest in regulated child care. This allowed the Klein government to intentionally avoid improvements in day care subsidization while at the same time trumpeting its commitment to low-income children. In contrast, however, the "Early Learning and Child Care" agreement signed by the federal and Alberta governments in 2005 resulted in significant improvements in the quality and accessibility of regulated child care.

The final operating allowances for day care spaces were paid for the month of March 1999. For almost nineteen years, the government of Alberta had used this program to lower the cost of licensed day care and thus promote this option over other types of child care, especially unregulated babysitters. The end of operating allowances meant that the government no longer identified regulated care as a favoured option for preschool children in Alberta, with the exception of children from low-income families who qualified for subsidies (since subsidies could only be used in a licensed day care or satellite FDH). The slow death of operating allowances was a significant element of the reprivatization of the care of young children in Alberta. As the provincial government withdrew from its previous funding commitments to regulated day care, families and markets were to fill the gap.

Beginning in the mid-1980s, deregulation and relaxations in standards worked together to place greater responsibility on Alberta parents to monitor the care of their preschool children. Deregulation moves previously regulated settings into the unregulated category, thus forcing families to assume full responsibility for monitoring that care. In contrast, when standards are relaxed in regulated settings, families are expected to take on greater responsibility but a formal monitoring procedure remains in place. Standards of care can be relaxed in two ways. First, the regulations can remain unchanged but the monitoring or enforcement of those regulations can be weakened. Second, a particular regulation can be formally weakened. Both types of relaxation in standards occurred in Alberta at the end of the twentieth century and are discussed below, as is the Klein government's important decision in 1994 to entirely deregulate medium-sized FDHs.

Alberta's political culture is defined by dominant myths about the province's history in Canada and dominant beliefs about the role of individuals, families, private enterprise, and governments in that history. One such belief celebrates private responsibility in all matters (including child care) and condemns government programs as "interference" in people's lives. In the 1960s and 1970s, commercial day care owners invoked this belief to promote free enterprise and lax government regulation in day care. Beginning in the 1980s, pro-family organizations have invoked this belief when demanding that the Alberta government reduce support for day care programs and do more to enable families (especially mothers) to care for preschool children.

It is important to realize that the belief in private responsibility is widely and passionately held in Alberta society, which is why pro-family and free enterprise groups have found fertile ground in the province. Evidence of this belief is found in the documented investigation of an unlicensed FDH in the central Alberta town of Blackfalds in 1983. The investigation was initiated after the Tory MLA for the area received a complaint from a woman who intermittently left her child at the day home and was disturbed that the operator occasionally looked after as many as eight children. At that time, a home-based service had to be licensed as a day home if it cared for four to six children and as a day care if it cared for seven or more children.

An inspector visited the day home and the operator indicated a willingness to apply for a license to operate as an FDH. However, one of her clients (a public health nurse, of all occupations) advised against making the application. In a letter to FSS Minister Neil Webber, she and her husband argued:

> We have recently come across a situation where the government is interfering in our personal lives.... We believe we are mature, caring parents and are capable of deciding—without government controls—on a home and babysitter best suited for our child.... We resent the interference of "government" particularly in the situation of people deciding to care for children in their homes, and in our choice, as parents, in choosing such situations. We do not approve of sending "inspectors" into these homes ... and checking what we believe are minor, insignificant things. This, we feel, is a waste of taxpayer money.[78]

Given this sentiment among the public, it is hardly surprising that later in the 1980s (during Connie Osterman's term as minister), the government committed itself to enhancing "parental responsibility and involvement in selecting and monitoring their child's care" (see the previous section). The first step in this process was the publication "Choosing a Day Care Centre: A Guide for Parents." It included a twenty-two-page checklist that parents were encouraged to fill out when they visited a centre. The checklist detailed hundreds of discrete characteristics and behaviours that parents were to observe. An obvious problem with the checklist was that it would take hours of observation to fill out properly—hours that most parents either do not have or are unwilling to commit. A second problem concerned the appropriateness of the checklist approach itself for the evaluation of the quality of care in a centre. Wendy Reid provided an example of this problem from her own in-depth observations in Calgary day cares. One of the items in the checklist was "Look for day care staff who smile and talk to infants they are changing or dressing." Reid had been in a centre where a day care worker had been doing just this, and a parent would have been justified in ticking that box on the checklist. At the same time this was happening, however, another infant was left unattended in a high chair for forty-five minutes without any attention whatsoever. Wendy Reid was only able to identify this problem because of extended observation in the centre that looked at the overall pattern of care of all children in a group rather than discrete activities with particular children; only a trained child care professional could carry out such observation effectively.[79]

Until 1996 parental use of the government's checklist had been voluntary. In that year, however, the Klein government began to enforce parental responsibility for inspecting a day care prior to the enrolment of a child. This was done through the use of a one-page form that acknowledged a parent had reviewed six aspects of the day care (e.g., program of daily activities). The parent had to sign the form along with the operator or director of the centre, and a copy of the form was placed in the child's file. The acting executive director of the Edmonton Social Planning Council, Christopher Smith, portrayed this checklist "as another example of our provincial government trying to download its responsibilities onto communities without providing the resources necessary to cope." It is interesting that when parents chose not to complete and sign the checklist, they were still expected to sign the form, acknowledging that they had been given the means and opportunity to review the centre.[80]

The mandatory parent checklist exemplifies one of the ways that the Klein government constituted a decisive break with previous provincial Tory governments. Parental responsibility had been an integral part of provincial day care policy for many years before Ralph Klein became premier in late 1992. Nevertheless, until Klein's regime, this did not mean the withdrawal of government from day care in favour of families but rather an active role for government in supporting families and dealing with issues that most families found difficult—a model for active collaboration between families and government. In contrast, the Klein government quickly defined parental responsibility as a preferred alternative to government responsibility and sought to download some of its duties in day care to families regardless of whether those families were prepared to assume such duties. Hence, the Klein government's approach to family responsibility had a neo-liberal sink-or-swim thrust. This stood in sharp contrast to the traditional Tory paternalism associated with the pro-family rhetoric of the Getty years.

The mandatory parent checklist was introduced approximately eighteen months after Alberta's ombudsman had released a report that was highly critical of the ways that provincial licensing officers investigated complaints about day cares. The Klein government was committed to reducing expenditures through reprivatization, so instead of following up on the ombudsman's findings by strengthening government's enforcement role, it formalized parental responsibility. The mandatory checklist was the government's way of acknowledging that standards had been relaxed because of weak inspection procedures; it communicated to parents the *caveat emptor* situation in day care.

The ombudsman's report, released in 1994, demonstrated that the government was not committed to the thorough investigation of complaints about day cares. It considered all 737 complaints that were made against day cares in 1993.

It is noteworthy that 25 percent of these complaints came from staff or ex-staff of day cares and fully 90 percent of the complaints involved commercial centres (Alberta Office of the Ombudsman 1994, 21–22).[81] The ombudsman's office found that "the gathering of evidence was erratic. Statements were rarely taken, and either none or not all witnesses were interviewed" (26). Furthermore, many complaints were not investigated immediately and 35 percent of the complaint files had been closed before they had reached a definitive conclusion. In light of these findings, it is not surprising that those who had complained about a day care were generally dissatisfied (29, 33, 38).

These inadequacies were a product of shortsighted funding decisions made in the 1980s. In 1981 the Alberta government had placed day care licensing and program consultation in one administrative unit (the Day Care Branch). It boasted that "when the 27 proposed staff positions are filled, Alberta will have the largest staff support service in Canada." Significantly, the plan included an almost equal number of consultants and licensing inspectors in the new branch: consultants would work collaboratively with day cares to improve programming while licensing inspectors would conduct routine regulatory inspections and investigate complaints.[82] Due to funding cutbacks, however, this neat division of responsibilities was abandoned shortly after it was introduced. For instance, in 1986 there were no consultants employed in the Calgary region. This meant that the four licensing inspectors in the region had to combine the licensing and consultant roles (Bagley 1986, 39–40). This situation persisted in the early 1990s. The problems identified in the ombudsman's review of complaints in 1993 stemmed largely from the same civil servants having to fill multiple, contradictory roles (25).

The ombudsman, former Calgary police superintendent Harley Johnson, had initiated this review in late December 1993 on his own accord (Alberta Office of the Ombudsman 1994, 4). Although this was within his statutory power, it was treated as an antagonistic action by the Klein government. One Tory MLA suggested that Harley Johnson had launched the review to get back at the government after a legislature committee had recommended a 20 percent cut in his office's budget. A second Tory MLA remarked, "Government must proceed cautiously on regulatory and legislative changes" because Albertans are "cautioning against interfering in the relationship between business and customers." Minister Mike Cardinal said he would "consider" the fifty-six recommendations made by the ombudsman but emphasized, "I didn't ask for this report, he went ahead on his own."[83]

Beginning in the 1980s and carrying through into the 1990s, some standards of care were also relaxed through formal changes in regulations. An early example concerned the calculation of "useable floor space." The Day Care Regulation of 1978 had stipulated that "every room or areas used for playing, resting or sleeping shall have a net floor area of not less than 2.5 square metres per child" (Alberta 1978, sec. 9.2). The Day Care Regulation of 1981 abandoned looking at net floor area on a room-by-room basis, and instead specified that the total floor area be no less that 2.5 square metres per child (Alberta 1981, sec. 7[c]). This relaxation of a standard was accompanied by a promise of an increase in the standard: on 1 August 1982, the minimum required area per child was set to increase to three square metres (sec. 7[f]). The effect of this increase in required indoor floor space was muted by a 1982 amendment that added the floor area of hallways and 50 percent of the floor area of washrooms into the calculation of overall net floor area (Alberta 1982). This sudden change in direction is another indication of the strong influence of commercial operators on policy during Bob Bogle's tenure as minister.

The new Day Care Regulation introduced in 1990 reversed direction again when it defined net floor area as "floor space that is appropriate for use by children when playing, resting, sleeping and eating" (Alberta 1991, sec. 11.2[a]). This excluded hallways and washrooms from the calculation. As a final concession to the commercial sector, day cares that were licensed by 30 November 1990 could include "unencumbered hallway space" in net floor area but not any washroom space (sec. 11.3).

The floor-space issue suggests that debates about the lowering or raising of standards in the 1980s were relatively fluid. Commercial operators did have the ear of government on the issue of indoor floor space, but so did civil servants and non-profit advocates. Therefore, rather than a clear and steady trend toward lower standards in these years, we see only controversy and ambiguity about what direction to take. The fact that civil servants convinced the provincial government to introduce a staff qualification system in 1990 is perhaps the best evidence that the pre-1993 Tory governments approached the question of formal standards in a pragmatic rather than an ideological manner.

In the mid-1990s, the Klein government conducted a "government-wide Regulatory Review." Following this review, amendments to the Day Care Regulation were put in place in February 1998. The one significant amendment increased the number of children that a single staff member could look after at the beginning and end of days: the previous maximum of three was increased to six, so long as none of the children was under nineteen months of age (Alberta 1998, sec. 17). Representatives of both provincial opposition parties criticized this regulatory change on the grounds that it put children at risk.[84]

As noted above, in the 1980s and early 1990s, there was no clear direction to the formal changes in day care standards, with some standards being relaxed while others were strengthened. Formal standards were viewed pragmatically by the provincial government and were revised in light of the input from many different groups. In contrast, from 1993 onwards, the neo-liberal Klein government presented lowered standards as a political imperative in day care, with parents expected to do more of the work of monitoring. Nevertheless, the formal changes made by the Klein government were modest in scope, undoubtedly because it came to understand that the wholesale gutting of standards would result in the same sort of political firestorms that had bedevilled Tory governments prior to the early 1980s. The Klein government instead pursued the reprivatization of child care by deregulating independent FDHs, reducing funding to regulated services and using tax policy to encourage care of young children by stay-at-home parents.

Almost immediately after winning the provincial election of 15 June 1993, the Klein government embarked on a "government-wide program for deregulation." All departments were instructed to complete an action plan by 1 September 1993 that would identify opportunities to "reduce government cost; accelerate decision making; and, to increase the effectiveness of the interface with the public." The Department of FSS hired a private consulting firm to survey day cares and advocacy organizations for ideas about cost cutting and deregulation. The survey was distributed in the middle of the summer and had a very short time for response, suggesting that it was more of a token consultation that a serious effort to canvass the views of the day care community.[85]

The AAYC's reply expressed some "grave reservations" about the possibility of deregulation of day care. It pointedly argued:

> The legislation which was originally introduced in the 1970s has done much to provide a guidepost for minimum standards. Although it does not address the issues of quality care, it ensures that the basic health and safety standards are met. Children are too vulnerable to not have this legislation in place.[86]

News of this consultation exercise on deregulation in day care did not appear in the Edmonton Journal until early November 1993. Minister Cardinal's comments at that time indicated that the deregulation of day homes was high on the government's list of priorities. He claimed to have heard from "many parents" who desired complete deregulation of FDHs. "We could allow parents to make that decision themselves to use private homes if they want without regulation," he said. "I'm looking at that. I have to give credit to parents. They'll make the choice."[87]

Prior to 1 December 1994, anyone who provided day care to more than three children in a private residence in Alberta was required to be licensed as long the caregiving relationship extended for at least twelve consecutive weeks (i.e., arrangements to cover school holidays were excluded). If the operator cared for four to six children, she was required to apply for a license for an FDH and had to meet some elementary safety standards specified in the Day Care Regulation. In contrast, if the operator cared for seven or more children, she was required to follow the much more stringent regulations for a day care. As of 1 December 1994, ongoing day care for seven or more children in a private residence still required licensing as a day care centre. However, the government deregulated mid-sized FDHs almost entirely (Alberta 1994): the only regulatory restriction on this sector was that no more than three children under the age of two years could be enrolled.[88]

Understandably, this development was greeted with consternation by advocates for licensed services. Upon learning of the government's intention, the Edmonton chair of the DCSA, Carolyn Lister, commented, "It's stunning, frightening news. We're taking huge steps backward in child care in this province." Lister expressed reservations about the ability of a single caregiver to look after six young children in a crisis, but her main concern was that the capacity of the unlicensed babysitting sector would now increase, thus causing a reduction of the cost of that service and putting greater competitive pressure on licensed services. At the time, approximately one-third of the licensed day care spaces in the province were vacant. "This is a money issue for me," said Lister. "I'm worried that we're going to lose children to babysitters."[89]

It must be remembered that this deregulation initiative only affected FDHs that operated independently, not those that were affiliated with and monitored by an approved agency. As noted earlier in this section, satellite FDHs were restricted to looking after no more than three children under three years of age, of whom no more than two could be under two years of age. Consequently, the deregulation of independent FDHs in 1994 created a disturbing regulatory disparity, as noted by the chair of the Alberta Association for Family Day Home

Services. In a letter to the editor, Wendy Yewman commented, "It is hard to understand a proposal that allows unregulated babysitters to care for twice as many children under the age of three as family day home providers in the regulated sector, who are screened, certified in first aid, monitored regularly (both scheduled and unannounced) to government standards, and offered training and support."[90]

As part of a significant overhaul of provincial tax policy, Provincial Treasurer Stockwell Day (a social-conservative supporter of the pro-family movement) introduced three significant modifications in Alberta tax policy in the late 1990s that affected families with children. The first was a refundable child tax credit introduced in 1997 that complemented the national child tax benefit paid to low- and middle-income families. On 1 July 1998, the maximum credit was raised to $500 per child with a maximum of $1,000 per family. In 2003, 160,000 families received an average of $500 from this measure: this was a very modest credit that could not play a decisive role in most families' decisions about child care. However, by dispersing this money in relatively small amounts to 160,000 families rather than investing it in the regulated child care system, the Alberta government encouraged families to find their own private solutions to child care needs.[91]

The other two significant changes to Alberta's tax policy were proposed by the Alberta Tax Review Committee (ATRC), which was struck in February 1998 and reported in October of that year. One of the issues addressed by the committee was tax differences between one- and two-income families. The ATRC received many submissions from the pro-family movement on this issue and offered quotes from both the Kids First newsletter and the National Foundation for Family Research and Education in its final report, which stated, "The majority of submissions on this issue argued that the tax system should remove the current differences and recognize the benefits of having one parent stay at home to care for their children" (1998, 20–21).

This is an issue where a superficial notion of equality leads to one conclusion while a more considered analysis leads in an entirely different policy direction. The superficial notion of equality argues that a single-income family with $60,000 total income should end up with the same after-tax income as the two-income family with $60,000 total income. In its final report, the ATRC reported that in 1998 the two-income family with $60,000 total income and $5,000 in deductible payments for child care would have ended up with $46,569 after taxes compared to only $42,313 for the one-income family that also had $60,000 total income but no payments for child care that could be deducted from income.

The basic assumption in this argument is that the two families are equal for the purpose of tax analysis simply because they have the same total income. This is an untenable assumption, however. The one-income family with $60,000 in income is clearly more privileged than the two-income family with the same income because the one-income family has the ability to significantly increase its total income if the second adult entered the paid labour force. Put differently, in order to generate its $60,000, the two-income family must engage in many activities and incur many expenses that the one-income family does not. Therefore, the meaningful income measure for comparisons between the two families is discretionary income, not after-tax income. The ATRC learned from civil servants that "working couples paying for child care already have less discretionary income than one earner couples" (and this was before any changes to the provincial tax system!).[92] The committee was at least honest enough in its final report to note that, in its hypothetical example, the two-income family's $4,256 advantage in after-tax income turned into a $744 disadvantage once child care fees were paid (Alberta Tax Review Committee 1998, 20). However, it did not attempt to quantify how other additional expenses associated with having a second person in the labour force (extra transportation, better clothes, purchase of more restaurant meals and other household services, etc.) would extend that disadvantage in discretionary income. Neither did it attempt to quantify the economic costs (in lost productivity and the recruitment and training of new staff) when highly trained mothers (and sometimes fathers) withdraw from the labour force for extended periods of time in order to be stay-at-home parents.

The ATRC chose to shift advantage in the provincial tax system toward one-income families by recommending that the amount of the spousal exemption be more than doubled and pegged at the same level as the personal tax exemption (1998, 2). The province accepted this recommendation and announced on 11 March 1999 that the spousal exemption would increase from $6,055 to $11,620 when a new provincial tax system was introduced in 2002 (later moved up to 2001). The interesting thing about this change is that it helped all single-income families, not just those with children, and can thus be seen as general support for the one-earner family rather than specific support for parents who stay at home to care for young children. The province avoided this issue since, as Edmonton Journal columnist Mark Lisac pointed out, "no one explained why the province would choose a permanent spousal deduction rather than a child tax credit that benefits one-earner couples only while they are raising children."[93]

The third significant change in provincial tax policy was a single rate of tax, initially proposed to be 11 percent and later lowered to 10 percent. The new single rate of tax was of greatest benefit to taxpayers with higher incomes. In 1998 the ATRC reported that with an 11 percent single rate and the changes in personal and spousal exemptions noted above, Albertans earning over $100,000 would realize 29 percent of the total provincial tax reduction even though they only controlled 18 percent of the total income (4). The new tax system also increased the exemption levels for paying taxes, a change that benefitted lower-income taxpayers.

Although both the poor and the privileged gained relative advantage from the new tax system, middle-income Albertans were disadvantaged. The disadvantage was pronounced for middle-income, two-earner families and middle-income singles, neither of whom qualified for the generous spousal exemption.

Each of these three changes to Alberta's taxation system removed money from the hands of the provincial government (money that could have been used for discretionary spending on day care or any other provincial program) and redistributed it to individuals and families. Therefore, these taxation measures amounted to a subtle form of reprivatization. Funding for regulated child care services remained in place, albeit significantly diminished compared to its high point in the late 1980s (see the inflation-adjusted figures in table A.5). But the new taxation measures encouraged parents to find private solutions for their child care needs rather than access the regulated day care system.

For middle-income, two-earner families with children in day care, tax savings were largely negated by the cancellation of operating allowances in 1999. Even more than in the 1980s and 1990s, these families were forced to look at lower-cost options when it came to child care. This is a classic example of a tax cut failing to provide a net benefit for the middle class because the cost of services increases, thus forcing these families to either pay more for those services or look around for a cheaper alternative.

Finally, the provincial tax changes increased the disposable income for employed low-income families, but the increase was not sufficient to dramatically affect their decisions about child care. The maximum subsidy levels for day care in Alberta in the late 1990s pushed families toward cheaper, marginal-quality centres, and the tax savings were nowhere near enough to allow these families to pay extra so their children could attend higher-quality centres. Furthermore, many low-income families only qualified for a partial subsidy and thus found that it made sense to forego the subsidy and to secure care in an unlicensed day home. For low-income families as a group, public funding for high-quality day care services (such as existed under the PSS program in the 1960s and 1970s, and the municipal continuations of the PSS system into the 1990s) provided much greater benefits than the modest provincial tax savings introduced by the Klein government.

In conclusion, the new provincial tax system unveiled between 1997 and 1999 made a powerful contribution to the reprivatization of day care in Alberta, working in tandem with the reduction in funding to regulated services. Significantly, reprivatization increased the options among high-income families and some middle-income families, both of which already had some financial leeway in how to handle day care, and now they had more. But for the remaining families, reprivatization narrowed their universe of choices in day care and usually left them with undesirable options. Therefore, the partially reprivatized child care system constructed by the Klein government served to extend economic and social inequalities in the province rather than compensate for those inequalities. The lofty egalitarian goals of the PSS approach to day care were a distant and seemingly forgotten memory for the new generation of neo-liberal/social-conservative politicians.

STAFF QUALIFICATION REQUIREMENTS: A RAY OF HOPE?

At the end of the 1990s, Alberta's day care system was in decline. The number of licensed day cares in the province had peaked in 1991 at 671 and had decreased by 20 percent to 538 by 1999 (table A.3). During this same period, the satellite FDH system expanded slightly (the annual average number of enrolled children increased by 254, or 4 percent),[94] but this did not come close to compensating for the loss of almost seven thousand licensed day care spaces. Meanwhile, total provincial spending on regulated preschool child care had peaked in 1987 and by 1999 had declined by 29 percent after adjusting for inflation (table A.5).

This chapter has investigated some of the key changes in the late 1980s and 1990s that help us to understand the decline in Alberta's day care system. From the standpoint of accessible, high-quality child care, the story of these years is fairly grim: the end of provincial operating allowances for day care spaces, the end to federal cost sharing of regulated child care for children from families with below average incomes, some deregulation and relaxation in the standards of care, growing political influence by pro-family groups, increasing emphasis on parental rather than societal responsibility for young children, and regressive changes to the tax system that favour higher-income earners and couples where one partner is dependent on the other partner's income.

Nevertheless, there appears to be a "good news" story for quality child care on an otherwise bleak political landscape: the 1990 introduction of staff qualification requirements in day care. What was the impact of this new regulation on day care in Alberta in the 1990s?

The staff training requirements of 1990 fell far short of what had been recommended by the ADCAC in 1981 (see chapter 5). Under their proposal, fully 50 percent of the staff of day cares would have been required to have a two-year diploma in ECE, while the 1990 regulation only required a centre's director to have this level of training. Furthermore, the ADCAC proposed a minimum ratio of three staff with education certificates to one staff without such a certificate; the 1990 regulation exactly reversed the ratio, requiring a minimum ratio of one staff with an education certificate to three staff without.

Besides requiring centre directors to have an ECE diploma (a Level 3 qualification), the 1990 regulation required 25 percent of primary staff to have at least a one-year ECE certificate or equivalent (a Level 2 qualification). Furthermore, other primary staff were expected to have completed a fifty-hour orientation course (a Level 1 qualification). The requirements were phased in and did not fully apply to all day cares in the province until 1 September 1995 (Alberta 1991, sec. 32–34).

Alberta's new staff qualification standards fell short of the standards in Ontario and British Columbia. In 1995 each of these provinces required at least one of the staff members working with a particular group of children to have advanced training in ECE (using Alberta's terminology, Level 3 qualification was required in Ontario and Level 2 in British Columbia). Manitoba also had more stringent training standards, requiring two-thirds of day care staff to have advanced training compared to the 25 percent in Alberta; however, Manitoba counted completion of a competency-based assessment program as equivalent to a diploma in ECE. Among the other provinces, the standards of Quebec and Nova Scotia were somewhat higher than Alberta's, while the standards of the other four provinces were lower (CRRU 1997, 96–98).

If the new requirements for trained staff had been fully enforced, there would have been a significant tightening of the labour market for day care workers. As a consequence, average wage rates would have increased, particularly for workers with Level 2 or 3 qualifications, and it is likely that a number of day cares would have been forced to close since they were not generating enough revenue to cover increased wage costs. However, the provincial government prevented this from happening by granting staff-qualification exemptions to day cares.

In early 1995, there were approximately 6,200 staff in the 630 or so day cares across the province. At that time, there were 1,030 total staff exemptions (17 percent of all staff), and 434 day cares had at least one exemption. An exemption for a particular level was granted on the condition that an individual was working toward completing the requirements for that level.[95]

Level 1 exemptions ensure that day cares can continue to hire untrained staff on the spot at very low wages. The number of Level 1 exemptions was initially very high since existing staff were given exemptions until they completed the fifty-hour orientation course. In December 1993 there were 670 Level 1 exemptions across the province. This had fallen to 360 by February 1995 but had risen to 442 by December 1996, demonstrating that day cares continued to have the latitude to hire completely untrained workers. It is therefore not surprising that the average wage rate of "assistant teachers" in Alberta day cares in 1998 was only $7.90 per hour, ranked ninth of the twelve provinces and territories (CRRU 2000, 115).

Levels 2 and 3 staff have considerably more training than Level 1 and are thus crucial to ensuring the quality of care in Alberta day cares. In December 1996 there were 172 Level 3 exemptions and 673 Level 2 exemptions. Level 2 exemptions are particularly problematic since they are granted to any worker with the Level 1 orientation course who is enrolled in a course leading toward Level 2 and they are renewed indefinitely as long as courses continue to be taken. In a 1995 interview, the director of day care staff qualifications for the province, Pauline Desjardins, indicated that she was particularly concerned about day cares with a "revolving door turnover of staff with one Level 2 exemption replacing another Level 2 exemption over and over."

The widespread use of staff qualification exemptions undermined the market power of trained day care workers, thus suppressing their pay levels. Consequently, the wages of trained employees in Alberta day cares were far below national averages in 1998. For example, teacher directors in Alberta earned an average of $9.90 per hour, compared to the national average of $14.54, and only Newfoundland and New Brunswick had lower average rates of pay for teacher directors (CRRU 2000, 115). Indeed, low wages and qualification exemptions were joined in a vicious circle since low wages encouraged trained workers to leave the field, thus making it necessary for day cares to apply for additional Level 2 and 3 exemptions, which in turn put further downward pressure on wages. Exemptions allowed day cares to skirt the staff qualification regulation and meant that the original intent of the regulation—to guarantee that every licensed day care has a core of staff with advanced training in ECE—was never realized in the 1990s.

As staff qualification requirements became established in Alberta in the 1990s, the DCSA continued to operate the Early Childhood Academy (ECA) as a private vocational school. In 1995 the ECA offered a program that qualified graduates for Level 2 certification and was attempting to get the province to approve an additional program that would qualify graduates for Level 3 certification. Pauline Desjardins noted that civil servants found it difficult to get the ECA to adopt a curriculum that met the standards established by the public colleges. She also stated that there was a strained relationship between the ECE programs in public colleges and private training programs such as the ECA. The public colleges refused to recognize the ECA Level 2 training program as equivalent to the first year of a two-year ECE diploma program even though the province's staff qualification bureaucrats had effectively granted equivalency. As a consequence, when a graduate of the ECA's Level 2 training program wished to pursue Level 3 certification at a community college, she did not receive any credit for her work at the ECA.

Commercial operators associated with the DCSA had vigorously pursued the establishment of their own staff training program in the 1980s. If day care had remained as lucrative an investment in the 1990s as it had been in the 1980s, and if the labour force needs of commercial day care had continued to expand, it is likely that the DCSA would have continued to directly sponsor the ECA. However, with the decline in the size and profitability of commercial day care in the 1990s and with the ready availability of qualification exemptions, the DCSA saw things differently at the end of the 1990s. The ECA ceased to operate and its programs were turned over to The Career College, the "longest standing private vocational college in Alberta." It was part of the IBS (International Business Schools) Group of Colleges and in 2001 offered training programs in both Edmonton and Calgary that led to Levels 2 and 3 certification.

"The difference between Mount Royal and The Career College," stated DCSA president Traudi Kelm in 2002, "is predominantly that The Career College has more immigrant students that wouldn't necessarily be successful at Mount Royal College." At that time, The Career College advertised its ECE program as "a practical approach to child care learning through lectures, small group discussions, demonstrating, observations and Audio/Visual." Alberta's Career Colleges were renamed CDI College Campuses after the IBS Group was purchased by CDI

Educational Corporation in 2001. The made-in-Alberta ECE program developed by the ECA did not readily fit into CDI's national curriculum, which was divided into the areas of business, technology, and health care. However, the Level 2 and Level 3 ECE programs continued to be offered in 2009 as part of the CDI's School of Health Care.[96]

The establishment of the ECA as a private vocational alternative to Alberta's public college programs in ECE was one of the first major thrusts of privatization in the early 1980s. The availability of the ECA's "practical approach to child care" through CDI College some thirty years later is a significant long-term success for the DCSA. It means that day care owners do not necessarily have to hire staff trained at public colleges for Level 2 and 3 positions. Furthermore, the exemption system meant that an employee of a commercial centre in the 1990s could qualify for a Level 2 exemption as long as she was enrolled as a part-time student in a course offered by CDI College. The consequence was that some employees with Level 2 or Level 3 certificates (or with Level 2 or Level 3 exemptions) did not have the breadth and depth of knowledge of ECE that is obtained through programs at public colleges. This is yet another way in which the intent of the staff-qualification regulation to improve the quality of day care was somewhat undermined in its practical implementation in the 1990s.

In conclusion, the staff-qualification regulation was introduced at a particularly difficult time for day care in Alberta; as a result, it did not have the uniformly positive impact on the quality of care in the 1990s as it would have had in propitious circumstances. Nevertheless, the logic of the new regulation ran counter to the provincial government's policies of cutbacks, deregulation, and reprivatization in day care and thus served to highlight the limitations of this approach. Staff-qualification requirements were a ray of hope because they posed administrative problems that could then be politicized by the proponents of quality child care.

8. Municipalities and Lighthouse Child Care, 1980–99

Municipal governments had taken the lead in building the Preventive Social Service (PSS) system of day cares in Alberta in the late 1960s and 1970s. As a consequence, many municipal bureaucrats and politicians strongly opposed the provincial government's unilateral decision, announced in 1978 and fully implemented in 1981, to end all dedicated provincial funding for the PSS day cares. In the early 1980s, five of Alberta's six largest cities showed their disdain for the provincial government's policies on preschool child care by defiantly stepping in to support "lighthouse" or model programs in their communities.[1] Their actions helped to ensure that the values and practice of the PSS program lived on at the same time that custodial commercial day care became the norm in Alberta. During the 1980s, federal funding sustained the different approaches taken by Alberta's largest municipalities to support quality care for both preschoolers and school-aged children. It set the stage for the 1990s, when each of the five municipalities that had championed lighthouse child care for preschoolers in the 1980s ended or substantially restricted its commitments. At the provincial level, the reversal was the product of the relative weakness of the movement for quality child care in the 1990s as well as the shift to the Right in Alberta politics. Simultaneously, important local factors in each of the cities affected the timing, basis, and final shape of the decision to end support for model child care programs. I comparatively investigate these local factors.

FIVE CITIES SUSTAIN MODEL CHILD CARE IN THE 1980s

At the same time that municipalities grappled with sustaining model child care for preschoolers without provincial cost sharing, they were faced with deciding on how much to emphasize the development of out-of-school care (OOSC) in their communities. However, it was only in Edmonton and Calgary that the two priorities clashed in a significant way. The demand for OOSC was not particularly strong in Grande Prairie, Red Deer, and Medicine Hat, and Lethbridge decided, soon after the inauguration of the new provincial day care system, not to use any municipal tax revenue to support preschool child care. In contrast, a strong commitment to model day care in Edmonton and Calgary co-existed with not only a strong demand for OOSC but also a history of municipal funding for dedicated OOSC centres.

Minister Bob Bogle acted in great haste in 1980 when he ended municipal participation in the provincial day care system. As a result, the provincial government inherited responsibility for OOSC programs on 1 August 1980 even though it did not have a plan in place for what to do with them. The plan soon became to give the OOSC programs back to municipalities as quickly as possible. When the minister announced the new operating allowance program for day cares on 4 September 1980, he also announced the "reassignment of after school programs, with appropriate financial support, to Preventive Social Services."[2] The problem with this plan, however, was that it was up to the discretion of each municipality whether or not to sponsor any PSS program, including OOSC. Therefore, whether a municipality accepted this reassignment from the minister was subject to negotiation between the two levels of government, and in the meantime, the province was left administering a program it had not wanted to administer in the first place. Ironically, Minister Bogle acted in haste because he was sick and tired of negotiating with Edmonton over day care policy and funding (see chapter 5) but his decision guaranteed many more months of negotiations with Edmonton and Calgary over the future of their OOSC programs.

Edmonton: Large Investments in OOSC and Support for Model Day Cares

When the provincial government assumed full responsibility for day care subsidies on 1 August 1980, municipalities saved money since they no longer had to cover 20 percent of the cost of the subsidies. In the case of Edmonton, the province estimated the annual net savings to be $391,000. On 14 May 1980, Edmonton City Council reaffirmed its "commitment to preserve community day care services for children and families in the municipality." However, the savings were not enough to maintain all aspects of the city's extensive program, and, as a result, Edmonton accepted the province's offer to assume responsibility for the municipally run family day home (FDH) program on 1 August.[3] Nevertheless, the savings were such that Edmonton made a substantial investment in model day cares. In 1981, $741,000 was allocated to twelve of the old PSS centres, now known as "municipally approved day care centres." Furthermore, an amount in excess of $300,000 was spent on subsidizing care through the city-run Glengarry Day Care and FDH project.[4]

The city's willingness to spend so much on lighthouse day care at this juncture partially reflected a desire "to put its money where its mouth was" in its political disagreement with the Lougheed government over the direction of day care in Alberta. However, it also reflected a significant political miscalculation: the city expected Minister Bogle to honour his previous commitment to phase out deficit funding for the old PSS day cares over a number of years. While the municipal government did receive a phase-out payment of $420,000 from the province on 1 August 1980, a payment of $328,000 that should have been made on 1 August 1981 never arrived. It was not until 4 March 1982 that the city learned the minister had unilaterally discontinued deficit phase-out payments from the time operating allowances were introduced in September 1980.[5]

The intrigue over when to phase out deficit payments for the old PSS day cares in Edmonton occurred in the context of yet another significant intergovernmental dispute—the future of OOSC programs. The sticking point in the transfer of the programs back to Edmonton and Calgary was funding. While the provincial PSS budget had been increased by $1.4 million in 1980 to accommodate the return of OOSC programs to PSS, this extra money would have not have covered the projected cost of OOSC in Calgary, let alone in both major cities. It is therefore not a surprise that neither Calgary nor Edmonton accepted the province's initial funding offer. The provincial government was negotiating from the position that OOSC in 1980–81 should cost $100 per month, with a low-income family being required to cover $40. However, the actual cost was $175 per month or more.[6] By the end of the 1980–81 school year, the future of OOSC in Alberta's two major cities was as much up in the air as it had been at the beginning of the year, with neither city having agreed to include OOSC in their roster of cost-shared Family and Community Support Services (FCSS) programs. (FCSS officially replaced PSS on 2 June 1981.)[7]

Behind the scenes, however, Minister Bogle was working on a dramatic reorganization of OOSC that would have ended, once and for all, formal municipal involvement in child care. In a policy initiative that was apparently never revealed to municipal governments, in June 1981 the department of Social Services and Community Health formally proposed to cabinet that the responsibility for OOSC be transferred to school boards. The proposal projected a cost per child at "less than one-third of existing program cost per child." The Request for Decision (RFD) on the proposal was submitted to the Executive Council office and treasury on 12 June 1981. It predicted possible opposition from school boards, municipalities, teachers, school janitorial staff, parents, and the general public. The possibility of this level of controversy must have concerned senior bureaucrats and politicians since the RFD was withdrawn by Minister Bogle before it was discussed at the Social Planning Committee of cabinet. Instead, the committee decided to add $570,000 to the FCSS budget (over and above the $1.4 million already committed) in order to give the minister a fighting chance of convincing Calgary and Edmonton to take over responsibility for OOSC. Interestingly, the inner circle of the Lougheed government was only interested in a short-term political solution to this problem and made it clear that it did not have a long-term commitment to expanding the availability of subsidized OOSC for Alberta's children. When he informed Minister Bogle of the $570,000 increase in the FCSS budget, the deputy minister to Executive Council stated, "Provincial government support is not to be increased to cover subsidies for new applicants to the program beyond 1981/82."[8]

Bob Bogle used this extra money to convince both Calgary and Edmonton to assume responsibility for OOSC starting in September 1981. Calgary was offered $800,000 to cover $120-per-month subsidies for 675 children over the course of the 1981–82 school year. It reluctantly accepted the offer even though it meant that the city would have to spend $300,000 of its own tax dollars on OOSC programs. Under the terms of its deal with the province, Edmonton projected having to spend over $1 million of its own tax revenue on OOSC in 1982–83.[9]

Consequently, during the first part of the 1981–82 school year, it appeared that OOSC programs would soon prove to be an unbearable financial burden for Calgary and Edmonton. It was at this point that the federal government came to the rescue. In a letter to Edmonton Alderman Jan Reimer, federal Health Minister Monique Begin indicated that the federal government was prepared to split the cost of municipal spending on subsidized not-for-profit day care and OOSC on a 50-50 basis, with the Alberta government's only role being to submit the claims. This was the genesis of an innovative political arrangement known as flow-through funding that would help Alberta municipalities in the 1980s to expand their OOSC programs and carry on with lighthouse day cares and FDH programs.

As mentioned in chapter 7, in early 1982 the Alberta government had finally gotten around to making Canada Assistance Plan (CAP) claims for eligible expenditures on child care between 1979 and 1981. In so doing, however, it had only asked for cost sharing on its own expenditures and any municipal expenditures that fit the terms of the PSS or FCSS programs. Therefore, no claims were made for discretionary municipal expenditures on OOSC or day care. Grant Notley, leader of Alberta's New Democratic Party (NDP), effectively criticized the government for this oversight. When the matter was first raised, Bob Bogle attempted to deflect the criticism by saying that "the real issue is that after-school care in Edmonton is unnecessarily expensive." Within a week, however, he was taking the matter very seriously and promised that if lawyers ruled that flow-through funding did not contravene provincial law, "we will take advantage of it."[10]

Alberta's municipalities had to wait until 1983 before the province finally allowed them to make flow-through CAP claims for their own independent expenditures on not-for-profit child care. In September 1983, they learned that their claims for expenditures incurred between 1980 and 1982 had been approved by the federal government. The amount of money involved was significant: for example, Edmonton received $1.2 million; Calgary, $480,000; and Medicine Hat, $378,000. It is important to recognize that although the dispute over inadequate provincial funding for OOSC programs had prompted the flow-through arrangement, municipal expenditures on lighthouse day cares and FDH projects were also eligible for CAP cost sharing.[11]

The receipt of a $1.2 million windfall from CAP in late 1983, plus the promise of additional CAP transfers every year, did not lead to Edmonton looking at expanding its support for model day cares. This is partly because close to half of the windfall had to be used to cover the shortfall caused by the province's early termination of deficit phase-out payments for PSS day cares. Furthermore, the economic recession caused by the fall in oil prices in 1982 had greatly reduced Alberta's royalty revenue and caused the province to limit transfers to municipalities at a time of high inflation. Most importantly, however, the demand for subsidized OOSC was growing rapidly; this raised the question of whether Edmonton should reallocate some or all of its spending on model day cares to expanding the availability of OOSC subsidies for the school-aged children of working families.

Between 1981 and 1984, the number of "full-year equivalent" OOSC subsidies in Edmonton grew from 400 to 1,134, and annual spending on OOSC increased four-fold to $2.7 million (table 8.1). The provincial FCSS grant to Edmonton did not keep pace with this growth. (Indeed, in real terms, the grant decreased

TABLE 8.1 Out-of-School Care in Edmonton, 1981 to 1991

Year	Licensed centres	Not-for-profit centres	Subsidized children[a]	Total cost
1981	22	22 (100%)	400	$0.6 M[b]
1982	64		611	$1.5 M
1983	97		900	$1.9 M
1984	93		1,134	$2.7 M
1985	106	26 (25%)	1,356	$3.3 M
1986	122		1,618	$3.7 M
1987	128		1,854	$4.4 M
1988			2,011	$5.1 M
1989	134		2,083	$5.5 M
1990			2,310	$6.2 M
1991	154	50 (32%)	2,471	$6.8 M

SOURCES: "The Historical and Political Perspective of the City of Edmonton's Out-of-School Care Program," Edmonton Children's Services, 13 February 1990 (ECFS, Children's Services, 1991, box 1, file 1.2); "The Municipality's Role in Child Care and Children's Services," Community and Family Services, Children's Services Section, April 1991, Appendix I (ECFS, Children's Services 1991, file 6.3).

[a] Number of full-year-equivalent children.
[b] Administrative cost for 1981 is estimated at $100,000.

between 1982 and 1990.) During these years, the city continued to fund the deficits of its original PSS out-of-school care centres but also subsidized the care of low-income children in any other licensed centre. As a consequence, in 1984 more than half of subsidized children were enrolled in commercial centres. This created an additional financial headache since any city spending on subsidies in commercial centres was ineligible for CAP cost sharing.[12]

The growth in demand for OOSC in Edmonton in the early 1980s was a direct consequence of the rapid expansion of day care during those same years. As is recorded in table 5.1, there were 135 licensed day cares in Edmonton at the beginning of 1982 with a licensed capacity of 5,611. Stimulated by operating allowances, the number of licensed spaces in Edmonton's day cares grew rapidly to 12,127 by July 1986 (an increase of 116 percent in four and a half years); at that point, 29 percent of the licensed capacity was filled by subsidized children. Parents who had placed their children in a day care centre often looked for an OOSC centre when their children went to school, and, as a consequence, the number of licensed OOSC centres in Edmonton also grew very rapidly in the early 1980s: from twenty-two in 1981 to ninety-seven in 1983 and 122 in 1986 (table 8.1). Parents whose children received a provincial subsidy for day care expected to receive a subsidy for OOSC and were directed to the city by the hundreds when they enrolled in the new commercial OOSC centres that were growing like mushrooms throughout Edmonton.[13]

Freezing the availability of OOSC subsidies was one way that Edmonton could control its OOSC costs when demand was growing so quickly. The first such freeze was introduced in the summer of 1983, although it was lifted after a short time. As an alternative, Edmonton looked to reduce its spending on model day care. In 1984 the quality-enhancement grants to the twelve municipally approved day cares were reduced by 17 percent compared to 1983. An equivalent cost saving was realized by the city's decision to end municipal sponsorship of the Glengarry Day Care. The cost of care at the municipal centre was relatively high compared to other non-profit day cares in the city but only because the workers were represented by Local 52 of the Civic Service Union and were thus paid wages that somewhat approximated the value of their work relative to other unionized city workers. The 1984 budget for the Glengarry Day Care projected a deficit of $397,000, half of which would be recoverable from CAP. The net cost to the city, therefore, would have been $198,500, or $275 per child per month.[14]

At this point, the costs of the Glengarry program became a subject of public ridicule. Even Alderman Jan Reimer, daughter of former provincial NDP leader Neil Reimer, bashed the municipal centre. "The costs to keep a child [in Glengarry] have gone out of line," she stated. "The city would be better off hiring a nanny for each child." It is important to note that there had been a changing of the guard in leadership at Edmonton Social Services (ESS), and the department in early 1984 seemed to pander to the critics of the municipal day care. For instance, the Edmonton Journal reported the following just after the budget committee had recommended that Glengarry be closed: "Department officials said it costs at least twice as much per year—approximately $10,000—to keep a child in the unionized daycare centre as it would in a non-union community agency." What department officials failed to emphasize was that the net cost to Edmonton taxpayers was only $3,300 per year for a child, a far cry from $10,000. This episode indicated that while modelling quality care continued to be part of Edmonton's conception of a lighthouse program in 1984, modelling quality compensation for workers had fallen out of favour.[15]

The city's initial decision was to close the Glengarry Day Care outright. Shortly after that decision was made, John Lackey was hired as the new general manager of ESS. Lackey, it will be remembered, was a former director of PSS for the province. Under Lackey's leadership, ESS soon crafted an alternative to closure that saw the Glengarry Day Care turned over to a non-profit community board effective 1 July 1984, and it immediately become eligible for subsidization as a municipally approved day care. Whereas the city would have saved almost $200,000 a year by closing the centre, the saving from the new arrangement was estimated at $150,000. (The difference between these two figures was Edmonton's 50 percent share of the $96,000 subsidy provided to the Glengarry Day Care Society, with the other 50 percent share covered by CAP.) Interestingly, however, the proposal included a commitment by ESS to donate all of the municipal centre's furnishings and toys to the new society and to spend $400,000 to renovate the city-owned building that housed the day care. The city also agreed to continue to operate the small FDH based at Glengarry as a direct municipal service so that the society could concentrate on the day care. Therefore, ESS eventually did everything it could to ease the transition of the Glengarry Day Care from municipal to community not-for-profit auspice. This ensured continuity of care for children and enabled the day care to maintain relatively high standards. Indeed, the only real losers were the twenty or so workers at the Glengarry Day Care who had their wages slashed in an exercise that had a great deal of symbolic meaning but very little effect on the city's bottom line.[16]

The end of municipal sponsorship for the Glengarry Day Care in 1984 was the nadir for Edmonton's support of lighthouse day care in the 1980s. The following year, ESS conducted a thorough review of its day care, OOSC, and FDH programs. The recommendations that emerged from the review provided a solid programmatic rationale for city support of particular day cares and resulted in an increase in the number of approved day cares from thirteen to eighteen. The recommendations also led to a significant reorientation of the municipal OOSC program and to the transfer of the small FDH program to the Glengarry Day Care Society on 1 September 1986.[17]

During the 1985 program review, opposition to the city's funding for lighthouse day cares was expressed by both commercial operators and the Edmonton Committee for Quality Child Care. The latter group recommended ending support for model day cares and reallocating the funds to OOSC programs.[18] Instead of supporting this move, however, Edmonton's child care subcommittee recommended that municipal funding be used to support "specialized Child Care Family Resource Centres" (CCFRCs), which would provide a range of "special functions" including parent training and support services, coordinating the range of services required by high-needs children, and operating a toy-lending library. On top of these special functions, a CCFRC was expected to operate a model day care that met improved city standards and to make itself available for practicum training by early childhood education (ECE) students. All in all, this was a surprising recommendation that went far beyond the opinions expressed during the public consultation process. A story in the Edmonton Journal maintained that if the CCFRCs came into existence, they would represent "a dramatic change from the current situation." This was not entirely accurate, however, since the recommendation was consistent with the spirit of the PSS approach to day care as a total community service. Furthermore, as was noted at the time by the director of one of the municipally approved day cares, "those preventive programs are occurring at centres now," albeit neither as systematically nor as thoroughly as they could have been.[19]

By the middle of 1986, the city had adopted a list of expected specialized services based upon the subcommittee's recommendations. ESS stipulated, "It is expected that Municipally Approved and Funded Centres will demonstrably provide most or all of these elements within their programs." But even though municipally approved day cares (MADCs) were now expected to serve as resource centres as well as provide quality child care, the "resource centre" label did not enter Edmonton's lexicon at that time.[20]

The city also followed the subcommittee's recommendations that the competition for municipal funding be opened up to any non-profit day care, that a Children's Services Sub-Committee (CSSC) be constituted on a permanent basis to make recommendations on the allocation of municipal funds to day cares, and that the city "update and revise its municipal daycare standards" and then require day cares to meet these standards as a basis for supplemental funding. A competitive process, managed by the CSSC, occurred in late 1986 for the 1987 budget year. It led to the number of MADCs growing from thirteen to eighteen, but due to a lack of funds, the number was frozen at eighteen in 1987.

On paper, it looked like the review process of the mid-1980s had propelled Edmonton to substantially increase its support for quality preschool child care: not only were there more MADCs, but each centre was expected to provide a long list of specialized services to families and the community, and was monitored to ensure that it followed the city's quality standards. Unfortunately, however, funding for the program did not keep pace with this ambitious plan. In 1983 the city provided an average of $1,761 per year for each of the 423 subsidized children in its MADCs. (There were 121 additional licensed spaces in the centres that were filled by unsubsidized children.) By 1988 the amount had fallen to $1,694 for each of 538 subsidized children. (After correcting for inflation, the 1988 subsidy was $1,450, or 18 percent less than in 1983.) Both the CSSC and city bureaucrats realized that this amount was inadequate and lobbied for a $250,000 increase in the city's grant to day cares in 1989. They were unsuccessful. In 1991 Edmonton provided $1,680 per year for each of 505 subsidized children. (In 1983 dollars, the 1991 subsidy was down to $1,232, or 30 percent less than in 1983.)[21]

Increased expectations in combination with declining subsidies put both the service providers (the MADCs) and their overseer (the CSSC) in a very difficult situation. In its first year for assigning subsidy money (1987), the CSSC had gone as far as to rank all applicants in terms of the range of specialized services they promised to offer. Three years later, however, no such ranking was undertaken. Instead, the subcommittee pragmatically focussed its attention on using some of the city's grant to supplement the wages of trained workers.[22]

The 1985 program review also addressed OOSC and significantly reoriented Edmonton's involvement in this area. The lead recommendation was "that City Council confirm its commitment to make Out-of-School Care available to all children who require the service." Although city council "struck" this recommendation at its 13 August 1985 meeting, it did immediately add $370,000 to the budget in order to expand the availability of OOSC subsidies. Furthermore, Edmonton regularly increased its spending on OOSC for the rest of the decade, even though increases in the province's FCSS grant did not keep pace (table 8.1). Indeed, in 1990 Edmonton spent approximately $17.5 million on FCSS programs, $6.2 million of which went to OOSC. In that same year, its provincial FCSS grant was only $7.7 million. Had Edmonton held to the expected 80 percent/20 percent cost-sharing formula for FCSS programs, it would have contributed only $1.9 million in 1990. Instead it contributed $9.8 million, or 56 percent of the total. If we use this percentage to calculate the city's share of the OOSC budget, then Edmonton contributed about $3.5 million toward OOSC in 1990, considerably more than the $916,000 it put into MADCs.[23]

Another important recommendation from the 1985 review was "that City Council financially support only those programs which meet City of Edmonton standards." A consultative process led to the introduction of a new set of OOSC standards for the 1987–88 school year and the establishment of a children's services section to monitor and consult with OOSC centres. While all licensed centres continued to be eligible for subsidies during the next two years, centres that met the city's standards received a higher subsidy rate than other centres.[24] "By the end of 1988 approximately 50% of all subsidized children were being cared for in licensed OOSC centres meeting the City's approved standards." At this time, the municipal government ended deficit funding of its original community OOSC centres and instead directed all of its spending into portable OOSC subsidies and consultative services.[25]

The fact that CAP did not allow for cost sharing of OOSC subsidies in commercial centres was another focus of the 1985 review. The advisory subcommittee recommended "that City Council work toward maximum utilization of Canada Assistance Plan funding." ESS in turn recommended "that the City encourage expansion of OOSC under non-profit auspices" by persuading existing not-for-profit groups to establish OOSC programs, helping to organize not-for-profit societies that would be solely focussed on operating OOSC programs, and assisting groups to secure funds from foundations and service groups. This recommendation was immediately accepted by city council (13 August 1985) and had a significant impact on the development of OOSC in Edmonton for the rest of the decade. Between 1981 and 1985, almost all of the rapid growth in OOSC had been in the commercial sector. However, between 1985 and 1991, the number of not-for-profit OOSC centres almost doubled, and the net growth in the two sectors was exactly equal at twenty-four centres apiece. By 1991 almost one-third of the OOSC centres in Edmonton were run on a not-for-profit basis (table 8.1).[26]

Given Edmonton's leadership role in day care in Alberta during the PSS years, it is not surprising that the city carried on this role in the 1980s and spent a great deal more on lighthouse day care and OOSC that any other Alberta city. Indeed, in 1992 Edmonton's per capita spending on child care was $14.37 compared to $8.56 in Medicine Hat, $3.56 in Lethbridge, and $2.41 in Red Deer. I estimate the comparable figures for Calgary and Grande Prairie at $6.75 and less than $1.00, respectively. Furthermore, Edmonton had a broad commitment to quality children's services beyond its MADC and OOSC programs. Specifically, in 1990 almost $800,000 in FCSS funding was allocated to Head Start and other forms of early intervention programs for preschoolers from disadvantaged families. Consequently, when the federal and provincial governments began to emphasize public spending on early intervention programs rather than on day care in the 1990s, the city was primed to move in this direction. This shift will be detailed later in this chapter.[27]

Calgary's Three Municipal Day Cares

Because Calgary had been the first city to commit itself to the new provincial system of cost-shared portable subsidies, it was spending far more on day care subsidies in 1980 than Edmonton was. Therefore, Calgary saved approximately twice as much as Edmonton ($800,000 vs. $391,000 annually) when, beginning in the summer of 1980, Bob Bogle unilaterally excluded municipalities from participation in the provincial day care system. Within a week of the minister's announcement of the new policy, the director of Calgary Social Services (CSS), Sam Blakely, publicly raised the possibility "of using municipal money, which will be saved by the provincial government's takeover of subsidy payments, to improve local day care standards."[28] Early the next year, the department prepared a detailed report on day care and OOSC in the city. It recommended an ambitious program to "provide daycare programs of all types with financial incentives to provide an enhanced quality of care." To qualify for incentive payments, centres would have to meet city standards that exceeded the province's licensing standards. The department proposed municipal funding of $1.8 million for this incentive program in 1981–82.[29]

At the time this recommendation was made, Calgary was at the beginning of a period of rapid growth of day care, sparked by the new provincial operating allowances. In May 1980, there were 5,534 licensed spaces in the city. Just twenty months later, the number of licensed spaces had grown to 7,258, an increase of 31 percent. This sort of growth meant that Calgary's idea of a broad-based financial incentive program for day cares would have potentially cost far more than initially budgeted. Eventually Calgary chose to restrict its involvement in lighthouse day care in the 1980s to ongoing sponsorship and subsidization of the three municipal day cares: Shaganappi (including a satellite FDH program), Bridgeland, and Connaught. The workers in these municipal day cares were all unionized; therefore, unlike Edmonton, which closed its only municipal day care in 1984, Calgary remained committed to a model of quality compensation for day care workers throughout the 1980s. As a consequence, in 1991 the City of Calgary spent $1.9 million on its three municipal day cares and FDH program while Edmonton spent less than $900,000 on its eighteen MADCs. While these figures are not directly comparable because Calgary's appears to include consultative services while Edmonton's does not, it is nonetheless apparent that Calgary had chosen a starkly different approach to lighthouse day care than Edmonton had.[30]

Like Edmonton, Calgary also put considerable effort into the development of subsidized OOSC after agreeing to include it as an FCSS program for the 1981–82 school year. In May 1980, there had been only 177 licensed OOSC spaces in Calgary, all in not-for-profit centres. Three years later, the city temporarily froze the number of OOSC spaces it was prepared to subsidize at 850 because of budget restraints. OOSC grew very rapidly in 1982–83, when Calgary's unemployment rate jumped because of a drop in oil prices. A city report explained this phenomenon: "Operators, faced with declining enrollments in preschool spaces [because unemployed parents do not tend to use day care], have turned increasingly in recent months to offering care for school-aged children as an alternative source of revenue in order to maintain their cash flow. This has coincided with an apparent increase in interest on the part of working parents to utilize supervised child care services for their elementary school-aged children."[31]

As was noted in the previous section, Edmonton provided subsidies for OOSC in any provincially licensed centre right up until 1989. Calgary, however, adopted municipal OOSC standards in 1982 and thereafter required subsidized children to enrol in a program that met those standards. Calgary's standards were not particularly stringent but undoubtedly excluded low-quality commercial centres and therefore helped to limit the growth of OOSC subsidies relative to Edmonton: while the number of subsidies in Edmonton grew by 175 percent between 1983 and 1991 (table 8.1), the number of OOSC subsidies in Calgary grew by only 36 percent over the same eight-year interval. In 1991 Edmonton's director of children's services, Kathy Barnhart, argued that another reason for the relatively high number of OOSC subsidies in Edmonton was that the participation rate of low-income families in the provincial day care program was much higher in Edmonton than in Calgary, and subsidized parents tended to move their children from day cares to OOSC programs when they entered grade 1. The main consequence of the differential growth rates in subsidized OOSC in the two cities was that Edmonton's 1991 budget for OOSC of $6.8 million (table 8.1) was more than twice the $2.6 million spent by Calgary.[32]

Overall, in 1991 Edmonton spent approximately $7.7 million on children's services while Calgary spent $4.4 million. Interestingly, however, Calgary spent considerably more on lighthouse day care, concentrating its spending on three municipal day cares and an FDH program. This contrasts with the lighthouse model in Edmonton, where far less money was spread over a relatively large number (18) of community-run, not-for-profit day cares. Calgary's model for lighthouse day care was certainly the better of the two in recognizing the value of the labour of trained child care workers. However, Calgary's model was also more vulnerable to political attack since its subsidy was benefiting relatively few children and employees.

Continuing to sit on Calgary City Council throughout the 1980s was perhaps the biggest critic of Calgary's municipal day care program. In 1980 Alderman Barbara Scott was the only member of the community services committee to oppose allocating $150,000 to subsidize the municipal day cares.[33] Later in the decade, however, Scott's philosophical aversion to direct municipal provision of social services began to attract greater support. Her concerted campaign to privatize or close Calgary's municipal day cares is detailed in the next section.

One additional factor complicated the future of Calgary's municipal day cares in 1989–90. After auditing Calgary's municipal day care program for adherence to the terms of CAP in the late 1980s, the federal government held off from processing the city's claims for 1988 and 1989, and "requested a portion of previous claims to be returned." The problem was that the city did not charge anyone the actual cost of the service and thus ended up subsidizing high-income parents as well as parents of more limited means, while CAP specifically forbade the universal subsidization of day care. Fortunately for the municipal government, it was not counting on CAP transfers to fund the ongoing operations of its municipal day cares (unlike Edmonton) and could thus live with a long delay in getting CAP reimbursements.[34] Nevertheless, the federal government's action contributed to questions about the sustainability of Calgary's municipal day care system and demonstrated that the federal government did not share CSS's enthusiasm for the universal subsidization of day care costs.

Patterns of Support for Lighthouse Child Care in Other Municipalities

At the zenith of municipal sponsorship of lighthouse day care in the 1980s, there were eleven municipally run day cares in Alberta's six largest cities (line 1, table 8.2). This was two more municipal day cares than had existed in the late 1970s, with Red Deer being the new municipal operator. The other major Alberta city that expanded its direct involvement in the provision of child care in the 1980s was Grande Prairie. When the end of PSS funding forced Awasis Day Care to move to a smaller facility, it could no longer continue to run a satellite FDH program. The municipality took over the program and ran it on a break-even basis

TABLE 8.2 Support for Lighthouse Child Care, 1980 to 1992

	Edmonton	Calgary	Medicine Hat	Red Deer	Grande Prairie	Lethbridge
Maximum number of city-run day cares during the 1980s	1	3	5	2	0	0
Number of city-run day cares in 1990	0	3	3	0	0	0
City-run FDH program during 1980s?	Yes	Yes	Yes	Yes	Yes	No
City-run FDH program in 1990?	No	Yes	Yes	No	Yes	No
Number of day cares receiving support in 1990	18	3	3	2	2	0
Approximate per capita spending on day cares and FDHs in 1992 [a]	$1.40	$2.50	$6.05	$1.40	$0.30	$0
Approximate per capita spending on OOSC in 1991	$11.05	$3.45	$1.00	$0.35	$0	$3.56

SOURCES: The first five entries in each column are based upon information recorded in the text. The financial data come from: memo from William Ardiel to Barbara Scott, "Comparison of Social Service Budgets for Edmonton and Calgary," 28 March 1991 (ECFS, Children's Services 1991, file 11.4); and Medicine Hat 1992, 108.

[a] Any reimbursements from CAP have not been deducted.

throughout the 1980s. This FDH program was very popular with many parents because it had the highest standards in Grande Prairie and it strictly enforced those standards.[35]

Edmonton turned its only municipal day care over to a not-for-profit community board in 1984 and did the same with its only FDH program in 1986. Red Deer, which had begun the 1980s by becoming the operator of two day cares and an FDH program, followed Edmonton's lead on 1 January 1990, when both of its day cares and the FDH program were turned over to a not-for-profit society. Red Deer remained committed to lighthouse day care at that time, however, since the facilities were leased to the society without charge and the city provided a yearly quality-enhancement grant of almost $100,000. At the beginning of the 1980s, therefore, the City of Red Deer strove to emulate the Calgary/Medicine Hat model of running lighthouse day cares under municipal auspice. At the end of the 1980s, however, Red Deer switched to the Edmonton model of providing subsidies for model day cares run by community groups (Medicine Hat 1992, 109).

Although Medicine Hat ran fewer day cares in 1990 (three) than in 1980 (five), it too remained committed to providing day care as a municipal service. In 1992, just after the city had opened a new municipal centre at Medicine Hat College, the municipal sector controlled 33 percent of the 619 licensed spaces in the city; the commercial sector, 41 percent; and two day cares run by churches, the remaining 26 percent. At the same time, there were three commercial FDH agencies in Medicine Hat with 321 homes, more than twice the 140 homes affiliated with the municipal FDH agency (Medicine Hat 1992, 20). The two cities that spent the most per capita on preschool day care in the early 1990s (table 8.2)—Medicine Hat and Calgary—were the only cities that, at that time, operated day cares as direct municipal services.

Medicine Hat took full advantage of CAP flow-through funding in the 1980s to sustain its direct involvement in preschool child care. In September 1983 the city received a backdated CAP reimbursement of $378,000 for its expenditures on child care between 1980 and 1982. For the years between 1983 and 1990, Medicine Hat received flow-through funds ranging from a low of $184,000 (1983) to a high of $256,000 (1990). In total, the federal government transferred $2.1 million to Medicine Hat for its day care services between 1980 and 1990 (Medicine Hat 1992, 22). Adjusting for inflation, the transfer was $3.7 million in 2006 dollars. The city used the CAP money to pay higher wages and require higher standards than its competitors. For instance, beginning in 1986, all new hires in city-run day cares had to have at least a one-year early childhood development (ECD) diploma (16), whereas the province's licensing standards at that time did not cover staff training.

In the late 1980s, federal officials became concerned that all families with children in municipally run day cares in Alberta were being subsidized: CAP rules mandated that only low- to middle-income families be subsidized. This problem was solved in 1991 when Medicine Hat introduced a sliding fee scale that had been approved by CAP officials. It made clear that "once a family income exceeds Canada Assistance Plan's likelihood of needs, then that family no longer qualifies for a City subsidy and is required to pay the City's unit cost" (26). However, the city included an exception to this rule that was approved by CAP: "In order to ensure that Day Care services will be affordable, a ceiling was placed on the parent fee to ensure that no family would have to pay more than 15% of their net income on Daycare services" (26). One consequence of the 15 percent ceiling was that an upper-middle-income family with three children in city-run child care programs would receive a subsidy from the city. This feature of Medicine Hat's subsidy system became a political liability when a new right-wing city council was elected in October 1992.

Medicine Hat's involvement in child care in the 1980s went well beyond spending large sums on its day care centres. For instance, in 1983 a cost-recovery Mother's Day Out program was initiated at the Crescent Heights centre after the early childhood services program previously run at the centre was transferred to the school system.[36] This particular initiative was similar to Grande Prairie's FDH program, begun at approximately the same time: both programs met important community needs for child care by drawing upon the professional expertise of municipal civil servants but did not cost taxpayers any money. The success of the two programs suggests that child care programs directly administered by local governments can sometimes be innovative, efficient, and highly popular.

Another new program initiated in Medicine Hat in the 1980s was a dedicated group-care program for school-aged children. Beginning in 1988, an OOSC program serving twelve children was established at one of the day cares to complement the city's traditional approach of placing school-aged children in FDHs (Medicine Hat 1992, 36–39). Nevertheless, the demand for OOSC during the 1980s in Medicine Hat and other smaller Alberta cities was nothing like the demand in the larger cities. In 1992 Medicine Hat spent approximately $1 per capita on OOSC, and Red Deer and Grande Prairie each spent less (line 7, table 8.2). Indeed, in the 1980s and early 1990s, Grande Prairie tried, on three occasions, to establish an OOSC program, but each time there was not enough interest to warrant a permanent program. For one of its pilot projects, Grande Prairie only charged parents $15 per month but "only three or four kids showed up."[37]

Municipal involvement in OOSC was a more pressing issue in both Edmonton and Calgary in the 1980s than municipal support for model day care. It is not surprising, then, that in 1992 each of these municipal governments spent more on OOSC than on model preschool child care (line 7, table 8.2); indeed, Edmonton's spending on OOSC was almost eight times what it spent on quality-enhancement grants for its municipal day cares. The pattern of spending by Medicine Hat was almost the exact reverse, with spending on preschool child care being six times greater than OOSC spending. This indicates that Medicine Hat's large spending on municipal day care in the 1980s and early 1990s, while consistent with the

historical trajectory of the development of day care in the city, was also a consequence of not facing intense pressures to expand the availability of subsidized
OOSC spaces. Furthermore, in the 1980s, Medicine Hat's per capita FCSS grant
was frozen at a level that was higher than any of the other large Alberta cities,
thus making it easier to run its modest OOSC program without extra contributions from property taxes.[38]

It is useful to add together the figures in lines 6 and 7 of table 8.2 to get
each city's total per capita spending on child care in 1992 (minus miscellaneous
programs). Medicine Hat ranked second on this statistic at $7.05 per capita,
well behind the $12.45 spent by Edmonton and just ahead of Calgary's $5.95.
Red Deer and Grande Prairie spent the least of the six cities, and both fit the
pattern of Medicine Hat in spending more on preschool services than OOSC.
Lethbridge, however, fit the pattern of the two large cities in spending relatively
more on OOSC. In fact, although Lethbridge spent nothing on day care or FDHS,
it ranked fourth overall since it spent $3.56 per capita on OOSC, slightly ahead
of what Calgary spent on OOSC ($3.45 per capita) and second only to Edmonton
($11.05 per capita) in the entire province.

In the first decade of the PSS program, Lethbridge had the deserved reputation of being the most conservative city in the province and, consequently, the
city where public spending on child care ran into the most opposition. But
based on provincial election results, by the end of the 1970s, it was no longer
accurate to think of Lethbridge's political culture in these terms (see chapter
4). Lethbridge's relatively high spending on OOSC in the 1980s confirms this
interpretation. The lack of spending on day care in the 1980s was a historical
legacy of the earlier period, while active municipal support for OOSC subsidies in
the 1980s was in keeping with Lethbridge's more moderate political ethos. It is
noteworthy that municipal tax dollars accounted for 36 percent of the total cost
of Lethbridge's OOSC program in 1992, far more that the 20 percent required to
fully access FCSS funds from the province (Medicine Hat 1992, 109).

In summary, a decade after the province had unilaterally eliminated municipal governments' formal responsibilities for preschool child care, four of
Alberta's large cities continued to provide significant funding for lighthouse
day cares. The province refused to share the costs of these municipal programs, but the federal government covered half of each city's net costs for
low-income children since the province had assented to a unique flow-through
funding deal between the federal and municipal governments. Furthermore,
although Grande Prairie's financial contribution to the two old PSS day cares

in that community was limited, it did run a municipal FDH program on a cost-recovery basis.

Things would change in the 1990s, however, as each of these cities abandoned their experiments with model child care for preschool children. The remainder of this chapter investigates why this happened, with attention to the intersection of national, provincial, and city-specific factors.

LARGE CITIES ABANDON THEIR LIGHTHOUSE PROGRAMS

The Best Is Attacked First: Business Owners and Right-Wing Aldermen Unite

In the summer of 1992, Howard Clifford bicycled through Alberta during a 5,800-mile "vision quest" for quality child care that took him from Prince Rupert to Inuvik to Winnipeg. During his brief stay in Medicine Hat, the national child care consultant was interviewed by a reporter for a local radio station. "I was asked what I thought of the day care program in Medicine Hat," Clifford wrote a short time later.

> The city historically has been an oasis for day care. If I was asked to name the most progressive community in Alberta in terms of child care, Medicine Hat would win hands down. In fact I would rank it the equal of any community in Canada. One of the reasons the day care program is of such high quality is that years ago the city opted for a number of municipally operated centres. Being municipal, the salary levels are better (still not what they ought to be) and the standards set by these centres provided a leadership thrust.

> I doubt the citizens of the City fully appreciate what a nice childcare system they have.... Later I was to hear that there are some in the community grumbling about the cost of day care and feeling that the private sector could do it cheaper. I hope, for everyone's sake, their vision isn't sold out.... Twenty years ago I believed that if you once got your foot in the door and established a good program, it was relatively safe. Sadly I have been proved wrong. (1993, 221–22)

As it turned out, the "grumbling" to which Howard Clifford referred had powerful political forces behind it. In the year of Clifford's vision quest tour, the municipal government operated four day cares at a net cost of $468,000 prior to CAP reimbursement. Four years later, the city had turned three of its day cares over to other operators. Furthermore, while it still operated the day care at Medicine Hat College, it only had to provide a small subsidy because of savings from management reorganization and a larger financial contribution extracted from the college.[39] Therefore, in the short span between 1992 and 1996, day care in Medicine Hat underwent a fundamental change as the municipal government drastically scaled back its involvement.

Two events in 1989 signalled problems for Medicine Hat's continued sponsorship of model day cares. The first was the formation of the Medicine Hat and District Independent Day Care Operators' Association (hereafter the Independent Operators' Association, or IOA). In a 1995 interview, long-time Medicine Hat Alderman Graham Kelly stated, "The major reason behind the formation of the Independent Operators' Association was to get the City of Medicine Hat out of the daycare business." He identified the owners of a struggling commercial centre as the spark for forming this organization. According to Alderman Kelly, the struggling day care was established in a neighbourhood that did not have very many young children. Instead of coming to the sensible conclusion that the day care should be moved to a neighbourhood with more young children, the owners and chamber of commerce blamed unfair competition from municipal centres for the day care's high vacancy rate.[40]

Also in 1989, the *Medicine Hat News* reported that "a couple of aldermen are working behind the scenes to have the [municipal day care] service privatized." Both prior to and after the 1989 municipal election, however, the aldermen who supported cutting what the city spent on model day care formed a minority on a council led by Mayor Ted Grimm (a former union employee who had run for the NDP in Medicine Hat in the 1967 provincial election) and Alderman Kelly (a high school principal). For instance, at the city council meeting on 4 May 1992, a motion put forward by Aldermen Kathy Mandeville and Wayne Craven to cut the city's spending on day care by $54,000 in 1992 was defeated, with six members of the nine members of council voting against.[41]

However, the political climate throughout Alberta and British Columbia changed markedly in the early 1990s, and this had a significant impact on municipal politics in Medicine Hat. During these years, the Reform Party of Canada, led by Preston Manning, the son of former Alberta Social Credit premier Ernest Manning, skilfully promoted provincial rights, fiscal conservatism, and traditional family values, and capitalized on growing disenchantment with the federal Progressive Conservative government of Brian Mulroney. Among the prominent members of the Reform Party in Medicine Hat was Alderman Kathy Mandeville, who on 11 April 1992 narrowly lost the Reform nomination for the riding of Medicine Hat to Monte Solberg. Solberg went on to handily win the riding in the federal election in 1993 with 55 percent of the vote. In that election, the Reform Party won 22 of the 26 ridings in Alberta and 24 of the 32 ridings in British Columbia.[42]

Julie Friesen was one of the three sitting aldermen who were defeated in their bids for re-election in the October 1992 municipal election. She described the politics of the period in these terms:

> In my opinion, the feeling of the people both municipally, provincially and federally was a very right-wing view: "We are not willing to support any social service kinds of areas, or soft service kinds of areas or human service kinds of areas. We are only willing to support those absolutely destitute types but anyone else can darn well start paying their own way. We shouldn't be in those kinds of businesses when the private sector can do it."[43]

The IOA made two astute moves in its campaign against the city-run day cares. First, it convinced the two church-run day cares in Medicine Hat to join, thus allowing the IOA to frame the debate as "independent vs. government" instead of "commercial vs. not-for-profit."[44] This anti-government theme tied in very nicely with the Reform Party's message. Second, as noted by Wally Regehr, who ran unsuccessfully for alderman in 1992, the IOA secured the support of the chamber of commerce, which he described as "a force in Medicine Hat politics." A 1991 letter to Mayor Grimm made it clear that the chamber's concern went beyond the municipal day care program: "The Community Services department is clearly out of control with a four year compound growth rate of 9.3%, almost double that of transportation services which averaged 5.4%."[45]

As noted in the first part of this chapter, in 1991 Medicine Hat introduced the rule that no family with children in city-run centres should spend more than 15 percent of its net income on day care. The next year, the Medicine Hat and District Chamber of Commerce featured this policy in an appraisal of city-run day care services. It described the situation of a hypothetical family with three young children aged seven, five, and three years, and $3,000 of monthly net income. Such a family would have paid $704 per month for day care at a commercial day care or $803 per month for municipal day care according to the city's sliding fee scale. However, the 15 percent rule meant that the family would only be charged $450 per month by the city. The Chamber of Commerce used this example to make the point that the city's 15-percent-of-net-income rule resulted in a subsidy "not only to low income groups but upper income as well."[46]

Agitation by the IOA and Medicine Hat and District Chamber of Commerce would have made day care an issue in the 1992 municipal election regardless of any other developments. However, day care was a much bigger issue in that election than it otherwise would have been because of the work of a day care policy review committee in the preceding months. Indeed, the committee released its final report on 6 October 1992, just two weeks before election day. The fact that this program review culminated when it did instead of being delayed until after the election was a tactical error; it suggests that the majority of those on city council between 1989 and 1992 did not fully appreciate how the growing strength of the Reform Party would affect municipal politics.

The policy review of 1992 was bureaucratically rather than politically initiated. Municipal FCSS recommended an internal review after noting that the day care program had last been reviewed in 1983. When the matter was put to city council, however, the recommendation was changed so that the review would be conducted not by civil servants but by a special public committee, and participation of the IOA on the committee was mandated.[47]

The IOA set the tone for the policy review with an aggressive presentation to city council on 16 March 1992 that concluded, "We can meet the total child care needs of the community without the use of municipal tax dollars." The review itself got underway the next month; it was chaired by Gitta Hashizume, a strong supporter of Medicine Hat's model day cares, but it did include among its five members a representative of the IOA.[48]

Many organizations and individuals wrote or made a presentation to the policy review committee in support Medicine Hat's system of quality day cares. Besides the IOA and the Medicine Hat and District Chamber of Commerce, the only organization that questioned the city's involvement was the Southview Church of God, operator of a not-for-profit day care. Pastor Mel Wagner did not call for Medicine Hat to withdraw from the field of day care, but he did note, "There are some among our board and congregation who feel the City ought not be operating a daycare service in the community.... The basis of their private belief is based upon the principle of free enterprise and/or the actual cost to the taxpayer."[49]

Most of the individuals who wrote to support the city's involvement in child care were parents with children in city-run facilities (thirteen letters) or FDH providers in the municipal satellite system (nineteen individuals). However, there were two long, thoughtful letters from other citizens who supported the city's child care system and a pithy letter of opposition from a stay-at-home mother, Jo-ann Petro, who made two main points. First, she objected to paying taxes "for the care of other people's children" and claimed that she would not be able to remain as a stay-at-home parent "if the taxes keep going up because of people who could stay at home but consider their careers a priority." This was the sort of argument that was being popularized throughout Alberta at this time by the pro-family group Kids First (see chapter 7). Second, Petro questioned why taxpayers' money had been used to try and mobilize parents with children in city-run day cares and FDHs to write to the review committee. It so happened that the city's day care advisory committee had prepared a form letter that was favourable to the status quo and had distributed the letter to all parents with children in city-run facilities, asking them to sign, add personalized comments, and submit it to the policy review committee. The dollars spent on the mobilization campaign were fairly small, covering the cost of printing about five hundred copies and mailing two hundred letters to satellite FDH clients (the material was handed out in person at the municipal day cares). Yet the question of whether this was an appropriate use of tax dollars was an important one and led to a prominent story in the *Medicine Hat News*.

Alderman Brian Stein reacted to the incident in a way that would resonate with the majority of citizens. The *News* quoted him as saying, "I didn't particularly like what was done. I didn't like that it seemed to be coming from within the city." Stein also told the paper that "the tone of the form letter was 'pretty well slanted.'"[50] In 1994 defeated aldermanic candidate Wally Regehr presented this incident as an important part of the politics of day care in 1992. He stated that the IOA and their supporters "effectively put doubt in people's minds whether in fact the city day care people, the administration, were playing fair with the privates. And that was pretty effective.... The city had perceived and put itself forward as the high-quality, squeaky clean, good operation and it kind of tainted them I'd say."[51]

The City of Medicine Hat's *Footsteps to the Future: Day Care Policy Review* recommended that the city scale back its involvement in model day care by closing one of its four centres and turning a second centre over to the public school district or a not-for-profit society. Hashizume stated that these suggestions "did not involve large conflicts" and were taken "in response to the political environment." At the same time, the report affirmed the need for the city to provide "some level of direct service" in day care in order to "maintain a positive influence on the standard of group care" and recommended that Medicine Hat continue to operate its satellite FDH project (Medicine Hat 1992, 47–48).

The IOA organized a special candidates' forum on day care just five days before the election. Mayor Ted Grimm was facing a token challenger in the 1992 election, and neither he nor his opponent appeared at this forum. However, thirteen of the seventeen candidates for the eight aldermanic positions did attend: three of the seven incumbents who were running for re-election and all ten of the other candidates. They were asked to respond to the question "Considering how much is spent, should the city get out of day care, yes or no?" It seems likely that this question provided an election focus for some voters. When the dust had settled on election night, only two of the nine members of council (Ted Grimm and Graham Kelly) were strong supporters of city-run model day care; six members were opponents and one supported a middle ground.[52]

The shift to the Right on Medicine Hat City Council in 1992 was in step not only with the rise of the Reform Party on the federal scene but also with a strong swing to the Right in provincial politics. Between 1989 and 1993, the NDP held sixteen seats in the provincial legislature. However, in the 15 June 1993 provincial election, the party failed to elect a single candidate. Nevertheless, it was the intersection of local and extra-local factors that explains the municipal election results of October 1992.

The election of a right-wing city council in Medicine Hat in 1992 elicited two responses from the supporters of the city's involvement in the provision of model day care. On the one hand, there were different forms of protest action, including a speedy move by the thirty-nine child care workers employed by the city to join the Canadian Union of Public Employees (CUPE), thoughtful letters to the editor of the *Medicine Hat News*, and collective action by a group of twenty people, some with placards, who sat in the public gallery during the city council meeting of 21 December 1992.[53] The other response was a finesse move by Mayor Grimm and Alderman Kelly: they attempted to use city council's committee structure to neutralize the power of the majority on council.

The tradition in Medicine Hat at the time was for the mayor to assign council members to standing committees. After the 1992 election, Mayor Grimm struck a public services committee consisting of the only two aldermen who supported continuing municipal investment in model day care (Graham Kelly and Ken Sauer) along with the most outspoken critic of municipal day care services, chamber of commerce manager and newly elected alderman John Hamill. This committee structure had the potential to neutralize Hamill's opposition if he could be convinced to publicly support a compromise hammered out in the committee. Later, Graham Kelly commented that "Hamill was safer on the committee than off."[54]

At first it looked like this finesse strategy might work. The initial recommendation of the public services committee called for the city to continue to operate three of its day cares and review whether it should continue to operate its fourth centre, located at Medicine Hat College. Furthermore, it recommended that the amount spent on subsidizing the model day cares be reduced without setting any specific targets or timetable. Of note, Alderman Hamill was quoted as saying he agreed with the recommendations although he commented that "yearly deficits of $300,000 cannot continue."[55]

But the finesse strategy of Grimm and Kelly collapsed at a heated meeting of city council on 7 December 1992. The majority on council refused to endorse the recommendations of the public services committee and sent the matter back to the committee to "develop a solid mission statement [for city involvement in day care] accompanied by financial figures." At that meeting, John Hamill broke with his colleagues on the committee and "suggested the city phase out day care completely in three years."[56]

Even when faced with defeat, however, Mayor Grimm and Alderman Kelly skilfully manoeuvred to minimize the long-term damage to quality day care in Medicine Hat. Behind the scenes, a compromise was crafted whereby civil servants would have four years to gradually reduce the city's spending on preschool day care to zero (spending on other child care services was not an issue at the time). Graham Kelly commented that he supported the compromise because "it is what I felt would pass. Given the council it seems the alternative was to be out of day care completely in a few months." Not realizing the tight spot that Kelly and Grimm were in, supporters of municipal day cares were taken by surprise that this recommendation passed by a vote of nine to zero at the city council meeting of 21 December; they had not yet realized that, given the conservative slant of the new council, a phased withdrawal was the best possible outcome.[57]

By the end of 1993, Medicine Hat continued to operate its four day cares and FDH program; however, it had substantially reduced its subsidy to the day care at Medicine Hat College by getting the college itself to add $58,000 in yearly contributions. In 1995 the city turned the management of its Crescent Heights Centre over to a commercial operator, and at the beginning of 1996, the public school board took over the operation of the Herald Centre. Later that year, after

Medicine Hat contemplated closing its John Millar Centre, the YMCA agreed to become the operator. Therefore, by the end of 1996, four years after city council's decision to eliminate the deficit in day care, the administration had largely accomplished this task (although agreements with the school board and college made the city responsible for small amounts of transitional costs).[58]

Two additional actions in subsequent years completely eliminated the city's direct involvement in the provision of child care for preschoolers. First, in 1998 management of the college centre was turned over to a non-profit society. Second, the city ended its operation of a satellite FDH agency, with the YMCA and College Child Care Society filling the gap as operators of not-for-profit satellite FDH agencies.

Although Medicine Hat ended its direct sponsorship of lighthouse child care for preschoolers in the 1990s, it managed to find new operators for all of its former services. Indeed, in 1998 the Crescent Heights Centre was taken over by the YMCA from the commercial operator who had run it since 1995, thus putting all four former city day cares in the control of stable not-for-profit organizations. Similarly, not-for-profit agencies filled the gap created by the exit from the FDH field. In the end, the municipal government's withdrawal from preschool child care was managed in such a way as to preserve a strong not-for-profit alternative to commercial child care in Medicine Hat.

Looking back, it is unfortunate that day care was the lightning rod for the right-wing majority elected to city council in Medicine Hat in 1992, since there was probably sufficient support in the community, even at the height of the right-wing populist wave sweeping Alberta, for continuing this unique municipal system of child care. Mayor Grimm, for one, did not see the campaign against the municipal day cares as having a strong community basis. In a 1995 interview, he stated, "The day care issue was brought into the 1992 election as a means of attacking any social programs and their supporters. It was not necessarily an issue that was important to the community."[59]

It is significant that the attack on lighthouse day care in Medicine Hat occurred well before the end of flow-through CAP funding for Alberta municipalities. Had Medicine Hat not made the decision it did in 1992, it would have been faced with deciding how to respond to the end of CAP funding in 1996. Some cutbacks were inevitable given that CAP transfers for the municipal day cares in Medicine Hat were over $200,000 per year. Nevertheless, it is conceivable that the city could have comfortably supported a reduced municipal program of lighthouse child care after 1996.

My conclusion is that a crucial legacy of the PSS era was lost when the City of Medicine Hat privatized its four day cares and FDH program in the mid-1990s. Fortunately, each of these services continued under not-for-profit auspices, albeit without the ability to model as high a standard of child care or employee compensation as would have been possible with city subsidization.

Ending Municipal Day Care in Calgary: A Settling of Political Scores

At the end of the 1980s, Calgary was the only other Alberta city that ran as many as three municipal day cares. Although the city ended financial support for its day cares at about the same time as Medicine Hat, the circumstances of Calgary's withdrawal were much different, in keeping with local political factors.

Barbara Scott was elected to her seventh consecutive term as a Calgary alderman in 1989. After the municipal election, city council produced a strategic plan to guide its actions in the 1990s. The social issue highlighted in the plan was "How will we address social disparities and multicultural diversity?" As would be expected in a document of this type, many of the strategies proposed to address the city's "social challenges" were very general without any specific policy implications and, as a result, uncontroversial. An example was "Develop programs to help new Calgarians." However, one of the eighteen social strategies stood apart from the rest: it was the only one that took the form of an "instruction" to CSS and bore the unmistakable fingerprints of Alderman Barbara Scott: "Instruct the Social Services Department to change its role by reducing its involvement in direct services and to offer new, experimental programs, evaluate them and when appropriate turn them over to commercial or volunteer organizations" (Calgary 1990, 7). In an interview in 1995, Sam Blakely reported, "Privately I was told by one alderman that [Scott] developed the plan and the rest of them simply rubber stamped it." Any ambiguity about Barbara Scott's role in crafting this particular strategy or its implications for the municipal day cares was dispelled shortly after the strategic plan was released: Alderman Scott met with the staff of the municipal day cares, telling them that although no action would be taken right away, she expected the city would get out of running the day cares in about five years.[60]

Following on from its strategic plan, in late 1989, city council passed a motion proposed by Scott that CSS "review in total the operation of the municipal day care centres." That review, submitted in September 1990, demonstrated that the three municipal centres continued to be located in neighbourhoods with relatively high needs and offered many support services beyond child care. The review also argued that the city's required staff qualifications for its municipal centres (all staff had to hold an ECE diploma or certificate) resulted in a much higher standard of care than in other nearby day cares. The review concluded by pointing to "the City of Calgary's positive role in influencing the development and maintenance of high quality day care, and leadership in fair labour practices." In 1990, therefore, CSS bureaucrats defended the municipal day cares in the face of those (especially Barbara Scott) who wanted the city to get out of the direct provision of day care. Their resistance contrasts with what happened in Edmonton in 1984, when civil servants seemingly abandoned the city's only municipal centre (Glengarry) rather than pick a fight with local politicians.[61]

In Alderman Scott's view, CSS "was mostly an agency organization" (i.e., involved in the direct provision of services) and its managers (led by Sam Blakely) "weren't using their staff well. The research and planning components, for example, were totally missing; community development was totally missing."[62] It was some time, however, before Barbara Scott hit upon a process that would back CSS into a corner and force them to close or privatize the municipal day cares.

> We set up a social challenges implementation committee and again talked about community development, talked with a whole bunch of people including parks and rec and others. And social services was very, very slow on the draw. You know the bureaucrats rule—the elected officials have power to state but in terms of implementation it's very, very tough if bureaucrats don't want to implement. And so we got promises from the [laugh] department that in order to develop this community development they'd have to do reports. So they did report after report after report and it took a long time to do the reports. [more laughter] And so we were having no progress whatsoever. The social services department was one of very few departments that had not had a value-for-money [VFM] audit done. And as the audit committee was looking at the various departments for a VFM audit they came to me and said "What about social services?" and I said "Great."

The evidence indicates that Alderman Scott managed (some might say manipulated) this particular VFM audit in order to get a recommendation to close the municipally run day cares. First, she agreed to chair the audit task force. Second, she personally recruited Alderman Sue Higgins to be the vice-chair knowing that Higgins, as a fiscal conservative with little expertise in social services, could be counted upon to be sympathetic to the sorts of facile arguments against city-run day cares that were routinely offered by owners of commercial day cares. Indeed, Alderman Higgins said she found the decision to recommend closure of the municipal day cares to be a relatively easy one compared to decisions she had made in VFM audits of other departments: "We had statistics to prove that there were four hundred vacant day care spaces in the private sector. Well, government should not be providing the same services in competition with the private sector because all of our services are subsidized by the taxpayer."[63] Alderman Higgins gave no indication in her interview that she appreciated what constituted quality day care or recognized that Calgary's municipal day cares provided a substantially higher standard of care than most commercial centres.

Third, the two citizen members of the audit task force were nominated and selected by the other members of the task force, thus ensuring that neither of the citizen members would be a strong advocate for continuing municipal involvement in preschool child care.[64] Fourth, Alderman Scott allowed the VFM audit to proceed with minimal input from CSS and almost no input from the staff and clients of Calgary's municipal day cares. The first step in the audit was a study by a consulting team "to identify and recommend opportunities for cost reduction and service improvement." The consulting team, which included representation from the city's management audit staff, was led by two partners of the large accounting and audit firm KPMG. A manager in CSS reported that his department "was hardly consulted at all" by the consulting team. Furthermore, the line staff, co-ordinators, and supervisors in the day cares "were not consulted." In contrast, in VFM audits of departments conducted at the City of Calgary prior to 1993, staff were involved to a much greater degree.[65]

The task force did not organize and mediate a dialogue between the consulting team and department aimed at achieving a consensual set of recommendation. "My sense of the [audit task force report]," remarked Calgary Alderman Bob Hawkesworth, "is that the consultants had their day in court and that the department was left to try and influence things at the very end but didn't really have that much of a voice in the formulation of the final recommendations that went forward."[66]

Conducting a VFM audit of the City of Calgary's model child care programs in 1993–94 was a difficult and highly political task since there is no standard or simple measure of the "value" of quality child care. The task was complicated by the fact that the consultants were directed to compare the value of existing programs (such as municipal day cares) with the value of proposed new programs (such as community development and research). One of the KPMG partners reported that Barb Scott's audit task force "clearly wanted us [the consultants] to express an opinion" on whether the city should be running direct social services.[67] The consultants would have known Barb Scott's view on this question from the start of the exercise; it is hard to believe that the way they approached the audit was not shaped by this knowledge.

A CSS manager argued that this "was not a value-for-money audit in the strict sense of the word (improvements, efficiency, value for money, etc.)." Rather, the manager thought the process was "driven by an ideology and particular point of view" and included "elements of personal vendetta." ("One of the aldermen on the task force was at odds with the director on a lot of issues.") Sam Blakely believed that "essentially the decision to close the [municipal day cares] had been made some time ago. And I was never convinced that the audit team had anything in mind other than to privatize everything, or privatize as much as they could." In his view, Alderman Scott's push to end the department's role in the provision of services was not merely "a change of direction" but rather "a dismantling of the department." Sam Blakely retired prior to the conclusion of the VFM audit because he did not want to be part of a decision he saw as a "giant step backwards."[68]

The VFM audit task force prepared a list of forty-three recommendations for Calgary's audit committee. The recommendation on day care read, "That the Social Services Department find alternative means for the delivery of direct childcare services and the Department bring forward to Audit Committee an implementation plan describing how this will be accomplished, no later than November 1994." Ending the city's model preschool child care would free up $1.3 million (later estimated at $1.4 million) for reallocation to other priorities.[69]

The audit committee itself was composed of a citizen representative and seven aldermen, only one of whom had been a member of the task force (Sue Higgins). The meeting focussed on the recommendation to get the city out of running day cares and featured a presentation by Noreen Murphy of the Calgary Regional Association for Quality Child Care, who defended the efficacy of the municipal day cares. She stated, "Your services have been the model for the rest of us." In particular, she highlighted the fact that Calgary's day cares have been "able to deal with special needs cases which other centres can not easily handle."[70]

The audit committee supported the task force's recommendation that the city cease operating child care services, with two dissenting votes. The recommendation was then forwarded to city council. The task force had also recommended that the city close its juvenile probation service for a saving of $895,000, although it said it would withdraw this recommendation if it could be demonstrated that the rate of juvenile recidivism in Calgary was superior to that in Edmonton, where the municipal government did not run its own service.[71] In fact the recommendation was withdrawn when the evidence of the superiority of Calgary's service was reported. The supporters of Calgary's municipal day cares hoped that a similar opportunity to prove their worth would be offered by city council. When the audit committee recommendations came before council later in May 1994, Alderman Hawkesworth "made a motion that we apply the same test or the same opportunity to all the other potential outsourced programs [as had been applied to Juvenile Probation]. That motion failed by one vote."[72]

It is significant that the vote in council on this "stay-of-execution" motion was so close. It indicates that there was relatively soft support among Calgary's elected politicians for Barb Scott's vision of a revamped social services department.

It would be an understatement to say that the staff members at the municipal day cares were disappointed with the city's decision to close or privatize their centres and with the process that led to the decision. Laurie Doyle, the senior planner at the Shaganappi Day Care, remarked that the staff at her centre "felt very devalued. They felt cheated because no one actually came here to interview staff or to compare our care to other people's care. All they did was phone some private day cares and said, 'What are your regulations? And what are ours?' They didn't compare quality at all. Quite angry. And disappointed." In the view of a social services manager, the disappointment of the city's child care workers was doubled when "they were not given the opportunity to demonstrate their effectiveness, etc. as the juvenile probation program was."[73]

Part of the reason for the disappointment of city employees was that they were losing excellent jobs that would be very difficult to replace. Tammy Baldwin, a supervisor at Connaught Day Care, understood this. After graduating from Mount Royal College in 1985, she had been hired as a supervisor in a commercial day care. She soon learned that there were staff in that centre "who were very inappropriate with children." She also "realized quite quickly that it was a very unrecognized field by society. I became very angry almost in a sense when I would hear that people would pay their cleaning lady ten dollars an hour but the most anybody was prepared to pay me to look after their children was five or six, at that time. I felt very underpaid." Within a year of her graduation in ECE, Tammy Baldwin left the field. She returned five years later when she got a job in a city-run day care. "Finally I really felt that I was making a difference because people appreciated what I was doing," she stated. "I was able to learn from the people around me because they were all very professional and finally being paid appropriately for what I was doing. I would have to say that the last four and a half years for me working for the City of Calgary has been the very best part of my career in early childhood."

Tammy Baldwin's comments highlight the importance of Calgary's municipal day cares as a model for employee compensation and treatment. Just as important, the day cares were models of quality care that made a huge difference in the lives of children and their families. As disappointed as Baldwin was at losing her own job in a city-run day care, she was even more disappointed in the needless loss of a service that made a real difference in day care in Calgary.[74]

After city council's decision in May 1994, the initial plan was for the city to continue its involvement in preschool child care until the end of 1996. The proposed transition period of approximately thirty months was somewhat shorter than the four years taken in Medicine Hat but probably would have allowed civil servants to organize the transfer of all of the city-run services (the three day cares plus the Shaganappi FDH program) to stable not-for-profit organizations. In late 1994, however, the processes of privatization in the two cities diverged sharply when Calgary announced it would end its support for lighthouse child care on 31 August 1995. In Medicine Hat, sympathetic members of city council worked in concert with municipal civil servants between 1993 and 1996 to ensure that the rich legacy of municipal involvement in day care was not entirely lost. This did not happen in Calgary.

Calgary hired a new director of social services in September 1994. Judy Bader came to her position from the Northwest Territories. She was praised by the staff in the day cares for pushing the city to offer an excellent severance package, including generous opportunities for counselling and retraining. However, she lacked the commitment of her predecessor to the city-run day cares and thus failed to insist upon a transition timeline that would have given a public institution, the YMCA, or a community association time to plan for a takeover of a service. A big difference between Medicine Hat and Calgary at this time is that none of the right-wing councillors in Medicine Hat pushed for the speedy closure or privatization of the municipal day cares while in Calgary, Alderman Scott was unsympathetic to any delay since she saw the end of the municipal day care system as unfinished business from the 1970s. The withdrawal date of 31 August 1995 conveniently fell just prior to Barb Scott's retirement from municipal politics, meaning that Scott would not have to worry about a new council having second thoughts on the matter once she was gone.[75]

On 31 August 1995, two of Calgary's municipal day cares closed (Shaganappi and Connaught) while the third day care (Bridgeland) and the Shaganappi FDH program were taken over by organizations headed by groupings of staff. Bridgeland went to a new not-for-profit association directed by two former city employees, Christine Sheppard and Nora Capithorn. They reported working many nights until midnight on the details of the takeover, and even then they barely had enough time to get everything done by 1 September 1995. This is further evidence of the folly of the municipal government's decision to end its involvement in day care on such short notice. All of the staff initially hired by Sheppard and Capithorn had formerly worked in city-run centres. The new, privatized Bridgeland Day Care paid them 35 percent less than the city had and offered no benefits. At first the CUPE local that represents Calgary's inside workers continued to represent the employees of the privatized day care. In 1995 Nora Capithorn reported that the negotiations with the union had gone well; to facilitate the transition, the union waived the workers' union dues for one year. By the end of the 1990s, however, the union had been decertified.[76]

Calgary originally established its three municipal day cares in the 1970s as PSS projects in high-needs areas. The idealistic thinking at the time was that preschool children with readily identifiable special needs should not be ghettoized: PSS day cares should serve the full range of children in their communities. Another important feature of PSS day cares was that, guided by the insights of social work and ECE, they recognized and responded to a wide range of special needs in children.

By the early 1990s, however, much narrower definitions of prevention and special needs were at play. Laurie Doyle noted that although city aldermen professed concern for what would happen to the special needs children enrolled in the municipal day cares,

they were looking at special needs children as just the ones with the visible handicaps. They weren't looking at our special needs children who are children who have difficulty in any aspect of their learning, whether it's their social skills or their cognitive skills, and they're the ones who fall through the cracks, and nobody was interested in what happened to those children.[77]

The truncated policy debate in Calgary between 1993 and 1995 centred on the question of whether high-quality day care for a clientele of predominantly poor children was a good enough reason for the provision of public subsidies. The same issue had been raised almost a decade earlier in Edmonton when the city began asking MADCs to become family resource centres and provide a range of preventive services, on top of high-quality day care. As was noted in the first part of this chapter, some of the MADCs were quicker to respond to the new expectations than others, but the city did not impose significant financial penalties on the recalcitrant centres in the 1980s. This changed in the mid-1990s.

Bending in the Political Wind of the Mid-1990s: Repackaging or Abandonment?

In both Medicine Hat and Calgary, the initiative for ending municipal support for lighthouse day care came from elected members of council. In Edmonton, however, the initiative came from municipal civil servants who argued that it was necessary to pre-emptively transform how the city spent money on pre-school children rather than risk losing the money entirely. A further key difference between Edmonton and the other two cities concerned the strength of the lobby for continued municipal funding of day care. Although in the early 1990s Edmonton spent less money on day care than either Medicine Hat or Calgary, it spread its spending over eighteen MADCs compared to the three municipal centres funded by Calgary and the four by Medicine Hat. This meant that Edmonton had a fairly large group of parents, staff, and board members with a vested interest in continued city funding of the MADCs. In turn, this interest group benefited from the fact that advocates for quality child care played a much more important role in Edmonton's civic culture than they did in either of the other cities. Among these advocates were city councillor Michael Phair, who was a former president of the AAYC, and the executive director of the Clifford E. Lee Foundation, Judy Padua.

A 1985 review of day care in Edmonton proposed that MADCs supply a range of specialized services (such as parent training) in addition to quality day care. The 1985 review was conducted shortly after long-time provincial civil servant John Lackey had become the general manager of ESS. In the late 1970s and early 1980s, the leaders of ESS presumed that their city had a duty to support lighthouse child care since the provincial government was doing so little to promote quality care. Lackey, however, came to the job with a provincial bureaucrat's view that cities had no jurisdiction over day care per se and with a relatively high opinion of the quality of commercial day care given that his wife, Barbel Lackey, was the owner-operator of a small commercial centre in Edmonton.[78]

Kathy Barnhart was hired as the manager of children's services for the City of Edmonton in 1990. In a 1996 interview, she reported that from the time she started her job, the internal discussion in the department "has always been, 'Why are we funding day cares?'" Furthermore, she indicated that there was a consensus among the managers in the department in the early 1990s that the MADC system could not be sustained because day care was no longer a city service. Their message to the existing MADCs was "You've got to do something different. You've got to package what you're doing in a way that is going to be politically correct in order to save it."[79]

Lana Sampson was hired as the executive director of the Edmonton Northwest Child Care Society in 1993. The society had opened a PSS day care in 1977 and later added an OOSC centre at a neighbouring school. It considerably expanded its scope in 1987 when it won the contract to manage integrated day care in the entire Edmonton region and later became the major agency in Edmonton organizing therapeutic and rehabilitative services for preschoolers with special educational needs. (This is the community preschool education program funded by the province's education department.) In a 1998 interview, she recollected that "John Lackey told us four, five years ago, if you don't start calling yourselves child and family resource centres you're never going to get anywhere because as long as you continue to call yourself 'day care,' people are going to have this idea about what it is you do." Her organization "jumped on it [John Lackey's vision] immediately," renaming itself "Community Options: A Society for Children and Families"; a second day care, started in 1997, was called a "Child and Family Resource Centre."[80]

The recollections of Kathy Barnhart and Lana Sampson indicate that from at least 1990 and probably before then, senior municipal civil servants in Edmonton were uncomfortable with the orientation of the MADC program. This explains why ESS (renamed Edmonton Community and Family Services [ECFS] in 1989)[81] never championed and advocated for the MADCs under John Lackey's leadership the way that it had under Keith Wass and Ande Dorosh (see chapters 3 to 5). It also indicates that although situational factors in the early to mid-1990s are important to understanding what happened to Edmonton's program of lighthouse day cares, the underlying impetus for change was a longstanding policy agenda of municipal civil servants.

There is a definite parallel between what transpired in Calgary and Edmonton: in both cities frustrated policy entrepreneurs took advantage of favourable situational conditions to launch attacks on municipally supported model day cares. In Calgary, the policy entrepreneur was the longest-serving alderman (Barb Scott) while in Edmonton, it was the leaders of Edmonton Community and Family Services (ECFS). However, while Alderman Scott utilized a VFM audit process in order to attack Calgary's municipal day cares, Edmonton's civil servants utilized a special preschool task force (PTF) to attack the existing system of MADCs. Hence the process in Edmonton was conducted in a more democratic forum than in Calgary, making for a more complex political struggle.

The first situational factor that affected the political debates over the future of MADCs in Edmonton was a growing interest among more senior levels of government in early intervention programs for children. The decision of Brian Mulroney's federal government against pursuing a national child care program after being re-elected in 1988 created a policy vacuum in the area of children's programs. It was filled by the Brighter Futures initiative, announced in May 1992. The inclusive-liberal philosophy of this initiative was that government programs for young children should assist children with the greatest needs instead of being universal in coverage. The Child Tax Benefit officially replaced universal family allowances as a means to redistribute income for the care of young children (Young 2000, 32). The second main component of the initiative was the Community Action Program for Children (CAPC), which provided funding for demonstration community-initiated early intervention projects aimed at high-risk children.

The governments of Canada and Alberta signed a protocol in August 1993 that made CAPC money available for projects in Alberta. It specified "that programs be targeted to children at risk because of factors such as low income, remote or isolated living conditions, youth or inexperience of parents, family breakdown and abuse or neglect." Slightly over $4 million per year was promised for each of the first four years of CAPC in Alberta. At a time when the provincial government was slashing its spending on social services (including day care; see chapter 7), this modest investment seemed like a big deal to community groups and municipal governments. However, the first round of competition funded only twelve projects and exhausted $11.2 million of the $17.4 million that had been committed until 1997. These initial funded projects in Alberta were representative of the "crazy quilt of programs" that CAPC created across Canada. They included a play program for children staying at a women's shelter in Lloydminister, programs for teenage mothers in both Edmonton and Calgary, and parenting classes in Fairview and High Level. The sort of program that was most frequently funded, however, was Head Start preschools for children from disadvantaged families.[82]

The provincial government soon jumped on this bandwagon. In 1995 it began its own early intervention program and committed $50 million over three years, with half of the money reserved for Aboriginal programs. These policy initiatives indicated that early intervention and Head Start were as much in favour in Alberta as day care was out of favour. In 1998 Lana Sampson wryly observed, "If we [the MADCs in Edmonton] had all changed our names to Head Start we'd have nothing but money."[83]

The second situational factor was the dire financial straits of both day cares and the City of Edmonton. Day cares were attempting to cope with the reductions in operating allowances that had begun in 1990 (table 7.1). Meanwhile, the city was faced with massive cuts in transfer payments as the Klein government attempted to eliminate the provincial deficit. The municipal assistance grant was cut by 77 percent over three years, starting in 1994, and the FCSS grant was decreased by 14 percent in 1994 as part of an 18 percent cut to Family and Social Services (Mansell 1997, 58). The reduction in the FCSS grant meant that ECFS had to cut either FCSS programs or other taxpayer-supported programs. In early 1995, Kathy Barnhart wrote, "Preschool day care, while seen as an important service in the community, is one service area that the Department proposed could be cut." To compound the problem, the city received $4 million a year in flow-through federal funding that would disappear when CAP was terminated in 1996.[84]

In 1994 Maria David-Evans was the manager of the operations branch of ECFS. She was also a longstanding member of the board of the Clifford E. Lee Foundation. As a consequence, the leadership of the foundation was very well informed that municipal civil servants were not prepared to support the status quo when it came to the MADC program. Furthermore, the foundation was in the advantageous position of having the confidence of the directors of the MADCs because it had provided so many grants to these day cares over the years. It thus came to realize that the centres and the bureaucrats were, in the words of executive director Judy Padua, "on a collision course." While the bureaucrats insisted on change,

a lot of them [MADCs] are reluctant to plan for it because they didn't think it should happen. They ran a good centre, they had trained staff, they had needy children, they had families that needed them. They weren't doing anything wrong and they had to have that money to continue to operate. So I think their strategy was just to try and convince the city that they shouldn't change anything. And the city kept saying, we have to change things.

The leadership of the foundation believed that "the boards and the directors of the [municipally] funded centres were not prepared for what was going to happen when the City downsized.... So we thought, these centres have to wake up to the fact that things are going to change big in the next few years, and they have to have a plan to do that." Consequently, the foundation initiated and funded an extensive strategic planning process. Unfortunately, the process concluded with a summary of discussions and questions instead of a strategic plan.[85]

In April 1994, the Community Services Committee of Edmonton City Council requested that ECFS report back on the results of the MADC strategic planning. Kathy Barnhart prepared a fairly innocuous, brief report for the municipal politicians. She used the occasion, however, to make two recommendations that were designed to lead to the significant changes that the department advocated. The first was for the establishment of a PTF with a mandate that assumed the end of the MADC system as it then existed: the PTF was "to direct municipal funding to preventative services targeted at a broader range of children and families in poverty commencing January 1, 1996." The second was for a review of the terms of reference of the Children's Services Committee, which just so happened to be controlled by supporters of the MADCs.[86]

The MADC lobby correctly perceived these recommendations as an end run and tried to get city council to refer the recommendations "to the Children's Services Committee and the Municipally-Approved Day Care Centres Association for their comments." Left-wing councillors Tooker Gomberg and Sherry McKibben sponsored this amendment at the council meeting of 8 November 1994; the amendment lost by a vote of eleven to two. In the vote on the main motion to establish a PTF, only Gomberg voted in opposition.

Despite this vote, the MADC lobby continued to object to the process. For instance, on 21 November 1994, the executive director and board chair of one of the city-supported day cares, the Oliver School Centre, copied a letter of protest to all members of council. They accused the municipal bureaucrats of claiming to have consulted the MADCs on the idea of a PTF even though no such consultation took place. They then suggested that, rather than constitute a new task force, "the existing Strategic Planning Group continue and that other interest groups join in this already working body." That same day, Lana Sampson of Edmonton

Northwest Child Care Society distributed a letter that made similar points using even stronger language. For instance, she argued "that the Department misled the Council by allowing them to believe the Department's recommendations were somehow related to the Strategic Planning already in process, when in fact, the recommendations were a negation of what has been an exemplary exercise in community development that is actually yielding some constructive results."[87]

Apparently the lobbying had some effect, since the question of whether to proceed with the PTF was discussed at a city council retreat held on 23 January 1995. In briefing notes prepared for the retreat, ECFS reviewed the federal and provincial initiatives in the area of early intervention and concluded, "There is no question that early intervention strategies that help disadvantaged children get off to a good start are a wise investment for the municipality." The PTF was presented as a way for the city to move in this direction, but the objections to the PTF at the council retreat were sufficiently loud that John Lackey felt it necessary to argue in favour of proceeding as planned in a memo to Mayor Jan Reimer dated 27 January 1995. Shortly thereafter, the department was given the go-ahead and the first meeting of the PTF was held on 15 February.[88]

As part of its deliberations, the PTF considered the extent to which MADCs served children living in poverty. They relied upon data provided by the department and came to conclusions that were surprisingly superficial and biased. For instance, they used "number of subsidized families" as an indication of the number of low-income families in a day care when, because the "break-even points" for subsidy qualification were so low in Alberta at the time (table A.6), many of the unsubsidized families might well have been low income. Even then, however, only four of the sixteen MADCs had more unsubsidized than subsidized children.

More disturbingly, the MADCs were dismissed because many of their subsidized clients were students or welfare recipients. The department reported to the PTF that 21 percent of the spaces in the MADCs in May 1995 were occupied by children from student families and an additional 7 percent were occupied by children from welfare families, and that these two groups of children were subsidized by city taxpayers in the amount of $387,930. At the 4 May meeting of the PTF, Chair Doris Badir stated, "These two scenarios could be funded from other sources, i.e., Student Loans and Provincial Day Care Subsidies. The time has come for us to focus on how to redirect funding available for the benefit of children at risk." Given that the MADCs were obliged to accept all applicants from subsidized families without discrimination, it is hard to fathom that these statistics were held against the MADCs. Furthermore, it is disturbing to see the

PTF engaged in the invidious exercise of distinguishing the deserving from the undeserving categories of poor children. Finally, it is fair to ask why the department did not break down the clientele of the MADCs by family status since many of those supposedly privileged children from student families would have been in female-headed, lone-parent families.[89]

The fact that the PTF wanted to end Edmonton's support for model day cares (although certain day cares might secure funding for early intervention components of their programs) engendered some critical submissions in the late spring and summer of 1995. The most important written submissions received by the PTF came from two veteran advocates for quality child care. The first, from former AAYC president Eva Roche, was dated just a few weeks before her death from cancer. She argued for "retaining, and enhancing, models of quality day care as benchmarks towards which parents and the system can work." In a classic defence of the lighthouse system, Roche asked: "If there are no quality day-care centres for parents to observe, how can parents demand good care for their children? What will be the incentive for centres to improve the quality of care they offer? How will they know what good day care is?"

The second submission was from Judy Padua on behalf of the children's subcommittee of the Clifford E. Lee Foundation Board. She offered general support for concentrating city support on children living in poverty, but added, "It is of vital concern to us that low income families continue to have access to good quality child care and related programs and that a 'critical mass' of demonstration and 'lighthouse' centres continue to be assisted by the City, albeit a smaller number than is currently the case." The reason for continuing to support such centres was that "such centres demonstrably have served to elevate the overall quality of childcare services to children in Edmonton." In 1998 Judy Padua commented, "I can understand why people think you should only subsidize low income parents, but if you don't in some way make the infrastructure survivable, you're no help to the subsidized parents, there won't be a service there to pay for." She also noted, "Everyone steers away from day care. It's got so much baggage attached to the name that they don't look at it as a site where you might have 60 or 70 kids, many of whom come from families with lots of problems."[90]

There is no evidence that these thoughtful defences of the lighthouse system of day cares were taken seriously by either department officials or the members of the PTF. The final report of the PTF made no mention of the need for lighthouse day care and did not even acknowledge that there was a plausible case for continuing to fund some day cares as model centres.

The recommendations of the PTF were presented to city council just after the October 1995 election that saw the defeat of three members of council's left-wing (Mayor Reimer and Councillors Gomberg and McKibben). In Medicine Hat, a swing to the Right on city council in 1992 had been the decisive factor in the decision to end the municipal day care program. The 1995 municipal election results had no direct bearing on what happened in Edmonton, however, since the old council, like the new one, would have voted overwhelmingly in support of the PTF recommendations. Indeed, Sherry McKibben had been a member of the PTF and was an unequivocal supporter of those recommendations.

The MADCs were given a final year of transitional funding and then had the option, starting in 1997, of competing with other organizations for early intervention program funding through FCSS. In 1998, ten of the original eighteen MADCs received FCSS funding. Of the eight centres that no longer received city funding, some had voluntarily withdrawn because they did not have a large number of subsidized children and some "were told not to bother to apply." One of the centres that continued to receive supplemental funding from the city was Edmonton Northwest/Community Options, which received an enhancement grant of $68,000 in 1998 for quality features of its day care that exceeded provincial licensing standards, such as a cook to provide breakfasts and hot lunches, and the requirement that all staff have an ECE diploma. That same year, the Community Day Nursery (CDN) received an enhancement grant of $74,000. It is noteworthy that these enhancement grants were each within $3,000 of the grant each day care had received from MADC funding in 1995 (ECFS 1995, 27). Therefore, although a new funding mechanism was in place, historical commitments to former MADCs were apparently being respected when those day cares served a high proportion of subsidized children.[91]

Nevertheless, relations between the city and the MADCs were far from smooth in 1998. Key members of the Children's Services Committee resigned after council accepted the recommendations of the PTF, the Children's Services Committee was once again classified as a subcommittee, and, in the words of Lana Sampson, "the Children's Services Sub-Committee somehow got lost in the shuffle and basically didn't have a job to do anymore." In turn, FCSS funding recommendations were turned over to the Community and Family Services Advisory Committee (CAFSAC). Whereas the members of the Children's Services Committee had been relatively knowledgeable about quality child care and sympathetic toward the MADCs, some of the members of CAFSAC were neither knowledgeable nor sympathetic.

Edmonton Northwest/Community Options' application for an FCSS grant for its main day care was approved without a hitch in both 1997 and 1998. Executive Director Lana Sampson was uneasy with how the city was proceeding at that time. She lacked confidence in the judgement of some of the members of CAFSAC and was disturbed by the cavalier way that CAFSAC had rejected Community Options' application for a second FCSS grant in the 1998 competition.[92]

Lana Sampson also reported that some of the old MADCs were treated rudely when they presented their funding proposals to CAFSAC in late 1997. This surprised her "because we've had such a really good relationship with the Children's Services Sub-Committee. These people were our friends. We were in this business together.... This was a longstanding relationship, twenty-five years.... We certainly don't feel collectively the support or the commitment or anything else from this new order that was felt from the Children's Services Sub-Committee, not by a long shot."

One of the day cares that expected but did not receive collegial treatment was the CDN (renamed the CDN Family Support Centre to keep in step with the times), which was required to appear twice before CAFSAC in late 1997. According to the day care's director, Mary Hull, CAFSAC members "drove home to us the importance of board and staff fundraising." Their message was "Don't ask us for money; apply to foundations." She commented that the experience got under her skin since the general tone of CAFSAC was "you do it or else." In Mary Hull's view, something was wrong in the relationship between Edmonton and the MADCs in 1998: "All we've ever done is program enhancement. We're preventive programs, we've always been that." Yet, she added, "nobody has recognized what these day cares have done."

Although the CDN received the same program-enhancement FCSS grant in 1998 as it had in 1997, Mary Hull was not particularly optimistic about the future prospects of the day care when I spoke to her in March 1998. The city had recently increased the day care's rent by $300 a month (23 percent) and turned down a request for a grant to help the CDN pay for its rent and utilities. Furthermore, both the CDN and the Glengarry Day Care were under threat to begin paying municipal property taxes, something they had never done; for the CDN, the tax bill would have amounted to approximately $10,000 per year. Meanwhile the day care was having trouble coping with the decrease in provincial operating allowances since "we can't in all conscience surcharge our parents" to make up for the loss in revenue; the parent surcharge had just been increased by $15 per month (to $65) in February 1998. Mary Hull also noted that the CDN was not attracting any new Level 3 (ECE diploma) staff since the starting salary of $1,400 per month was so low. Most ominously, she reported that experienced, qualified workers were being paid far less in 1998 than they had been in 1978. "Maybe it is time for Community Day to close," she said.[93]

At the time, I found this possibility to be improbable. The CDN had been the first day care in Alberta to receive provincial funding, and Mary Hull had been the first person in Edmonton to demonstrate how young children could learn through play in a group setting. Furthermore, the CDN continued to offer a superb program in the same converted city garage into which it had moved in 1966. Even if the members of CAFSAC seemed to have no sense of history and could not see the incredible community value of what had been happening at the CDN for over ten thousand days of operation, I fully expected some group to intercede and ensure that the CDN would continue.

But I was wrong. The CDN closed on 30 March 2001 after over thirty-five years of operation, including thirty-four and a half years with Mary Hull as the director. In the months before the closure, enrolment had fallen to approximately thirty children compared to forty-five children in 1998, fifty in 1995, and over sixty in the 1970s. The enhancement grant from the city had been cut to reflect the decline in the enrolment after 1998. Mary Hull commented at the time of the closure, "In this era of per capita funding and volunteer fundraising, the nursery could no longer make a go of it."[94]

It is also fair to say that the CDN under Mary Hull's leadership resisted playing the game expected of Hull by the city's bureaucrats in the 1990s, and the day care suffered as a result. Hull's daughter Rae captured this aspect of the CDN's last few years in an astute newspaper commentary:

> You were old-fashioned in some ways, sceptical of a bureaucracy and government that paid lip-service to those values you lived by every day. You winced at the introduction of programs that were resplendent in policy and process but bereft of true creativity or common sense. You stood firm. When you might well have benefited from becoming more proficient lobbyists, or creators of revenue-generating streams to augment critically short budgets, you knew what you did best. You were highly skilled and trained in the care and the development of tiny human beings entrusted to you.

The stories on the closure of the CDN called it "a very special place," "a gem," and a place of "magic." Rae Hull even made the bold statement that the child care provided by the CDN was done "as well as it has ever been done anywhere in the world." The Community Day Nursery was indeed an exceptional centre and deserves to be remembered as one of the finest examples of day care in Alberta's history.[95]

The CDN was one of the four former MADCs that folded between 1995 and 2005. However, fourteen of the eighteen original MADCs remained open in 2005, and nine of these centres received FCSS funding from the city that year. Indeed, the total of the FCSS grants provided to these nine centres in 2005 (about $859,000; see table 8.3) was not appreciably lower than the funding provided through the MADC program in 1995 (about $913,000). At first glance, one might be tempted to conclude that Edmonton continued to offer significant support to quality day cares in 2005 although it hid that support within a larger FCSS funding envelope. The reality is not quite so straightforward, however. Two points must be noted.

First, between 1995 and 2005, the share of city grants going to day cares fell from 37.4 percent to 9.5 percent. This was a period when the pot of money available for grants to social service agencies grew from $2.4 million to $9 million (table 8.3). The growth of funds was such that the municipal government could have reinstituted a modest lighthouse day care program (say, involving five day cares, each subsidized at $200,000) and still had plenty of new money for other agencies. The failure to take this step is confirming evidence that Edmonton stopped supporting lighthouse day cares because of policy convictions rather than mere financial exigencies.[96]

Second, although all of the money provided through MADC grants in 1995 went toward directly enhancing the quality of day care centres' programming, most of the money provided through FCSS grants in 2005 went toward community outreach or family support programs. Indeed, only one of the nine day cares (Beverly) clearly specified that it was using some of its grant to enhance the quality of care in its day care (although the descriptions of four of the other funded FCSS projects were sufficiently vague that some of the money could well have been funnelled into their day cares). Therefore, my conclusion is that most of the FCSS money received by the nine former MADCs in 2005 was not going into their day cares. Thus, the City of Edmonton's support for lighthouse day cares had ended in practice as well as in name.[97]

As was the case in Medicine Hat and Calgary, Edmonton's decision to end municipal support for model day cares involved important local political actors and issues. At the same time, because Edmonton's decision was made with the

TABLE 8.3 Supplemental Funding for Edmonton Day Cares, 1995 and 2005

	1995	2005
Centres with MADC funding in 1995 and FCSS funding in 2005		
Beverly	$99,999	$133,566
West End (City West)	$63,793	$107,115
Edmonton NW (Community Options)	$65,517	$126,232
Fulton Place	$58,621	$57,390
Glengarry	$73,275	$66,000
Jasper Place	$60,345	$119,512
Lansdowne	$68,965	$70,000
Oliver School Centre	$67,762	$110,416
Primrose Place	$43,103	$68,763
Former MADC centres still open in 2005 but without FCSS funding		
Garneau/University	$0	$0
Students' Union (University of Alberta)	$47,790	$0
Oliver (Glenora)	$34,483	$0
King Edward	$15,000	$0
Hospitals and Community	$31,035	$0
Former MADC centres closed in 2005		
Malmo	$10,560	n.a.
Community Day	$75,862	n.a.
South Edmonton	$55,172	n.a.
Grant MacEwan South Campus	$42,000	n.a.
Total	$913,282	$858,994
Total FCSS funding, Edmonton	$2,444,537	$9,018,329
% of total FCSS funding spent on programs run by these day cares	37.4%	9.5%

SOURCES: For a list of MADCs in 1990: memo from David Gilbert to Kathy Barnhart, "Report of a Brief Visit," 23 August 1990 (a copy of this document is available from the author). For funding in 1995: ECFS 1995, 27. For funding in 2005: "City of Edmonton 2005 FCSS-Funded Programs" (document, dated 9 February 2005, was downloaded from the City of Edmonton's website and is available from the author).

end of CAP flow-through funding just around the corner, with the city already dealing with the Klein government's cutbacks to municipal grants, and with funding for new federal and provincial early-intervention programs in place, national and provincial factors were referred to much more frequently in Edmonton than in the other two cities. This is partly because the national and provincial factors were somewhat more germane in 1995 than in 1992 (Medicine Hat) or 1994 (Calgary), but mainly because Edmonton's bureaucrats faced stiff opposition in their move to end the MADC program and hence had to draw upon all available arguments in an attempt to make their case. Their basic argument was that funding for the MADCs would not survive for long in this new economic and political environment, and hence there was no choice but to consider an alternative. This turned out to be a very effective rhetorical move. However, in retrospect, it is easy to see how a scaled-down lighthouse day care program, along the lines suggested by Eva Roche and Judy Padua in 1995, could have survived in this environment if city bureaucrats had backed this option and worked with advocates to pressure city councillors. In the end, it was the determined actions of local political players in Edmonton, just as in Medicine Hat and Calgary, that constituted the primary impetus to end the city's support for lighthouse day cares.

Ideological Commitment Rules the Day in Grande Prairie

Grande Prairie was an outlier among Alberta's six major cities in 1991 because it spent next to nothing on child care. Indeed, its spending of $0.30 per capita was less than one-fifth of the per capita spending by the next lowest ranked city, Red Deer, and was only about 4 percent of the per capita spending by Medicine Hat (calculated from data in table 8.2). However, the city continued to be involved in model child care for preschoolers by operating an FDH program.

This was a small, stable satellite program that never had more than twenty FDHs. Tanice Jones became the coordinator of the program in 1983 and stayed in that position until it closed in 1996. She indicated that the city maintained a high-quality standard by being very choosy about who to take on as FDH providers. "We really emphasize a lot the professionalism," she stated in 1996, noting that somewhat less than 50 percent of the prospective providers who submitted formal applications were ultimately hired by the municipal program. She went on to explain what she looked for in a provider:

I've hired people who don't think that their house is very nice and this kind of thing, but you know that they value child care very, very, very much. And they're not just saying, "I love children." Because a lot of times you get that, "I love children. I just think they're the greatest." And they go on and on and on and on. But somebody who truly, like you can tell, truly, truly thinks of this as very important work, you know, those are the type of people we are looking for. It's a style, I guess that's what it is. And it's that professionalism. Like this is a job.

People that understand what the responsibility is of child care. Like they're with those people's children more waking hours that their parents are. The responsibility that they have in raising those children is so important. And the people who already know that are the people I am most interested in.

The city's FDH agency was relatively well staffed compared to other agencies, with a coordinator and a home visitor who worked three-quarter time. This staffing for twenty or fewer homes meant than each home got a minimum of two visits a month, one of which concentrated on the provider and the other on the children.[98]

In 1995 Grande Prairie charged parents $18.75 per day for care in one of its day homes. In a month with twenty-one days of service, parents would be charged $393.75. Since the maximum available subsidy from the province for FDH care was $260 per month, low-income families with a full subsidy would be faced with paying the city $133.75 per month. Undoubtedly, some low-income parents pursued child care that was less costly than that offered by the city, but this was not a concern to municipal civil servants since their goal was to provide a model service and they always had an excess of applicants for the number of quality providers they could find. A large proportion of the families using the service made too much to qualify for subsidization and paid the full fee themselves.

Grande Prairie City Council voted to privatize its FDH program in early December 1995. It made this decision even though the program was hugely popular with citizens and was budgeted to return a surplus of more than $18,000 to city coffers in 1995, even after paying city administration costs of 9.5 percent. Therefore, unlike the situations in Medicine Hat, Calgary, and Edmonton, where spending reductions and ideology were intertwined concerns, in Grande Prairie, spending on model child care was never an issue. The privatization decision was made strictly on ideological grounds.

"It was a philosophical decision to get out of direct service delivery," explained Grande Prairie's FCSS administrator, Chris Henderson, in 1996. City council's strategic plan "was not to be in direct service delivery if there was someone else in the community who could do it." In line with this philosophy, Grande Prairie had turned over the ownership of hockey rinks to community groups and had stopped offering skating lessons because the Grande Prairie Figure Skating Club could assume that role. More significantly, in the mid-1990s, the city had contracted out the transit system bus driver jobs. The company who won the first "Transit Operator Provision Contract" lost the contract to a lower bidder the next time it was tendered. Consequently, the privatization of the bus driver jobs resulted in a great deal of disruption in the lives of the workers, in addition to downward pressure on their salaries and benefits. The closing of the city satellite FDH agency created similar disruption in the lives of children, parents, and providers. City council went ahead with its decision even though it acknowledged that the program was superior to other programs in Grande Prairie, and even though parents had "pleaded to council to keep the program because it was operated so successfully by the City."[99]

Grande Prairie's satellite FDH agency was a true model program. Over the years, it had willingly provided guidance to people in other communities who wanted to establish quality FDHs. Chris Henderson explained that if anyone phoned her for advice on how to proceed, she asked them to come to Grande Prairie "to work with us for a week." Furthermore, both the providers and the parents in the program were very well educated about what constituted quality child care. The loss of this education role worried Tanice Jones in 1996: "As much as we educate these parents, they're going to go away and people are going to become used to a standard that's not quite as high as they could get if they pushed, but if they don't know what to push for ..."[100]

The City of Grande Prairie had helped to build a strong system of PSS day cares in the 1970s. In the mid-1990s, however, Grande Prairie lagged behind other large Alberta cities in its commitment to social services. For instance, it was the only one of the six large cities that did not qualify for a flow-through payment from CAP in 1995. This indicates that Grande Prairie, unlike the other cities, was spending not a nickel more on preventive social services than it had to in order to qualify for the maximum FCSS grant from the province. Indeed, a number of smaller communities such as Banff and Fort Saskatchewan received flow-through payments that year, indicating that Grande Prairie was out of step with the priority that most Alberta municipalities placed on social services.

The End of an Era

By 1997 only Red Deer among Alberta's largest cities still maintained a program that explicitly supported lighthouse child care for preschool children. Specifically, the city provided over $125,000 per year to enhance the quality of care in the two day cares that had been municipal centres in the 1980s. With other Alberta cities abandoning their lighthouse programs in the early to mid-1990s, it is understandable that the future of Red Deer's program was called into question. Debates ensued and finally, in late 1999, Red Deer City Council voted by a six-to-three margin to begin reducing the subsidy in 2001, with a targeted date for elimination being 2004.

In opposing the decision, Councillor Larry Pimm argued, "If we have done it for 18 or 20 years, we can continue to do it. We can find the resources." Of course, he was correct since the amount being spent by Red Deer on day care in 1999 was relatively small ($133,000, or $2.08 per capita). But what Pimm failed to acknowledge was that the politics of day care in Alberta had changed markedly over the two decades since the province had unilaterally assumed control of the provincial day care system. In 1981 municipal social services departments had a great deal of expertise in quality day care, and city councils were enthusiastic about doing something to demonstrate the inadequacies in the province's new day care system. Yet by 1999 municipal expertise in child care had eroded because civil servants had moved to new jobs or retired, and day care had long been surpassed as a key issue of contention in provincial-municipal relations. On top of this, as noted at different points in this chapter, the movement for quality child care was fairly quiescent in the 1990s. In light of these factors, perhaps the most surprising aspect of the decision in Red Deer was that it did not happen sooner.[101]

The end of Alberta cities' support for lighthouse day cares and FDH programs was a definite setback for the movement for quality child care. It resulted in the closure of some wonderful programs such as the CDN in Edmonton, the Connaught Day Care in Calgary, and Grande Prairie's satellite FDH program. It also meant that the surviving centres had to make do with less as they struggled to offer the best possible care to their children. They still served as lighthouses, but not all of their lights burned quite as brightly without the support of municipal governments.

The lighthouse model is not completely dead in Alberta. The small municipalities of Beaumont and Jasper have operated municipal day cares for many years, and in 2008 Drayton Valley opened its own ECD centre.[102] Furthermore, a number of not-for-profit organizations (such as post-secondary institutions and churches) partially subsidize the cost of particular day cares. Nevertheless, these examples are isolated and have nothing like the impact that Edmonton's eighteen MADCs or Medicine Hat's five municipal day cares once did.

At the end of the 1990s and into the first decade of the new millennium, Alberta's cities and towns still had the option of supporting OOSC in their communities with PSS funding. In 2005 there were fifty-six OOSC programs throughout Alberta, funded jointly by the province and municipalities through FCSS. Municipalities had the authority to develop their own OOSC regulations that had to be followed for an OOSC centre to be eligible to enrol subsidized children, and Alberta's largest five cities had developed such regulations.[103] However, in September 2008, the provincial government introduced an income-tested provincial subsidy system for OOSC. This brought to an end more than four decades of power-sharing collaboration on child care between the province and municipalities. The finality of municipalities' exit from governance responsibility for child care was demonstrated when Calgary announced that it would be closing its Community and Child Care Standards Unit on 31 August 2008.[104]

9. Day Care into the Future
Trends, Patterns, Recent Developments, and Unresolved Issues

It is going on fifty years since the government of Ernest Manning broke new ground by committing funds to the Community Day Nursery (CDN) in Edmonton. This was the first time that day care was financially supported by the Province of Alberta, and it was far from a routine governmental decision. Prior to the province being asked for money, there was an intense public controversy in Edmonton, sparked by the Edmonton Creche Society's shocking decision to close the creche that it had been operating on a charitable basis since 1930. When the matter of funding for the CDN came to the provincial cabinet, many ministers insisted that public money should not subsidize child care for parents who could otherwise afford the service.

A wide variety of provincial programs now support child care financially, some of which (like staff wage enhancements) universally benefit all children in regulated care; others (like subsidies for children from low-income families) benefit targeted groups. Governmental enhancements, allowances, grants, and subsidies have helped to make day care much more of an institutional fixture in contemporary Alberta than it was when the CDN opened. At the same time, however, just as was the case in the mid-1960s, day care policy questions continue to provoke controversy in the public realm and among Alberta's political elite. Furthermore, contemporary policy debates often rehash arguments that were just as eloquently expressed by Albertans in the 1980s, the 1960s, or even during the wartime day nurseries dispute in 1943–44.[1] Perhaps the emotions associated with today's debates are not quite as raw as they were in the late 1960s, when Howard Clifford could never be sure whether he should extend a hand in greeting or duck when someone addressed him as Edmonton's "Mr. Day Care" (see chapter 3). Nevertheless, many individuals and groups continue to feel passionate about day care. In 1975 Al Hagen wrote to a former colleague that "the daycare controversy seems to continue endlessly in Calgary."[2] All these years later, Alberta's day care controversy still appears endless.

What accounts for the durability of day care as a controversial issue? In my view, it is because different policy preferences for the care of young children are based upon competing conceptions of what a good society looks like, as well as upon competing sets of foundational beliefs about class privilege, gender inequalities, and the quality of children's lives in an adult-centric world. Any issue that simultaneously evokes notions of class, gender, and generational justice is bound to be highly salient for a great many people. That salience has been amplified by the determined work of contending advocacy organizations, with a broad-based movement for quality child care taking the initiative and gaining many successes in the 1960s and 1970s, only to be forced onto the defensive, first by day care capitalists and a provincial government sympathetic to free enterprise and second by pro-family organizations and neo-liberal politicians committed to spending cuts, deregulation, and reprivatization. But just when it seemed that neo-liberals and pro-family organizations had gained a decisive upper hand in the advocacy battles, the provincial government, in the first decade of the new century, introduced and rapidly expanded a wage-enhancement program for workers in day cares and approved FDHs and even extended the enhancements to workers in out-of-school care (OOSC) programs. This breakthrough renewed the movement for quality child care, as demonstrated by the founding of the Alberta Child Care Association (ACCA) in 2009.

The goal of this chapter is to update the story of day care in Alberta in a way that puts recent developments and unresolved issues in a broader context. The first section looks at trends. I begin by outlining the significance of the demographic and labour-force changes that have occurred since 1976 in Alberta society, and then consider how the patterns of non-parental child care changed in Alberta between 1994–95 and 2002–3 in comparison to the changes experienced in other large provinces. Finally, I identify changes in the number of day cares and licensed spaces that accompanied the end of operating allowances in 1999, broken down by region and auspice. The second section highlights some of the mechanisms that have patterned the development of day care in Alberta over the past few decades, and the third analyzes recent developments in child care in Alberta up to 2009. I conclude by highlighting the major unresolved issues for quality child care and the four distinctive blueprints that compete to define child care's place in Alberta society: social liberalism, inclusive liberalism, pro-family conservatism, and free enterprise conservatism.

TRENDS

Demographic and Labour Force Changes, 1976–2006

In chapter 3, I considered the changes in Alberta society after World War II that helped to set the stage for the rapid development of both commercial and Preventive Social Service (PSS) day care in the late 1960s. These changes (1946 to 1971) are recorded in table 3.1. I constructed table 9.1 as an update of that earlier table: it covers changes in the same variables between 1976 and 2006. (It also includes a few data points for 2008.) In combination, tables 3.1 and 9.1 give a picture of key changes in Alberta society during a period of sixty years.

Alberta's population doubled in size in the twenty-five years between 1946 and 1971, and doubled again in the thirty-five years between 1971 and 2006. In the latter period, population growth has followed the fortunes of the fossil fuel industries: the increases were large between 1976 and 1981, much smaller in the period 1981–96, and large again after 1996. The rapid process of urbanization between 1946 and 1971 slowed in the 1970s, but the percent urbanized still continued to grow: in 2006, 82 percent of the population lived in urban areas, the vast majority in Edmonton and Calgary.

The baby boom after World War II created a population pyramid with a large proportion of young children; indeed, in 1961, 14 percent of the total population was four years of age or younger, and 26 percent was nine or younger. This latter percentage fell to 17 percent in 1976, stabilized for fifteen years, and then gradually decreased from 16 percent in 1991 to 12 percent in 2006. In the latter year, only 6 percent of the population was less than five years of age. But even though this was less than half the 1961 peak percentage for children under four, because of overall population growth, there was actually a greater number of preschool children in Alberta in 2006 (203,000) than in 1961 (180,000).

Between 1991 and 2001, the number of preschoolers in Alberta actually declined. However, by 2006 this trend had reversed because the economic opportunities created by Alberta's vibrant economy for most of the first decade of the new century had attracted many migrants in their childbearing years: between 2001 and 2006, the number of preschoolers in Alberta increased by seventeen

TABLE 9.1 Demographic and Labour Force Changes in Alberta, 1976 to 2008

	1976	1981	1986	1991	1996	2001	2006	2008
Population	1,838	2,238	2,366	2,546	2,697	2,975	3,290	3,596[a]
% urbanized	75%	77%	79%	80%	80%	81%	82%	
Calgary	470	593	636	754	822	951	1,079	
Edmonton	461	542	574	838[b]	863	938	1,035	
Together, as % of total Alberta population	51%	51%	51%	63%	62%	63%	64%	
Lethbridge	47	55	59	61	63	67	95[b]	
Medicine Hat	33	41	42	53[b]	57	62	69	
Red Deer	32	46	54	58	60	68	83	
Grande Prairie	18	24	26	28	31	37	72[b]	
Together, as % of total Alberta population	7%	7%	8%	8%	8%	8%	10%	
Newborns to 4 year olds	153	188	205	208	194	186	203	
% of total Alberta population	8%	8%	9%	8%	7%	6%	6%	
5 to 9 year olds	163	174	183	207	210	208	204	
% of total Alberta population	9%	8%	8%	8%	8%	7%	6%	
Divorces per 100,000 people	310	376	404	329	282	277	246 (2005)	
Lone-parent families, old concept	41	57	73	83	92	117		
Lone-parent families, new concept[c]						130	134	
% of all families, old concept	9%	10%	12%	12%	13%	14%		
% of all families, new concept						15%	14%	
Females in labour force	330	476	554	635	677	769	879	933
Participation rate	50%	58%	63%	66%	66%	67%	67%	68%
% of total labour force	38%	40%	43%	45%	46%	46%	45%	45%
Married women in labour force[d]	211	285	345	404	429	484	539	
% of married women	49%	56%	64%	69%	69%	69%	70%	

SOURCES: Alberta Bureau of Statistics, 1981 (for 1976 only); Statistics Canada Catalogues nos. 92-901, 93-921, 93-111, 93-324, 93F0053XIE, 94F0006XCB (CD), and 95F0377XCB2001003; Statistics Canada profile reports for Alberta using PCensus for MapInfo; Statistics Canada CANSIM tables 051-0001, 053-1997, 053-0002, 101-6501 (divorces), 153-0037 (urbanization), and 111-0009 (family characteristics); Statistics Canada Labour Force Survey table 282-0002; Statistics Canada population figures for Alberta cities, 1996–2006, online table; civic census population results provided by municipal civil servants.

NOTE: All raw numbers are in thousands.

[a] Statistics Canada estimate, CANSIM table 051-0001.

[b] Changes in the census boundaries for Edmonton and Medicine Hat between 1986 and 1991 and for Lethbridge and Grande Prairie between 2001 and 2006 contributed to large increases in the population figures.

[c] A change of concept increased the number of lone parents between 1996 and 2001 by approximately 10 percent (Catalogue 93F0053XIE). The figures for the new concept in CANSIM Table 111-0009 are taken from Labour Force surveys.

[d] Figures for 1976 include women who are married but separated; figures for 1981 to 1996 include only women who are married, with spouse present; figures for 2001 include women in legal or common-law marriages; figures for 2006 include only women in legal or common-law marriages with spouse present.

thousand. Nevertheless, the economic recession that brought about a rapid increase in the unemployment rate in Alberta in 2009[3] is likely to cause both a downward trend in the number of births and the out-migration of families with young children. Such fluctuations in the number of preschoolers are to be expected in a resource-based economy like Alberta's and suggest that a significant proportion of day cares should be located in facilities that can be easily converted to other uses when demand drops. Schools, recreation centres, and seniors' centres readily come to mind as ideal locations for such convertible spaces.

One important trend shown in table 3.1 that has continued throughout the years covered by table 9.1 is the increase in the number of lone-parent families. The 23,000 lone-parent families in 1961 had increased to 57,000 by 1981, when the Alberta government used operating allowances to dramatically increase the supply of licensed spaces. By 2006 the number had grown to 134,000. Even if lone-parent families in proportion to all families stabilizes at around 15 percent in future years (a possibility suggested by the percentages for 2001 and 2006 in table 9.1), the size of this group alone is large enough to make day care services a crucial, ongoing policy issue. Quality day care has the unique capacity to provide unobtrusive but comprehensive social support to parents engaged in the difficult job of caring for and educating young children without the assistance of a partner.

Between 1951 and 1971, the proportion of women in the labour force more than doubled, led by the rapid increase in the participation of married women. These trends continued until 1991, when the overall female participation rate was 66 percent and that of married women was 69 percent. Between 1991 and 2006, however, the rates increased only marginally, even with an economic boom at the end of the period; this suggests that women's labour force participation had reached at least a temporary plateau. Nevertheless, with the considerable growth in Alberta's population between 1991 and 2006, the absolute number of married women in the labour force grew substantially, even with a stable participation rate: in 2006 there were 539,000 married women in Alberta's labour force, one-third more than in 1991.

In the late 1990s and early 2000s, the Alberta government instituted tax changes that favoured couples with a single income. This was meant to encourage more women (and occasionally men) to become stay-at-home parents. During the same period, the Quebec government rapidly expanded the number of licensed day care spaces to meet the demand created by its promise that day care would only cost parents $5 per day (later raised to $7 per day). Data from Statistics Canada indicate that Alberta's tax policy may have contributed to a very small decrease in the labour force participation rate of married women with young children, while Quebec's $7 day care definitely increased the participation rate of this same group. In Alberta the participation rate of married women with young children was stable at around 67 percent between 1995 and 1999; fell slightly in each of the four years after that, hitting a low of approximately 64 percent in 2003; but rose to around 65 percent in 2004 and 2005. In Quebec the participation rate of married women with young children was about 64 percent before the government introduced its program of affordable day care. Between 1996 and 2005, however, the participation rate of this group rose steadily to over 75 percent.[4]

The divergent Alberta and Quebec experiments in family policy suggest that it may be easier for governments to increase than to decrease the participation rate of married women in the labour force. Therefore, whatever the Alberta or federal governments do to try to encourage stay-at-home parenting by couples, it is highly unlikely that the participation rate of married women with young children would fall by more than a few percentage points. Reprivatization policies do not appear to have any hope of making the pressing public issue of quality child care go away.

The Use of Day Care and Other Types of Non-Parental Child Care, 1994–95 to 2002–3

The National Longitudinal Survey of Children and Youth can be used to study the changes in the use of different types of child care in Alberta that occurred during the period when the neo-liberal Klein government was deliberately pursuing policies of funding cuts, privatization, and deregulation in day care. The first wave of the survey was in 1994–95, just when the Klein Revolution was kicking in. At that time, 39 percent of young children (six to seventy-one months) were in some type of non-parental child care. Eight years later, this percentage had risen to 43 (panel 1 of table 9.2). The increase in the percentage of children in non-parental child care over these years was also relatively modest in Ontario (6 percent increase to 50 percent), which, like Alberta, was governed by a neo-liberal political party. The increase was greater in other large provinces, particularly in British Columbia (13 percent) and Quebec (23 percent). As a consequence, in 2002–3 a smaller percentage of Alberta young children were in non-parental child care than in any of the other five largest provinces (even though the gap was 10 percent or less between Alberta and each of the other provinces except Quebec).

TABLE 9.2 Children in Non-parental Child Care, 1994–95 and 2002–3

| | Children in any type of non-parental child care | | Main provision for non-parental child care | | | | | | | |
| | | | Day care (%) | | Family day home run by non-relative (%) | | Relative (%) | | Non-relative in child's home (%) | |
	1994–95	2002–3	1994–95	2002–3	1994–95	2002–3	1994–95	2002–3	1994–95	2002–3
National	42	54	20	28	43	30	22	29	14	8
Alberta	39	43	24	19	46	39	18	34	12	8
British Columbia	36	49 [a]	13	20	40	26 [a]	26	43	21	11
Manitoba	42	53 [a]	14	27 [a]	51	35	24	31	11	6
Ontario	44	50 [a]	19	22	44	34	24	35	13	9
Quebec	44	67 [a]	25	52 [a]	43	26 [a]	19	16 [a]	13	6

SOURCE: National Longitudinal Survey of Children and Youth as reported in Bushnik 2006, tables 1, 1b, 2, and 4a-4e. The children included in this survey were aged 6 to 71 months at the time of the interview (p. 40). An additional category of non-parental child care was measured: "'other' care, which includes nursery school or preschool, before or after school programs, or other unspecified non-parental care" (p. 13). Data for this category are usually not reported by Statistics Canada owing to small sample sizes. The only exception in this table is the 2002–3 national data, in which the percentages total 95% because the remaining 5% are in the "other" care category.

[a] The 95% confidence interval for this provincial estimate does not overlap with the 95% confidence interval for the Alberta estimate.

These National Longitudinal Survey statistics suggest that the Klein government's policies in the 1990s had a stronger impact on Alberta parents' choices about child care arrangements than on their choices about whether to participate in the labour force or not. Specifically, as public support was withdrawn from day cares and satellite FDHs, Alberta parents with young children were more likely than comparable parents in other large provinces to find ways to look after their children all on their own. It must be emphasized, however, that the Alberta government's policies slowed but did not reverse the trend of an increasing percentage of young children in non-parental care. This is further evidence that the pro-family movement and its supporters in conservative governments are fighting an uphill battle when it comes to reversing a strong societal trend away from exclusive parental (usually maternal) responsibility for the care of young children. In 2006–7, the new federal Conservative government of Stephen Harper recognized that half measures would not work to promote the stay-at-home family; consequently, as is detailed in the final section of this chapter, it committed almost $4 billion per year to pro-family programs. It remains an open question, however, whether even this sort of spending can substantially increase the percentage of children who are cared for by stay-at-home parents.

Between 1994–95 and 2002–3, interesting shifts occurred in the percentages of Alberta children utilizing different types of non-parental care. Given the reduction and then ending of operating allowances for day cares throughout the 1990s, it is not surprising that day care declined in importance as the main child care arrangement for children in non-parental care (from 24 percent to 19 percent); Alberta was the only large province where day care declined in relative importance during these years (table 9.2). Care in a family day home (FDH) and by a non-relative in the child's home (this includes nannies) also declined in importance in Alberta, in line with the national trends. To compensate for these three percentage decreases, care by a relative as the main child care arrangement jumped from 18 to 34 percent. There was an identical increase in child care by relatives in British Columbia, more modest increases in Manitoba and Ontario, and a small decrease in Quebec.

The increased importance of child care by a relative in Alberta in 2002–3 was consistent with the reprivatization thrust of the Klein government. Nevertheless, the economic boom between 2005 and 2008 restricted the capacity of this sort of non-parental care. For one thing, fewer relatives were available for child care because of the abundance of jobs in the labour market. In addition, many of the migrants drawn to Alberta by economic opportunities did not have any relatives nearby. As a consequence, the boom caused a sharp increase in the demand for regulated day care and FDH spaces. There were many signs of this heightened demand. For example, Kids & Company, a Toronto-based day care chain that caters to corporate clients, opened two Calgary centres in 2005 and later expanded to five. A number of news stories documented a shortage of spaces and long waiting lists in 2006 and 2007. In February 2007, Ralph Klein's replacement as premier, Ed Stelmach, announced a special $1 million investment to increase the number of child care spaces in Fort McMurray. Later in 2007, 123 Busy Beavers, a corporation with links to the Australian-based ABC Learning Centres, moved into Alberta by purchasing a number of existing centres, including six former Panda chain centres in Calgary and two former Peter Pan chain centres in the Edmonton region.[5]

Between 2006 and 2009, therefore, the day care system entered a modest expansionary phase after fifteen years of decline (table A.3). By happy coincidence, the new public investments in day care in Alberta in 2005 resulting from the federal Liberal government's short-lived Early Learning and Child Care (ELCC) program coincided with the economic boom, day care's re-emergence as a hot political issue, and a change in Alberta's premiership. As a result, the provincial government formally maintained and even expanded these new program initiatives after the federal Conservative government elected in 2006 cancelled the ELCC program.

Changes in Day Cares, 1995–2002

Between 1991 (the high point in day care capacity) and 2005, the number of day cares in Alberta decreased by 26 percent and the number of licensed spaces decreased by 27 percent (yearly changes are recorded in table A.3). This huge loss in the capacity of the day care system was inconsistent with the overall change in the number of newborns to four year olds in the province: although the number of young children decreased by 22,000, or 11 percent, between 1991 and 2001, it increased by 17,000, or 9 percent, between 2001 and 2006, in step with the rapid growth of Alberta's economy.

My goal here is to better understand the nature of the decline in the day care system in the 1990s and early 2000s. Table 9.4 presents a detailed accounting of the changes in the day care system during the period defined by the provincial government's reduction and then elimination of operating allowance payment for day cares. It is based on an analysis of the changes in the distribution of licensed day cares and spaces between 1995 (table 6.2) and 2002 (table 9.3).

In the seven years covered in table 9.4, the provincial day care infrastructure shrank by about 15 percent. I have bolded figures in the table where the shrinkage was considerably greater than 15 percent. First, larger chains declined by about 30 percent with all of the decline taking place in Calgary, where most of the larger chains were located in 1995. Second, the smaller chains sector was the hardest hit: it declined by almost 40 percent, with the percentage decrease being somewhat larger in Edmonton than in Calgary. Overall, chain day care in Alberta decreased by about one-third between 1995 and 2002. Operating a commercial day care in Alberta was certainly no longer the "license to print money" that it had been in the 1980s. Third, while the overall decline in the independent commercial sector was 15 percent, the decline in this sector outside of the two major cities was about 35 percent. One reason why the independent commercial sector did not decline as much in Calgary and Edmonton as in the rest of the province is that in the cities, independent owners took over a number of the locations that had previously been operated by chains. Fourth, while the overall decrease in the commercial sector (including commercial chains and independent commercial

TABLE 9.3 Licensed Day Care in Alberta, 2002, by Region and Auspice

Auspice	Edmonton			Calgary			Rest of Alberta		
	Number	Licensed capacity	Average size	Number	Licensed capacity	Average size	Number	Licensed capacity	Average size
Larger chains[a]	10 (5%)	577 (6%)	58	32 (21%)	2,163 (24%)	68	2 (1%)	140 (2%)	70
Smaller chains[a]	19 (9%)	1,047 (11%)	55	23 (15%)	1,501 (17%)	65	8 (5%)	430 (6%)	54
All chains	29 (14%)	1,624 (17%)	56	55 (36%)	3,664 (40%)	67	10 (6%)	570 (7%)	57
Independent commercial	132 (62%)	5,709 (61%)	43	60 (39%)	3,116 (34%)	52	62 (40%)	2,957 (39%)	48
Total commercial	161 (75%)	7,333 (78%)	46	115 (75%)	6,780 (75%)	59	72 (46%)	3,527 (46%)	49
Total not-for-profit	53 (25%)	2,092 (22%)	39	39 (25%)	2,288 (25%)	59	84 (54%)	4,138 (54%)	49
All centres	214	9,425	44	154	9,068	59	156	7,665	49
Region as % of total for Alberta	41%	36%	n.a.	29%	35%	n.a.	30%	29%	n.a.

SOURCE: Spreadsheet provided by Alberta Children's Services, Child Care Information System.

[a] For definitions, see tables 6.1 and 6.2.

day cares) was about 22 percent, the decrease in the commercial sector outside of the two major cities was much larger at approximately 35 percent. The economics of operating a day care without operating allowance payments were clearly not as favourable in smaller cities, towns, and villages as they were in Edmonton and Calgary.

After the introduction of operating allowances in the early 1980s, the primary business task confronting commercial investors had been to establish new day cares and expand existing day cares as quickly as possible. In the difficult economic conditions of the late 1990s and early 2000s, however, the primary business task confronting these same investors was to downsize or even exit the day care business without losing too much money. The gradual and steady downsizing of

TABLE 9.4 Changes in Day Cares, 1995 to 2002, by Auspice and Region

	Number of day cares	Licensed spaces
Province-wide	-93 day cares (-15%)	-4,894 spaces (-16%)
Larger chains	-17 (-28%)	-1,237 (-30%)
Edmonton	+1	-3
Calgary	-18 (-36%)	-1,278 (-37%)
Rest of Alberta	0	+44
Smaller chains	-32 (-39%)	-1,732 (-37%)
Edmonton	-15 (-44%)	-876 (-46%)
Calgary	-31 (-36%)	-601 (-29%)
Rest of Alberta	-4	-255
Total chains	-49 (-34%)	-2,969 (-34%)
Edmonton	-14 (-33%)	-879 (-35%)
Calgary	-31 (36%)	-1,879 (-34%)
Rest of Alberta	-4	-211
Independent commercial	-44 (-15%)	-2,237 (-16%)
Edmonton	-16	-853
Calgary	+9	+227
Rest of Alberta	-37 (-37%)	-1,611 (-35%)
All commercial	-93 (-21%)	-5,206 (-23%)
Edmonton	-30	-1,732
Calgary	-22	-1,652
Rest of Alberta	-41 (-36%)	-1,822 (-34%)
Not-for-profit	Unchanged	+312 (+3%)
Edmonton	-3	-60
Calgary	+1	+107
Rest of Alberta	+2	+265

SOURCE: Calculated from Tables 6.2 and 9.3.

the Kidsland chain in Calgary illustrates this point. Kidsland had grown to thirteen centres after it bought six of the old Kindercare centres from the receiver in 1994 and another centre in 1995. Between 1995 and 2002, the chain converted one of its day cares into a seniors' residence and sold five centres to other operators. This would have left the chain with seven day cares except for the fact that the company had built a new day care in 2000–2001 in a rapidly growing area of north Calgary. Between the end of 2002 and the end of 2005, the downsizing of the Kidsland chain continued, decreasing from eight to five day cares. One of the three closed centres was sold to an independent commercial operator while the other two (including the original Kidsland centre opened in 1983) were closed. Then, in the summer of 2006, Kidsland closed its centre in the community of Montgomery that operated from an old church; the property was sold to a real estate developer. From its peak of thirteen centres in 1995, Kidsland had strategically downsized to four centres by the middle of the next decade. Significantly, a number of the properties sold by the Kidsland chain were no longer operated as day cares in 2007.[6]

Perhaps the most interesting finding shown in table 9.4 is that there was no net loss of not-for-profit day cares between 1995 and 2002 even though the commercial sector declined by more than 20 percent during that period. This summary statistic camouflages important changes within the not-for-profit sector, however. I define "traditional" not-for-profit operators as dedicated associations or societies (e.g., Bowness-Montgomery Day Care Association) and local governments. Between 1995 and 2002, the number of day cares run by these traditional operators fell from 114 to 96, a decrease of 16 percent. This reflects the decision of many local governments to abandon their financial support for lighthouse programs and the difficulties that a number of dedicated day care societies had in trying to independently operate a quality program during these years. Among the notable closures of old PSS centres that were being run by day care societies were the Awasis Day Care in Grande Prairie, the High Level Children's Centre, and the Little People's Community Day Care in Calgary.

As was described in the last chapter, day cares formerly run by the City of Medicine Hat were taken over in the mid-1990s by Medicine Hat College, the Public School District, and the YMCA. Across the entire province between 1995 and 2002, the number of day cares run by public educational institutions increased from eight to twelve and the number of day cares run by the YMCA/YWCA increased from eleven to seventeen. Public educational institutions and the YMCA/YWCA had the capacity to partially subsidize the operations of quality day cares and thus keep them viable in difficult times.

The largest increase in the not-for-profit sector was in day cares run by First Nations: from fourteen in 1995 to twenty-two in 2002. This occurred because of special funding for day cares on reserves in Alberta provided by a number of federal government departments. For instance, in 2002–3 Indian and Northern Affairs Canada ran a program in Alberta that supported 812 licensed preschool and OOSC spaces in seventeen day cares. The financial subsidy was $2.665 million, which worked out to a very modest $274 per month for a space. Funding for First Nations day cares in Alberta was also available from the Aboriginal Human Resources Development

Strategy of Human Resources Development Canada and the Early Childhood Development Initiative. The five Treaty Seven nations in southern Alberta used money from all three programs to support seven day cares with 369 licensed spaces in 2002. Three years later, they operated ten day cares with 422 spaces.[7]

Therefore, the growth in the number of First Nations day cares in Alberta between 1995 and 2002 was due to special funding initiatives of different branches of the federal government and did not reflect the general conditions for not-for-profit day cares in the province during these years. Aboriginal day cares were first established in Alberta in the early 1970s in the spirit of the PSS program and continue to hold great potential along this line. In 2005 the child care coordinator for the Treaty Seven nations in southern Alberta, Violet Meguinis, noted that quality day care supports the well-being of families on reserves and allows children with special needs to be identified and receive special programs. She also noted that day care is the ideal forum in which to introduce young Aboriginal children to traditional languages and culture. However, there is a need for substantial extra resources, including capital and operational funding, if Aboriginal day cares are to reach their potential as preventive and educational organizations.[8]

PATTERNING MECHANISMS

At different points when working on this book, I was struck by how particular sequences of events echoed earlier sequences and by how both the supporters and opponents of public investment in day care constructed arguments that had already appeared in the historical record. Events and discourse, then, sometimes fit patterns that have recurred over time in the history of day care in Alberta. In this section, I discuss seven of these recurring patterns. My goal is to consider not only the nature of the patterns but also their causes, or generating mechanisms. Understanding these seven patterns and their generating mechanisms should help us to anticipate elements of day care's future in Alberta.

Advocates Argue That Day Care Costs Less Than Welfare

At many points in this history, advocates for day care have been faced with a conservative provincial political elite that is ideologically uncomfortable with government support for day care. In this circumstance, the one argument that sometimes gets through to such an elite is that public investment in day care actually saves the government money because day care subsidies are far less expensive than welfare payments. It was this argument that secured the support of Public Welfare Minister L.C. Halmrast for day care funding in the mid-1960s, and the argument regularly reappears in the historical record. For example, a KPMG consultant's report in 2002 quantified the annual savings in welfare costs because of subsidized child care at more that $15 million, almost one-quarter of the total spending on subsidies at that time (Cleland 2002, 10–11); this report was instrumental in convincing the provincial government to introduce a program of wage enhancements for day care workers in 2002. Furthermore, an ingenious piece of research by provincial civil servants in 1981 showed that the savings in welfare costs because of day care subsidization are actually greater than are estimated using conventional assumptions. They discovered that 17 percent of the subsidy caseload in May 1981 (a total of 950 families) had income levels low enough to qualify for social allowance payments, in addition to a child care subsidy, but had not applied. A senior civil servant argued that the child care subsidy gives such families enough to survive and that they would rather not have to apply for stigmatized welfare payments.[9] Therefore, child care subsidies result in hidden savings in the welfare budget in addition to the easily measured savings that happen when families fully or partially move off of welfare because of the availability of child care subsidies to support employment.

This history has shown that many arguments in favour of the public subsidization of day care seem to have little persuasive power with conservative political elites, particularly those who favour stay-at-home parenting. When faced with such unsympathetic decision makers, civil servants and advocates in Alberta have learned that day care only looks good to those elites when it is compared to an even more despised program (welfare) and that estimates of substantial immediate cost savings tend to get the attention of fiscal conservatives and even pragmatic social conservatives.

Government Advances Policy to Quell Opposition to Other Initiatives

Between 1935 and the time of this writing (2010), Alberta experienced only one change in its governing political party, and every provincial election yielded a majority government. As a consequence, advocates for quality child care have not been able to use stiff party competition and regular changes of government to leverage policy advances. Furthermore, except for the Progressive Conservatives' first term in office (1971–75), when the party closely identified with urban reform movements, and the beginning of Ed Stelmach's premiership (2007–8), when it looked like the Liberal Party would challenge the Progressive Conservatives' urban support base, provincial political elites have been decidedly reluctant supporters of day care at best. It is hard to imagine a provincial political environment that could be less conducive to advocacy for quality child care.

Nevertheless, there have been significant advances in programs and policies over the years, in part because progressive initiatives have sometimes been introduced by the provincial government not out of deep-seated conviction but in an attempt to quell opposition to some other initiative central to the government's agenda.

An early example is the Preventive Social Service (PSS) program. It was begun at the same time that the provincial government took over child welfare services from municipalities and can be seen as a move by civil servants to blunt opposition to a more centralized model for the delivery of welfare services from both senior Social Credit cabinet ministers and municipal social services bureaucrats. A second example is the introduction of training requirements for day care directors and workers; this finally happened in 1990 in conjunction with the provincial government's plan to systematically reduce operating allowances for day care to $50 per space. Later that decade, in conjunction with a new plan to entirely eliminate operating allowances, the government twice made improvements in the day care subsidy program. After the opposition to the end of operating allowances had dissipated, however, no further improvements were made to the subsidy program for six years (1999–2005) even though federal money provided through the National Child Benefit could have been used to increase and/or extend the eligibility for day care subsidies.

At many times in Alberta's history, advocacy for quality child care has seemed like a futile gesture. When this compensatory mechanism operates, however, a policy advance may occur in conjunction with a policy reversal. Unfortunately, this mechanism does not lead to programmatic, progressive reform but rather to sporadic, piecemeal policy advances.

Advocates Make Alberta Look Bad Compared to Other Provinces

At a rally at Calgary City Hall in 1978, a protester carried a placard with the question, "Must Alberta Always Have Lowest Day-Care Standards?" Such advocacy through embarrassment tries to evoke the pride (and perhaps even the conceit) that Albertans have about the importance of their province in the Canadian federation. The logic of this approach is that neither political elites nor the general public will be happy with Alberta trailing other provinces because it contradicts their provincial identity of Alberta as a national leader.

An early example of this approach was an investigative report that Karen Harding published in the *Edmonton Journal* in 1966. Titled "Day Nurseries Contrast: Higher Standards Observed in Toronto's Subsidized Centres," the story was based upon Harding's first-hand observations of Toronto's subsidized day nurseries compared to the day nurseries that were then operating in Edmonton. In 1979 the *Edmonton Journal* again investigated how the standards of day care in Alberta compared to the standards in other provinces and reported "that Alberta ranks last in one crucial area, the ratio of staff to children, which determines the amount of personal attention a child receives." The sensitivity of the Lougheed government to this sort of unfavourable interprovincial comparison was demonstrated by the four studies it commissioned between 1978 and 1982 (two by civil servants and two by Price Waterhouse) and by the decisive action it took in 1980 to significantly improve the minimum required staff-to-child ratios.

Unfavourable interprovincial rankings also spurred the government to introduce minimum training standards for day care workers in 1990 and contributed to the decision made in 2002 to start enhancing the wages of day care workers. In the latter case, the "You Bet I Care!" national survey of 1998 found that the annual turnover of staff in day cares was considerably higher in Alberta than in any other province (Doherty et al. 2000a, xxi). The year after the release of the results of the national survey, the provincial government hired KPMG Consulting to assist an advisory committee "to examine ways to provide additional support to Alberta's Day Care Professionals." The consultant confirmed the validity of the "You Bet I Care!" survey results and reported that Alberta was one of only three provinces (the others being New Brunswick and Newfoundland) that did not enhance the wages of the staff in day cares as of March 2001 (Cleland 2002, 1, 4–5). Once again, Alberta's laggard position on the national stage had a significant impact on the political process. It provided a focus for intense lobbying both during and after the 2001 provincial election. It also helped to finally convince both the government and the Conservative caucus that a policy initiative was needed: a modest wage-enhancement program was announced in December 2002.[10]

Nevertheless, there is an important limitation on the operation of this mechanism. In the 1980s, Alberta was among the provincial leaders in per capita spending on day care. In the mid-1990s, however, Alberta significantly decreased its spending on day care (tables A.4 and A.5). In 1992 the province still ranked third in per capita spending, but by 1995 it had fallen to fifth, in 1998 it ranked seventh, and by 2003–4 Alberta ranked last among the ten provinces (CRRU 2005, 209). As was described in chapter 7, the neo-liberal government of the day prided itself on deregulation, privatization, and cutting government spending on social services. Therefore, Alberta's fall throughout the 1990s in the interprovincial rankings on spending for day care was a source of pride rather than embarrassment for the political elites. It turned out that they could only be embarrassed by evidence that Alberta children suffered because of low government spending or weak government regulation.

Finally, embarrassment through unfavourable interprovincial comparison can only work when other provinces are doing better on a salient criterion. This points to the importance of a complementary mechanism: the innovations of model programs tend to positively influence other day cares, even if that influence is only realized after a process of public embarrassment.

Model Programs Function as Exemplars

This book has documented many examples of the positive impact of lighthouse day cares and FDH programs. For instance, the satellite FDH program run by the City of Grande Prairie in the 1980s and 1990s was a blueprint for the establishment of a number of other FDH programs in northwestern Alberta. Model programs influence other programs in at least three different ways. First, as described in the previous subsection, they can trigger embarrassment for governments that support programs that are inferior when compared to the model programs; sometimes this causes those governments to improve the quality of care in the inferior programs. Second, the model programs can be an inspiration and a source of learning for people committed to providing quality child care: it is far easier to develop a quality program when an exemplar is available for emulation. Third, model programs can be a source of competitive pressure since other day cares or FDH programs may lose customers if their services are vastly inferior to what is available through the lighthouses.

In Alberta, large municipalities experimented with model day care and FDH programs in the 1980s but abandoned those experiments in the neo-liberal political climate of the 1990s. In general terms, the most influential model municipal programs were those that constituted a relatively large proportion of the day care and/or FDH capacity in a community. This is why the City of Calgary's three municipal day cares had a much smaller impact on the quality of day care in Calgary than the City of Edmonton's eighteen municipally approved day cares had in Edmonton.

On the national stage, the Province of Quebec's commitment to financially accessible day care for preschool children has served as an important model reference program since the late 1990s. Quebec's approach has functioned as a "radical flank," causing other provinces to think about doing something new in child care even if those provinces reject the universalistic and heavily subsidized approach of Quebec. Furthermore, because Quebec is a relatively large province with a major impact on national politics, its universalistic approach undoubtedly made it increasingly difficult for the federal Liberal government to ignore its own 1993 election promise to introduce a national child care plan. The framework for a national system of ELCC was finally approved in 2004, and federal-provincial agreements were signed in 2005. However, these agreements fell short of the Quebec model since, as noted by Wendy McKeen, they "gave provinces considerable leeway to choose between the principles of universality and targeting, as well as between public and for-profit" (2007, 161).

It is worth considering whether the Alberta Child Care Accreditation Program (ACCAP), announced in 2002 and implemented in 2005, is a similar model program on the national stage. In its press releases, the provincial government proudly notes, "Alberta is the only province that has a child care accreditation program."[11] There is little doubt that in the context of Alberta politics, the ACCAP has been highly significant. It served as a means for advocates to leverage a wage-enhancement program from the provincial government at a time when day cares and FDH agencies were reeling from the loss of operating allowances. Furthermore, given the government's reluctance to move to higher licensing standards, particularly in the important area of staff training requirements, the ACCAP was a roundabout way to eliminate programs with very low-quality standards and at the same time re-establish a positive consultation process throughout the entire child care system.

The ACCAP provides accredited centres and agencies with financial incentives and thus penalizes those programs that either eschew accreditation or are unable to make the accreditation standard. In 2002, when the accreditation program was announced, these incentives were laughably small, including a wage enhancement for Level 3 staff of only $0.62 per hour.[12] Two factors, however, led to huge increases in wage enhancements between 2005 and 2008. The first was money provided to Alberta by the federal government through its ELCC program. As a consequence, in September 2005, the wage enhancement for Level 3 staff in accredited centres was increased to $2.96 per hour. The second factor was the economic boom between 2005 and 2008 that created not only a spike in the demand for day care but also a child care labour crisis since, because of the overall shortage of workers, even routine service jobs were being paid more than Level 2 and Level 3 child care staff. To stabilize the child care labour force, the enhancement for Level 3 staff in an accredited centre was increased to $4.14 per hour effective 1 January 2007 and to $6.62 per hour effective 1 April 2008.[13] After these increases, the wage enhancement for a child development supervisor (the new name for Level 3 staff) amounted to approximately $13,000 per year. Since there is no regulatory requirement that a program hire child development supervisors to work with children, this particular supplement had no impact on unaccredited centres. However, by April 2008, the other financial incentives for accreditation were substantial. They included wage enhancements of approximately $8,000 per year for a child development worker (the new name for Level 2 staff) and $4,000 per year for an untrained child development assistant (the new name for Level 1 staff), and an operating grant of $7,500 per year. Incentives of this size meant that unaccredited programs now bordered on being economically uncompetitive. They were consequently faced with three stark options: work to improve the quality of programming so as to attain accreditation and access the government funding, sell the centre to an individual or organization who would go after accreditation, or close the centre.

Accreditation is granted by the Alberta Association for the Accreditation of Early Learning and Care Services. Once a centre or agency joins the accreditation process, it qualifies for technical assistance grants that can be used to pay for advice, training, and mentoring through the Alberta Resource Centre for Quality Enhancement. This resource centre was established in late 2004 by Alberta Children's Services in partnership with four child care organizations including the Alberta Child Care Network (ACCN) and the Canadian Child Care Federation. Sixty percent of the accreditation test score is based upon adult/child interactions. The resource centre supplies mentors to work with front-line staff to improve the quality of those interactions prior to formal observation for accreditation.[14]

Far from guaranteeing excellence, accreditation in the Alberta system simply means that a program exceeds the rock-bottom quality that is possible given lax licensing standards related to staff training. This was shown by the fact that, as of early January 2010, the success rate on first-site visits was 86 percent and on second-site visits, an almost perfect 98 percent. Therefore, programs that commit to the accreditation process are almost guaranteed to succeed. This helps to explain why by the end of 2009, the vast majority of Alberta's day cares and FDH agencies (504 in total) had been accredited even though there is undoubtedly great variability in the quality of care among these programs. In light of this track record, the ACCAP is unlikely to serve as a model for other provinces unless they too are seeking a way to eliminate the poorest-quality programs without introducing higher licensing standards.[15]

Money Talks in Disputes Between the Federal and Alberta Governments

At three crucial points in this history, the Alberta government had a vastly different approach to the direction of social policy than did the federal government. The first was in the mid-1960s, when the federal government established national medical care insurance, the Canada Pension Plan, and national standards for welfare services funded through the Canada Assistance Plan. The Alberta government was deeply suspicious of the entrenchment of large, centralized welfare state programs. The second was in 1987–88 when the Progressive Conservative federal government of Brian Mulroney pushed its "National Strategy on Child Care." At that time, the pro-family movement in Alberta had begun to have a significant influence on the provincial government of Don Getty. As a consequence, the Alberta government favoured new spending for stay-at-home parents ahead of new spending for regulated child care. The third was in 2004–5, when the Liberal government of Paul Martin worked to put in place its own ELCC national program. The Alberta government argued, contrary to the federal Liberals, that government subsidization should be available to unlicensed/unregulated programs.

It is noteworthy that Alberta's opposition at each of these junctures was overcome because the federal government offered Alberta so much new money for program spending that standing on principle and walking away from the federal proposal was out of the question. For example, under the terms of the 1987–88 child care plan, the federal contribution to Alberta's total spending on day care would have increased to 51 percent, far above the 12 percent reimbursement Alberta had received in 1985–86. And in 2005 the federal government offered $70 million of new funding for child care in 2005–6, an amount that exceeded the total amount that Alberta had spent on child care in the year ending in 2004 (table A.4). Even better, the agreement with the federal government projected that transfers to Alberta would increase to $117 million by the third year of the plan. With this sort of money at stake, it is little wonder that Alberta signed an ELCC agreement in July 2005 that promised it would use the new federal funding to "develop and enhance its regulated early learning and child care system." Public Interest Alberta later determined that the combined federal transfers for child care through the ELCC agreement and the Canadian Social Transfer exceeded total provincial spending on child care by $14.9 million in 2005–6 and fell but $6.8 million short of the provincial total in 2006–7.[16]

These examples demonstrate that the federal government is in a much better position to strike a deal with recalcitrant provincial governments when it is in good fiscal shape and can promise to increase transfer payments by a significant amount. The Canadian federal system is highly decentralized and, as a consequence, it is difficult to come to any sort of national agreement. The events detailed in this book indicate, however, that generous amounts of new money for a province can pave the way for provincial acceptance of a federal initiative it might otherwise reject.

The Cadillac Metaphor: Opponents Frame Quality Child Care as a Luxury

In 1971 an oil industry executive described Calgary's new PSS day cares as "gold-plated," a metaphor that resonated with many segments of the public because it associated the publicly subsidized, high-quality PSS centres with luxury that was beyond the means of ordinary citizens. In 1978 Minister Helen Hunley used an equally evocative metaphor to justify the provincial government's plan to set an upper limit on the amount it would pay to subsidize a child's day care costs: "She stressed the government will refuse to finance 'Cadillac service.'" In the Cadillac metaphor, the recipients of the government-subsidized Cadillac service are set up as a reference group in a process of invidious social comparison.

Framing quality child care as a luxury is a politically expedient means to limit government financial support for such child care. It encourages a backlash by families with middle incomes against the provision of high-quality, subsidized day care to children from low-income families. In doing so, it disregards the potential of child care to compensate for some of the inequalities in family-class situations, thereby preventing some of the problems that disadvantaged children may run into later in life as well as promoting overall societal integration. It also fails to question whether the quality of care received by all preschoolers should be substantially improved as part of change to a less adult-centric society. Therefore, framing quality child care as a luxury serves to dramatically limit the range of policy options that can be fully considered.

The Labour of Child Care Is Undervalued

In 1917 the Children's Aid Society of Edmonton employed a staff of three to care for thirty-two children in a day nursery located in a former hotel. "No high salaries are paid at the Nursery," noted a newspaper story at the time, "and in this respect the total salaries do not represent the work that is actually done by the staff."[17] Similar arguments were made eighty-five years later in Edmonton by those lobbying the provincial government for the introduction of a wage-enhancement program for child care workers. For example, one worker wrote, "I often wonder why the daycare system and its hard-working and poorly paid caregivers seem to be neglected by both the federal and provincial governments." Furthermore, at one commercial day care in Edmonton, the director talked about organizing a union drive that would culminate in a province-wide strike, if necessary, to back the demand that the provincial government double the wages of workers in day care.[18]

Eight main factors account for the systematic undervaluing of the work of child care in Alberta's regulated day cares, satellite FDHs, and OOSC centres. The first is market pressure from unregulated alternatives. As long as many parents are required to pay all or a significant proportion of the cost of regulated child care, alternatives will place downward pressure on the wages paid in the regulated system. In contemporary Alberta, one type of market pressure comes from unlicensed FDHs that can legally care for up to six children: these FDHs tend to be less costly than regulated care. The second type of market pressure comes from foreign workers recruited as nannies on special work visas. While nannies are not usually cheaper than regulated care, they are often cost effective for higher-income families since they provide a range of services besides child care and can be called upon to work extended hours. Nanny services compete with day cares for upper-middle-income and upper-income clients, and thus draw a significant amount of revenue away from the day care system.

As already noted, in 2005 the Alberta and federal governments signed a bilateral agreement that promised significant new funds for regulated child care. This led to important new public investments in the day care and satellite FDH systems. The maximum subsidy rate was increased for the first time since 1999 (table A.6), as were the turning point for receiving a full subsidy and the break-even point for receiving a partial subsidy. In addition, the government made significant improvements to the wage-enhancement program it had introduced in late 2002.[19]

Low-income Alberta families have the option of pursuing subsidized, regulated child care or unsubsidized, unregulated child care. The improvement to the subsidy system in November 2005 made regulated care the best financial choice for a larger group of low-income families. Indeed, the number of families receiving child care subsidies increased from 8,699 in September 2005 to 12,021 in May 2006.[20] This increase in the subsidized population served to modestly lessen the downward pressure that unregulated providers place on workers' wages in regulated care.

At the same time, an income-based subsidy system with much higher turning and break-even points would be that much more effective in making licensed services affordable for a wider cross-section of the population. Universal allowances are also efficacious in drawing significant numbers of families away from the unregulated sector and therefore limiting the ability of that sector to exercise downward pressure on workers' wages. Between 1980 and 1999, Alberta's operating allowances had this effect on the competitive playing field, even though workers' wages in the regulated sector did not generally benefit due to other undervaluing factors. The wage-enhancement program introduced in 2002 and generously expanded between 2005 and 2008 similarly made regulated services more affordable, thereby lessening the competitive pressure from the unregulated sector. It had the added bonus of placing public subsidies directly in workers' hands rather than in the hands of operators (although it created the possibility of operators limiting future wage increases to workers in an effort to indirectly appropriate a portion of the wage enhancements). Alberta's wage-enhancement program has now been joined by a second universal allowance of note, the latest version of an operating allowance program. Introduced in May 2008, it pays $150 per month, but only for infant spaces.[21]

Even with these two universal allowances in place, however, Alberta parents are still required to pay a substantial amount out of their own pockets for better-quality day care or satellite FDH care. As a result, unregulated FDH homes continue to be a competitive threat to the regulated sector and consequently exert a downward pressure on workers' wages.[22] Only a program with a much higher level of universal allowance, such as Quebec's $7-per-day child care, can eliminate such pressure since no unregulated, unsubsidized provider can compete with such a low price.

The second undervaluing factor stems from the high proportion of subsidized children in Alberta's day care system and the fact that the provincial government controls the maximum monthly amount that this segment of the market can pay. Subsidized children typically have made up 30 percent or more of all preschool children in regulated care in Alberta. As was documented in chapter 4, when the provincial government introduced a new portable subsidy day care system in 1978, it set a maximum subsidy level that was far less than the cost of high-quality PSS day care. This was a deliberate strategy: it forced the PSS centres that mainly served subsidized children to slash workers' wages since the only other way to balance their budgets—get parents to pay more out of their pockets—was unrealistic for a subsidized clientele.

Although in constant 2006 dollars the maximum subsidy levels in 2008 were somewhat higher than the subsidy levels that had been frozen in place between 1999 and 2005, they still fell far short of what would be required to run an excellent early learning program that was completely staffed by early childhood education (ECE) graduates. Therefore, subsidized parents are forced to look for a day care that charges close to the maximum subsidy level rather than a day care that offers a superior program but significantly "extra bills" parents. The provincial government could eliminate this source of undervaluation by setting a maximum subsidy level that equals the cost of care in high-quality programs. Such a strategy would have the extra benefit of maximizing the capacity of child care to lessen class inequalities.

The third undervaluing factor involves the substitution of "babysitting" (relatively unskilled) labour for skilled ECE labour in a group setting. As was noted in the first section of this chapter, when the Alberta government's support for day cares and FDH agencies was reduced at the end of the 1990s, many parents responded by calling upon relatives for child care. This sort of labour substitution happens in many fields of life: for example, people might get a friend or relative to help with mechanical repairs to a car instead of hiring a mechanic. But while the success or failure of a do-it-yourself repair job is usually easy to discern (i.e., the car runs well or it does not), the same cannot be said for the substitution of babysitting for trained child care. The benefits of ECE training in a high-quality day care or the drawbacks of loosely organized babysitting are not always discernible on a daily basis and involve characteristics and capacities that often do not register with parents. Therefore, the inability to record a telling difference in a child encourages parents to substitute relatively unskilled for skilled labour in child care.

The ready substitution of unskilled for skilled labour devalues skilled labour in any field of human activity. When this sort of substitution occurs for technological reasons in a goods-producing industry, the devaluing of skilled labour is usually lamented but accepted as a component of societal progress (increasing productivity, standard of living, etc.). When unskilled labour is substituted for skilled labour in a human service like child care, however, a different dynamic is at play: the substitution almost always results in a decline in the quality of the service.

Substitution of unskilled for skilled labour in child care is not a new phenomenon, but it has taken on renewed importance since the early 1980s as a new regime of capitalist accumulation, usually called post-Fordism, has taken root across the capitalist world. Post-Fordism is characterized by labour market flexibility, flexible production systems, and the service of niche markets utilizing decentralized organizations (Munck 2002, 93–99). Post-Fordism uses two paradigmatic types of flexiworkers. First, there are multi-skilled, autonomous, and highly motivated workers who work in regularized jobs in core sectors of the economy. Second, there are relatively unskilled workers where flexibility describes the terms of their employment relationship: ad-hoc, contingent, temporary, and/or part time. In light of this pattern, Ronaldo Munck has argued that the new capitalism has both a "high road" and a "low road" for workers (2002, 98). It is also important to note that some of the jobs on the "high road" involve elements of the flexibility seen on the "low road" (e.g., temporary contracts).

What implications does post-Fordism have for the valuing of the labour of child care? This is the fourth factor to be considered in this section. Looking first at the "high road," Munck notes that "behind the new male 'flexiworker' giving his all to his high-powered City job lies someone (usually female) who in a very 'flexible' way is caring for his household needs" (2002, 97). In the new capitalism, household tasks, including child care, are more difficult to manage and accomplish in combination with full engagement as a high-powered flexiworker. Dual-career couples need more help with child care and household tasks than is available through a day care or satellite FDH. This explains the popularity of nannies and care by relatives. It also explains why one member of the couple (usually a woman) may opt for a job that has the built-in flexibility needed to leave time and energy to care for household needs. In the latter situation, the family only needs part-time child care and is relatively cost conscious when purchasing that service because they have far less disposable income than if both partners were working full time. Therefore, the career demands in post-Fordism make it more likely that the professional-managerial class will substitute relatively unskilled child care (by a parent, other relative, nanny, or part-time babysitter) for the skilled child care of an ECE professional in a regulated facility. This post-Fordist tendency toward an increase in the substitution of unskilled for skilled labour in child care puts further downward pressure on the value of skilled labour.

For many segments of the working class, flexible capitalism means lower wages, limited or no benefits, and greater insecurity. These conditions in themselves impel such flexiworkers to find flexible and low-cost unregulated child care. Given this dynamic, post-Fordism would have had a devastating impact on the value of labour in child care except for the fact that low-income families in Alberta qualify for child care subsidies that can only be used in regulated programs. However, the post-Fordist dynamic does indeed apply to those working-class families who fail to qualify for a sizeable subsidy. Once again, post-Fordist employment relations tend to encourage labour substitution, thus undermining the value of skilled labour in child care.

Undervaluing the labour of child care negatively affects two groups: children who need care and the workers who care for them. This suggests the fifth factor that contributes to the undervaluing of labour in this field: despite widespread lip service to the well-being of young children, children themselves are relatively powerless in our adult-centric world and are systematically disadvantaged in the distribution of resources across generations. Undervaluing the labour of child care thus reflects a deep-seated undervaluing (and under-resourcing) of young children in our society. This statement applies in particular to children from lower-income families for whom class and generational inequalities combine to create particular disadvantages.

Proponents of ECE argue that there are long-term societal benefits from investments in ECE. For example, Jacques van der Gaag (2002) maintains that ECE strengthens a society's human capital (education and health) and social capital (social integration), lessens inequality, and ultimately promotes economic growth. Such an instrumental argument, however, does not value children for who they are and what they contribute today but rather for who they will become and what they will contribute as adults. Consequently, it does not address the fundamental undervaluing of children's lives that lies behind the undervaluing of the work of child care. Sociologist William Corsaro offers a more radical prescription for addressing generational inequalities. He argues, "We need to enrich children's appropriations from the adult world, to encourage their constructions of their own peer culture, and to better appreciate the contributions that children can and do make to our adult worlds" (2005, 310). In this framework, high-quality child care is an important means of creating a society that values young children's social worlds to the same degree that it values adults' social worlds.

As discussed in chapter 1, a gender order involves institutionalized power relations between women and men along with prevailing cultural notions of masculinity and femininity. When we look at the entire gender order instead of at gender as an element of individual identity and experience, we are able to recognize that gender relations influence what happens in every sphere of human life. Three of the undervaluing factors I have already discussed in this section are economic: market pressure from unregulated providers, substitution of unskilled for skilled labour, and the rise of a new type of flexible capitalism (post-Fordism). Each of these factors is gendered in the sense that gender relations contribute to how each factor operates to undervalue the labour of child care. For example, gender relations play an important role in the way that unregulated providers exert market pressure on wages in the regulated system. Women have the major responsibility for looking after young children in our current gender order, and unless they are well educated, their prospects for paid employment tend to be limited to low-paying, female-dominated occupations. As a consequence, many women with their own young children find looking after several additional children in their own home to be the best economic option for their family. Market pressure would not be an important devaluing factor without a large pool of women who are available and compelled to operate an unregulated FDH.

The sixth devaluing factor—the virtual absence of men in the labour force in day cares and satellite FDHs—involves the gender order in a more obvious way than do the other factors. Researchers have found that "through occupational segregation certain jobs have become identified as 'women's work,' and these jobs pay less because they are feminized and deemed 'unskilled'" (Figart 2005, 510). Analyses of survey data from both the United States and Canada have found that "men are represented stereotypically as productive, accomplished, and up for any type of challenge" while females are associated with a set of traits that are seen as relatively powerless and bad, including foolish, unstable, unambitious, and weak (Langford and MacKinnon 2000, 41–42). The existence of these gender stereotypes helps to explain why the labour of female-dominated occupations such as child care worker is devalued.

Nevertheless, it is important not to exaggerate the influence of occupational segregation and gender stereotypes on the undervaluing of the labour of child care. In 1994 fully 97 percent of day care workers in Sweden were women (Jensen 1996, 31); this was virtually identical to the percentage in Canada at that time (Doherty et al. 2000b, 23–24). Yet despite this similarity in occupational segregation, trained child care workers tended to be paid at a much higher level in Sweden than in Canada. This observation indicates that however desirable it might be to get more men working in the field of child care and to fundamentally reorient the gender order at the level of entrenched stereotypes (European Commission Network on Childcare 1994), it should be possible to substantially revalue the labour of child care without waiting for these momentous changes to take place.

Child care workers' low level of economic and political power is the seventh undervaluing factor. The fact that very few child care workers are unionized is an indicator of this power deficit. As a consequence, with very few exceptions, workers lack the institutional means to directly bargain for a distribution of resources that better reflects their valuable contributions to child care.

Since unionization of small workplaces like day cares is a daunting if not an impossible task given the current state of labour relations law in Alberta, over the years child care workers have sensibly pursued their collective interests through interest groups and social movement organizations. The modest successes of the Alberta Association for Young Children (AAYC) in the 1970s and the ACCN in the first decade of the 2000s demonstrate that at opportune moments, child care workers and their allies are able to win political victories. Such victories, however, have been exceptions rather than the rule.

The eighth and final undervaluing factor is that governments are reluctant to systematically address the problem because to do so would be very costly. There is no way around the fact that the care of young children is labour intensive. In a typical elementary school, a single kindergarten teacher might be responsible for a group of eighteen children who are five or six years old. In comparison, in a day care in Alberta, a minimum of three workers must be assigned to care for a group of eighteen children who are two to three years old. Therefore, pay equity in child care requires adjustments to the wages of a relatively large number of workers relative to the number of children served. Furthermore, the higher the average skill level of the labour force, the more government spending is needed to redress the systematic undervaluing. This factor therefore also helps to explain the resistance of the Alberta government to more rigorous training standards for all child care workers.

It was aggregate-cost considerations that caused the government of Peter Lougheed in 1978 to set a relatively low maximum amount for subsidies (chapter 3) and then in 1982 to abandon its promise to introduce a staff-qualifications regulation (chapter 4). Cost considerations were also front and centre in the province's policy agenda of reprivatization and deregulation for child care in the 1990s (chapter 7).

The increase in spending on child care in Alberta occasioned by the ELCC agreement signed with the federal government in 2005 gave the day care and satellite FDH systems their first sizeable financial boost since the 1980s. When this agreement was cancelled in 2006 by the incoming federal Conservative administration, the provincial government could have rolled back the initiatives supported by federal ELCC money. Because of large provincial surpluses and an overwhelming demand for child care during the 2005–8 economic boom, however, the provincial government not only replaced federal ELCC money with provincial money but committed the province to major new expenditures on programs such as wage enhancements and a new operating allowance for infant spaces. Economics alone does not explain the good fortunes of regulated child care in Alberta at that time: equally beneficial was the ascendancy of a new Progressive Conservative premier. Ed Stelmach governed during the boom years in a distinctly more centrist and activist fashion than had his predecessor, Ralph Klein, and selected child care as a priority issue from the outset of his premiership.[23] Nevertheless, to thoroughly address the undervaluing of the labour of child care, the provincial government would have to both increase its spending by many times beyond the levels committed to by Premier Stelmach during the economic boom and adopt policies that minimize the impact of market pressures on workers' wages. There is little chance that this will happen as long as a right-of-centre party forms the government.[24] Probably the best that can be hoped for in the coming years is that the valuation gains of 2005–9 will not be rolled back and that incremental changes will gradually improve the valuation of labour in the field.

Undervaluing the labour of child care is the strongest and most persistent pattern in this history. It has been sustained by the wide range of economic, social, and political mechanisms identified in this section. Until neutralized by new public policies, these mechanisms can be expected to contribute to how the work of child care in Alberta is valued.

The changes made to Alberta's child care system between 2002 and 2009 did not quite match the momentous changes made in the late 1970s and early 1980s, but they were significant nonetheless, especially those in the 2007–9 period. Some of the new programs and policies have already been discussed while others will be identified here for the first time.

The policy changes can be organized into three types. The first is new programs of universal financial support: wage enhancements, grants to support the accreditation process, operating allowances for infant spaces, and space-creation start-up grants. The Space Creation Innovation Fund is the only one of these programs that I have not previously mentioned. Announced in 2007, it paid up to $1,500 toward the costs of business planning, minor renovations, and equipment to open up a space in a day care, approved FDH, OOSC program, or preschool. The goal identified for the program in 2008 was to create 14,000 new child care spaces between 2008 and 2011, in addition to the 3,500 spaces created in 2007–8. In 2008–9, 9,449 new spaces were created, including 2,558 in day cares.

In the larger scheme of things, this is a relatively insignificant program: it involved one-time rather than ongoing funding, was a short-term commitment, and covered only a small proportion of the capital costs of creating a truly new space. The most notable feature of the program was its faulty design: because it subsidized the cost of opening new spaces but did nothing to preserve the continuation of existing spaces, the net gain of spaces was significantly less that the number of spaces created. For example, although the program subsidized the creation of 2,558 day care spaces in 2008–9, the net gain in day care spaces that year was only 354 (table A.3).[25]

Second, the provincial government finally assumed full responsibility for OOSC programs and in so doing ended the long-standing arrangement whereby municipalities had primary responsibility for OOSC even though it was funded jointly by the province and municipalities through Family and Community Support Services.[26] A number of factors explain the provincialization of OOSC in 2008. A systemic problem with the old system was that subsidized care was unavailable in some smaller municipalities around Alberta. It also seemed that it was only a matter of time before municipalities would lose control of OOSC programs in light of two administrative developments. The first was the establishment at the end of the 1990s of regional Child and Family Services Authorities to administer child welfare, day care, and a variety of other social services for children and families. Leaving OOSC in the hands of municipalities seemed to be a case of glaring administrative duplication. The second was the introduction in 2004 of provincial licensing standards for OOSC in response to a court case.[27] Finally, two factors specific to the 2007–8 period are crucial. The first was the strong demand for OOSC during the economic boom. The second was an unintended consequence of the wage-enhancement system for workers in day cares and satellite FDHs: the wage enhancements caused many OOSC workers to quit their jobs in favour of work that was eligible for the enhancements.[28]

In September 2008, an income-tested provincial subsidy was first offered to families with children in OOSC. At the same time, the province provided a small staff-retention allowance to stabilize the workforce in OOSC centres. A few months later, a full-blown OOSC centre accreditation plan was unveiled along with hourly wage enhancements that equalled those available to those working with young children. Furthermore, in order to encourage OOSC in close proximity to elementary schools, the province committed $42 million over three years so that school districts could buy modular buildings for OOSC programs. Whereas OOSC had formerly been a poor cousin to the day care and satellite FDH systems, it was now accorded equal status under full provincial jurisdiction.[29]

The third type of policy change involved the province opening the door to major corporate investments in day care by removing the regulatory limit of eighty on the size of a day care facility (Alberta 2007, 219). This change was made without fanfare in May 2007 at a time when there was a severe shortage of day care spaces. It meant that the economies of scale associated with very large centres were now available in Alberta for corporations to exploit. The deregulation of facility size made possible a plan by a real estate investment company headed by Leslie Wulf, the Canadian Education Property Fund, to provide the funds to build eighty new day cares in Alberta, each with a capacity for 175 children. Wulf's company committed to raising $300 million for the project but asked the provincial government to guarantee the leases made with operators (in effect guaranteeing a return on the fund's real estate investment). When the government refused this request in December 2008, the plan collapsed.[30]

In early March 2009, Leslie Wulf maintained that the Canadian Education Property Fund was not affiliated with 123 Busy Beavers, the Alberta day care chain that had been created in 2007 by an Australian corporation with many contracting ties to ABC Learning Centres. Indeed, Leslie Wulf maintained that the fund's "goal is to provide capital to not-for-profit agencies, municipalities, or private agencies that seek to build and operate child-care facilities." Later that year, however, he emerged as the chief executive officer of Edleun Inc., a private company "involved in acquiring, developing and operating high quality community based learning and child care centres throughout Canada." As its first acquisition, Edleun Inc. purchased the 123 Busy Beavers chain in Alberta. It is noteworthy that the president of Edleun, Mark Davis, had been "responsible for the acquisition and establishment of 123 Busy Beavers Limited" in the Canadian market.[31]

An immediate consequence of the deregulation of facility size was that a number of commercial day cares applied for space-creation grants in order to expand their licensed capacities in existing facilities beyond the former maximum of eighty. For example, the 123 Busy Beavers chain added 132 spaces in two existing centres in Calgary, and Cancare Children's Centre in Calgary added 32 spaces to an existing centre. In addition, the Kids & Company chain received space-creation grants in 2008–9 to create 120 day care spaces and 30 OOSC spaces in a single facility.[32] Buildings with combined day care and OOSC licenses for 200 spaces or more should soon be part of the child care landscape in Alberta's largest cities. The conjunction of a deregulated facility size and generous universal allowances could well make Alberta a magnet for corporate investors in the coming years unless regulatory action is taken.

UNRESOLVED ISSUES AND FOUR COMPETING BLUEPRINTS

The list of major unresolved issues for quality child care in Alberta is short: (1) blocking the spread of corporatized day care; (2) strengthening staff training standards so that all program staff in a child care centre are required to hold a degree or diploma in early childhood development and education; (3) finding sources of capital to establish and maintain facilities for not-for-profit programs; (4) expanding the early learning opportunities available through the school system, particularly the establishment of province-wide full-day kindergarten and junior kindergarten; and (5) incrementally increasing provincial funding for universal programs like wage enhancements as well as the income-targeted subsidy system.

For many years now, there have been four distinctive blueprints for child care in Alberta, each with its supporters and detractors. The preceding list of unresolved issues is written from the perspective of the social liberalism that guided the rapid expansion of high-quality, community-oriented PSS day cares in the late 1960s and 1970s, and continues to be promoted by many ECE professionals and advocates based in the not-for-profit sector. If social liberalism were the organizing principle of Alberta's current social welfare regime, then substantial progress could be made on the unresolved issues without much contention or controversy. The existence of three alternate blueprints, however, and the fact that each of the alternates enjoys more support among Alberta's elites than social liberalism, explains why Alberta's day care controversy is far from a thing of the past.

The alternates to social liberalism are inclusive liberalism, which supports quality child care as a means to develop human capital and ensure that less people become dependent on state transfer payments; pro-family conservatism, which favours the care of children by stay-at-home parents; and free enterprise conservatism, which promotes market mechanisms and the unfettered involvement of private businesses in the provision of child care. Underlying each blueprint for child care are competing conceptions of what a "good society" looks like.

Social liberalism posits quality child care as a building block for greater gender, class, and generational equality. Because it has such ambitious, transforming goals for child care, social liberalism puts particular emphasis on the educational qualifications of the staff. It has consistently objected to the large proportion (approximately 40 percent in 2008) of the workforce in Alberta day cares who are essentially unschooled in early childhood development. It has also objected to the province's moves during the recent economic boom to circumvent the existing training requirements by granting certification equivalencies to "people with no background in early childhood development" and to consider an apprenticeship system of training as an alternate to college programs in ECE.[33]

Especially in its fullest expression, it is hard to distinguish social liberalism from collectivist approaches such as communitarianism. Social liberalism is therefore quite distinctive from the three other blueprints current in Alberta, all of which are individualist in their conceptions of a good society. The AAYC's classic 1974 statement best represents the full scope of social liberal aspirations for day care: "It is a total service providing for the needs of children, and the needs of parents, contributing to the prevention of family problems, and problem families, contributing to the growth and development of children, of parents, of families and of society."[34]

Social liberalism conceives of day cares as tools for building community rather than simply as providers of a service. This is why establishing public and not-for-profit centres is a priority in social liberalism, beyond the concern that the well-being of children might sometimes come second to the pursuit of profit in commercial centres. Since 1980 the not-for-profit sector in Alberta has had to scramble to find money to maintain existing facilities and establish new ones. Beginning in the early 1990s, advocates for quality day care began to pursue the possibility of getting a share of the proceeds from Alberta's burgeoning gambling industry as a partial solution to this problem. After years of lobbying, not-for-profit day cares were finally granted eligibility for gaming licenses in 2003 (a gaming license for a casino can yield $75,000 or more for a two-day shift by a team of volunteers, once every two years).[35] Even before this breakthrough, however, day cares had been accessing some gambling money through granting programs. While most of the revenue that the Alberta government generates from VLTs, slot machines, and ticket lotteries (an estimated $1.3 billion in 2006–7) is utilized for general government expenditures, a modest amount (13 percent in 2006–7) is distributed by the Alberta Lottery Fund to not-for-profit community groups through a variety of granting programs. These programs include the defunct Community Lottery Boards, the Community Facility Enhancement Program, and the Community Initiatives Program. Between 1998–99 and 2006–7, seventy-two child care organizations (mostly day cares but including a few OOSC centres) secured a total of 170 gambling-funded grants with a total value of $2.8 million. Many of these grants were less than $10,000 in size and used to purchase equipment or undertake minor repairs or renovations to infrastructure. For example, Bowness-Montgomery Day Care Association in Calgary secured a grant of $5,500 in 1999–2000 to "re-shingle and tar roof." However, a number of organizations received grants for major repairs and renovations of existing facilities, and in a few cases, grants were used to construct or purchase/renovate new facilities.[36]

Relying upon gambling money to provide capital for not-for-profit child care is a travesty, but given the lack of alternatives, it is better than nothing. Such has been the hold of free market conservatism over the provincial government since 1980 that the idea of a dedicated capital program for not-for-profit operators seems to have never been given serious consideration. Indeed, in 2008 the provincial government refused to provide special relocation funds to one of Alberta's oldest day cares, Primrose Place, when it was forced to move out of a building owned by the Catholic Church. A last minute rental deal with the Edmonton Catholic School Board was the only thing that saved Primrose Place from closing.[37] Furthermore, since the 1980s, the provincial government has consistently opposed any federal money being used in Alberta to the exclusive benefit of not-for-profits. It thus seems that there is no magic governmental fix to this problem on the horizon. Instead, not-for-profit associations are going to have to continue to rely upon their own devices and their ties to the broader community to patch together the grants, donations, and fundraising schemes needed to keep existing centres going and new ones coming into existence.

Among the three alternate blueprints for child care in Alberta, inclusive liberalism is the closest to social liberalism (see Mahon 2008, 345). Inclusive liberalism assigns child care a positive role in creating its version of a good society. That society is individualist and highly competitive in character, so quality child care, just like quality education, is a means to create individuals with the skills and aptitudes to be successful in such a competitive environment. The inclusive liberal blueprint has gained more support among business and political elites in recent years as they have come to realize the importance of knowledge work in the post-Fordist globalized economy. The Alberta government's recent investments in wage enhancements and centre accreditation, as well as the provincialization of OOSC, are consistent with an inclusive liberal concern about the quality of young children's experiences. It is noteworthy that these investments were well supported by social liberals but drew criticism from those operating with free enterprise or pro-family perspectives.[38]

Another initiative that is consistent with both inclusive liberalism and social liberalism is the inclusion of both full-day kindergarten and junior kindergarten in the School Act, thus making their delivery mandatory across the province. These two recommendations were among the ninety-five recommendations tabled by the Alberta Commission on Learning in October 2003. The commission specified that the programs should be taught "by certified teachers with expertise and training in early childhood education" (2003, 46–47).

In the end, the provincial government accepted eighty-six of the ninety-five recommendations by the commission.[39] Given the strong influence of the pro-family movement on the Klein government, it is not surprising that the recommendations for full-day kindergarten and junior kindergarten were rejected. Nevertheless, the commission made a compelling case for this expanded mandate. In the intervening years, a few Alberta school districts have voluntarily introduced full-day kindergarten programs, although in doing so, they have had to take resources away from other parts of the education system. An example is the Medicine Hat School District, which in 2004 began offering the first full-day kindergarten program in the province. In 2009 full-day, every-day kindergarten was offered at every elementary school in the district, with part-day kindergarten also offered at some schools. At the Herald School, where the school district runs a day care that it took over from the municipal government in the mid-1990s, full-day kindergarten is seamlessly integrated with before- and after-school care. This is a forward-thinking exemplar.[40]

There have also been important developments in other provinces: British Columbia has initiated a full-day kindergarten program and Ontario has moved toward full-day kindergarten that is integrated with before- and after-school care along the lines of what happens at the Herald School in Medicine Hat.[41] A similar initiative on a province-wide basis is not beyond the realm of possibility for Alberta, especially given the province's new-found commitment to OOSC in 2008–9. Perhaps the ultimate lighthouse to guide the comprehensive development of high-quality day care for very young children and high-quality OOSC for school-aged children will be new ELCC programs for four and five year olds offered on a statutory basis by school districts.

Pro-family conservatism is the third contending blueprint for child care in Alberta. It emphasizes traditional family relations as the template for a good society. In this ideal society, young children are cared for by a stay-at-home parent and governments use their taxation powers to support the ideal. Pro-family conservatism is the only one of the four perspectives that is generally unsupportive of the regulated child care system.

In the late 1990s, the Alberta government slashed its spending on day care (mainly by ending operating allowances). At the same time, it promoted greater private responsibility for child care by introducing a tax credit for children and increasing the spousal tax exemption to the same amount as the personal exemption. These measures were very popular with stay-at-home parents and were praised by the pro-family movement. The pro-family perspective even shaped the Klein government's initiatives after signing an ELCC accord with the federal government in 2005. One of the programs introduced the next year was specifically geared to the children of stay-at-home parents: Stay-at-Home Parents Support offers an income-tested subsidy of up to $100 a month per young child for fees in "an approved early childhood development program," subject to the condition that at least one parent must be a stay-at-home parent (defined as not working, volunteering, or attending school for more than twenty hours per week). A better version of this program would make subsidies available to all children regardless of parental income and employment status. This change would make early childhood development the unambiguous objective of the program, encourage enrolment in approved programs regardless of family status or caregiving pattern, and give higher-income families a stake in the program. As it stands now, Stay-at-Home Parents Support disallows subsidization if young children are being primarily looked after by nannies, relatives, or unregulated FDH providers. From an ECE perspective, this is illogical since these children would benefit from preschool programs as much if not more than children who are being cared for by a stay-at-home parent.[42]

Public subsidization of quality child care is not logically incompatible with "baby bonuses," tax credits, and other tax measures that favour families with children. It is not even incompatible with public subsidization of stay-at-home parents. Since all of these types of family policy are costly, however, investing in one policy limits a government's financial ability to pursue a second approach (and, perhaps as important, gives a government a convenient financial excuse for not pursuing the second approach). This sort of policy trade-off was in evidence after the federal election in January 2006, won by the Conservative Party of Stephen Harper. One of the Conservatives' major election planks was a new universal "baby bonus" of $100 per month for all children under six years of age. (Its name, the Universal Child Care Benefit [UCCB], is a misnomer since families are not required to use the government transfer for child care). This newest incarnation of a universal baby bonus was projected to cost the federal government $2.1 billion in the 2007–8 fiscal year. The new government covered over half of the cost of the UCCB by cancelling the ELCC agreements that the previous government had negotiated with the provinces in 2005.[43]

The UCCB is a particularly crafty pro-family policy because while it appears to provide equivalent benefits to all families with young children, it provides the greatest benefits to two-parent families with a stay-at-home parent because the UCCB is taxed in the hands of the lower-income parent. Therefore, the family with a stay-at-home parent gets to keep most of the $1,200 yearly benefit even if the family has a very high total family income.[44]

The federal Conservative government extended its pro-family agenda with the 2007 budget, which contained two pro-family taxation measures that had been part of the Alberta tax reforms in the late 1990s: a child tax credit and a spousal tax exemption equal to the basic personal exemption. The total cost for these two measures in 2007–8 was approximately $1.75 billion. Altogether, the price tag for the UCCB, the child tax credit, and the higher spousal exemption in 2007–8 was projected to be in the neighbourhood of $3.85 billion—more than triple the $1.2 billion that would have been spent on regulated child care in 2007–8 under the terms of the cancelled ELCC agreements. The Harper government's spending commitments in the 2007 federal budget showed that it could have easily honoured the ELCC agreements signed by the Martin government and at the same time implemented its new baby bonus. Cancelling the ELCC agreements was a point of principle rather than a financial necessity: it simultaneously expressed the new government's pro-family conservatism and its belief that the federal government should not use its taxation power to take a leadership role in areas of provincial jurisdiction.[45]

While it is true that in the late 1990s, the Alberta Progressive Conservatives pioneered some of the pro-family policies later adopted by the federal government of Stephen Harper, Ralph Klein's government was reluctant to commit to the heavy spending that would have been necessary to firmly entrench a pro-family mix of policies. Stephen Harper's Conservatives demonstrated no such reluctance in 2006 and 2007. Nevertheless, at least during their first four years in office, Harper's Conservatives refrained from adopting the two most costly of pro-family ideas. The first was promoted by the Action démocratique du Québec during the Quebec provincial election in March 2007: a government payment of $100 per week to each child under six years of age not in subsidized day care. The second is income splitting among the adults in a family unit, a measure that would result in an estimated $5 billion in tax savings for couples where one partner is in a high-income bracket and the other has much less income (this includes all stay-at-home parents). Adoption of either of these policies would result in a major new ongoing financial commitment from the federal government. Large subsidies to stay-at-home parents of young children and income splitting at tax time would not only limit the federal government's ability to fund new programs in early learning and child care but would also strengthen the allegiance of many Canadians to elements of the pro-family movement's program. This is why such aggressive and costly pro-family policies constitute a threat to the further development of quality child care in Alberta and other provinces.[46]

The fourth blueprint, free enterprise conservatism, conceives of a good society as individuals participating in competitive marketplaces. While it shares inclusive liberalism's individualism and emphasis on competitiveness, free enterprise conservatism assigns a much narrower role for government: government intervention in the ideal marketized society is only supported when it enhances rather than limits the growth and profitability of private businesses. According to free enterprise conservatives, child care is like other commodities:

it can be efficiently developed and delivered by private investors competing with one another for the allegiance of customers. Therefore, whereas social liberalism actively promotes the decommodification of child care by supporting public and not-for-profit programs, free enterprise conservatism actively promotes its commodification. This helps to explain why proponents of these two perspectives have so often been at loggerheads over the years.

Between the late 1970s and the late 1980s, free enterprise conservatism was the organizing principle of Alberta's day care system. It was superseded by pro-family conservatism in the 1990s, but developments between 2007 and 2009 indicated that the Stelmach government looked favourably on the assumptions of free market conservatism at the same time as it pursued elements of the inclusive liberal blueprint. This was shown, first, by the eligibility of for-profit businesses for space-creation grants. These grants added to the capitalization of businesses and thus amounted to a transfer of wealth from the provincial government to business owners. Second, the deregulation of the maximum facility size for day cares in 2007 demonstrated a political openness to corporate investment in day care that had not existed in Alberta since 1980.

In the early 1980s, civil servants and the Alberta Day Care Advisory Committee proposed two anti-corporatization regulations aimed at preventing U.S.-based corporations like KinderCare Learning from entering the Alberta market and limiting domestic chains from growing beyond a capacity of five hundred children. As described in chapter 6, the provincial government refused to enact the first recommendation and then failed to enforce the second after it was enacted in 1983. As a result, only the regulation that limited the size of day cares to eighty children diminished the possibility of corporate investments (since corporations prefer much larger centres that reduce the fixed costs per child and consequently improve profitability).

Eliminating the maximum facility size in 2007 was a disappointingly short-sighted move that failed to take into account the historical lessons of corporatization of day care, both in Alberta and other jurisdictions. Chapter 6 detailed how in the 1980s the largest day care corporation in the United States, KinderCare Learning, compromised the quality of children's care by squandering financial resources in other investments, including junk bonds. It also detailed the rise and fall of Alberta's leading day care corporation, Kindercare, between the late 1970s and mid-1990s. Kindercare's principal owner, Dennis Sorensen, likewise invested the profits he made in day care in other businesses and by so doing starved the children and workers in his chain of resources. My conclusion from these two examples is that in essential fields of human life (such as the care of young children), corporatization has public policy risks that are too severe to be tolerable. The collapse of ABC Learning Centres in Australia in 2008 with A$1.6 billion of debt on its books supports this conclusion—the lives of thousands of families were disrupted as the receiver almost immediately announced plans to examine the future of 386 centres (out of a total of 1,042). It is highly significant that the majority of the bankrupt chain's centres were eventually sold to a new not-for-profit corporation formed by four well-established Australian charities.[47]

The potential coalition against the corporatization of child care includes, at the very least, the owners of many smaller commercial centres as well as social liberals. Small owners may join the fight against corporatization because they fear the competition from chains and/or because they object to the profit-centred focus of corporations. In the latter case, small owners put the well-being of children ahead of profit considerations (along the lines described by Williams [2009, 72]) and are thus crucial allies in social liberalism's campaign to shift the balance of forces in Alberta child care away from commodification. Therefore, opposing corporatization in day care is a wedge issue that has the potential to split the commercial sector much as it was split in the early 1980s between the Day Care Society of Alberta, on the one hand, and a variety of other owners, on the other. Child care politics in Alberta are unique among the large Canadian provinces because of the relative weakness of social liberalism and the relative strength of both the pro-family and free enterprise blueprints. This is why recognizing and mobilizing sympathetic commercial owners is much more of a requirement for successful anti-commodification campaigns in Alberta than in the other provinces.

My concluding point concerns the marked growth of provincial power in the Canadian federal system since the 1970s. In years gone by, advocates for quality child care sometimes worked around a recalcitrant Alberta government by allying with the federal government or a sympathetic municipal government. Such an end run is no longer possible because all policy and program roads run through Edmonton. While the future may yet yield a federal government that uses its taxation power and a strong electoral mandate to establish a medicare-like, national early learning and child care system, it would be unwise for Alberta advocates to hold their breath waiting for the day. In the meantime, advocates can proceed with confidence by keeping in mind a number of lessons from the past:

1. Certain arguments, such as "Day care costs less than welfare," are effective in disarming opponents. Furthermore, studies that demonstrate the long-term economic benefits of high-quality child care (e.g., Heckman 2006) have the potential to win over those whose conceptions of a good society would not otherwise include extensive public investments in early learning and child care.

2. There is an opportunity for policy or program change whenever Alberta can be made to look bad compared to other provinces on a criterion that resonates with the public.

3. Model programs continue to be lighthouses for program change. Therefore, it is worth pursuing model programs not only for their own merits but also because they expand the range of viable policy options for other jurisdictions.

4. There is no guarantee that a regulation or funding program won't be cut, even if it is long-standing and at one time seemed unassailable. Two examples are the deregulation of the maximum facility size for day cares and the end of the original operating allowance program. Therefore, advocates must continually defend and even call for the extension of programs that are crucial to a quality agenda. Of note in this regard is staff wage enhancements.

5. A significant proportion of Albertans, including political leaders, continue to hold that an ideal society is one in which young children are cared for by a stay-at-home parent. Group care of young children has a very limited place in this pro-family ideal, and universal funding for day care is vehemently opposed. The continuing strength of pro-family conservatism over time is a prime reason for the endless quality of Alberta's day care controversy. It also means that Albertans with a social liberal conception of child care must always be prepared to pare down their demands and find common cause with inclusive liberals and/or free enterprise conservatives in order to counter the political influence of the pro-family movement.

In 1970 Dr. Jay Bishop, an educational psychologist at the University of Alberta, was interviewed for a story on the effects of poor-quality day care on young children. He offered this political observation: "We are still in a frontier province concerned with wheat sales and oil. The young child, here, is not considered relevant."[48] This sweeping condemnation of Alberta's myopic frontier mentality may well have had a degree of validity in 1970 and it certainly aligns with a common anti-Alberta stereotype. The reality today, however, is more complex. The young child is indeed relevant, but relevant in different ways for different groups of Albertans. Therefore, the task facing those who support making early learning and child care a governmental priority on par with the tar sands is to put the case to all Albertans in a respectful but insistent fashion. The Alberta Association for Young Children is defunct. Its mission is incomplete.

Appendix A
Supplementary Tables

TABLE A.1 Licensed Day Nurseries and Day Care Centres in Alberta, 1959 to 1977

Year	Licensed facilities	PSS day cares[a]	Year	Licensed facilities	PSS day cares
1959[b]	2		1969	78	7
1960	5		1970	98	
1961	29		1971	107	14 ($578,000)
1962	26		1972	135	13 ($658,000)
1963	34		1973	146	20 ($981,000)
1964	38		1974		($1,240,000)
1965	42		1975	219	46 ($1,998,000)
1966	50		1976	252	($3,271,000)
1967	62	1 ($74,800)[c]	1977	293	60 ($4,306,000)
1968	69	1			

SOURCES: Bella 1978, 70, 104; annual reports of the Department of Social Development and its successor departments; "PSS Day Care Operators and Addresses, May 1977" (CA, Social Services, box 9566, file: Day Care Staff Outline); Alberta Social Services and Community Health, List of Day Cares, 1 July 1975 (PAA, 83.386, file 12).

[a] PSS day cares (which came into existence only after the passage of the *Preventive Social Services Act* in 1966) were run on a non-profit basis by municipal governments or community agencies. Their start-up costs and yearly deficits were shared by the federal, provincial, and municipal governments on a 50-30-20 percentage basis. Dollar amounts in parentheses represent the cost to the province for PSS day cares in a given year, prior to the receipt of funds from the federal government. PSS day cares were licensed by the province and are a subset of all licensed facilities.

[b] For 1959–1969 and 1973 the counts of licensed facilities are for January. The source is a table found in the Provincial Archives of Alberta (83.836, file "Misc."). A comparison of the table's entry for 1970 with comparable data found in the 1969–70 annual report of the Alberta Department of Social Development suggests that the January counts included pending licenses as well as existing licenses.

For 1970–72 and 1976–77, the counts are for 31 March. Sources are the annual reports of the Department of Social Development (1970–71), the Department of Health and Social Development (1972), and the Department of Social Services and Community Health (1976–77).

The number of licensed facilities in 1974 was not recorded in any of the documents I consulted.

For 1975 the count is for a 1 July list of licensed day cares (PAA, 83.386, file 12) supplemented by information on day cares in the City of Calgary in 1974 (CA, Social Services, box 6290) since there were obvious omissions from the province's 1975 list. Facilities with as few as four licensed spaces were included in the 1975 list. Family day homes were not distinguished from day care centres until the establishment of the Day Care Regulation on 15 March 1978 (Alberta 1978).

[c] Provincial costs for PSS day cares include day care studies and municipal day care directors.

TABLE A.2   Licensed Day Care Centres and Family Day Homes in Alberta, 1978 to 1981

Year	Location	Licensed facilities	Licensed capacity	Licensed day cares	Day care capacity
1978	Outside Calgary	244	7,919		
	Calgary	108	4,924		
	Total	352	12,843		
1979	Outside Calgary	298	9,504	195 [b]	
	Calgary [a]	137	5,463	90 [b]	
	Total [a]	435	14,967	285	
1980	Outside Calgary	278	9,484	208	8,283 (January)
				215	8,966 (August)
	Calgary	165	6,002		
	Total	443	15,486		
1981	Outside Calgary			235	9,611 (January)
				232	9,714 (July)
	Calgary			117	6,401 (January)
				113	6,414 (July)
	Total	501	17,900	352	16,012 (January)
				345	16,128 (July)

SOURCES: Annual reports of Alberta Social Services and Community Health, 1978–79, 1979–80 and 1980–81. For 1980 and 1981, the published data have been supplemented by unpublished provincial licensing statistics for day cares (PAA, 92.150, box 1).

NOTE: Published data for the years 1978 to 1981 are not comparable to data for succeeding years since day care centres and family day homes were not treated as distinct categories at that time. For this reason I have reported data for these four years in a separate table.

[a] The City of Calgary ran its own licensing program in 1979 and 1980. The 1979 figures for Calgary and for the provincial total are estimates based upon the assumption that there were equivalent increases in facilities and licensed capacity in Calgary in 1978–79 and 1979–80.

[b] Memo from Catarina Versaevel to John Lackey, 29 August 1979, "Re: Minister's Briefing Book, Fall Session" (PAA, 90.301, file: Com. Soc. Ser. Briefing to Ministers.)

TABLE A.3 Licensed Day Care Centres in Alberta and Their Capacity, 1981 to 2009

Year	Licensed day cares	Yearly % change in day cares	Licensed capacity	Yearly % change in capacity
1981[a]	353	+13%[b]	16,163	+16%[b]
1982	365	+3%	17,037	+5%
1983	442	+17%	20,255	+19%
1984	482	+9%	22,152	+9%
1985	515	+7%	23,673	+7%
1986	579	+12%	27,194	+15%
1987	649	+12%	30,196	+11%
1988	661	+2%	31,656	+5%
1989	656	-1%	32,023	+1%
1990	669	+2%	32,839	+3%
1991	671	+1%	33,571	+2%
1992	651	-3%	32,690	-3%
1993	631	-3%	32,132	-2%
1994[c]	644	+2%	32,567	+1%
1995	629	-2%	31,503	-3%
1996	608	-3%	30,478	-3%
1997	572	-6%	28,557	-7%
1998	553	-3%	27,847	-2%
1999	538	-3%	26,709	-4%
2000[d]	567	+5%	28,038	+5%
2001	577	+2%	28,037	0%
2002	574	0%	27,723	-1%
2003	522	-9%	25,494	-8%
2004	522	0%	25,874	+1%
2004[e]	519	-1%	25,593	-1%
2005	497	-4%	24,561	-4%
2006	510	+3%	25,009	+2%
2007	504	-1%	25,279	+1%
2008	512	+2%	25,890	+2%
2009	556	+9%	26,244	+1%

SOURCES: Annual departmental reports of Alberta Social Services and Community Health (fiscal years 1981–82 to 1985–86), Alberta Social Services (1986–87 to 1987–88), Alberta Family and Social Services (1988–89 to 1998–99, except for 1993–94). For 1994: "Day-care Costs Under Microscope," *Calgary Herald*, 5 November 1993, A1. For 2000–2002: personal correspondence from Merrilyn Greig, Information Services Branch, Alberta Children's Services. For 2003: Alberta 2003. For first 2004 entry: Alberta 2004. For November 2004: telephone conversation with Bernard Trudell, Child Development Branch, Alberta Children's Services. For 2005–6: spreadsheet provided by Bernard Trudell. For 2007–9: spreadsheet provided by Leann Wagner, Child Development Branch, Alberta Children and Youth Services.

TABLE A.3 (continued)

[a] As of 31 March unless otherwise noted.

[b] These percentage increases were calculated on the basis of information presented in table A.2. From January 1980 to January 1981, the number of day cares outside of Calgary increased by 13% (from 208 to 235), as did the total number of day cares and family day homes in the province, including Calgary (from 443 to 501). For the same period, the licensed capacity of day cares increased by 16% outside of Calgary (from 8,232 to 9,611), as did the total licensed capacity of day cares and family day homes in the province, including Calgary (from 15,486 to 17,900).

[c] Early November 1993 instead of 31 March 1994.

[d] June 2000 instead of 31 March 2000.

[e] November 2004.

TABLE A.4 Provincial Spending on Preschool Child Care (in Actual Dollars, Thousands)

Fiscal year ending	PSS expenditures	Child care subsidy	Operating allowance	FDH agency fee	Total
1971	578				
1972	658				
1973	981				
1974	1,240				
1975	1,998				
1976	3,271				
1977	4,306				
1978	4,744				
1979					6,412
1980					9,349
1981			3,200 [a]		
1982		11,525	11,269		24,631 [b]
1983		13,731	15,586	735 [c]	31,461 [d]
1984		17,084	20,073	1,617 [c]	39,911 [e]
1985		20,675	26,458 [f]		48,112 [e]
1986		23,673	33,784 [f]		58,328 [e]
1987		25,823	37,566 [f]		64,944 [g]
1988					65,137
1989					64,168
1990			33,800 [a]		70,530
1991					73,941
1992		31,732	25,641	7,173 [h]	72,549
1993					71,017
1994					73,534
1995		39,848	19,222	6,787 [i]	73,832
1996					67,494
1997					61,878
1998		32,158	15,513	4,928 [j]	60,305
1999					63,770
2000					64,437
2001		49,800	0	5,600 [k]	63,875
2002					59,598
2003		44,000			61,300
2004		41,000		4,900 [l]	56,934
2006		49,750		4,820 [m]	78,300
2007					104,000
2008		61,327		5,234 [n]	116,000

TABLE A.4 (continued)

SOURCES: The principal sources for tables A.4 and A.5 are as follows: *Public Accounts of Alberta*, 1970–71 to 1996–97; Alberta Family and Social Services, annual reports for 1997–98 to 1998–99; Alberta Children's Services, annual reports for 1999–2000 to 2001–2; Alberta 2003 and Alberta 2004; and, for 2006-2008, http://www.child.alberta.ca/home/documents/childcare/chart_2005_06_to_2008_09.pdf (available from author; link active 5 September 2010). Data for 2005 were unavailable.

[a] Alberta FSS 1990a.

[b] The total for 1982 includes day care administration expenses of $1,837,000.

[c] The operating allowance and satellite family day home agency fee were separated in a document prepared for the Federal/Provincial/Territorial Working Group on Child Care, 28 January 1985 (PAA, 93.188, box 2, file: August 1984 to October 1985).

[d] Administration expenses for 1983 were $2,409,000.

[e] These totals are slight underestimates since the only administration expenses reported were for regional service delivery.

[f] Includes the family day home agency fee.

[g] This total includes expenditures of $1,208,000 for administration and $347,000 for the "appeal and advisory secretariat" (together equal to 2% of the total).

[h] The first three entries for 1992 are from CCRU 1993, 59.

[i] The first three entries for 1995 are from CCRU 1997, 56.

[j] The first three entries for 1998 are from www.childcarecanada.org/pt98/ab/ab4.html

[k] The first three entries for 2001 are from www.childcarecanada.org/ECECC2001/AB.pdf

[l] The first two entries for 2004 are from CRRU 2005, 121.

[m]The first two entries for 2006 are from CRRU 2007, 137.

[n] The first two entries for 2008 are from CRRU 2009, 119. Spending in 2008 included $33.2 million on accreditation and wage enhancements, $3.1 million on inclusive child care, and $0.8 million on stay-at-home parents support.

TABLE A.5 Provincial Spending on Preschool Child Care (in 2006 Dollars, Thousands) [a]

Fiscal year ending	PSS expenditures	Child care subsidy	Operating allowance	FDH agency fee	Total
1971	3,102				
1972	3,379				
1973	4,695				
1974	5,390				
1975	7,816				
1976	11,818				
1977	14,296				
1978	14,502				
1979					18,018
1980					23,840
1981			7,229		
1982		23,373	22,854		49,952
1983		26,487	30,065	1,418	60,688
1984		32,084	37,697	3,037	74,953
1985		37,711	48,259		87,756
1986		41,735	59,561		102,832
1987		43,796	63,712		110,145
1988					107,541
1989					101,706
1990			50,632		105,654
1991					104,257
1992		44,266	35,769	10,006	101,206
1993					97,861
1994					99,933
1995		52,958	25,546	9,434	98,122
1996					87,742
1997					78,771
1998		40,519	18,026	6,209	75,984
1999					78,437
2000					76,551
2001		57,867	0	6,507	74,223
2002					66,988
2003		47,344			65,959
2004		43,460		5,199	60,407
2006		49,750		4,820	78,300
2007					99,112
2008		56,666		4,836	107,184

SOURCES: See table A.4.

[a] Corrections for inflation for the years prior to 2006 are based upon the Statistics Canada table "Annual Inflation Rate—Alberta: 1971–2006." Corrections for inflation for 2007 and 2008 are based upon the Statistics Canada table "Annual Inflation Rate—Alberta: 1988–2008."

TABLE A.6   Selected Statistics on Child Care Programs in Alberta, 1979 to 2009

	Preschoolers with income subsidies	Operating allowance			Licensed out-of-school spaces	Children in satellite family day homes
		6-month-old	24-month-old	42-month-old		
1979	535 (non-PSS)					
1980	2,776 [a]	(payments began in September 1980)				
1981	6,456	55 (124) [b]	55 (124)	55 (124)	1,800	302
1982	6,710	180 (365)	110 (223)	70 (142)		1,124
1983	6,898	240 (463)	120 (232)	70 (135)	2,813	1,335
1984	8,478	257 (483)	131 (246)	78.50 (147)	3,564	2,549
1985	10,172	257 (469)	131 (239)	78.50 (143)	4,505	3,745
1986	11,625	257 (453)	131 (231)	78.50 (138)	5,441	5,050
1987	12,522	257 (436)	131 (222)	78.50 (133)	6,578	5,182
1988	12,491	257 (424)	131 (216)	78.50 (130)	7,510	4,936
1989	12,227	257 (407)	131 (208)	78.50 (124)	8,257	5,280
1990		257 (385)	110 (165)	78.50 (118)	10,669	5,812
1991		200 (283)	110 (156)	78.50 (111)	10,651	6,536
1992	11,848	180 (251)	100 (140)	78.50 (110)	10,958	6,811
1993	11,436	180 (248)	100 (138)	78.50 (108)	11,425	7,173
1994	12,550	170 (231)	90 (122)	70 (95)	11,954	
1995	13,554 [c]	170 (226)	90 (120)	70 (93)		7,800
1996	10,762 [c]	165 (214)	85 (110)	65 (84)		6,850
1997	10,980	160 (204)	80 (102)	60 (76)		6,415
1998	10,600	160 (202)	80 (101)	60 (76)	14,529	6,505
1999	11,575	58 (71)	29 (36)	22 (27)		6,610
2000	12,371	0	0	0	14,988	6,792
2001	12,067				15,442	7,039
2002	11,013				16,222	6,975
2003	10,158					
2004	10,600					
2005					17,313	
2006	11,932				18,506	6,775 (10,102) [d]
2007					18,925	11,427
2008	10,616				19,506	11,667
2009					22,039	10,696

	Maximum monthly subsidy		Turning point[e] for a family with 1 parent, 1 child	Break-even point[e] for a family with 1 parent, 1 child
	6-month-old	42-month-old		
1979	210 (590)	190 (534)		
1980	210 (536)	190 (484)		
1981	175 (395)	175 (395)		
1982	175 (355)	175 (355)		
1983	195 (376)	195 (376)		
1984	195 (366)	195 (366)	13,560 (25,466)	17,532 (32,925)
1985				
1986	195 (344)	195 (344)		
1987				
1988	195 (322)	195 (322)	13,560 (22,388)	17,532 (28,945)
1989	240 (380)	240 (380)		
1990				
1991	240 (339)	240 (339)		
1992	240 (335)	240 (335)		
1993	330 (455)	260 (358)		
1994	330 (448)	260 (353)	16,560 (22,505)	24,480 (33,268)
1995	330 (439)	260 (346)		
1996	330 (429)	260 (338)		
1997	330 (420)	260 (331)		
1998	330 (416)	260 (328)	16,560 (20,866)	24,480 (30,845)
1999	435 (535)	340 (418)	19,560 (24,059)	29,400 (36,162)
1999 (second increase)			20,520 (25,240)	30,720 (37,786)
2000	475 (564)	380 (451)	20,520 (24,378)	31,680 (37,654)
2001	475 (552)	380 (442)	20,520 (23,844)	31,680 (36,812)
2002	475 (534)	380 (427)	20,520 (23,064)	31,680 (35,608)
2003	475 (511)	380 (409)	28,080[f] (30,214)	38,990[f] (41,953)
2004	475 (504)	380 (403)		
2005	475 (494)	380 (395)		
Nov 2005	575 (575)	500 (500)	35,100[g] (35,100)	54,900[g] (54,900)
2006				
June 2007	607 (578)	528 (503)	35,100[g] (33,450)	56,076[g] (53,440)
Sept 2008	628 (580)	546 (505)	35,100[fg] (32,432)	58,827[g] (54,356)
2009				

TABLE A.6 (continued)

SOURCES: Various statistics for 1992: CRRU 1993; various statistics for 1995: CRRU 1997; various statistics for 1998, CRRU 2000; various statistics for 2004, CRRU 2005; various statistics for 2006, CRRU 2007; various statistics for 2008: CRRU 2009.

Additional subsidy information. For 1979, Catarina Versaevel, 29 August 1979, "Re: Minister's Briefing Book, Fall Session" (PAA, 90.301, file: Comm. Soc. Serv. Briefing to Ministers). For reduction in 1980, *Calgary Herald*, 6 May 1980, B1. For 1982, Medicine Hat Child Care Services, "History of the Medicine Hat Day-Care Services," June 1989, p. 22. For 1983: Province of Alberta response to questionnaire from the National Day Care Information Centre, 21 July 1983 (PAA, 93.188, box 2); and "Day Care Programs" (PAA, 93.188, box 2, file 9.1.2). For 1984: Federal / Provincial / Territorial Working Group on Child Care, 28 January 1985, "Phase One: Province of Alberta Data" (PAA, 93.188, box 2, file: August 1984 to October 1985); and Melane Hotz, director, Day Care Branch, 24 May 1984, "Alberta Day Care Program Issues," 24 May 1984 (PAA, 93.188, box 2, file: May 1984 to December 1984). For 1993: information posted on government web page (in the author's possession). For increases in 1998–2000: 2 March 1999 press release from the province (in the author's possession) and the Winter 1997 issue of *Day Care Matters* (Alberta Family and Social Services). For 2001: "National Child Benefit in Alberta," July 2001, distributed to recipients of the benefit. For 2003: Alberta 2003: 32. For 2004: Alberta 2004, 32. For 2005: table on website of Calgary and Area Child and Family Services Authority (in the author's possession). For 2007 and 2008: figures calculated using the on-line estimator tool provided through the provincial government's website (on 5 September 2010 it could be found at http://www.child.alberta.ca/home/1190.cfm).

For children on subsidies, licensed out-of-school spaces, and children in satellite family day homes: Annual Reports of Alberta Family and Social Services and its predecessor departments. For 1981 out-of-school spaces: "F.C.S.S. Program Children's Programs" (PAA, 93.188, box 2). For 2000–2002: personal correspondence from Merrilyn Greig, Information Services Branch, Alberta Children's Services.

For operating allowance levels: Alberta Cabinet docket RFD-M4-81, 14 April 1981; documents referenced in chapter 7; and *Day Care Matters*, Winter 1997 (Alberta Family and Social Services).

For OOSC spaces in 2000 (June), 2001 (March), and 2002 (March): personal correspondence from Merrilyn Greig, Information Services Branch, Alberta Children's Services. For OOSC spaces and contracted FDH spaces in 2006: spreadsheet provided by Bernard Trudell, Child Development Branch. For OOSC spaces and contracted FDH spaces in 2007–9: spreadsheet provided by Leann Wagner, Child Development Branch.

[a] This is the estimated number of preschool children with a subsidy as of 29 February 1980. The estimate assumes that the percentage increase in preschoolers with a subsidy between 29 February 1980 and 31 March 1981 is the same as a reported percentage increase in school-age children with a subsidy over the same time period (132.6%). This allowed me to take the reported number of pre-schoolers with income subsidies on 31 March 1981 (6,456) and extrapolate backwards to the estimated number of 2,776 on 29 February 1980.

[b] When dollar figures are reported in this table, the first number is unadjusted and the number in brackets is the inflation-adjusted equivalent in 2006 dollars.

[c] These are estimates. Estimates are needed since the numbers of preschoolers receiving subsidies in 1995 and 1996 were not reported. The estimates are calculated using the assumption that the percentage change in the number of subsidized preschoolers in a set time period (e.g., 1994 to 1995), is equal to the percentage change in the number of subsidized families in the same time period.

[d] Contracted FDH spaces, not the number of enrolled children.

[e] The turning point is the maximum income a family can earn to be eligible for a full subsidy; the break-even point is the income at which a family no longer qualifies for a partial subsidy. Prior to 2003, turning and break-even points were calculated using net income. There are different turning points and break-even points depending upon the number of parents and children in a family. This table reports just one set of turning and break-even points—that for a family with one parent and one child.

[f] Beginning in 2003, turning and break-even points were calculated using gross income rather than net income. Therefore the figures for 2003 onward are not directly comparable to the earlier figures.

[g] Calculated for an infant less than 18 months of age. Prior to 2005, the turning point and break-even points did not vary with the age of the child.

Appendix B
Taped Interviews

ALBERTA

Pauline Desjardins, 3 March 1995
Joanne Guinet, 13 June 1995
John Lackey, 12 April 96
Caterina Versaevel, 25 April 1996
Judy Padua, 3 March 1998 and 14
    August 1998
Dennis Maier, 5 March 1998
Sylene Syvenky, 13 November 1998

CALGARY

Wendy Reid, 23 June 1993
Noreen Murphy, 18 August 1993 and
    22 August 1995
Billie Shepherd, 30 March 1995
Brian Corbishley, 12 July 1995
Barb Scott, 12 July 1995
David Bronconnier, 13 July 1995
Bob Holmes, 17 July 1995
Bob Hawkesworth, 19 July 1995
Norm Bilodeau, 29 July 1995
Bill Ardiel, 27 July 1995
Sue Higgins, 27 July 1995
Judy Bader, 9 August 1995
Loreen Huras, 8 July 1997
Traudi Kelm, 16 August 1995 and 11
    December 2002
Peter Marsden, 29 August 1995
Laurie Doyle, 31 August 1995
Tammy Baldwin, 15 September 1995
Christine Sheppard and Nora Capithorn,
    22 September 1995
Sam Blakely, 27 September 1995
Annette LaGrange, 10 August 1995
Maria Valenti, 31 July 1997 and 29 July 1998
Irmtraud (Irma) Walter, 18 December 2002
Nizar Daya, 19 December 2002

EDMONTON

Jennifer Wolfe, 3 March 1995
Howard Clifford, 20 and 23 February 1996
Bruce Ryan, 11 March 1996
Avril Pike, 9 April 1996
Mary Hull, 10 April 1996 and March 1998
Kathy Barnhart, 10 and 25 April 1996
Keith Wass, 13 April 1996
Al Hagan, 16 April 1996
Sheila Campbell, 17 April 1996
Sheila Campbell (with Ellen Derksen),
    25 April 1996
David Gilbert, 21 August 1997
Lana Sampson, 5 March 1998
Conny Hippe, 6 March 1998

MEDICINE HAT

Gita Hashizume, 15 December 1994
Karen Charlton, 15 December 1994 and
    25 April 1995
Susan Costea, 15 December 1994
Walter Regehr, 15 December 1994
Graham Kelly, 4 January 1995
Julie Friesen, 4 January 1995
Melinda Arthur, 4 January 1995
Mayor Ted Grimm, 24 April 1995
Patti Drysdale, 24 April 1995
Dorothy Samuel, 24 April 1995
Diane Buchignani, 25 April 1995
Robert Wanner, 25 April 1995

GRANDE PRAIRIE

Marg Valiquette, 18 April 1996
Tanice Jones, 18 April 1996
Chris Henderson, 19 April 1996
Nancy Hall, 19 April 1996

PRO-FAMILY ORGANIZATIONS

H. Dykxhoorn, 4 May 1998
Mark Genuis, 19 May 1998
J. Woodard, 19 May 1998
Cathy Perri, 20 May 1998
Beverley Smith, 26 May 1998
B.R. Beyer, 5 June 1998

Notes

1. Introduction

1   Until recently, "day care" was the umbrella term used in Alberta to refer to the group care of young children (Alberta 1991, 2–3). In November 2008, the term "child care" replaced "day care" in the title of the regulation that accompanied a new licensing act. Nevertheless, "day care program" was retained as the name for the care of a group of eleven or more young children "for four or more consecutive hours" (Alberta 2008, 1, 15).

2   Langford (2002) cites theoretical sources for the neo-Marxist/neo-Weberian class schema presented here.

3   The operators of satellite FDHs are classified as workers because of their exclusive affiliation with an FDH agency. They are like industrial home workers who, while ostensibly independent, are in a captive relationship with a single employer. In contrast, the operators of independent FDHs control all aspects of their business and are thus members of the old middle class.

4   Small business owners are a "middle class" in the sense that they are neither workers nor capitalists. They are called the "old" middle class because they were the predominant middle-class grouping during the early decades of capitalism.

5   Nevertheless, some historical background on the development of "Indian day care" can be found in chapter 4. Racialization refers "to those instances where social relations between people have been structured by the signification of human biological characteristics in such a way as to define and construct differentiated social collectivities" (Miles 1989, 75). The parallel process of ethnicization involves the construction of differentiated social collectivities through the signification of cultural characteristics.

2. Early Efforts to Organize Day Nurseries, 1908–45

1   The practice of seizing children from single mothers was outlined and critiqued by the Calgary Children's Aid Department in a brief to the 1947–48 Judicial Commission of Inquiry (Rooke and Schnell 1982, 14).

2   "The Edmonton Creche," Edmonton Bulletin, 5 December 1908; Alberta Bureau of Statistics 1981, table 4; Canada 1953, table 19.

3   "Is Not the Proper Maintenance of this Institution Worth a Thousand Dollars Annually to Edmonton?" Edmonton Bulletin, 17 April 1909.

4   "Taking Over the Creche," Edmonton Bulletin, 26 January 1910.

5   Alberta Bureau of Statistics 1981, table 4; City of Edmonton Planning and Development, "City of Edmonton Population, Historical," table available through the City of Edmonton Internet portal; "Nearly Thirty Children Are Being Taken Care of in Day Nursery," *Edmonton Bulletin*, 24 February 1917.

6   Neither Sheila Campbell (2001, 82) nor Larry Prochner (2000, 46) record the existence of the dedicated day nursery run by the Children's Aid Society between 1912 and at least 1917. This day nursery is especially significant because of its relatively large size (thirty-two children) in 1917. In comparison, the new Edmonton Creche established in 1930 "rarely [had] more than eighteen children per day" at any point during the 1930s (Prochner 2000, 47).

7   "An Act Granting Assistance to Widowed Mothers Supporting Children, assented to April 17, 1919," *Revised Statutes of Alberta*, 1919, chap. 6, pp. 59–62. Cohen (1927, 18) mistakenly reported that in 1926 Alberta extended coverage to mothers with totally disabled husbands. In fact, this amendment was passed but never proclaimed. In 1942 the coverage of the *Mothers' Allowance Act* was broadened to include mothers deserted "without reasonable cause" by their husbands for five or more years (*Revised Statutes of Alberta*, 1942, vol. 3, chap. 302, p. 3941).

8   "City of Edmonton Population, Historical."

9   "Memorandum re Creche," n.d. [1951] (City of Edmonton Archives [hereafter cited as EA], RG 11, class 32, file 11).

10 Letter from Hugh R. Elston, vice principal of Edmonton College Inc., to Edmonton Mayor and Council, 26 March 1951 (EA, RG 11, class 32, file 11).

11 Zwicker 1985, 71–75; "Population Gains and Losses," *Edmonton Journal*, 4 July 1944, 4; Alberta Bureau of Statistics 1950, 36. The combined population of the two major cities in 1941 was 182,721, with Edmonton having about 4,000 more residents than Calgary (39).

12 Zwicker 1985, 69, 77–88; "More Women Getting Jobs," *Calgary Albertan*, 11 May 1944, 9.

13 The meeting with Premier Manning is recorded in Enid McCalla, "Nursery Story, World War II," 1966 (EA, MS 323, class 2, file 27). McCalla was a member of the Edmonton Day Care Committee in 1943–44. Minister of Health W.W. Cross sent an unsigned copy of the agreement to the City of Edmonton on 31 August 1943 (EA, RG 11, class 32, file 7). Order-in-Council PC 6242, 20 July 1942, authorized "the Minister of Labour, on behalf of the Dominion to enter into an agreement with any province, in accordance with an attached draft, for the provision of day nurseries, creches and recreation centres for children." Ontario and Quebec had been involved in drafting the terms of PC 6242 and consequently signed agreements within two weeks. Other provinces were sent a copy of the draft agreement and invited to participate (Pierson 1986, 51). McCalla reports that the draft agreement had been sent directly to Ernest Manning on 9 July 1942 and that when no reply was received, a follow-up inquiry was sent in March 1943 ("Nursery Story, World War II"). The agreement between Alberta and the federal government was officially dated 7 September 1943 (see draft agreement on funding between the Province and the City of Edmonton, EA, RG 11, class 32, file 8).

14 Premier Manning's 9 May 1944 press release is found in Provincial Archives of Alberta (hereafter cited as PAA), 69.289, file 882, as is the 27 April 1944 statement by the provincial advisory committee. The press release was reprinted in "Day Nursery Plan Now Is In Abeyance," *Edmonton Bulletin*, 9 May 1944, 9.

15 This half-day kindergarten was founded in 1939 by a women's organization, the Calgary Stagette Club, in an effort to "keep children off the streets." It was run out of a classroom in the James Short elementary public school. The Calgary Board of Education assumed responsibility for the kindergarten in 1941 at the request of the Stagette Club (Prochner 2000, 37).

16 Submission of the Calgary Day Nursery Committee (CDNC) to the Provincial Day Nursery Advisory Committee, April 1944 (National Archives of Canada [hereafter cited as NAC], RG 27, vol. 611, file 6-52-9).

17 "Information re. Need of Day Care for Children in Edmonton," presented by the Day Care Committee of the Edmonton Council of Social Agencies to the Provincial Advisory Committee, April 1944 (NAC, RG 27, vol. 611, file 6-52-9).

18 Memo from Mrs. Rex Eaton to Mr. A. MacNamara, "Setting Up of Day Care Units in Other Provinces," 16 August 1943 (NAC, RG 27, vol. 609, file 6-52-1, pt. 1); Submission of the CDNC (NAC, RG 27, vol. 611, file 6-52-9).

19 EA, RG 11, class 32, file 7.

20 F. Eaton, 18 January 1944, "Report—Day Nursery Situation, Calgary, Alta." (NAC, RG 27, vol. 60, file 6-52-2, vol. 3).

21 EA, RG 11, class 32, file 7.

22 Letter from Deputy Mayor Ainlay to W.W. Cross, 9 September 1943 (EA, RG 11, class 32, file 7).

23 Commissioners Report to Finance Committee, 6 October 1943; "Finance Committee Report no. 14, section 1" (EA, RG 11, class 32, file 7).

24 "Information re. Need of Day Care for Children in Edmonton," April 1944; memo submitted to Edmonton City Council by Alderman Ainlay, 10 January 1944; Commissioners Report No. 4, sec. 4, "Day Nurseries," including council decision of 24 January 1944 (EA, RG 11, class 32, file 8).

25 Submission of the CDNC and letter from Adelaide Hobson to Mrs. Eaton, 13 January 1944 (NAC, RG 27, vol. 611, file 6-52-9); letter from W.W. Cross to Humphrey Mitchell, 29 December 1943 (NAC, RG 27, vol. 610, file 6-52-2, vol. 3).

26 Cross to Mitchell, 29 December 1943.

27 The definition of "war industry" in the cost-sharing agreements was very broad, but the term "war industry" itself suggested a narrow focus on the munitions and armaments industries. Beginning in 1943, "war industry" was defined according to the manpower priority classification system that had been established on a nationwide basis in 1942 and was being continually updated by the Department of Labour based upon reports by employers. Specifically, a mother was classified as working in a war industry if either the industry in which she worked or the firm where she was employed had a priority A (very highly essential) or B (highly essential) rating for women workers (letter from Humphrey Mitchell to the Chair of the Toronto Board of Education, 18 May 1943 [NAC, RG 27, vol. 610, file 6-52-2, vol. 1]; Stevenson 2001, 28–29).

28 Fraudena Eaton, 18 January 1944, "Report—Day Nursery Situation, Calgary, Alta." (NAC, RG 27, vol. 610, file 6-52-2, vol. 3).

29 Letter from A. MacNamara to W.W. Cross, 10 March 1944 (NAC, RG 27, vol. 611, file 6-52-9). A copy of provincial Order-in-Council 355/44 is found attached to a letter from Marjorie Pardee to Fraudena Eaton, 6 April 1944 (NAC, RG 27, vol. 611, file 6-52-9).

30 Letter from R.W.R., "Why the Day Nursery Delay?" 14 April 1944, p. 4. Maude Riley had been the president of the Calgary Council of Child Welfare since the 1920s and had been actively involved in the Canadian Welfare Council. Despite her opposition to the establishment of day nurseries in 1944, she was no shill for the Social Credit government: she supported Charlotte Whitton's critical views on Alberta's child welfare practices (Rooke and Schnell 1987, 128). Nevertheless, Riley's nomination to the advisory committee in 1944 is perhaps the best indication that W.W. Cross chose to stack the committee with negative votes.

31 Receipt of Drayton's nomination is recorded in a letter from W.W. Cross to Mayor John Fry, 7 February 1944 (EA, RB 11, class 32, file 8).

32 Pardee to Margaret Grier, 28 March 1944 (NAC, RG 27, vol. 611, file 5-52-9).

33 Pardee to Eaton, 6 April 1944 (NAC, RG 27, vol. 611, file 6-52-9).

34 Pardee to Eaton, 27 April 1944 (NAC, RG 27, vol. 611, file 6-52-9).

35 Pardee to Eaton, 6 April 1944 (NAC, RG 27, vol. 611, file 6-52-9).

36 This quotation is from Frank Drayton's report to Edmonton's City Commissioners, 6 April 1944 (EA, RG 11, class 32, file 9).

37 For instance, the advertisement ran continuously in the Calgary Albertan between 18 and 24 April. It read, "MOTHERS employed in WAR INDUSTRIES, who will undertake to place their children under the age of SIX years in DAY NURSERIES if such were in operation, are requested to fill in the blank form below and mail it not later than 22nd April, 1944 to The Secretary, Advisory Committee on Day Nurseries, 134 Administration Building, Edmonton, Alta." Interestingly, the advertisement ran on Monday, 24 April (p. 8) even though the deadline for mailing in the form had passed. An identical version of the advertisement ran on 25 April in the Calgary Herald (p. 2), three days after the stated deadline for mailing. The failure to ensure that the content of the advertisement was consistent with its appearance dates in the newspapers is a small indication of the ineptness of the provincial advisory committee.

38 "Information re. Need of Day Care for Children in Edmonton," April 1944.

39 "Information Regarding the Wartime Day Nursery Situation in Edmonton. Presented to the City Council of Edmonton by the Day Care Committee of the Edmonton Council of Social Agencies," 12 June 1944 (EA, RG 11, class 32, file 9).

40 Pardee to Eaton, 27 April 1944 (NAC, RG 27, vol. 611, file 6-52-9).

41 "Information re. Need of Day Care for Children in Edmonton," April 1944; "'Albertans Unequalled,'" Calgary Albertan, 24 April 1944, 2.

42 Pardee to Eaton, 26 April 1944 (NAC, RG 27, vol. 611, file 6-52-9).

43 "Day Nurseries," Edmonton Bulletin, 29 April 1944, 4; "Day Nurseries," Edmonton Bulletin, 4 May 1944; "Some Day Nursery Questions," Edmonton Journal, 1 May 1944, 4; "For All Working Mothers," Edmonton Journal, 2 May 1944, 4.

44 Letter to the editor from "A Working Mother," Edmonton Bulletin, 6 May 1944, 4; Ladies Jay Cee Club, letter to the editor, and University Women's Club, letter to the

editor, *Edmonton Bulletin*, 8 May 1944, 4; "Two Organizations Protest Decision Against Nurseries," *Edmonton Journal*, 6 May 1944, 11.

45 "Day Nursery Report to Be Under Review," *Edmonton Bulletin*, 1 May 1944, 11.

46 PAA, 69.289, file 882. See the reports on the 6 April meeting written by Frank Drayton (EA, RG 11, class 32, file 9) and Marjorie Pardee (NAC, RG 27, vol. 611, file 6-52-9).

47 Letter from Mayor Fry to Minister Cross, 27 June 1944, quoting a city council resolution from 12 June (EA, RG 11, class 32, file 9). Copies of letters from many groups are found in this file and in PAA, 69.289, file 882.

48 "3,088 Jobs Open at End of Week," *Edmonton Journal*, 13 May 1944, 11; "Need 2,735 Men for Work in City," *Edmonton Journal*, 20 June 1944, 9; "Labor Lack Here 'Worst in Canada,'" *Edmonton Journal*, 27 June 1944, 9; "More Women Getting Jobs," *Calgary Albertan*, 11 May 1944, 9.

49 Mary Livesay to M. Shannon, 16 August 1944 (NAC, RG 27, vol. 611, file 6-52-9); "Community Nursery to Assist Mothers," *Calgary Herald*, 6 July 1944.

50 Hazeldine Bishop to Margaret Grier (NAC, RG 27, vol 611, file 6-52-9).

51 Letter to A. Miller, 22 April 1944 (EA, RG 11, class 32, file 9).

52 Committee on Day Care for Children of Working Mothers, "Brief to be Submitted to City Council," 24 September 1943 (EA, RG 11, class 32, file 7).

53 "Still Unsatisfactory," *Edmonton Bulletin*, 10 May 1944, 4.

54 Letter to Premier Manning, 5 May 1944 (PAA, 69.289, file 882).

55 Submission of Calgary Day Nursery Committee to the Provincial Day Nursery Advisory Committee (NAC, RG 27, vol. 611, file 6-52-9).

56 The Calgary Day Nursery Committee offered a particularly thoughtful labour-market analysis: "It so happens that the most desired group to draw back into industry is the young marrieds, usually young mothers. They are trained in present day business methods, business experiences are fresh and they have good health" (Submission to the Provincial Day Nursery Advisory Committee, NAC RG 27, vol. 611, file 6-52-9).

57 Soroptimist's letter, 16 May 1944 (PAA, 69.289, file 882); "Day Nurseries Are Much Needed in Calgary," *Calgary Herald*, 26 May 1944, 4.

58 Pardee to Eaton, 6 April 1944 (NAC, RG 27, vol. 611, file 6-52-9).

59 *Edmonton Bulletin*, 3 May 1944, 10. This Dix column dealt with young mothers who shopped and went to the movies when they found someone to look after their kids. An inattentive headline writer, however, provided a different moral message in the subtitle "A Woman Has No Right to Leave Tiny Children with Grandparents, Neighbours or Friends While She Goes Off to Work."

60 "Council Deprecates Discrimination Against Employment of Wives," *Edmonton Journal*, 21 June 1944, 10.

61 "Canadian Women May Demand a New Deal," *Calgary Herald*, 19 June 1944, 4.

3. The 1960s

1 An early public opinion survey confirms that a majority of Canadians expected married women to have a very restricted role in post-war Canada. In 1956 the Gallup Poll asked a national sample of 1,410 Canadians: "Do you think married women should be given equal opportunity with men to compete for jobs, or do you think employers should give men the first chance?" Fifty-nine percent answered that men should be given the first chance (including 53 percent of working-class women respondents) while 32 percent favoured equal opportunity for married women. (The other 14 percent provided a qualified answer or were undecided.) In contrast, when the same question was asked by Gallup in a 1985 national survey of 1,029 Canadians, only 19 percent answered that men should be given the first chance while 76 percent favoured equal opportunity (including 82 percent of working-class women respondents). These data are taken from Gallup Polls 248K, May 1956 and 494:1, February 1985. Code book preparation and data cleaning were completed by the Carleton University Social Science Data Archives, under the auspices of the Machine Readable Archives Division of the National Archives of Canada. These organizations provided the data but cannot be held responsible for the analyses presented here nor any problems with the data.

2 "Memorandum re: Creche," n.d., and letter from Hugh R. Elston, vice principal of Edmonton College Inc., to the Mayor and Council, City of Edmonton, 26 March 1951 (EA, RG 11, class 32, file 11).

3 Letter from John W. Clark to Commissioner Menzies, 26 April 1951 (EA, RG 11, class 32, file 11).

4 "The Creche Problem," Edmonton Journal, 25 April 1951; letter from Kathleen Moar to Commissioner Menzies, 25 April 1951; letter from the city commissioners to Kathleen Moar, 30 April 1951 (EA, RG 11, class 32, file 11).

5 Census of the Prairie Provinces, 1946, Census of Alberta, table 21, "Population by age groups for census subdivisions," 1946 (Ottawa: Dominion Bureau of Statistics, 1949); Census of Canada, 1956, Bulletin 1-9, Age Groups, table 19, "Population by five-year age groups and sex, for incorporated cities, towns, villages, and other municipal subdivisions of 10,000 and over, 1956."

6 Sheila Campbell, interview by Tom Langford, 17 April 1996, tape recorded.

7 Memo from Edmonton Council of Community Services to the Commissioners of the City of Edmonton, "Day-care Services in Edmonton," 9 April 1957; and memo from E.S. Bishop, superintendent of the Welfare Department to the City Commissioners, "Re: Day-care Services in Edmonton," 25 June 1957 (EA, RG 11, class 32, file 13).

8 Norquay had relocated to Toronto by 1963. She co-hosted the CBC current events show "Take 30" with Adrienne Clarkson between 1963 and 1967, and in 1971 had the distinction of being a central contributor to the first Open College university-level credit course for radio. She was the program director of CJRT-FM in Toronto between 1974 and 1985. A brief history of Norquay's career was found at http://archivesfa.library.yorku.ca/fonds/ON00370-f0000176.htm (active 1 August 2010).

9 Campbell, interview, 17 April 1996.

10 "Report to the By-Laws Committee of the City of Edmonton from the Study Group on Family Welfare Services," 8 December 1960 (EA, MS 323, class 2, file 18).

11 "Report to the By-Laws Committee," 8 December 1960; Michel (1999, 155) gives further detail on Bowlby's research findings, and Campbell (2001, 87) notes that the applicability of Bowlby's research to day care began to be seriously questioned in the early 1960s. Before this development, however, the members of day care committees and study groups might well have been opponents of rather than advocates for day care for young children. An example is Dr. Julius Guild, an Edmonton psychologist who was one of the eight original members of the Council of Community Services Day Care Committee (EA, MS 323, class 2, file 19). The next year he was quoted as saying there is seldom an adequate substitute for a mother. He argued that the absence of the mother up to the age of five can lead to such problems as withdrawal, delinquency, apathy, intense depression, and loss of weight ("Edmonton Psychologist Disapproves Day Care," *Edmonton Journal*, 1 September 1962).

12 "Minutes of Edmonton Citizens Concerned about Day Care," 23 March 1961 (EA, MS 323, class 2, file 19).

13 "Resume of Meeting Held at the Bonnie Doon Day Nursery ... May 22, 1963" (EA, MS 323, class 2, file 21).

14 "Report to the By-Laws Committee," 8 December 1960.

15 "Edmonton Psychologist Disapproves Day Care."

16 Irmtraud Walter, interview by Tom Langford, 18 December 2002, tape recorded.

17 Minutes of Day Care Committee, 24 May 1961 (EA, MS 323, class 2, file 19).

18 "Report of the Edmonton Creche and Day Nursery Exploratory Committee," 25 October 1962 (EA, MS 323, class 2, file 20).

19 Letter to the editor, name withheld (126th Street), Edmonton Journal, 11 May 1964.

20 "Final Chapter Written in the History of the Edmonton Creche and Day Nursery," Edmonton Journal, 4 December 1968.

21 "Creche Board Explains Closure," Edmonton Journal, 15 May 1964, 7.

22 "Society to Give Creche Reprieve," Edmonton Journal, 7 April 1964.

23 "Welfare Council Supports Creche in Stay-Open Bid," Edmonton Journal, 6 May 1964; "Edmonton Welfare Council. Edmonton Creche & Day Nursery," 22 April 1964 (EA, MS 323, class 2, file 22); "Society Shuns City Nursery," Edmonton Journal, 12 May 1964. The equipment was eventually turned over to the UCF, and the assets of the Creche Society, valued at between $60,000 and $70,000, were given to the city in 1968 when the society decided to disband. Interestingly, the stipulation on the gift was that it be "used for further extension of daycare centres in capital expenditures such as furniture and equipment," demonstrating that the Creche Board was much more sympathetic to the value of publicly funded day cares in 1968 than it had been in 1964. Mrs. H.H. Stephens admitted later that "had there not been so much trouble at the time [1964] we would have turned over the assets then" ("Final Chapter Written in the History of the Edmonton Creche and Day Nursery," Edmonton Journal, 4 December 1968).

24 Memo from R.E. Swenarchuk, Public Relations Director, UCF to B.D. Stanton, President, UCF, "Re: Community Day Nursery," 31 March 1966 (EA, RG 11, class 32, file 17); Minutes of EWC Day Care Planning Committee meeting, 21 April 1965 (EA, MS 323, class 2, file 25).

25 Letter from L.C. Halmrast to V. Dantzer, 7 June 1965 (EA, RG 11, class 32, file 16).

26 The next section of this chapter will examine the peculiar character of the PSS Act that encouraged the development of high-quality, not-for-profit day cares in Alberta despite the fact that provincial Social Credit politicians never had much enthusiasm for day care per se.

27 Answer to Alderman Dent's Inquiry on the Creche, 25 October 1966 (EA, RG 11, class 32, file 16); Mary Hull, interview by Tom Langford, 10 April 1996, tape recorded; Edmonton Welfare Council, Day Care Planning Committee, "Brief to the City of Edmonton on the Establishment of Day Care Services," March 1966 (EA, RG 8.6, class 155, file 1); Family Service Association of Edmonton, "Day Care Study," March 1966 (EA, RG 8.6, class 155, file 1); letter from Jessie Holmes to the chairman and members of the board, Community Day Nursery, 24 March 1966 (EA, RG 11, class 32, file 17).

28 I discuss the closure of the Community Day Nursery in chapter 8.

29 Campbell, interview, 17 April 1996; Hull, interview, 10 April 1996.

30 FSA of Edmonton presentation to City Council, "Day Care Services for Children," 19 June 1967 (EA, RG 8.6, class 155, file 1).

31 Revised Statutes of Alberta, 1980, chap. P-15; Acts of the Parliament of Canada, 1966/67, vol. 1, 14–15 Elizabeth II, chap. 45.

32 Keith Wass, interview by Tom Langford, 13 April 1996, tape recorded.

33 Al Hagan, interview by Tom Langford, 16 April 1996, tape recorded.

34 City of Edmonton, Social Service Department, "An Approach to Preventive Services," n.d. (City of Calgary Archives [hereafter cited as CA], box 28427).

35 John Lackey, interview by Tom Langford, 12 April 1996, tape recorded. John Lackey's own place on the political spectrum provides an interesting footnote to this quote. Following his retirement from the provincial civil service, Lackey ran as a Green Party candidate in the constituency of Edmonton-Riverview in the provincial election held on 22 November 2004.

36 Hagan, interview.

37 Howard Clifford, interview by Tom Langford, 20 February 1996, tape recorded.

38 Edmonton Welfare Council, "Day Care: A Position Paper," 9 July 1964 (EA, MS 323, file 23). The December report, titled "An Assessment of the Need for Day Care Services for Children of Employed Mothers in Edmonton," is included as the appendix to the Planning Committee's "Brief to the City of Edmonton on the Establishment of Day Care Services," March 1966 (EA, RG 8.6, class 155, file 1).

39 "An Assessment of the Need," 4–5, iv, and 1.

40 "A Nursery Story 1: Working Moms' Pre-Schoolers Get 'Supervision' Only," Edmonton Journal, 18 January 1966, 9; "A Nursery Story 2: Just What Should a Good Day Care Centre Provide?" Edmonton Journal, 19 January 1966, 11.

41 "Day Nurseries Contrast: Higher Standards Observed in Toronto's Subsidized Centres," Edmonton Journal, 4 February 1966.

42 Family Service Association of Edmonton, "Day Care Study," March 1966 (EA, RG 8.6, class 155, file 1).

43 "City Commissioners Report to the Aldermen of the City of Edmonton," 4 July 1966 (EA, RG 11, class 200, file 1). This report represented the end of the FSA challenge for pre-eminence in the development of day care in Edmonton. Keith Wass recalled that the FSA, under the leadership of its executive director, Jackson Willis, "had designs to become a massive agency and they were going to use PSS and they were going to run the day care and they were going to run the counselling and they wanted us [the city's Social Service Department] just to be the channelling agency that would fund them" (interview). On this competition "for control of preventive social service funding" in Edmonton, see Bella (1978, 185–92).

44 "'We're Being Penalized,' Parents Say," *Edmonton Journal*, 30 May 1967, 17; "Day Care Centre Wins Welfare Aid," *Edmonton Journal*, 26 August 1967, 17.

45 Department of Social Services, City of Edmonton, Annual Report, 1966, 2.

46 Clifford, interview, 20 February 1996.

47 Bruce Ryan, interview by Tom Langford, 11 March 1996, tape recorded. Bruce Ryan quit his job as a psychometrist at the psychiatric hospital and started graduate studies in educational psychology at the University of Alberta in 1967. He received his PhD in 1971, and, after a short period in New Zealand, joined the Department of Family Studies at the University of Guelph in 1975.

48 Clifford, interview, 20 February 1996. Unless otherwise noted, the statements of Mr. Clifford quoted in the remainder of the chapter are from this interview.

49 "'We're Being Penalized'"; Clifford, interview, 20 February 1996.

50 "Day Care Facilities for Working Mothers Beginning to Move," *Edmonton Journal*, 8 June 1967.

51 "Co-operative Development of District Recreational and Day Care Centres," C.R. No. 32, 12 June 1967 (EA, RG 11, class 200, file 2); Ryan, interview.

52 "Province-Backed Day Care Plans 'Are for the Birds,' Says Hooke" and "Manning Rekindles City Hopes on Glengarry Day Care Centre," *Edmonton Journal*, 23 October and 25 November 1967, respectively.

53 All letters are found in PAA, 77.173, file 702. Carson's articles included "Day Care Workers Mobilize" and "The Day Care [Words Missing]: Mothers May Have to Quit Jobs," both 24 October 1967.

54 In the spring of 1967, the CBC decided "to turn over all documents from a previous investigation into corruption in Alberta" to the provincial NDP, who made the documents public. Although the CBC had gathered the documents as part of an investigation, its management had decided against airing any reports because of the political sensitivity of the issue (Turcott 2002, 123). The CBC's documents were a major reason why Premier Manning was forced to call a Royal Commission into allegations of corruption involving his government. This may well be the "kerfuffle" mentioned by Mr. Clifford.

55 Letter from Minister Hooke, 12 March 1968, and memo from Wass to Dantzer, 9 January 1968 (EA, RG 11, class 200, file 3).

56 "Day Care Centres Given Support," *Albertan*, 1 November 1968.

57 Letter from Hilde Bloedow to Premier Manning, 8 February 1968, with two attachments: (1) copy of a letter to Rev. Harry Meadow, 5 February 1968, and (2) copy of unpublished

submission to the *Edmonton Journal*, December 1967. The data on commercial centres are from the unpublished submission. Edmonton Day Nursery Association submission to Premier Manning, n.d., received 22 November 1967 (PAA, 77.133, file 702).

58 "Private Nurseries Are Not Inferior, but the Public Has a Negative Attitude," *Edmonton Journal*, 11 July 1967; letter from Hilde Bloedow to Premier Manning, 8 February 1968, with attached copy of a letter to Rev. Harry Meadow, 5 February 1968 (PAA, 77.133, file 702).

59 Campbell, interview, 17 April 1996.

60 Ibid. Howard Clifford's version of this story is found in *Let's Talk Day Care* (1972), 124–25.

61 Letter from Hilde Bloedow to Premier Manning, 8 February 1968; letter from Hilde Bloedow to Edmonton Mayor Dent and City Council, 22 February 1971 (EA, RG 8.6, class 151, file 1).

62 Letter to Manning, 8 February 1968, both attachments (PAA, 77.133, file 702).

63 "Day Care Supervisor Attacks Public Prejudice," *Edmonton Journal*, 11 October 1967, 23; Edmonton Social Service Department, Annual Report, 1968.

64 "History of the Medicine Hat Day-care Services," prepared by a STEP student in June 1989; untitled history of PSS programs in Medicine Hat, 21 October 1970; "Day Care Centre to Operate in '69," *Medicine Hat News*, undated clipping from early January 1969 (documents provided by Medicine Hat Children's Services).

65 "New Calgary Day Care Centre Sets Example for Future," *Edmonton Journal*, 7 April 1966.

66 Barbara Scott remained involved in the politics of day care in Alberta for thirty years. Following her research jobs in Edmonton and Calgary, she served on Calgary City Council between 1971 and her retirement in 1995.

67 "Bowness-Montgomery Day Care Program: City of Calgary Preventive Project Submission," August 1969, 4 (CA, box 28431, binder: Preventive Services Reports).

68 The recommendations are appended to the city's submission to the province for the PSS project, "Day Care Counsellor for the City of Calgary," 10 July 1968 (CA, Board of Commissioners, ser. 5, box 207, file 6000).

69 "Bowness-Montgomery Day Care Program: City of Calgary Preventive Project Submission," 2.

70 "Bowness-Montgomery Day Care Program: City of Calgary Preventive Project Submission," 14–15; "Public Day Care Centre in Bowness," *North Hill News*, 27 November 1969, 1.

71 "Bowness-Montgomery Day Care Program: City of Calgary Preventive Project Submission," 9–10, 12.

72 For example, Vancouver's contemporary "hub vision" of child care is consistent with the Bowness-Montgomery program. A 2005 report states, "Participants in the City of Vancouver's 2002 consultation process emphasized the importance of services for school age as well as young children. As a result, the City's hub vision integrates child care for children under age 12 with other child development services families might need or choose, rather than focusing solely on early childhood development services for children under age six." Furthermore, the Vancouver hub model links child care centres and family day home providers (Anderson 2005, 2n2, 3).

73 "Bowness-Montgomery Day Care Program: City of Calgary Preventive Project Submission," Appendix A.

74 Day Care Association of Calgary, Submission to City Council, 26 January 1970 (located in the files of the Bowness-Montgomery Child Care Association).

75 "Bowness-Montgomery Day Care Program: City of Calgary Preventive Project Submission," Appendix A.

4. The 1970s

1 Lackey, interview.

2 Seminar program found in AAYC Archives.

3 "New Concept in the Development of Day Care," keynote address (copy provided by Nancy Hall).

4 Panelist Dr. Jean Nelson, "Program Content—Varieties of Care" (copy provided by Nancy Hall). Biographical information on Jean Nelson was found on the website of the Alberta Public Health Association, which offers a memorial award in her name. Dr. Nelson's career was cut short by cancer. She died in 1979.

5 "Day Care Centres Given Support," *Albertan*, 1 November 1968; Hagan, interview.

6 This analysis draws upon Langford (2001).

7 "A Brief to the Government of the Province of Alberta. Recommendations Pertaining to Young Children and Child Development Programs in the Province of Alberta, December 1972" (AAYC Archives, 1972). See also Campbell (1997, 8).

8 Letter from Gloria Milligan, president of the AAYC, to Education Minister Hyndman, 30 April 1973; "The Need for Consolidation and Improvement of Legislation Pertaining to Programs for Young Children," brief presented to the Legislative Committee on Regulations, Government of Alberta, 6 September 1973 (AAYC Archives, 1973); AAYC Information Bulletin, n.d. [1974], 6 (AAYC Archives, 1974).

9 "Standards for Child Development Programs, Including Day Care Centres and Family Day Homes," AAYC, April 1973 (AAYC Archives, 1973).

10 AAYC Archives, 1974.

11 Letter from Mel Finlay, 15 May 1974 (AAYC Archives, 1974); Campbell 1997, 8.

12 Letter "For General Circulation," 6 November 1974 (CA, SS box 6290, file: Child Care, Oct.–Dec. 1974).

13 In 1985 Helen Hunley became the first woman to be appointed as the Lieutenant Governor of Alberta (http://www.assembly.ab.ca/lao/library/lt-gov/hunley.htm) (active 1 August 2010).

14 "Submission of the Alberta Association for Young Children in Response to the *Proposals for Day Care Standards and Licensing*," November 1976; memo from S. Campbell to Dr. M. Horowitz, "Re: Meeting Friday with M. Finlay, et al.," 1 March 1976 (AAYC Archives, 1976).

15 "Submission," November 1976, 15–17.

16 Memo from Hoebarth to Blakely, 8 August 1977; "Minutes of the Task Force on Day [Care]," Edmonton, Alberta, 10 August 1977 (CSS, file: Day Care Task Force, 1976–77); Minutes of the Alberta Provincial Cabinet Discussion of Day Care, 13 September 1977, with supporting documentation (obtained by a freedom-of-information request to Alberta Executive Council).

17 Minutes of the Alberta Provincial Cabinet Discussion of Day Care, 13 September 1977.

18 AAYC, "Submission of the Alberta Association for Young Children in response to the 1978 Day Care Regulations and Subsidy to Low Income Families," May 1978 (AAYC Archives, 1978).

19 Clifford, interview, 20 February 1996.

20 Edmonton Social Services, "Policy Guidelines Regarding the Expansion of Day Care Services in Edmonton," September 1975 (ECFS Records); "'Edmonton Needs 10 More Subsidized Care Centres,'" Edmonton Journal, 20 February 1971.

21 "'Edmonton Needs 10 More Subsidized Care Centres'"; letter from Hilde Bloedow, 22 February 1971 (EA, RG 8.6, class 155, file 1).

22 Clifford, interview, 20 February 1996.

23 Research since 1971 has confirmed Clifford's assertion that the preschool years are critical. In an article in Science in 2006, James Heckman noted that "decades of independent research in economics, neuroscience, and developmental psychology" had established that "the mastery of skills that are essential for economic success and the development of their underlying neural pathways follow hierarchical rules. Later attainments build on foundations that are laid down earlier" (p. 1900). Heckman reported that for one preschool program for disadvantaged three and four year olds, the benefits-to-costs ratio was 8.74 to 1. He concluded, "Investing in disadvantaged young children is a rare public policy initiative that promotes fairness and social justice and at the same time promotes productivity in the economy and in society at large" (p. 1902).

24 Edmonton Journal, 25 July 1972.

25 Campbell, interview, 17 April 1996. Sheila Campbell was a faculty member at the University of Alberta until 1980, specializing in the organization of space in day care centres. While at the University of Alberta, she had taken a leave to begin her PhD at the University of Texas. She completed her dissertation in 1981. Sheila Campbell's research involved detailed observations at an Edmonton kindergarten over an entire year with the aim of identifying the combinations of factors that promoted good learning opportunities. During the remaining years of her professional life, Dr. Campbell worked as a consultant on day cares.

26 Community Task Force on Day Care, Edmonton Social Planning Council, Information on Day Care, November 1973 (ECFS records).

27 Edmonton Social Services, "Policy Guidelines Regarding the Expansion of Day Care Services in Edmonton."

28 Biographies are available from the Edmonton Public Library at www.epl.ca/Elections/ Results/EPLBiographies.cfm (active 1 August 2010).

29 Edmonton Social Services, "Policy Guidelines Regarding the Expansion of Day Care Services in Edmonton," 14, 17, 25–26. A 50 percent annual growth rate would have yielded 149 percent more subsidized spaces by 1980 than a 25 percent growth rate (10,441 versus

4,186; p. 16). However, the cost projections for a 50 percent growth rate would have been so unpalatable to the provincial government that they were not reported in this document.

30   "Changes in Canada Assistance Plan Pertaining to Day Care," AAYC *Newsletter*, Winter 1973.

31   Letter from Mike Day to Eric Haffenden, 6 February 1975 (CA, Social Services, box 6290, file 0542). Edmonton Social Services also recommended setting aside a parcel of land for a day care in each new housing development of twenty thousand residents and that the city purchase these parcels.

32   "Funding Curbs May Mean Cut in Day Care," *Edmonton Journal*, 9 June 1976. The percentage increases in the Consumer Price Index for Alberta were 11.1 in 1975, 8.3 in 1976, and 8.8 in 1977 (Statistics Canada, CPI Table—Alberta: 1971 to 2001).

33   "Day Care Restraints Criticized," *Edmonton Journal*, 21 September 1976; "Funds for Two Day Care Centres Killed from Budget," *Edmonton Journal*, 25 January 1977.

34   Leadbeater to Commissioner A.H. Savage, 14 September 1977, with attachment F.2.r, 6 September 1977 (ECFS, Children's Services 1975–78, box 5, file: City Council Correspondence and Memos). Leadbeater did not run for re-election in 1977.

35   Gilbert to Dorosh, Milne, and Levin, 11 August 1977 (ECFS, Children's Services 1975–78, box 5, file: Policy Statements).

36   "Background Information for Mayor's 'State of the City Address'—1978," attached to a memo requesting the information, dated 8 December 1978 (ECFS, Children's Services 1975–78, box 5, file: Commissioners' Correspondence/Memos). The number of PSS centres had fallen back to fifteen by March 1978 (Edmonton Social Services, Day Care Branch, "1977 Year End Report: Project JC241—Day Care" [PAA, 84-270, box 3, file 77]).

37   "'Bad' Day Care Standards Could Worsen, Expert Says," *Edmonton Journal*, 22 March 1978; "Attention Parents" leaflet, n.d. (ECFS, CRC 92J0404B); "A Petition to be Submitted to the Mayor and Aldermen of the City of Edmonton by Parents Using Subsidized Day Care Services," received 29 March 1978 (ECFS, CRC 92J0404B, file: City Council Correspondence).

38   "Brief to the Hon. Helen Hunley … Respecting the City of Edmonton's Position on the Day Care Regulation: March 1978," April 1978 (ECFS, CRC 93J040B, file: Briefs).

39   Mayor Purves to Minister Hunley, 7 June 1978; Public Affairs Committee Report No. 8, 15 May 1978; David Gilbert to Commissioner A.H. Savage, 8 June 1978; Catarina Versaevel to John Lackey et al., "City of Edmonton Day Care Program Recommendations," 16 June 1978; City Commissioners to Mayor and Members of Council, "Day Care Program," 23 June 1978 (ECFS, CRC 92J040B, files: City Council Correspondence and Provincial-Municipal Correspondence); ESS Day Care Branch, "Day Care Aldermanic Update," 6 March 1979 (ECFS, CRC 92J040B).

40   "Subsidy to Low Income Families and Standards of Care," 6 July 1978 (ECFS records).

41   Dorosh to Savage, 5 December 1978, with attached report on day care prepared by the Corporate Policy Planning Office, 28 November 1978; "Day Care Aldermanic Update," 6 March 1979; Mansbridge to Hunley, "Report: Day Care Progress," 13 December 1978 (PAA, 90.301, file: Briefing to the Minister—Day Care, 1978–79).

42   Lackey to Mansbridge, 18 December 1978 (PAA, 90.301, file: Day Care Unit—Policy Discussions).

43 Lackey to Versaevel, 8 January 1979 (PAA, 90.301, file: Day Care Unit—Policy Discussions); "Day Care Aldermanic Update," 6 March 1979.

44 "Day Care Aldermanic Update," 6 March 1979.

45 Hagan, interview; Calgary Social Services, file 0542.2, file 1, to 1974.

46 City of Calgary Preventive Project Submission, "Shaganappi Day Care Centre and Social Service Unit," September 1969; Pleasant Heights Day Care Association, "Proposal for a Community Day Care Centre in North Calgary," November 1969; "Staff Report and Recommendations to Social Service Committee, Mount Royal College Day Care Centre," 10 March 1970 (CA, box 28431, binder: Preventive Services Projects); "Day Care Centre Approved," *Calgary Herald*, 28 January 1970; "First Community College Day Care Centre in Canada," *The Reflector*, 3 April 1970, 14.

47 Nancy Hall, interview by Tom Langford, 19 April 1996, tape recorded.

48 Mary Selby, "The Bowness Montgomery Day Care Centre," *Junior League Lasso Magazine*, November 1970.

49 "Gingerbread Play House Makes a Hit," *Albertan*, 6 November 1970.

50 *Calgary Herald*, 7 January 1971; Hall, interview. Nancy Hall recollected that Ralph Klein's reports generally favoured PSS day cares over their critics in the commercial sector. Nancy Hall's expertise quickly became valued throughout southern Alberta. "Pretty well all the daycare centres that went in south of Edmonton, I went out and consulted with," she stated. This included holding "an annual Indian day care workshop for a week.... We were able to have a really good group of women that really wanted to learn and were very, very anxious to do a good job. And I consider that a very successful start to Indian day care."

51 "'Day Care Has Turned Full Circle,' Says City Consultant," *Calgary Herald*, 3 August 1978; "Campaign Heats Up to Obtain Day Care Centre at U of C," *Calgary Herald*, 9 September 1970, 20; "Students Change Day Care Tack," *Calgary Herald*, 15 September 1970, 39; "Facts of Life," *Albertan*, 22 September 1970.

52 "Day Care Centre Costs Criticized," *Calgary Herald*, 19 January 1971; "The City of Calgary. NOTICE. Day Care Study Group," *Calgary Herald*, 15 February 1971.

53 CA, Social Services, box 9566, files: Parents' Group Committee, batch 1 submissions, items 19 and 25; batch 2 submissions, items 14 and 15; batch 3 submission, item 3; batch 4 submission, item 1.

54 "Council Approves Day Care Subsidy," *Calgary Herald*, 21 September 1971.

55 Walter, interview.

56 Copy of letter to Mary Poppins Child Centre, 19 September 1974 (CA, Social Services, box 6290).

57 Hall, interview.

58 Hagan, interview.

59 "Commissioner's Report. Re: 1974–75 Preventive Social Service Day Care Program," 4 November 1974 (CSS files).

60 "Table: The Status of Day Care in Calgary, Approved Centres and Spaces" (CA, Social Services, box 6292, file: Child Care Statistics, 1976–77).

61 Letter from Bruce Rawson, chief deputy minister, to Sam Blakely, 29 June 1973 (CA, Social Services, box 6290, PSS Division, 0540).

62 "Report to the Community Service Committee," May 1974, 10; "How Hillhurst-Sunnyside Beat High Cost of Day Care," *Albertan*, 10 September 1974.

63 "Community Centre Continues to Evolve," *Hillhurst-Sunnyside Voice*, April 2003.

64 "Minutes of a Special Meeting of the Standing Policy Committee on Community Services Held December 2, 1974" (CA, Social Services, box 6290, file 0542); "Day Care Operators Want Change in Law," *Albertan*, 4 December 1974; Hall, interview.

65 Letter from Barbara Scott, 15 September 1970 (CSS, file 0542.2, file 1, to 1974). In September of 1974, Sam Blakely told the city's chief commissioner that over the preceding year, his staff had "spent literally hundreds of man hours on answering [Scott's] direct inquiries quite apart from those formally made through committees and council." The chief commissioner chastised Scott for her actions: "I think you will agree that the Social Service Department is a busy one and the delivery of approved services and programs must take precedence over individual requests by aldermen for information." He went on to request that future inquiries from Ms. Scott should be put in writing (Chief Commissioner Denis Cole to Barbara Scott, 23 September 1974 [CA, Social Services, box 6290]).

66 "Day Care Standards Boost Rejected," *Albertan*, 21 January 1975; "Memorandum to Community Services Committee from Alderman Barbara Scott, Re: Day Care," 17 January 1975 (CA, Social Services, box 6292, file 0542.2/B Child Care Standards 1975); Hagan, interview.

67 "Provincial Government Blamed over 'Bad Day Care' Centres," *Calgary Herald*, 20 February 1975; "Less Rigid Subsidized Day-care Standards Recommended," *Calgary Herald*, 23 July 1975; "Note on Day Care Standards," *Albertan*, 26 August 1975.

68 Alderman Barb Scott realized in 1976 that some of the PSS day cares were operating with fewer children than would be expected given the 1975 change in staff-to-child ratios. She asked CSS why this was the case. Memo from Eric Haffenden to Barbara Scott, 12 April 1976 (CA, Social Services, box 6290, file: Child Care, Jan.–May 1976).

69 "After-School Centres Get Money from City" and "Subsidized Day Care," two undated articles from *North Hill News* (CA, Social Services, box 6290). The money for the OOSC centres was committed sometime after the release of the Day Care Task Force report in April 1977, probably prior to the start of school in September 1977.

70 "City Will Subsidize Day Care for 700 Additional Children," *Calgary Herald*, 18 January 1978; "Province Must Act Before City Moves," *Calgary Herald*, 19 January 1978.

71 Letter found in records of ECFS, 92J04013, file: Alberta Municipalities.

72 "Day Care Standards Lowest in Canada, Blakely Charges," *Calgary Herald*, 3 June 1978; "Calgary Mothers Force Day-care Showdown," *Albertan*, 14 June 1978, 3; "Day Care 'Smear' Charged," *Albertan*, 5 June 1978; Gertrud deWiel, letter to the editor, *Albertan*, 6 June 1978; "Row Over Standards Has Hurt Reputations," *Calgary Herald*, 8 June 1978; R. Petrowitsch, letter to the editor, *Calgary Herald*, 14 June 1978; D. Samulak, letter to the editor, *Calgary Herald*, 20 June 1978.

73 "Day Care Vote Leaves Critics Surprised," *Calgary Herald*, 28 June 1978; "Provincial Standards for Day Care Accepted," *Albertan*, undated clipping; "Subsidy System Operational Soon," *Calgary Herald*, 20 September 1978; "City 'Pushed' into Dirty Day Care Job," *Calgary Herald*, 27 September 1978.

74   "History of Medicine Hat Day-care Services," June 1989 (MHCS); Medicine Hat Day Care Centre, Annual Reports, 1970, 1971, 1972.

75   "Medicine Hat Day Care Centre Survey, May 1972, Summary Report" (MHCS).

76   "History of Medicine Hat Day-care Services"; Medicine Hat Day Care Centre, Annual Report, 1973.

77   "History of Medicine Hat Day-care Services"; Medicine Hat Day Care Centre, Annual Report, 1976; Robert Wanner, interview by Lynne Malmquist, 23 April 1995, tape recorded.

78   It is worth adding that Jim Horsman could legitimately claim to be a friend of PSS day care: his wife, Betty, had served as a member of the board of directors of the Medicine Hat Day Care between 1970 and 1972.

79   "History of Medicine Hat Day-care Services."

80   "Preventive Social Services Director's Annual Report," 1973, 17 (MHCS).

81   "Integration Proposal Gets Sharp Reactions," Medicine Hat News, 27 April 1977; Early Childhood Services Program Highlights, March 1977 (MHCS); Bill Sass, "ECS-Parents vs. the City?" Medicine Hat News, undated [sometime between May and October 1977] (MHCS).

82   The date of the ECS transfer is recorded in Footsteps to the Future (Medicine Hat 1992).

83   Medicine Hat Day Care Centre, Annual Report, 1973; Susan Costea, interview by Lynne Malmquist, 15 December 1994, tape recorded.

84   Karen Charlton, interview by Lynne Malmquist, 25 April 1995, tape recorded; Medicine Hat Day Care Centre, Annual Report, 1972; Medicine Hat Day Care Services, Annual Report, 1975 (MHCS).

85   Charleton, interview, 25 April 1995; Medicine Hat Day Care Services, Annual Reports, 1977, 1978; "History of Medicine Hat Day-care Services," 15.

86   Medicine Hat Day Care Services, Annual Reports, 1978, 1979.

87   Mansbridge to Hunley, 13 December 1978 (PAA, 90.301, file: Briefing to the Minister—Day Care 1978–79); "History of Medicine Hat Day-care Services," 17.

88   "Red Deer Rejects Day Care Centre," Calgary Herald, 13 January 1971; "PSS Project 661. The Red Deer Day Care Society. The Red Deer Day Care Centre," Report for 1977 (PAA, 84.270, box 3, file 28); "Chairman's Corner," AAYC Newsletter (Winter 1972).

89   "The Alberta Association for Young Children Information Bulletin" (AAYC Archives, 1974).

90   "Ad Hoc Committee Report on Day Care Services in Lethbridge," 17 October 1975 (Lethbridge Public Library, Local History Collection, pp. 1 and 11). On 1 July 1975 there were four not-for-profit day cares in Lethbridge with spaces for ninety children. The operators were Lethbridge Community College, YWCA, the University of Lethbridge Students' Society Council, and Lethbridge Preschool Services (PSS supported). Two commercial centres had sixty spaces at that time. By 17 October there were three commercial centres licensed for 125 children (p. 4).

91   "Ad Hoc Committee Report," 6–8.

92   Catarina Versaevel, director, Day Care Unit, to Gordon Thomas, executive assistant, Minister's Office, 14 November 1979, "Municipal Phase-Out of the Deficit Method of Funding" (PAA, 90.301, file: Briefing to the Minister—Day Care, 1978–79).

93 "Projected Project. Red Deer & District Day Care Coordinator" (PAA, 84.270, box 3, file 28).

94 "Subsidy to Low Income Families," 7.

95 Red Deer, Preventive Social Services Department, "Report on Day Care Services," esp. "Appendix C. History of Day Care in Red Deer" and "Appendix D. City of Red Deer. Day Care Resolutions," May 1980 (ECFS, 92J040B, box 3, file 9).

96 Grande Prairie PSS Director's Annual Report, 1974, 10–12 (PAA, 84.270, box 1, file 12).

97 "News from the Regions," AAYC Newsletter (March–April 1976).

98 Funding a commercial centre in this way appears to have violated the terms of the Canada Assistance Plan.

99 Grande Prairie PSS Director's Annual Report, 1976, and Grande Prairie and District Day Care Summary of Activities, 1976 (PAA, 84.270, box 1, file 12).

100 "Issue for Minister's Briefing Book," n.d. [1977] (PAA, 90.301, file: Comm. Soc. Serv.: Briefing to Ministers).

101 Versaevel to Gordon Thomas, 14 November 1979 (PAA, 90.301, file: Briefing to the Minister—Day Care 1978–79); Chris Henderson, interview by Tom Langford, 19 April 1996, tape recorded.

102 Henderson, interview.

103 Memos from Pieter de Groot to Catarina Versaevel, 11 October 1978, and Dennis Maier to Catarina Versaevel, 6 October 1978 (PAA, 90.301, file: Day Care Unit—General).

104 Lesser Slave Lake PSS Advisory Board brief, pp. 1–2 (CA, Social Services box 6290, file: Child Care, May–August 1975).

105 Alberta Social Services and Community Health, Homes and Institutions Branch, "Day Care Centres Operating in the Province of Alberta as of July 1, 1975" (PAA, 83.386, file 12); "PSS Day Care Operators and Addresses, May 1977" (CA, Social Services, box 9566, file: Day Care, Staff Outline); Grande Prairie and District Preventive Social Services, "Day Care Administration. Annual Report 1976–1977," 6 (PAA, 84.270, box 1, file 12).

106 Memo from Catarina Versaevel to File, 18 April 1980, "Meeting with Mr. Bogle, April 17, 1980," with attached deficit figures (PAA, 90.301, file: Briefing to the Minister, Day Care).

107 "Summary of Day Care Evaluations," n.d. [probably 1982] (Clifford E. Lee Foundation records). The estimated date comes from an interview with Judy Padua by Tom Langford, 3 March 1998, tape recorded.

5. Years of Turmoil, 1979–82

1 "Opposition Hits Cabinet's Size," Calgary Herald, 24 March 1979, A2; Dennis Maier, interview by Tom Langford, 5 March 1998, tape recorded.

2 In March 1980, the provincial government appointed a board of review under the Public Inquiries Act, chaired by Justice J.C. Cavanagh, to investigate the child welfare system in Alberta. Minister Bogle was responsible for child welfare as well as day care. The inquiry report was highly critical of Bob Bogle's management style and his relations with civil servants (Cavanagh, Allison, and McCoy 1983, 1–6, 216–17).

3   Hunley did not run for re-election in 1979, and Crawford was a member of the inner circle of cabinet ministers after the 1979 election, holding the attorney-general portfolio as well as being government house leader ("Complete List of Ministers," *Calgary Herald*, 23 March 1979, A2).

4   John Lackey, director-general, Community Social Services, to David Stolee, acting deputy minister, Health Services, "Saskatchewan Day Care Advisory Board" memo, 8 May 1979 (PAA, 90.301, file: "Briefing to the Minister—Day Care 1978–79"); Catarina Versaevel, director, Day Care Unit, to Lackey, "Day Care Advisory Committee" memo, 8 June 1979; Lackey to Stolee, "Alberta Day Care Advisory Committee" memo, 18 June 1979 (PAA, 93.188, box 2, file 9.7.4).

5   "Beleaguered Bob," *Edmonton Journal*, 7 April 1980, A5; "Remaking the Cabinet," *Calgary Herald*, 8 November 1982, A4.

6   "Parents Start Petition over 'Ridiculous' Day-care Rule," *Edmonton Journal*, 3 April 1979; "Parents, Owners to Protest the 'Bungling' of Day Care," *Edmonton Journal*, 4 May 1979.

7   "MLAs' Help Sought in Day-care Struggle," *Edmonton Journal*, 23 May 1979, B6; "Protest Rally over Day-care Dilemma," *Edmonton Sun*, 27 May 1979.

8   David Gibson, interview by Tom Langford, 21 August 1997, tape recorded.

9   Day Care Branch, Edmonton Social Services, "Alderman Norris re: Agreement for Day Care Centres," attached to a memo from Dorosh to Savage, 12 April 1979 (Edmonton CFS files).

10   "City May End Role in Day-care Service," *Edmonton Journal*, n.d. [April or May 1979].

11   "Gov't Won't Negotiate Day Care," *Edmonton Journal*, 1 June 1979; letter from A.H. Savage to Stanley H Mansbridge, 7 June 1979, and letter from Purves to Bogle, n.d. [August 1979] (Edmonton CFS files).

12   Letter from Purves to Bogle, n.d. [August 1979].

13   Bogle to Purves, 17 September 1979; Purves to Bogle, 15 October 1979; Purves to Bogle, n.d. [but later] (Edmonton CFS files).

14   Versaevel to all PSS directors, 19 November 1979 (CA, Social Services, box 9564, file: Day Care Budget and Deficits, 1979); "Response of Department of Social Services and Community Health Day Care Unit to Tentative Directions Raised by the Honourable Mr. Bob Bogle on February 11, 1980" (PAA, 90.301, file: Briefing to the Minister Day Care).

15   Bogle to Purves, 17 September 1979.

16   Mansbridge to A.H. Savage, 12 March 1979 (Edmonton CFS, 92J040B, file 6-14).

17   City of Edmonton Social Services Department, "Day Care Subsidy to Family: Policy Statement," January 1980 (Edmonton CFS files); Catarina Versaevel to David Gilbert, 11 February 1980 and "Day Care Program—Update as of February 20, 1980," Day Care Branch, Edmonton Social Services (Edmonton CFS, 92J040B box 2, file 6-14[a]). A clause on "discipline" was added to the Day Care Regulation in 1981, but it did not forbid corporal punishment. It read: "Staff in every day care facility shall discuss methods of disciplinary action with the parents of each child ... and shall ensure that the discipline used corresponds to that of a kind, firm and judicious parent" (Alberta 1981, 637). Similar language was included in the 1990 version of the Day Care Regulation (Alberta 1991, 10). Corporal punishment was finally banned in the Child

Care Licensing Regulation of 2008: "A license holder must not, with respect to a child in the program, inflict or cause to be inflicted any form of physical punishment, verbal or physical degradation or emotional deprivation" (Alberta 2008, 7).

18 "Mayor's Office: Progress Report on Day Care Program," 11 December 1979; "Day Care—Update," 17 January 1980; letter from David Gilbert, 9 November 1979 (Edmonton CFS, 92J040B box 2, file 6-14-a).

19 Private Day Care Society of Alberta, Edmonton Branch, "Re: Day Care Subsidy to Low Income Parents. Letter from City Social Services, David Gilbert," 23 November 1979 (Edmonton CFS files).

20 "Day Care Assisted Everywhere but City," Edmonton Journal, 29 January 1980.

21 Memo from Catarina Versaevel to John Lackey, "Discussion with Dr. Anderson and Mr. Bogle on February 18, 1980," 19 February 1980 (PAA, 90.301, file: Day Care Unit—Policy Discussions). The MLA Review Committee also set in motion the process that led to Alberta's operating allowances, a matter that is the subject of detailed treatment in the next section.

22 "Response of Department of Social Services and Community Health Day Care Unit to Tentative Directions Raised by the Honourable Mr. Bob Bogle on February 11, 1980"; "City Day-care Centres Face 18% Subsidy Cut," Calgary Herald, 6 May 1980, B1.

23 My freedom-of-information request for cabinet discussions of day care did not produce any documents between 23 January 1979 and 16 December 1980.

24 "Operators Laud Day-care Plans," Calgary Herald, 7 May 1980, B3; "Province Stands Firm on Day-care," Calgary Herald, 14 May 1980, B1; memo from Versaevel to Lackey, "Minister's Briefing Book, Fall Session," 29 August 1979, 4 (PAA, 90.301, file: Com. Soc. Serv. Briefing to Ministers).

25 Minutes of Municipal/Provincial Day Care Meeting, 6–7 September 1979 (Edmonton CFS, 92J040B, box 3, file: Prov-City Daycare).

26 Memo from Versaevel to Lackey, "Minister's Briefing Book, Fall Session," 29 August 1979 (PAA, 90.301, file: Com. Soc. Serv. Briefing to Ministers).

27 The MLA Review Committee went through the motions of meeting with the board of directors of the AAYC on 12 October 1979 (AAYC Newsletter, December 1979). There is no evidence that the views of the AAYC had an impact on the work of the review committee.

28 "Social Services: Daycare Fights Seem Futile," Calgary Herald, 17 May 1980, A7.

29 Letter from Michael Phair to AAYC Board of Directors, 15 April 1980 (AAYC Archives, 1980).

30 In April 1980, Pieter de Groot was fired by Minister Bogle after complaining that his legal rights as director of licensing had been infringed upon by Gordon Thomas during the course of this appeal ("Director of Day-care Licensing Dismissed," Edmonton Journal, 2 April 1980, B1). Mr. de Groot sued for wrongful dismissal. The matter was settled in de Groot's favour in 1981 when he was offered the position of Edmonton regional director for the Alberta Alcohol and Drug Abuse Commission plus legal costs. Because of his principled stand on this matter, Pieter de Groot was highly respected by day care advocates in Edmonton. Until he left the city in 1987 for a position in Ottawa, Mr. de Groot served as a member of the advisory committee for Grant MacEwan College's ECE program.

31   "Response of Department of Social Services and Community Health Day Care Unit to Tentative Directions Raised by the Honourable Mr. Bob Bogle on February 11, 1980."

32   Government of Alberta News Release, 4 September 1980 (PAA, 93.188, box 2, file: Minister's Correspondence). The news release also announced limits on group sizes in day care. No such limits existed in the 1978 regulation.

33   "City Delighted with Bogle's Day-care Changes," *Calgary Herald*, 5 September 1980, B1; letter from Michael Phair to Bob Bogle, 10 October 1980 (AAYC Archives, 1980).

34   "Discussion with Dr. Anderson and Mr. Bogle on February 18, 1980" memo; "MLA Day Care Regulation Review (Typed from Dr. Anderson's Handwritten Notes)" (PAA, 90.301, file: Day Care Unit—Policy Discussions).

35   Day Care Unit, "Report. A Comparison of Selected Indicators in Day Care Licensing Regulations and Standards Among Provinces in Canada," August 1978 (PAA, 90.301, file: Briefing to the Minister—Day Care, 1978–79).

36   "Alberta on 'Poverty Line' with Day Care Facilities," *Calgary Herald*, 27 June 1979, B1. The report by the Day Care Unit was completed in July 1979 of that year ("Report Concedes Low Day Care Ranking," *Calgary Herald*, 5 June 1980, A5).

37   Memo from Catarina Versaevel to File, "Meeting with Mr. Bogle, April 17, 1980," 18 April 1980 (PAA, 90.301, file: Briefing to the Minister—Day Care). "Notley Condemns New Day Care Rules," *Calgary Herald*, 2 May 1980, A13; "Let's Look at Day Care in Alberta!" leaflet (AAYC Archives, 1981).

38   Dennis Sorensen, letter to the editor, "Phase-in for Improving Day Care," *Calgary Herald*, 18 February 1980, A8; "Privately-Operated Day Care Defended," *Edmonton Journal*, 13 June 1980.

39   "Father's Day-care Dispute Brings Daughter's Expulsion" and "Centre's Action Defended," *Calgary Herald*, 20 May 1980, B3; "Alderman Demands Daycare Intimidation Probe," *Calgary Herald*, 26 May 1980, B2.

40   "Socred Leader Urges Bigger Budget for Day Care," *Calgary Herald*, 23 May 1980, A18; "Official Opposition News Release," 22 May 1980 (Edmonton CFS file).

41   "Immediate Day Care Upgrading Sought by Some MLAs: Anderson," *Calgary Herald*, 4 July 1980, D15; "Day-care Improvements Soon," *Calgary Herald*, 5 July 1980, B2.

42   I did not find a copy of the 1980 Price Waterhouse study, but its main results were reported in a follow-up study conducted by the firm (see Price Waterhouse Associates 1982).

43   Letter from S.E. Blakely to Alderman Craig Reid, "Subject: Comparison of Provincial Day Care Standards," 26 September 1980 (Edmonton CFS, 92J040B, box 3, file 9).

44   Government of Alberta News Release, 4 September 1980; "Response of Department of Social Services and Community Health Day Care Unit to Tentative Directions Raised by the Honourable Mr. Bob Bogle on February 11, 1980"; "Discussion with Dr. Anderson and Mr. Bogle on February 18, 1980."

45   "MLA Day Care Regulation Review (Typed from Dr. Anderson's Handwritten Notes)"; memo from Dave Dewar, supervisor of licensing, southern Alberta region, to all licensing inspectors, southern Alberta region, "Maximum Capacity for Day Care Centres," 17 September 1980 (PAA, 92.150, box 2). The memo on day care capacity was received at the Red Deer office of the Social Care Facilities Licensing Unit. Since the Day

Care Regulation had not yet been amended to specify an eighty-child limit on centre capacity, civil servants anticipated some difficulty. A handwritten note at the bottom of the memo read: "May have exemptions—but do not advertise—ever [underlined four times]."

46 Provincial cabinet record of decision on RFD-M16-80, 16 December 1980; RFD-M16-80, subject title: "Day Care," 27 November 1980 (FOIP request to Executive Council).

47 Alberta Public Accounts, 1981–82, Alberta Treasury, Edmonton; "Surplus Budget Tops $6 Billion," Edmonton Journal, 3 April 1980.

48 Provincial Cabinet Record of Decision on RFD-M4-81, 14 April 1981; RFD-M4-81, subject: "Day Care Operating Allowance," 3 April 1981 (FOIP request to Executive Council). The rates reported here are the differential operating allowances plus the flat $5 space allowance.

49 RFD-M4-81, subject: "Day Care Operating Allowance"; "Lack of Day Home Aid 'Strange,'" Calgary Herald, 16 April 1981, C4.

50 "History of the Day Care Advisory Committee," 30 October 1982 (PAA, 93.188, box 2, file: Minister's Correspondence).

51 "History of the Day Care Advisory Committee," 30 October 1982; Government of Alberta News Release, 4 September 1980; letter from PDCS to Neil Clarke, director, College Program Services, 18 February 1982 (PAA, 90.438, file: Proposal PDCS).

52 "Operators Unhappy with Day Care Education," Calgary Herald, 12 May 1980, B1; "Students Defend Daycare Course," Calgary Herald, 22 May 1980, B4.

53 Minutes of ADCAC, 9 February 1984 (PAA, 93.188, box 2, file 9.1.2); "Day-care Operators Upgrading Training," Edmonton Journal, 13 February 1984.

54 Letter from Michael Phair to Bob Bogle, 10 October 1980; letter from Andrea Dinsmore to Bob Bogle, 7 May 1981 (AAYC Archives, 1981); "History of the Day Care Advisory Committee," 30 October 1982.

55 Audrey Griffiths' personal assessment of commercial day care was every bit as harsh as the typical ECE professional. Her assessment was recorded in the minutes of a meeting she had with the training subcommittee of the minister of Education's policy advisory committee on early childhood, 28 June 1983: "Dr. Griffiths felt that private daycare centres are totally inadequate; they have no philosophy. The approach seems to be simply custodial care with a minimum of flack from the public" (minutes attached to a 31 August 1983 memo from David Liles to Neil Clarke [PAA, 93.188, box 2]).

56 "Operators Unhappy with Day Care Education," Calgary Herald, 12 May 1980, B1.

57 Minutes of 18 December 1981 meeting between Judy Lathrop, dean of the Faculty of Community and Health Studies, Mount Royal College, and members of the education committee, Private Day Care Society of Alberta (PAA, 90.438, file: Correspondence, PDCS); minutes of the college's Early Childhood Programs Committee, 29 November 1982 (PAA, 90.438, file: Day Care Pgm [Gen]).

58 Report on 26 January 1981 meeting in AAYC Newsletter, February 1981; "Day-care Subsidies to Increase Substantially—Bogle," Lethbridge Herald, 19 February 1981 (repr. in AAYC Newsletter, March 1981).

59 "Briefing Materials—Meeting with Private Day Care Society of Alberta," 23 February 1982 (PAA, 90.438, file: Proposal PDCS); minutes, Alberta Day Care Advisory

Committee, 12 June 1981 (PAA, 93.188, box 2, file 9.1.2). The submission date of the first proposal is found on a copy of an agreement for the program (PAA, F95.128, box 5, FOIP 98-AA-02).

60 "Educational Standards for Early Childhood Workers. A Proposal Submitted to the Minister's Advisory Committee on Day Care," April 1981, Alberta Vocational Centre, Lac La Biche, Grande Prairie Regional College, Grant MacEwan Community College, Keyano College, Lakeland College, Medicine Hat College, Mount Royal College, Red Deer College (PAA, 90.438, file: Correspondence, PDCS); "Day Care Staff Recommendations," 16 March 1981 (AAYC Archives, 1981); "City of Calgary, Social Services Department, Position Paper for Day Care Advisory Committee," n.d. (PAA, 92.150, box 2).

61 Minutes, Alberta Day Care Advisory Committee, 8 December 1981 (PAA, 90.438, file: Correspondence, PDCS).

62 The cabinet discussion is mentioned in a memo from Advanced Education and Manpower Deputy Minister Henry Kolesar to Minister James Horsman, 8 January 1982 (PAA, 93.438, file: Day Care Pgm. General). The working meeting on 15 December is mentioned in the 8 December 1981 minutes of the ADCAC meeting.

63 "Private Day Care Society of Alberta—Education Committee Members" (PAA, 90.438, file: Correspondence, PDCS).

64 Memo from Judy Lathrop to Thomas Wood, "Meeting with Colleen White ... (December 18, 1981)" (PAA, 90.438, file: Correspondence, PDCS).

65 Letter from Jacqui Kallal to Ministers Bogle and Horsman, received by the Department of Advanced Education and Manpower on 21 December 1981; memo from Leslie Savage to Neil Clarke, "Preliminary Review—Program Proposal from Private Day Care Society of Alberta," 14 January 1982 (PAA, 80.438, file: Correspondence, PDCS).

66 Memo from Kolesar to Horsman, "Directive M-12. Letter from the Private Day Care Society of Alberta," 19 March 1982 (PAA, 90.438, file: Proposal PDCS).

67 Memo from Savage to Berghofer, 9 June 1982 (PAA, 90.438, file: Proposal PDCS); unsigned draft agreement for Day Care Worker Training Certificate Program, 1983 (PAA, F95.128, box 5, FOIP 98-AA-02). The minister agreed to cover two-thirds of the cost of the first year of operations of the certificate program, to a maximum of $39,000.

68 Memo from Melane Hotz, director, Day Care Program to Dr. C.D. Guenter, executive co-ordinator, Appeals and Advisory Secretariat, "Provincial Day Care Advisory Recommendations—September to November 1982," 2 December 1982 (PAA, 93.188, box 2, file: Day Care Advisory Committee); "Day Care Workers Lack Training, Says Report," Calgary Herald, 11 November 1982, C9.

69 Alberta Public Accounts, 1982–83, Alberta Treasury, Edmonton; Historical Labour Force Statistics, Statistics Canada Catalogue 71-201; "Economy Catches Up to Day Care," Calgary Herald, 22 September 1982.

70 "Notes Taken at Sheila Campbell's Session at the A.A.Y.C. Conference in Banff, 16 October 1982," prepared by Shirley Philippe, 21 October 1982 (PAA, 93.188, box 2, file: Day Care Advisory Committee).

71 Memo, "Resignation of Ann Moritz, Parent Member of Day Care Advisory Committee," 21 October 1982 (PAA, 93.188, box 2, file: Day Care Advisory Committee). Hotz also reported that two members of the advisory committee who attended the AAYC

conference, Lorraine Paskuski (the parent of a child in a commercial centre in Lethbridge) and Ray Petrowitsch (a Calgary day care owner and former PDCS president) "were incensed by Dr. Campbell's remarks." Their emotional reaction to Campbell's critical analysis is a good indicator of just how much the commercial sector's values and beliefs differed from those of ECE professionals.

72 Memo from Melane Hotz to Dr. Sheila Durkin, deputy minister, Health Services, "Release of Summary of Manpower Study by A. Moritz, Day Care Advisory Committee Member," 5 November 1982 (PAA, 93.188, box 2, file: Day Care Advisory Committee).

73 "Zaozirny Likely Star in Cabinet Game," *Calgary Herald*, 10 November 1982, A1; "Zaozirny Posting a Good Choice," *Calgary Herald*, 20 November 1982, A8; "Kids Mistreated, Says Ex-official," *Edmonton Journal*, 13 November 1982, A9; "Day Care Advisor Quits 'Facade,'" *Edmonton Journal*, 13 November 1982, B1.

74 This percentage is calculated from the data that Alberta submitted in response to a questionnaire prepared by the National Day Care Information Centre (21 July 1983, PAA, 93.188, box 2). It differs from the percentage that can be calculated from the Alberta data published in the *Status of Day Care in Canada* series. This is because the published data included spaces in out-of-school care programs, all of which were operated on a not-for-profit basis in 1983. Including these spaces in the Alberta calculation drops the commercial sector's share of the total spaces to 61 percent in 1983. This is behind Newfoundland, where 68 percent of all spaces were controlled by commercial operators (National Day Care Information Centre 1984, 11).

75 There were 405 day care centres in Dallas in 1984 with a licensed capacity of over 36,000. A study at that time noted that "much of the city's child care capacity is in proprietary chains and 'mom and pop' operations of relatively low standard." A similar situation existed in Houston. "The proprietary chains that seemed to be making a profit were enrolling 100 to 150 children. But everywhere staff-to-child ratios were low, groups were large, caregiver qualifications were very poor—and the salaries and fringe benefits were inadequate by any standard. Staff turnover was high" (Kahn and Kamerman 1987, 63–75).

6. From Corporatized Chains to "Mom and Pop" Centres

1 Dennis Maier, interview by Tom Langford, 4 March 1998, tape recorded.

2 Perry Mendel's decision to establish KinderCare was spurred by the prosperity of a small "mom and pop" operation. "A man he knew seemed to be living well without anything very obvious in the way of an occupation. Mendel asked how. His wife ran two daycare centres, the man explained" (Lelveld 1977). This anecdote is consistent with the seeming prosperity of small commercial day cares in Calgary in the late 1960s and early 1970s: owners were well enough off to hire a prominent Calgary lawyer, Irwin Blackstone, to act as an advocate.

3 "Companies Plan Day-care Centres," *Globe and Mail*, 2 December 1980; "Kinder Crunch: CUPE's Day Care Win Is a Free Market Loss," *Alberta Report*, 28 June 1982, 17; "Great-West Leaves Daycare Business," *Financial Post Western Business*, 17 July 1982, W3.

4 "Private Operators Alarmed at Prospect of Day-care Chain," *Calgary Herald*, 21 August 1980, B2. Caroline Kiehlbauch presented a fetching image of the "personal touch" in

community commercial day cares. Juxtaposed against this image is the fact that her own day care, Fairyland, was licensed for 104 children.

5 "Day-care Chain Has Calgary Plans," *Calgary Herald*, 3 December 1980, C4.

6 John Lackey to Dr. Sheila Durkin, deputy minister, Health Services, "Great-West Life and Mini-Schools," 19 February 1991 (PAA, 92.150, box 2).

7 The concern of the civil service was confirmed in an interview with John Lackey by Tom Langford, 12 April 1996, tape recorded.

8 Larry Taggart to John Lackey, 26 January 1981 (PAA, 92.150, box 2).

9 "Private Operators Alarmed"; "Kinder Crunch"; "Great-West to Drop Child-care Chain Link," *Winnipeg Free Press*, 1 June 1982.

10 "204 Customers Pull Benefits from Great-West," *Winnipeg Free Press*, 6 July 1981.

11 "Great-West to Drop Child-care Chain Link." It is at least conceivable that Great-West Life used the boycott as a convenient excuse to extract itself from a business relationship or business deal that had gone sour for other reasons. Without knowing the exact financial impact of the CUPE boycott on Great-West Life, it is difficult to evaluate this alternative explanation. However, in the first quarter of 1982, Great-West Life reported a 29 percent decrease in net income and an 84 percent decrease in net profit ("Great-West Leaves Daycare Business").

12 "Kinder Crunch."

13 Minutes, ADCAC, 14 August 1982, 2 (PAA, 93.188, box 2, file 9.1.2).

14 Ibid.; Melane Hotz to Dr. C.D. Guenter, "Provincial Day Care Advisory Recommendations—September to November, 1982," p. 1 (PAA, 93.188, box 2, file: Day Care Advisory Committee).

15 Neil Webber to Audrey Griffiths, 13 July 1983 (PAA, 93.188, box 2, file 9.1.2).

16 "Day Cares Can Set Cash Register Ringing," *Calgary Herald*, 20 November 1985, A1.

17 "Subsidized Day Care," n.d. [1977], *North Hill News* (CA, Social Services, box 6290). The article reported Sorensen's objection to the development approval for a new PSS centre, Connaught Day Care.

18 Melvin W. Finlay, "Situation Alert Memo: Temple Day Care Centre Calgary," 22 October 1984 (PAA, 93.188, box 1).

19 Minutes, ADCAC, 14 August 1982, 2.

20 "Day Cares Can Set Cash Register Ringing."

21 Ibid. The level of operating allowances in 1985 is recorded in table A.6. Assume that a Kindercare centre with a capacity for 120 children had an average occupancy rate of 75 percent for the year. Assume further that of the average attendance of ninety, nine children were infants, fifteen were toddlers, and the remaining sixty-six were preschoolers. In 1985 dollars, the monthly operating allowance payment to this centre alone would be almost $9,500. Over the entire year, the centre would receive a payment of approximately $113,500. Converting this to 2006 dollars, the yearly payment would be around $207,000. This sort of operating allowance payment would be repeated for each of the Kindercare centres.

22 "Situation Alert"; Decision of Appeal Board, 16 November 1984 (PAA, 93.188, box 1).

23 "Little Demand for Daycare," *Alberta Report*, 14 February 1994, 33.

24 Statistics Canada, *Historical Labour Force Statistics*, Catalogue 71-201.

25 Nizar Daya, interview by Tom Langford, 19 December 2002, tape recorded.

26 "Largest Day-care Operator Struggling," *Calgary Herald*, 25 January 1994, B2; "Little Demand for Daycare"; "In Bankruptcy," *Calgary Herald*, 11 April 1994, C3. Information on the ownership of the Dover Kindercare was obtained from a Land Registry search, title no. 941 178 849, 4315 – 26 Ave. SE.

27 Daya, interview.

28 "Kinder-Care Issue of $50 Million," *New York Times*, 29 July 1983; "Punished," *Forbes*, 3 February 1992, 12; "Guilty Plea in Tax Evasion," *New York Times*, 3 August 1991; "Kinder-Care Files for Chapter 11 Protection," *New York Times*, 11 November 1992.

29 Daya, interview.

30 This intention is stated in a letter from Minister Neil Webber to the chair of the ADCAC, Dr. Audrey Griffiths, on 13 July 1983 (PAA, 93.188, box 2, file 9.1.2). However, the published amendment was far more restrictive than this. It modified the wording suggested by the advisory committee in 1982, specifying the restriction in terms of a multiple of centres and aggregate capacity. There is no evidence that the original wording of the amendment was ever enforced, and the regulation was subsequently revised to state that the limit was an aggregate capacity of five hundred (Alberta 1991, sec. 9).

31 In a background report prepared by Larry Egger, 23 May 1986, attached to a memo from Deputy Minister M. Ozerkevich to Minister C. Osterman, 11 July 1986, regarding Regulation 144/81 Section 2(3) (PAA, 92.222, box 2).

32 "Situation Alert."

33 Larry Egger and Pauline S. Peters, Community Day Programs, "Material Prepared for Green Docket 85130-0098 June 28, 1985 and Updated May 21, 1986," 23 May 1986 (PAA, 92.222, box 2).

34 Ozerkevich to Osterman, 11 July 1986.

35 Memo from Executive Committee, Alberta Social Services, and Community Health to Honourable Neil Webber, "Proposed Day Care Act," 25 May 1983 (PAA, F95.128, box 5, FOIP 98-AA-00002).

36 Egger and Peters, "Material Prepared for Green Docket."

37 On union efforts to organize in the service sector in Ontario, see Yates (2000). The department store Wal-Mart has used a number of tactics to keep employees from unionizing. See "Wal-Mart—What's to Hate?" *Globe and Mail*, 19 February 2005, and "Wal-Mart Intimidated Unionists, Board Rules," *Globe and Mail*, 26 February 2005.

38 A research assistant contacted the following day care chains in the summer of 1998 and learned that none of their centres were unionized: Bright Horizons, KinderCare Learning, Children's World, Childtime, and Nobel Education Dynamics.

39 "Strike 'Threatens' Profitable Day Care," *Toronto Star*, 17 November 1982; "Contract Talks Break Down in Day-care Workers' Strike," *Toronto Star*, 3 December 1982; "Pair's Dream Turns to Nightmare," *Globe and Mail*, 12 March 1983; "Mini-Skool: Where Day Care Spells Big Business," *Globe and Mail*, 17 March 1983; "Eight-Month Strike Over at Mini-Skools," *Globe and Mail*, 1 June 1983.

40 Neil Webber's career after he left politics demonstrated that he was quite sympathetic to private sector involvement in child care and education. Webber was first elected to the legislature in 1975, representing the constituents of Calgary Bow. After leaving provincial politics in 1989, he founded the Webber Academy, an elite "university preparatory school" in Calgary. In 2003 the Webber Academy had 550 children ranging from junior kindergarten to grade 11. Tuition ranged between $8,000 and $9,200 per year and entrance tests were used to select students. In order to accommodate junior kindergarten children in a full-day program, the private school was licensed to run a day care for a maximum of twenty-one children. The elite thrust of the school was demonstrated by the following statement found in a discussion of class sizes on the Webber Academy website in 2003 (www.webberacademy.ca):

> When considering class sizes, one key thing to keep in mind is the range of abilities present within one classroom. Because there is a screening procedure in place at our school, the range of abilities represented in each classroom tends to be narrow. Therefore, teachers are able to appropriately cater to all students' needs.

41 Section 2 of DCSA notes for 14 February 1983 meeting with Minister Webber; Webber to Dr. Sheila Durkin, deputy minister, Health Services, 23 February 1983 (PAA, F95.128, box 5, FOIP 98-AA-02).

42 Webber to Kallal, 2 May 1983 (PAA, F95.128, box 5, FOIP 98-AA-02).

43 "Day Cares Scrambling for Qualified Staff," Calgary Herald, 18 June 1988, A1.

44 "CUPE Out to Unionize Day-care Centres," Calgary Herald, 14 December 1988, B1; "Day Care Fights Union Move," Calgary Herald, 15 December 1988, B2; "Union Wins Fight to Represent Day Cares," Calgary Herald, 16 December 1988, B1. In the 1986 Calgary Yellow Pages, Calgary Association for Quality Child Care listed all of its members. The members consisted of nineteen not-for-profit organizations (day cares, dayhome projects, and OOSC centres) and three commercial day cares: Brookside Village Daycare, Montgomery Day Care Centre, and Whitefield Day Care, the latter owned by Patti Penner. None of these three commercial centres was a member of the DCSA at the time. Penner was a former president of the Day Care Association of Calgary ("Day Care Needs Kids," Calgary Herald, 17 November 1983).

45 "Union, Day Care at Odds," Calgary Herald, 20 January 1990, B3.

46 "Day Care Union under Attack," Calgary Herald, 12 November 1989, B1; "Union's Future Hinges on Vote," Calgary Herald, 15 November 1989, B5; "Union Boss Undaunted by Day Care Ouster," Calgary Herald, 18 November 1989, B1. The Alberta Labour Relations Code is available online at www.qp.alberta.ca (active 1 August 2010).

47 "Union, Day Care at Odds"; supplementary information from Peter Marsden, CUPE Local 38 president, 16 May 2003.

48 "From Chicken Feed to $13M Best Western Hotel: Commercial Developers Favour Sherwood Park," Edmonton Journal, 26 May 2001, G1.

49 "Day Care Re-opens with All-New Look," Edmonton Journal, 14 April 1998, B3; "Day Care Closed Until It Cleans Up, Fixes Toys," Edmonton Journal, 13 March 1998, B3.

50 Unless otherwise noted, all information on the Rainbow chain and Conny Hippe is from my interview with her, 6 March 1998, tape recorded.

51 In 2009 Rainbow Day Care Ltd. continued to operate three centres (see CUPE's "Child Care Profile: Alberta" at http://cupe.ca/child-care/child-care-profile--alberta) (active 1 August 2010).

52 Unless otherwise noted, all information on Kidsland is from my interview with Nizar Daya. Details of the Educentres' bankruptcy are recorded in "Parents Scramble After 9 Day Cares Close," *Calgary Herald*, 25 September 1996, A1, and "Two Educentres Daycares Stay Open," *Calgary Herald*, 4 October 1996, B7.

53 This licensing development was a major item of business at the meeting of the Alberta Day Care Advisory Committee on 9 September 1985. The ADCAC objected that it "again was not informed of this change in policy in any official way" (Minutes, PAA, 93.188, box 2, file: More on Day Care Advisory Committee). At this time the committee had a very adversarial relationship with Minister Webber. In 1984 he had recommended that the ADCAC reduce their meeting frequency to twice a year (a recommendation that the committee appeared to ignore) and on 9 May 1985 had written that "there is currently very little activity for the Day Care Advisory Committee" (letter to Audrey Griffiths, PAA, 93.188, box 2, file: More on Day Care Advisory Committee). Nevertheless, in August 1983, Webber had approved a revised mandate for the committee. The first of five responsibilities in the mandate was "to review and advise me on Day Care standards for preschool children." Therefore, the members of the ADCAC had a legitimate reason to expect to be consulted about the decision to allow up to 108 children in a building, with eighty being the previous maximum. It is symptomatic of the lowly status of the ADCAC in 1985 that its 9 September meeting was attended by neither the minister nor the day care director at the time, Pauline Peters. The ADCAC was disbanded following the provincial election of 8 May 1986.

54 The main interview with Traudi Kelm, which I conducted, occurred on 11 December 2002. She was also interviewed on 16 August 1995 by Janine Bauman. All information on Marlborough Day Nursery comes from these interviews, both of which were tape recorded.

55 Marketwire News Release, "San Anton and Edleun Announce Proposed Business Combination," 18 November 2009 (http://www.marketwire.com/press-release/San-Anton-and-Edleun-Announce-Proposed-Business-Combination-TSX-VENTURE-TON.P-1079048.htm (active 1 August 2010).

56 All information on Charleswood Day Nursery comes from my interview with Irmtraud Walter, 18 December 2002, tape recorded.

7. Day Care in Question, 1984–99

1 I have borrowed this turn of phrase from a 1975 letter that Al Hagen wrote to a former colleague. He reported, "The daycare controversy seems to continue endlessly in Calgary" (Hagen to Norma Matheson, 19 February 1975 [CA, box 6290, file: Child Care, Jan–Apr 1975]).

2 Department of National Health and Welfare, Canada, "Policy Guidelines Relating to the Provision of Day Care Services for Children Under the Canada Assistance Plan," March 1974. Only in later years did the federal government insist that families with above-average incomes pay the full cost of day care. In the 1960s and early 1970s in Edmonton, no families paid the full cost. "This is way back at the beginning of the Canada Assistance

Plan," reported Howard Clifford, "and there was no outcry about it. Because what it says is 'likelihood of need' and 'likelihood of need' is interpreted according to what every bureaucrat wants to interpret it. We [in Edmonton] were interpreting it, and when I first went to the federal government I know we were too, as simply, the child's going to be unsupervised, they'll likely be in need regardless whether you're making $100,000 a year or not. So we weren't uptight at all about that kind of thing" (interview, 20 February 1996).

3 "Income vs Needs Testing for Day Care Subsidy in Alberta," briefing note prepared by Melane Hotz, attached to a memo from Minister Neil Webber to Deputy Minister Durkin, 3 January 1984 (PAA, F95.128, box 5, FOIP 98-AA-00002).

4 Memo from Judy Bennett (PAA, 92.150, box 2); "Infusion Calms Feud over Program Funds," Edmonton Journal, 30 March 1982.

5 "Income vs Needs Testing for Day Care Subsidy in Alberta."

6 "Income vs Needs Testing for Day Care Subsidy in Alberta"; "Conclusions and Recommendation" from a report by the Federal/Provincial/Territorial Working Group on Child Care (PAA, 93.188, box 2, file: August 1984 to August 1985).

7 The Alberta government spent about $17.1 million on day care subsidies in 1983–84 (table A.4). Forty-eight percent of the total qualified for cost sharing. This included all of the subsidized children in not-for-profit centres (approximately 30 percent of the total) and those children in commercial centres whose families were needs tested for general welfare benefits (approximately one-quarter of the remaining 70 percent of subsidized children = 18 percent). "The $12 Million Dollar Misunderstanding—Or, Giving Credit Where Credit Is Not Due," 10 May 1984 (PAA, 93.188, box 2, file: May 1984 to December 1984). This document corrects the preliminary calculations done by researchers working for the federal Task Force on Child Care. The corrected calculations seem to have been included in Blain (1985).

8 "Cost Sharing Day Care Expenditures. 1985/86 Actual Expenditures," Community Day Programs, 17 November 1986 (PAA, 92.222, box 2). The spending on subsidies reported in this document is slightly different than the figure reported in Public Accounts data (table A.4).

9 Between June 1982 and November 1984, 243 commercial centres opened in Alberta, compared to only twenty-seven not-for-profit centres. This was a ratio of nine new commercial centres to only one new not-for-profit centre ("Manitoba's Proposed Canada Day Care Act," attached to a memo from Melane Hotz to Don Axford, director, Federal/Provincial Coordination, Policy and Program Development, 21 November 1984 [PAA, 93.188, box 2, file: May 1984 to December 1984]).

10 Neil Webber's indifference is noted by Bagley (1986, 39). A civil servant commented that Webber was uncomfortable as the minister of Social Services, "a mathematician who wanted numbers and not much else."

11 "Osterman Vows Fight on Daycare," Edmonton Journal, 14 November 1986; "Osterman Considers Income-Assets Test," Edmonton Journal, 27 January 1987; "Province Could Set Rules for Income-Assets Test," Edmonton Journal, 28 January 1987; "Alberta Social Services Proposed Business Plan. Executive Overview," 10 March 1987 (PAA, 92.222, box 5, file: Social Services Executive Committee).

12 "Briefing Note. Issue: Meeting of Federal and Provincial Officials to Discuss Child Care Cost Sharing," 1 January 1988 (PAA, F95.74, box 6, FOIP 98-AA-02). The first version of

Bill C-144 favoured not-for-profit over commercial services. Howard Clifford provided an interesting account of how federal officials secured the Government of Alberta's support for that version of the bill:

> It's the kind of conniving that goes on in planning when we were doing C-144. Well, politically, federally, we knew that if some major provinces fought it, it's dead. And we wanted it non-profit—of course that's mainly me but others came on side. Well, Alberta, we knew would scream bloody murder and Quebec in our view would go on board with them. [Quebec] only wanted non-profit too, but it's another question and the question is provincial autonomy.... So if you got Quebec and Alberta, and probably one or two others come on board, we would have been dead on that issue. We had to fight it ahead of time. So what could we do. We knew Alberta didn't believe in day care anyway. So they're not interested in growth, but they are interested in catching up the fairness, what they considered the equity problem. So we had a thing, we will grandfather in all existing programs and share that cost and any new costs have to be non-profit. And Alberta was "Phew," getting a hundred million bucks out of this and they didn't care about new growth and they didn't believe in day care anyway and a hundred million bucks is a lot of money and it got us off the hook. (Interview, 20 February 1996)

13 "Briefing Paper on the Future of Day Care and Funding Options," 29 January 1988, draft prepared by Policy Development and Service Design (PAA, F95.74, box 6, FOIP 98-AA-02).

14 "Kid Care at Home Means Big Cash," *Calgary Herald*, 22 September 1988, A3. The story reported that "Dinning, who is also education minister, took on the family portfolio in a cabinet shuffle this month." The Getty government seems to have had a long-term strategy when they made the minister of Education responsible for day care. On 6 October 1988, Alberta and federal officials met to discuss the question, "How would cost sharing under the Canada Assistance Plan or the new *Canada Childcare Act* be affected if the Department of Education had responsibility for family issues?" This was an important initiative by the Getty government that had the potential to redefine day care in Alberta more as early childhood education (ECE) than a welfare service.

The federal officials reacted very negatively to the idea of integrating Alberta's day care program into the Department of Education. At the time, federal officials expected that federal-provincial cost sharing for child care would continue under the terms of CAP for two years before the Canada Childcare Act would take effect. The acting director of CAP attended the meeting and made it clear that "CAP has no intention of funding anything that resembles a nursery school or a kindergarten." Federal officials emphasized that "the Canada Assistance Plan is clearly 'welfare' legislation, not education legislation." They also stated how the federal government distinguished a child care service from an educational service. "Childcare programs are expected to meet the developmental needs of the child, but essentially exist to meet the needs of the parent [specifically, the needs of parents for child care while they engaged in paid labour]. Education, on the other hand, is a service which is clearly focussed on developing and educating the child."

In light of the federal position, Assistant Deputy Minister David Kelly indicated that an immediate transfer of the day care program to the Department of Education would put CAP cost-sharing revenue "significantly at risk." His overall portrayal of the federal response was highly negative, and it is little wonder that the Getty government gave up on its plan to move day care to the Department of Education. Following the 1989 provincial election, the Department of Social Services was renamed the Department of Family and Social Services (Kelly's note to File, 7 October 1988, PAA, F95.74, box 6, FOIP 98-AA-02).

15 Data for the fiscal years ending 1980 to 1997 are included in the calculation. Because expenditure data for 1980–81 are unavailable, an inflation-adjusted estimate of $25 million is used for this year. Using the data in table A.5, the total amount spent by Alberta on day care over these nineteen years was $1.439 billion in adjusted dollars. This total was then multiplied by 19.6 percent to get $282 million. I am concerned that this approximation may be high, so I rounded down by approximately 10 percent and came up with $255 million as a conservative estimate of the total forfeited amount.

16 "Special Committee on Child Care," AAYC Information Bulletin, 1986 (AAYC Archives, 1986).

17 "Kids First Fights for Parents," Calgary Herald, 7 June 1987, C5; "Day-care Plan Could Prove Fatal," Calgary Herald, 21 February 1990, A5.

18 Maier, interview.

19 Letter from Connie Osterman to Dorothy French, 30 September 1986 (AAYC Archives, 1986).

20 Ney's paper, and a one-page summary prepared by Marlene Jubenvill of Community Day Programs, were attached to a 24 September 1986 memo from Ozerkevich to Osterman (PAA, 92.222, box 2).

21 Based on an Internet search on Philip G. Ney, 2002.

22 "'Women's Movement Hurt Moms at Home,'" Calgary Herald, 7 June 1987, C5.

23 Joanne Loughlin, Acknowledgements and "Comments on the Report Entitled 'Watch Me Mama!, Watch Me Dad!'" 26 November 1987 (PAA, F95.74, box 6).

24 Underlying all pro-family arguments are the unexamined assumptions that (1) the care of young children in families is superior to all alternatives, and (2) the care of young children by a non-parent in a family-like setting is superior to group care. Beverley Smith recognized that parents need generous social support in the difficult task of caring for and educating young children. Yet she never problematized the quality of care in family-like settings, let alone in families. Such questioning would have undermined the simplistic assumptions stated above and would have challenged the core of the pro-family position.

25 "Stay Home Moms May Get Help," Calgary Herald, 8 December 1987; "Briefing Note. Working Group on Child Care Support for Women in the Home," n.d. [December 1987], prepared by Social Services staff (PAA, F95.74, box 6, FOIP 98-AA-02).

26 "PCs Would Be Wise to Reconsider Day Care," Calgary Herald, 5 June 1988, C1.

27 "Kid Care at Home Means Big Cash"; "Throne Speech Family Bonanza," Calgary Herald, 18 February 1989, A1; "PC Report Touts $42-Million Childcare Plan," Calgary Herald, 1 March 1989, A1; "Stay-Home Parents Unsure About Credit," Calgary Herald, 6 March 1989, B2.

28 "Is There a Crack in Tory Ranks?" Calgary Herald, 9 March 1989, A3; "Premier Helps Out Borrowers," Calgary Herald, 2 March 1989, A1; "Don Getty's Election Commitments: Here Are the Facts," advertisement, Calgary Herald, 13 March 1989, A12.

29 Conny Hippe, interview by Tom Langford, 6 March 1998, tape recorded; Noreen Murphy, interview by Tom Langford and Rachel McKendry, 18 August 1993, tape recorded. Ms. Murphy was the program director for the Churchill Park Day Care Society in Calgary and active in the Calgary Regional Association for Quality Child Care. Wendy

Reid, interview by Tom Langford and Rachel McKendry, 29 June 1993, tape recorded. Reid was the program director of Briar Hill Children's Programs in Calgary before the establishment of Choices in Childcare in 1989 following a successful application for a grant from Childcare Visions.

30 Minutes of Alberta Child Care Network (ACCN) meeting, 12 May 1988 (AAYC Archives, 1988).

31 Minutes found in AAYC Archives, 1987 and 1988, and in PAA, F95.74, box 6, FOIP 98-AA-02.

32 Letter, 31 March 1989 (AAYC Archives, 1989); Wendy Reid, interview, 29 June 1993. It is noteworthy that journalists had a much harsher view of Connie Osterman's record on day care than did Noreen Murphy, Wendy Reid, or Conny Hippe. See, for example, Linda Goyette's column, "Osterman's Absence from Day-care Meet Was No Loss," *Edmonton Journal*, 25 January 1987.

33 The minister's refusal to meet separately with the DCSA was reported by Wendy Reid in an interview.

34 A more critical view of Connie Osterman's politics was provided by Darryl Grams, one of the two AAYC representatives at the 25 June 1987 meeting that the network held with the minister. Following that meeting, he wrote:

> My admittedly biased impression of the meeting is that the minister is open to reviewing suggestions but that her basic value system regarding day cares is still one of a necessary evil to be tolerated but not supported lest it encourage women to enter the workforce to the detriment of their children's development. She therefore is wholly supportive of daycare for the less privileged families. Daycare funding would be directed towards providing help only to those in economic need or family crises, rather than for any universal support program. (Memo to AAYC Board, 25 June 1987, [AAYC Archives, 1987]).

35 Notes distributed with the minutes of the AAYC Board meeting held on 9 December 1988 (AAYC Archives, 1989).

36 "The Day-care Debate: At-Home and Working Moms Are Finding Some Common Ground," *Calgary Herald*, 18 February 1991, C1.

37 Eva Roche undoubtedly would have done much more to encourage the dialogue had her health allowed her to do so. In 1991 she was diagnosed with cancer and she died in 1995. Eva Roche, along with her husband, Douglas, were active in the social-justice branch of the Catholic Church. Douglas Roche was the founding editor of the Western Catholic Reporter, a Progressive Conservative member of Parliament from Edmonton (1972–84), Canada's ambassador for disarmament (1984–89), and a member of the Senate between 1998 and his retirement in 2004 ("Educator Eva Roche a Noted Kids' Advocate; Memorial," Edmonton Journal, 15 July 1995; http://roche.apirg.org, active 1 August 2010).

38 The province had a small net deficit in 1982–83 and a small net surplus in 1983–84 (Mansell 1997, 30). The deficit for 1982–83 reported in Public Accounts data was $2.1 billion. The net deficit was much smaller, however, because of the growth of the Alberta Heritage Savings Trust Fund (AHSTF). In that year, 15 percent of all resource revenues were transferred to the AHSTF, and for the first six months of the year, the fund retained the investment income on a balance of approximately $8 billion (Mansell 1997, 25).

39 Letter from Webber to Audrey Griffiths, 12 March 1984, and "Day Care Advisory Committee, Kindercare and Amended Staff Proposals to Cope with Day Care Budget

Cost Increases," Appendix IV of submission to Social Planning Committee, 23 May 1984 (PAA, 93.188, box 2, file 9.1.2).

40 Calculated from Alberta Public Accounts data, published by the Alberta Treasury, various years. The non-renewable resource revenue for 1983–84 was $4.2 billion, close to the previous peak year of 1979–80 ($4.5 billion).

41 "Incentive for the Development of Satellite Family Day Home System in the Province of Alberta," proposal by Health Services Division (Day Care Branch) to Management Committee, 8 June 1982 (PAA, 93.188, box 2).

42 "Extract from DCAC Minutes, 1 June 1982" (PAA, 93.188, box 2, file: DCAC).

43 "Federal/Provincial/Territorial Working Group on Child Care. Phase One: Province of Alberta Data," 28 January 1985 (PAA, 93.188, box 2, file: August 84 to October 85).

44 "Electoral Summary, 1905–2004," www.elections.ab.ca/Public%20Website/748.htm (active 1 August 2010). Percentage revenue decline calculated from Alberta Public Accounts data, published by the Alberta Treasury.

45 Minutes of Social Services Executive Committee, 14 October 1986 (PAA, 92.222, box 5).

46 "Day-care Cuts Blasted," Calgary Herald, 13 November 1986; "Osterman Vows Fight on Daycare," Edmonton Journal, 14 October 1986.

47 Minutes of the Social Services Executive Committee—Core, 25 November 1986 (PAA, 92.222, box 5).

48 Memo, "Minister's Policy on Freeze of Daycare Spaces," 16 April 1987 (PAA, F95.74, box 6, FOIP 98-AA-02); Alberta Social Services, Proposed Business Plan, Executive Overview, 10 March 1987 draft (PAA, 92.222, box 5, file: Social Services Executive Committee).

49 "Daycare Centres Seek Parents' Aid in Funding Battle," Calgary Herald, 9 January 1987.

50 UCCA material attached to the minutes of the first meeting of the Alberta Child Care Network, 8 May 1987 (AAYC Archives, 1987).

51 The importance of Griffin's workshop was emphasized by Wendy Reid in an interview on 29 June 1993.

52 "Flash" newsletter prepared by Paddi Solem, along with a report on the 8 May 1987 meeting, date stamped 22 May 1987 (AAYC Archives, 1987). Minutes of ACCN meetings with Minister Osterman, 25 June and 19 August 1987 (AAYC Archives, 1987).

53 Minutes of ACCN meetings with Minister Osterman, 25 June and 19 August 1987.

54 "Briefing Paper on the Future of Day Care and Funding Options," prepared by Policy Development and Service Design, 29 January 1988 draft (PAA, F95.74, FOIP 98-AA-02).

55 Minutes of ACCN meeting, 12 May 1988 (AAYC Archives, 1988).

56 Minutes of ACCN, 25 July 1989 (AAYC Archives, 1989).

57 Maier, interview.

58 Maier, interview; Alberta FSS (1990a, 21).

59 Government of Alberta, Caring and Responsibility: A Statement of Social Policy for Alberta, 28 March 1988, 7–8.

60 Maier, interview; Alberta (1991, sec. 30 and 34).

61 "Day Cares Take Issue with Proposed Fee Cutbacks," *Calgary Herald*, 8 February 1990, B4; "Parents Demand Day-care Subsidies," *Calgary Herald*, 13 February 1990, B2. The form letters are found in PAA, 92.404. More than 2,400 letters and phone calls were received in response to the White Paper's invitation to respond to the proposed reforms (Alberta FSS 1990b, 4). ACCN Minutes of Pre-Ministerial Meeting, 12 June 1990 (AAYC Archives, 1990); "It's Time the Tots Came First," *Calgary Herald*, 27 October 1991. The private meetings between Oldring and the DCSA were reported by Wendy Reid in an interview on 29 June 1993.

62 Board of Directors, Edmonton and Area Non-Profit Day Care Centres, "Meeting the Need ... A Fairer, Better System for Albertans: A Response to the White Paper on Reforms to Alberta's Day Care Program," 1990 (found in records of ECFS, Children's Services, 1991, box 1, file 2.2).

63 Minutes of ACCN Ministerial Meeting, 12 June 1990 (AAYC Archives, 1990).

64 "Day Cares Squeezed by Recession; But Enrolments at Non-profit Centres Healthier Than at Commercial Ones," *Edmonton Journal*, 13 March 1994, B2; Dennis Maier, comments, ACCN meeting, 17 January 1994 (AAYC Archives, 1994).

65 "Day-care Operators Cheer New Play Plan; Middle-Income Parents Better Brace Themselves, One Expert Warns," *Edmonton Journal*, 26 July 1992, A5; "Subsidy Hikes Reduced," *Calgary Herald*, 24 July 1992, B2.

66 These campaign promises were recorded in a card distributed to voters in the constituency of Calgary Varsity on behalf of the successful Tory candidate, Murray Smith.

67 "Parents to Face Higher Fees; Day Care," *Edmonton Journal*, 19 January 1994, B3.

68 Ibid.

69 "Day-care Rates Set to Rise as Gov't Ends Subsidies; Low-Income Earners to Get Extra Cash," *Edmonton Journal*, 25 July 1997, B3.

70 "Uproar Hits the Daycares: Government Subsidy-Trimming Leaves Working-Poor Moms Fuming," *Alberta Report*, 23 February 1998, 32.

71 "Reverse $30M Day-care Funding Cut, Government Urged at Public Forum," *Edmonton Journal*, 30 January 1998, B2.

72 A number of such letters were forwarded to the AAYC, which forwarded copies of the letters to Oberg, Klein, and local MLAs (AAYC correspondence files).

73 Sylene Syvenky, AAYC president, interview by Tom Langford, 13 November 1998, tape recorded.

74 Ibid.; Maier, interview.

75 "Alberta F&SS Budget Increased by 1.2%," *Community Action*, 16 March 1998, 3.

76 "More Funds Sought for Child-Benefit Plan," *Globe and Mail*, 7 October 1997, A6.

77 Initial money from the NCB clawback was also used to establish an extended health plan for low-income children that included coverage of dental, optical, and prescription drug services (Government of Alberta News Release, "More Families Eligible for Child Care Subsidy," 18 June 1998; "Funding Raises Income Ceiling for Day-care Subsidies," *Calgary Herald*, 19 June 1998, A16).

78 Letter to Neil Webber received on 16 May 1983 and background memo (PAA, F95.128, box 5, FOIP 98-AA-02).

79 Reid, interview. Day Care Programs also produced a companion booklet, "Choosing a Family Day Home: A Guide for Parents."

80 "Day-care Checklist Assailed as Gov't Cop-out," Edmonton Journal, 26 September 1995, A7.

81 In 1995 commercial centres made up 71 percent of all day cares in Alberta (calculated from data in table 6.2). Therefore, in the ombudsman's study, commercial centres generated considerably more complaints than would have been expected from their incidence in the population.

82 Alberta Day Care Branch, "Fact Sheet on Day Care," October 1981; Alberta Day Care Branch, organizational chart, October 1981 (PAA, 92.150, box 2).

83 "Much Ado About Nothing," Calgary Sun, 28 June 1994, 11; "Day Care Probes Slammed," Calgary Herald, 28 June 1994, A1.

84 Alberta FSS, Annual Report 1997–98, 20; "Staff Reduction Smacks of Day-care Deregulation, Critics Say," Edmonton Journal, 18 February 1998, A6.

85 Letter from William Page to AAYC, 21 July 1993 (AAYC Archives, 1993); "Province Looks at Ways to Cut Daycare Budget," Edmonton Journal, 5 November 1993, A1.

86 Letter from Connie Toporowski, AAYC president, to William Page (AAYC Archives, 1993).

87 "Province Looks at Ways to Cut Daycare Budget," Edmonton Journal, 5 November 1993, A1.

88 Letter from Dennis Maier to Joy Huebert, provincial coordinator of the AAYC, 18 October 1994 (AAYC Archives, 1994).

89 "Babysitting Legislation Shocks Child-care Workers," Edmonton Journal, 19 October 1994, A1.

90 "Six Tots Too Many for Lone Babysitter," Edmonton Journal, 26 October 1994, A15.

91 The Alberta government produced a brochure, "The National Child Benefit in Alberta," dated June 1998, that was distributed to recipients of the National Child Tax Benefit. It contained information on the Alberta Family Employment Tax Credit. More recent information is at www.finance.alberta.ca/business/tax_rebates/alberta_family_employment_taxcredit.html (active 1 August 2010). The total cost of the Family Employment Tax Credit increased from $80 million to $97 million in 2008 even though fewer families qualified for the tax credit in the latter year. This is because the government increased the maximum credit for families with two or more children.

92 "Informed Debate Needed on Income Tax; Single Rate Favours Upper-Income and One-Earner Families," Edmonton Journal, 19 January 1999, A12.

93 Government of Alberta News Release, 11 March 1999, www.finance.gov.ab.ca/whatsnew/newsrel/2000/n000224b.html (no longer online, 1 August 2010; available from the author); "Informed Debate Needed on Income Tax."

94 Calculated from statistics reported in Alberta FSS Annual Reports, 1990–91, 8, and 1998–99, 16.

95 Pauline Desjardins, interview by Rachael McKendry, 3 March 1995, tape recorded. All figures on exemptions come from tables provided by Day Care Programs staff in 1995 or 1997, or were cited by Desjardins.

96 Alberta Children's Services website, "Day Care Staff Qualifications," 28 December 2001; Kelm, interview, 11 December 2002; information on The Career College's Early Childhood Education program, 28 December 2002, www.nacc.ca/219a.htm (no longer online, 1 August 2010; available from the author); information on the CDI Education Corporation, 28 December 2002, www.cdieducation.com (no longer online, 1 August 2010; available from the author). The ECE programs offered by CDI Colleges in Alberta were listed on 1 August 2010 at www.cdicollege.ca/View/College_Programs/School_of_Health_Care.

8. Municipalities and Lighthouse Child Care, 1980–99

1 The term "lighthouse" was used by advocates like Sheila Campbell to refer to a day care with higher standards than most day cares in a community. It would thus serve as a navigational lighthouse for other day cares that sought to improve their standards (Campbell, interview, 17 April 1996).

2 Press Release (PAA, 93.188/box 2, file: Minister's Correspondence).

3 This is the only instance in Alberta history where the provincial government directly ran a service for preschool children. In the summer of 1982, there were seven provincial employees administering 150 FDHs. The province continued its administrative role until the payment of administrative fees encouraged the establishment of independent satellite FDH projects in Edmonton. Deputy Minister Sheila Durkin to Management Committee, SSCH, "Extension of Edmonton Family Day Home Project," 29 July 1982 (PAA, 93.188, box 2).

4 Letter from Chief Deputy Minister Mansbridge to Chief Commissioner Burrows, 2 June 1980; memo from A.I. Dorosh to A.H. Savage, 17 July 1980, including recommendation on the FDH program from the Day Care Branch; "Press Release re: Day Care" from the Office of the Mayor, 31 July 1980 (ECFS records); "Briefing Report and Background Information re: City of Edmonton's Involvement in Day Care," 22 July 1988 (ECFS, Children's Services 1985–89, file 2-2).

5 "A Synopsis of the City of Edmonton's Preschool Day Care Program for the Period 1966–1985," Edmonton Social Services, 11 September 1985 (ECFS files). I do not have the exact deficit for the Glengarry Day Care in 1981. However, the city budgeted for a deficit of $397,00 in 1984, which works out to a subsidy of $6,617 for each of the sixty licensed spaces. Information on deficit phase-out payments is found in letters from A. Dorosh to J. Lackey, 10 November and 15 December 1981 (ECFS files); an undated (April 1982) letter from Mayor Purves to Minister Bogle (ECFS files); and "Commissioner's Brief: Day Care and After School Care," ESS, 22 March 1982 (ECFS, 92J040B).

6 Children's Services Annual Report, 1980, Children's Services Section, ESS, March 1981 (ECFS, 92J040B); Bob Bogle to Lou Hyndman, 16 April 1981 (FOIP request to Executive Council). In 1982 the monthly cost per child for OOSC in Edmonton was $198 ("The Historical and Political Perspective of the City of Edmonton's Out-Of-School Care Program," Edmonton Children's Services, 13 February 1990 [ECFS, Children's Services, 1991, box 1, file 1.2]). In early 1981, the cost of OOSC in Calgary was approximately $175 per month ("After-School Care Strained," Calgary Herald, 11 April 1981).

7 "Province Offers After-School Funds," Calgary Herald, 28 April 1981; "City Must Accept Conditions: Bogle," Calgary Herald, 15 August 1981, B1.

8 RFD-M5-81 including "Record of Decision" dated 19 June 1981; Harry B. Hobbs to Bogle, 30 June 1981 (FOIP request to Executive Council).

9 "City Must Accept Conditions"; "City Saves After-School Program," *Calgary Herald*, 1 September 1981, B1; "Day Care Issues," ESS, 3 July 1984 (ECFS, 92J040B, box 4, file 1-1); "Commissioner's Brief: Day Care and After School Care." The actual spending by Edmonton on OOSC is recorded in table 8.1.

10 "Infusion Calms Feud over Program Funds," *Edmonton Journal*, 30 March 1982; "Notley Says Gov't Not Sharing Federal Funds for Child Care," *Edmonton Journal*, 31 March 1982; "Province Ignored Extra Funds for After-School Care," *Edmonton Journal*, 8 April 1982.

11 "Day-care Grant Falls Short," *Calgary Herald*, 7 September 1983; Medicine Hat (1992, 27).

12 In June 1985, there were ninety OOSC programs in Edmonton with a total licensed capacity of 2,466 children. Twenty-two of the programs were municipally approved (and thus eligible for higher subsidies than other centres), six were independent non-profit, and sixty-two were commercial. ("The Historical and Political Perspective of the City of Edmonton's Out-Of-School Care Program," Edmonton Children's Services, 13 February 1990, p. 10 and first enclosure. On the FCSS grant to Edmonton, see "Brief to the F.C.S.S. Ministerial Advisory Panel," April 1991 [ECFS, Children's Services, 1991, box 2, file 5.3.2].)

13 "Day Care Subsidy to Low-Income Families: The Historical Perspective," 10 November 1983 (PAA, 93.188, box 1); "Concerns and Recommendations with Additional Background Information Relating to Provincial Funding of Social Services," 16 October 1984, ESS (ECFS, 92J040B, box 4, file 8); "Edmonton City Council Approved the Following Recommendations at Its February 25, 1986 Meeting" (ECFS files); "The Historical and Political Perspective of the City of Edmonton's Out-Of-School Care Program," first enclosure.

14 "The Historical and Political Perspective of the City of Edmonton's Out-Of-School Care Program," 8; memo to Alderman White from John Lackey, 29 May 1984 (ECFS, 92J040B, box 4, file 614b).

15 "A Synopsis of the City of Edmonton's Preschool Day Care Program for the Period 1966–1985," ESS, 11 September 1985 (ECFS files); "City May Shut Glengarry Day-Care Centre," *Edmonton Journal*, 28 February 1984; "Educators, Parents Decry Centre's Closing," *Edmonton Journal*, 29 February 1984.

16 "Daycare Centre Given New Life," *Edmonton Journal*, 2 May 1984; memo to Alderman White from John Lackey, 29 May 1984 (ECFS, 92J040B, box 4, file 614b); "Briefing Report and Background Information," 22 July 1988.

17 "Briefing Report and Background Information," 22 July 1988.

18 "Day Care. A Summary Report of a Public Participation Process in the City of Edmonton," ESS, June 1985 (ECFS files).

19 "Day Care in the City of Edmonton," Social Services Advisory Committee, 9 July 1985 (ECFS, Children's Services 1985–89, file: Daycare Reports, 1985); "Switch Subsidy from Day Care, City Is Urged," *Edmonton Journal*, 2 July 1985; "Shift to Preventive Care Backed," *Edmonton Journal*, 4 July 1985.

20 "Municipally Approved Preschool Day Care Centres Specialized Functions," ESS, 21 July 1986 (ECFS, 92J040B).

21 The subsidy figures cited in this paragraph were cost-shared with CAP, so the city's contribution was 50 percent. "A Synopsis of the City of Edmonton's Preschool Day Care Program for the period 1966–1985," ESS, 11 September 1985 (ECFS files); "Briefing Report and Background Information," 22 July 1988; "Preschool Day Care in Edmonton—1991 Facts," Appendix VII to "The Municipality's Role in Child Care and Children's Services," April 1991.

22 "Report of the Children's Services Sub-Committee … ," 10 December 1986, and "Report of Activities of the Children's Services Sub-Committee for 1989 and Its Recommendations to Community and Family Services Advisory Committee Regarding 1990 Funding Allocations to Non-Profit Day Care Centres," 7 December 1989 (ECFS, Children's Services 1985–89, file 2-2). The rankings of applicants for 1987 indicated that some of the MADCs were able to quickly repackage themselves as family resource centres plus quality day cares while others seemingly resisted this change. Of the eighteen applicants, the four with the highest ranking were all old PSS centres: South Edmonton, Glengarry, Lansdowne, and Northwest. At the same time, three of the four applicants with the lowest rankings were old PSS centres: Fulton (ranked 15), Community Day (16), and Beverly (18). The low rankings resulted in these centres receiving grants that were somewhat smaller than requested. Nevertheless, Community Day received the highest supplemental grant in 1987, as it did in 1989. In 1990 Community Day's grant was the second largest, about $1,000 less than that for Beverly. "The Historical and Political Perspective of the City of Edmonton's Out-Of-School Care Program" ("Synopsis Update for Period 1986–1990").

23 Memo from J. Lackey to J. McAully, acting city manager, "Report of the Social Services Advisory Committee on Day Care in the City of Edmonton," 25 November 1985 (ECFS, Children's Services 1985–89, file: Daycare Reports 1985); "The Historical and Political Perspective of the City of Edmonton's Out-Of-School Care Program," appended table; "FCSS Review: A Brief Submitted to the FCSS Advisory Panel by Alberta Association for Young Children," April 1991 (ECFS, Children's Services 1991, file 5.3.2).

24 Report of the Emergency Working Committee, 30 March 1987 (ECFS 92J040B).

25 "Day Care in the City of Edmonton," 9; memo from J. Lackey to Alderman L. White, "Preschool Day Care and Out-of-School Care Situation," 24 June 1986 (ECFS, 92J040B); "Child Care Centres Win New Hearing," Edmonton Journal, 25 February 1987; "The Historical and Political Perspective of the City of Edmonton's Out-Of-School Care Program (Synopsis Update for Period 1986–1990)."

26 "Report of the Social Services Advisory Committee on Day Care," 25 November 1985. Appendix I to "The Municipality's Role in Child Care and Children's Services," April 1991.

27 Medicine Hat (1992, Appendix F). Calgary estimate is based on Appendix II to "The Municipality's Role in Child Care and Children's Services" and "Commissioners' Report to Community Services Committee," CS90-51, 18 September 1990, attached Social Services Department Report on Municipal Day Care Program, p. 003409 (City of Calgary). The per capita amounts cited in this paragraph include consulting expenses and therefore are higher than the sum of rows 6 and 7 in table 8.2.

28 "City Day-care Centres Face 18% Subsidy Cut," Calgary Herald, 6 May 1980, B1; "City Council Wants Full Control of Day Care," Calgary Herald, 13 May 1980, A1.

29 "A Report on the Status of Day Care and Out-of-School Care in the City of Calgary," Social Services Department, January 1981 (attached to Calgary Commissioners' Report [CCR] C.81-3, January 1981).

30 "A Report on the Status of Day Care and Out-of-School Care in the City of Calgary," 7; memo from William (Bill) Ardiel, acting research officer, City of Calgary, to Alderman Barbara Scott, "Comparison of Social Service Budgets for Edmonton and Calgary," 28 March 1991 (ECFS, Children's Services 1991, file 11.4).

31 "A Report on the Status of Day Care and Out-of-School Care in the City of Calgary," 7; "Child Care Fears Ease," Calgary Herald, 25 August 1983, B3; "CS83-37 Re: Out-of-School Care Subsidy Program Funding" (CCR to Community Services Committee [hereafter cited as CSC], 26 July 1983).

32 Executive Summary and Appendices I and II to "The Municipality's Role in Child Care and Children's Services," April 1991; "CS83-14 Re: Out-of-School Care Regulations—Review" (CCR to CSC, 22 March 1983); "CS83-37 Re: Out-of-School Care Subsidy Program Funding." A second factor helps to explain the overall disparity in OOSC spending. The average cost of an OOSC subsidy in Calgary in 1991 was $126 per month compared to $200 in Edmonton. Calgary's average was lower because it provided part-service OOSC subsidies (for example, just for after-school care) whereas Edmonton always provided full-service subsidies in order to allow "operators to maintain staff on a full-time basis and meet the Approved Standards" ("The Municipality's Role in Child Care and Children's Services," 3).

33 "City of Calgary's Involvement in Out-of-School Care Programs and Day Care Support," 4 November 1980 (CCR to CSC, CS.80-48).

34 CS90-51, p. 5. Al Hagan noted that Edmonton handled CAP flow-through transfers differently than did Calgary and Medicine Hat. Edmonton built the anticipated CAP reimbursements for the previous year's program into its current year's budget while both Calgary and Medicine Hat put CAP reimbursements into a "rainy day" account to be used for special expenditures on child care and social services (interview, 16 April 1996).

35 Chris Henderson, Grande Prairie FCSS director and acting director of Community and Social Services, interview by Tom Langford, 19 April 1996, tape recorded.

36 Karen Charlton, interview by Lynne Malmquist, 15 December 1994, tape recorded.

37 Henderson, interview.

38 The province introduced a per capita funding formula for its PSS program in 1980–81. In 1979–80, some municipalities received PSS grants that exceeded what they should have received under the new formula. The province decided that these municipalities would continue to receive the same per capita amount as they would have under the old, project-based funding method and these exceptions remained in place over time. In 1985–86, standard FCSS funding was $10 per capita in larger municipalities and $12 per capita in smaller municipalities. Calgary, Edmonton, Grande Prairie, and Red Deer each received the $10-per-capita grant while Lethbridge received $11 and Medicine Hat $13.86. If Medicine Hat had received the $10-per-capita grant instead of $13.86, it would have received $160,000 less in FCSS funds than it actually did. This was a significant sum of money given that it far exceeded what the city was spending on its modest OOSC program. Indeed, even by 1991, the city's net cost of OOSC was only $37,000. About fifteen other communities also benefited from per capita FCSS payments in 1985–86

that were higher than the provincial formula, including High Prairie ($15.89), Grande Cache ($22.71), and Fort Chipewyan ($47.98). "Inter-Municipal Task Force Report on Out-of-School Care," 1985, Appendix: Family and Community Support Services 1985/86 Allocations (ECFS, 92J040B); Medicine Hat (1992, 40).

39 Spread Sheet for the [Day Care] Transition Plan, Social Planning Department, City of Medicine Hat, 3 January 1995 (Medicine Hat Social Planning Department [hereafter cited as MHSPD]); "College Daycare Centre Still Under City Hall's Wing," *Medicine Hat News*, 1 June 1996, A3.

40 Graham Kelly, interview by Lynne Malmquist, 4 January 1995, tape recorded.

41 "Too Many Foxes in the Henhouse these Days," *Medicine Hat News*, 12 May 1989; "Day Care Funding Survives," *Medicine Hat News*, 5 May 1992, A1.

42 Electoral results printed in the *Globe and Mail*, 27 October 1993, A10–A11.

43 Julie Friesen, interview by Lynne Malmquist, 4 January 1995, tape recorded.

44 "City Council Presentation," Medicine Hat and District Independent Day Care Operators' Association, 16 March 1992 (copy provided by the association).

45 Wally Regehr, interview by Lynne Malmquist, 15 December 1994, tape recorded; Kelly, interview; letter from Rick Derbyshire, VP of Medicine Hat Chamber of Commerce, to Mayor Grimm and councillors, "Re: City of Medicine Hat's 1991 Operating Budget," 2 May 1991 (MHSPD). In a taped interview with Lynne Malmquist on 15 December 1994, Gitta Hashizume termed the Chamber of Commerce "a shadow council."

46 "Day Care Services. Preliminary Report for Medicine Hat & District Chamber of Commerce" and "Presented to Day Care Policy Review Committee" [by the Medicine Hat and District Chamber of Commerce] (Medicine Hat Social Planning Department). More accurately, the 15 percent rule meant that middle- and upper-middle-income families with three young children would be subsidized in addition to lower-income families. Truly high-income families (with $5,500 of monthly net income or more) in this circumstance would not be subsidized.

47 Hashizume, interview.

48 "Medicine Hat and District Independent Day Care Operators' Association City Council Presentation," 16 March 1992 (MHSPD); "City May Cut Role in Day Care," *Medicine Hat News*, 17 March 1992, A1; Hashizume, interview.

49 Written copy of Southview Church of God presentation, 13 April 1992 (MHSPD).

50 Copies of the letters were provided by the MHSPD. "Hatter Angered by Daycare Letter," *Medicine Hat News*, 21 April 1992, A3.

51 Regehr, interview.

52 "Candidates Queried on City's Daycare Role," *Medicine Hat News*, 15 October 1992; "Wally Regehr for City Council," *Medicine Hat News*, 17 October 1992, B4; "Candidates for City Council Speak on the Issues," *Medicine Hat News*, 17 October 1992, A3, A8; "Results," *Medicine Hat News*, 20 October 1992, A1; "Craven Tops, Renner Returns," *Medicine Hat News*, 20 October 1992, A3.

53 "City Daycare Workers Move to Unionize," *Medicine Hat News*, 28 November 1992, and "Council Tackles Daycare Issue," *Medicine Hat News*, 7 December 1992. Two such letters are "City Is Not Thinking About Children in Daycare Issue" and "Day Care Is Not an

Issue of Money," *Medicine Hat News*, 26 December 1992, A5; "Vote Surprised City Daycare Backers" and "Parents Peeved," *Medicine Hat News*, 22 December 1992, A3.

54 Peter Mossey, "Only on Monday," *Medicine Hat News*, 9 November 1992; Kelly, interview; Regehr, interview.

55 "Committee Forced to Address Daycare Report," *Medicine Hat News*, 2 December 1992, A3.

56 "Daycare Path Unsure: Aldermen" and "Kelly Asked to Resign," *Medicine Hat News*, 8 December 1992, A8; "Re-examining City's Role in Providing Day Care," *Medicine Hat News*, 3 December 1994.

57 "Deficit Cuts New Daycare Goal," *Medicine Hat News*, 17 December 1992, A3; "Vote Surprised City Daycare Backers"; "Parents peeved."

58 "Day Care Transition Plan: A Progress Report," Medicine Hat Social Planning Department, December 1994, and "Summary of Understandings Between the City of Medicine Hat and Children's Corner (D. Samuel)," 5 December 1994 (provided by MHSPD); "Board Running School Day Care," *Medicine Hat News*, 11 April 1995, A1; "College Daycare Centre Still Under City Hall's Wing."

59 Mayor Ted Grimm, interview by Lynne Malmquist, 4 April 1995, tape recorded.

60 Barbara Scott, interview by Janine Bauman, 12 July 1995, tape recorded; Sam Blakely, interview by Janine Bauman, 27 September 1995, tape recorded.

61 "CS90-51 Municipal Day Care Program," attached report from Social Services Department (CCR to CSC, 19 September 1990).

62 Scott, interview. All quotations from Barb Scott are taken from this interview, unless otherwise noted.

63 Sue Higgins, interview by Janine Bauman, 27 July 1995, tape recorded.

64 Bill Ardiel, interview by Janine Bauman, 27 July 1995, tape recorded. Mr. Ardiel, a senior research officer with CSS, pointed out that some other VFM audits had advertised for citizen members rather than directly recruiting them.

65 AC94-20. Social Services Value-for-Money Audit Task Force—Final Report, 4 May 1994. (provided to those attending the meeting of the Audit Committee); Brian Corbishley, interview by Janine Bauman, 12 July 1995, tape recorded; anonymous interview by Janine Bauman, 1995.

66 Bob Hawkesworth, interview by Janine Bauman, 19 July 1995, tape recorded.

67 Corbishley, interview.

68 Blakely, interview; anonymous interview, 1995.

69 AC94-20. Social Services Value-for-Money Audit Task Force—Final Report, 4 May 1994.

70 Minutes of Audit Committee special meeting, 4 May 1994. Details of the special meeting were recorded in notes taken by the author.

71 AC94-20. Social Services Value-for-Money Audit Task Force—Final Report, 4 May 1994.

72 Hawkesworth, interview.

73 Laurie Doyle, interview by Janine Bauman, 31 August 1995, tape recorded; anonymous interview, 1995.

74 Tammy Baldwin, interview by Janine Bauman, 15 September 1995, tape recorded.

75 Doyle, interview; "Calgary Gets Out of Day Care: All Its Chubbily Subsidized Centres Will Be Sold or Closed," *Western Report*, 2 January 1995, 16.

76 Blakely, interview; Christine Sheppard and Nora Copithorn, interviews by Janine Bauman, 22 September 1995, tape recorded; online records of the Alberta Labour Relations Board.

77 Laurie Doyle, interview, 31 August 1995.

78 Kinder House Day Care Centre was licensed for twenty-eight children in 1995.

79 Kathy Barnhart, interview by Tom Langford, 10 April 1996, tape recorded.

80 Lana Sampson, interview by Tom Langford, 15 March 1998, tape recorded.

81 See historical timeline of Edmonton's involvement in child care, Preschool Task Force (hereafter cited as PTF), 1995, Member's Binder, p. 26 (ECFS).

82 Government of Alberta News Releases, "Canada-Alberta Children's Agreement Signed," 23 August 2003, and "High Risk Alberta Children to Benefit from New Projects," 29 March 1994; "Ottawa Urged to Invest in Children," *Globe and Mail*, 13 December 1996, A10.

83 Government of Alberta News Releases, "Over $4 Million Allotted to Families and Children in Alberta," 20 December 1995, and "Additional $2 Million Approved to Help Local Children and Families," 27 February 1996; Sampson, interview.

84 "Background for Preschool Task Force," 15 February 1995 (ECFS).

85 Judy Padua, interview by Tom Langford, 13 August 1998, tape recorded; "Strategic Planning for Municipal Day Care Centres Report," September 1994, Shelley Williams Consulting (PTF 1995, Department Binder, ECFS).

86 "Municipally-Approved Day Care—Strategic Plan," 18 October 1994 (PTF 1995, Department Binder, ECFS).

87 Minutes of 8 November 1994 Edmonton City Council Meeting, pp. 123–25; letters dated 21 November 1994 found in the PTF 1995 Department Binder (ECFS).

88 "Child Care Strategies: Municipal Involvement," 18 January 1995 (ECFS); memo from Lackey to Reimer, "Preschool Task Force," 27 January 1995 (PTF 1995, Department Binder, ECFS).

89 Minutes of Meeting #9, PTF, p. 2 and attached table, "Municipally Approved Day Cares Preschool Task Force Survey Results, May 1995" (ECFS).

90 Eva Roche, "Submitted to the Edmonton Preschool Task Force," 7 June 1995, p. 3, and "Response to Preschool Task Force Preliminary Report From the Clifford E. Lee Foundation," 14 August 1995 (PTF 1995, Department Binder, ECFS); Padua, interview.

91 Sampson, interview; Mary Hull, interview by Tom Langford, March 1998.

92 Kathy Barnhart, interview by Tom Langford, 25 April 1996, tape recorded; Sampson, interview.

93 "New Tax System Threatens City Day Care; Non-profit Centre Faces Closure If It Is Forced to Pay $9,500 Levy, Director Says," *Edmonton Journal*, 1 February 1996, B5; "Tax Forgiven Two Non-profit Day Cares, but City Warns of Taxation Next Year," *Edmonton Journal*, 15 February 1996, B3; Hull, interview, March 1998.

94 "Closing of Community Day Care End of an Era: Edmonton's First Public, Non-profit Centre Provided Quality Care for Generations of Kids," *Edmonton Journal*, 30 March 2001, B2; Hull, interview, March 1998; Minutes of Meeting #9, PTF, attached table, "Municipally Approved Day Cares Preschool Task Force Survey Results, May 1995" (CFS).

95 "In an Ill-favoured Part of Town, a Magical Place: Beloved Day Care May Be Closed, but It Lives on in the Hearts of Thousands," *Edmonton Journal*, 11 April 2001, F2.

96 Between the 1992–93 and 1997–98 budget years, the provincial government cut FCSS grants to municipalities from $37 million to $31 million, a decrease of 16 percent. Over the next six years, FCSS grants were increased by $28 million to $59 million, with the largest single-year increase being $15 million in the 2002–3 budget year. This helps to explain why Edmonton was able to substantially increase the size of its grants to local agencies between 1995 and 2005. Alberta NDP Press Release, "Child Care Centre Closes due to Funding Cuts," 30 October 1997; Alberta Children's Services (2004, 9).

97 Edmonton Community Services, "2005 FCSS-Funded Programs and Agency Information" (retrieved from website; available from author); Sampson, interview.

98 Tanice Jones, interview by Tom Langford, 18 April 1996, tape recorded.

99 "Family Day Home Satellite Program," Grande Prairie FCSS, 24 November 1995 (provided by Chris Henderson); Henderson, interview; "Council Turns Cold Shoulder to FCSS Funding Increase," *Grande Prairie Herald-Tribune*, 8 December 1995. In 2005–6 the "Transit Operator Provision Contract" was held by Cardinal Coach Lines (Agenda of the Grande Prairie Council Meeting, 4 July 2005). This apparently was the only contract held by Cardinal Coach Lines to provide drivers for a public transit system (EXPRESS[ions], newsletter of the Canadian Urban Transit Association, 16 March 2005).

100 Henderson, interview; Jones, interview.

101 "Red Deer Cuts Day-care Aid for Poor Families," *Edmonton Journal*, 28 October 1999, B5; "City of Red Deer Community Profile and Demographic Analysis, Part One: City Wide Demographic Profile," June 2000, Red Deer Social Planning Department and Parkland Community Planning Services.

102 CUPE's "Child Care Profile: Alberta" at http://cupe.ca/child-care/child-care-profile--alberta (active 1 August 2010).

103 "Family and Community Support Services: Annual Overview 2005," Alberta Children's Services, December 2006, 19; "Review Could Debase City's After-School Care," *Edmonton Journal*, 10 June, 2005, B3.

104 In September 2009, the City of Calgary renewed its commitment to OOSC by launching Calgary AfterSchool in conjunction with a number of community organizations. Calgary thereby became "one of the first municipalities to approach the hours of 3 p.m. to 6 p.m. from a city-wide perspective." This initiative coordinates and enhances programs for children aged six to sixteen. The municipal government's involvement includes offering an online search tool that includes hundreds of supervised programs, improving the quality of particular community programs through larger FCSS grants, and offering its own programming at city-run pools and leisure centres. See http://content.calgary.ca/CCA/City+Hall/Business+Units/Community+and+Neighbourhood+Services/Children+and+Youth/Calgary+AfterSchool/Calgary+AfterSchool.htm, active 1 August 2010.

9. Day Care into the Future

1 One example was the lively set of letters published by the *Calgary Herald* in February 2007 in response to stories about a lack of day care spaces. One letter writer, Tanya Graham, took a pro-family perspective. She argued: "Perhaps the shortage could be alleviated if more parents chose their children over their careers and stayed home. How many of these parents actually need to work?" ("Just Stay Home," 7 February 2007, A15). In contrast, another letter writer offered a conciliatory position that echoed the approach taken by Eva Roche when she led the Alberta Association for Young Children in the late 1980s. Beth Banas wrote: "Once again, the battle begins between working parents and stay-at-home parents.... Haven't we figured out yet that we're all just trying to raise our children to the best of our abilities? Let's stop bickering and work together to solve the child-care problems" ("Live and Let Live," 11 February 2007, A15). A second example was the heated debate in 2009 occasioned by Iris Evans' public praise for her own adult children for understanding "perfectly well that when you're raising children, you don't both go off to work and leave them for somebody else to raise." Evans, a former minister of Children's Services, was Alberta's minister of Finance at the time ("Evans Stresses One Parent Should Stay at Home," *Edmonton Journal*, 18 June 2009, B5; "Evans's Parenting Advice Comes Under Fire," *Edmonton Journal*, 19 June 2009, A3).

2 Al Hagen to Norma Matheson, 19 February 1975 (CA, box 6290, file: Child Care, Jan–Apr 1975).

3 The Alberta unemployment rate rose from 3.7 percent in December 2008 to 7.1 percent in August 2009. The boom years were 2005–8, when the Alberta unemployment rate was less than 4 percent and even fell below 3 percent on five occasions between November 2006 and April 2008 (Statistics Canada, CANSIM table 2820054: three-month moving average rate, unadjusted for seasonality).

4 "The Boardroom or Romper Room?" *Globe and Mail*, 1 May 2006, A1.

5 "Day-care Policy at Centre of Heated Debate," *Business Edge*, 18 August 2005, 27; "Alberta Crying for Child Care: Parents Face Waiting Lists," *Calgary Herald*, 4 February 2007, A1, A3. On the Fort McMurray investment: Government of Alberta News Release, "Government Invests in People Who Serve Children, Youth and Families," 5 March 2007; "Big Box Operator Eyes Canada's Child Care," *People's Voice*, 16–30 November 2007, 3; "Learning Is Not Child's Play," *Courier Mail*, 25 November 2007 (http://www. news.com.au/couriermail); "Creep of Privatization into Health Care, Education Worries Lobby Group," *Edmonton Journal*, 5 April 2008, B3.

6 Nizar Daya, interview with Tom Langford, 19 December 2002, tape recorded. Data for the 2003–5 period were constructed from the Day Care Look-up available at that time through the Alberta Children's Services website and the classified advertisements in the Telus Yellow Pages, 2005–6. On the closing of the Montgomery Day Care, see "Parents Left Hunting for Scarce Day Care," *Calgary Herald*, 20 June 2006.

7 "Government of Canada Early Learning and Child Care Programs and Services," report for 2004, accessed at www.socialunion.ca/ecd/2004; 18 July 2006; "Treaty 7 Economic Development Corporation. First Nations and Inuit Child Care (Day Care) Initiative," accessed at www.t7edc.com/childcare.htm, 19 July 2006; "Child Care: Challenges and Successes," report by the Treaty Seven Economic Development Corporation, accessed at www.t7edc.com\childcare.htm, 21 July 2006; these three documents are no longer available at the above URLs but can be obtained from the author. See also "Aboriginal

Day-care Workers Gather at Their First Conference," Edmonton Journal, 21 February 2005, A6. In addition to the funding for First Nations day cares, the federal government provided funding for Aboriginal Head Start (AHS) programs both on reserves and in urban areas throughout Alberta. Most of the AHS programs run for only a half day and are thus licensed as preschools, but some run for a full day and are licensed as day cares. (For instance, the Grande Prairie Friendship Centre's AHS program held a day care license for twenty children in 2005.) Information can be found on Aboriginal Head Start page of the website of the Public Health Agency of Canada, www.phac-aspc.gc.ca/dca-dea/programs-mes/ahs_main-eng.php (active 1 August 2010). Information on the entire package of federal programs can be found in "Aboriginal Childcare Badly Run, Expert Says," National Post, 23 May 2003, A7.

8   "Aboriginal Day-care Workers Gather at Their First Conference"; "Child Care: Challenges and Successes."

9   Memo with supporting data from Vivien Lai, director of Social Services Research and Planning, to Dave Stolee, Rene Morrissette, and Catharine Arthur, "Number of Families on Day Care Subsidy Eligible for Social Allowance," 13 July 1981 (PAA, 90.301, file: Day Care General Information).

10 "Rally Highlights Day-care 'Crisis': Government Urged to Probe Staff Turnover, Conditions," Calgary Herald, 28 January 2001; "Low Pay Driving Away Day Care Workers: Parents, Day-care Workers Ask for Federal Dollars," Edmonton Journal, 10 February 2001, A6; "Day-care Workers Need Raises, Says Klein," Edmonton Journal, 22 February 2001, A6; "Low Pay Creates Revolving Door at Day Cares: Alberta's Turnover Rate Is Double the National Average," Edmonton Journal, 5 March 2001, B1; "5.6M Gift for Day-care Workers," Calgary Herald, 17 December 2002, A1.

11 Government of Alberta News Release, "Year One of Provincial Child Care Space Creation Initiative Sees Great Success." Backgrounder: Improving Access to Quality, Affordable Child Care—Progress Made to Date, 12 May 2009.

12 "$5.6M Gift for Day-care Workers"; Alberta Children's Services, n.d., "Alberta Child Care Accreditation Funding Guide for Day Care Centres."

13 Increases in the wage enhancements are recorded in the Alberta Children's Services brochure, "Our Children, Our Future," November 2005, and two Government of Alberta News Releases: "Government Invests in People Who Serve Children, Youth and Families," 5 March 2007, and "Provincial Child Care Plan Will Create More Quality Child Care Spaces for Children up to 12 Years of Age," 9 May 2008.

14 Information was taken from documents found on each organization's website: Alberta Association for the Accreditation of Early Learning and Care Services (AELCS) and Alberta Resource Centre for Quality Enhancement (ARCQE). Among the documents with useful information were "Accreditation Child Care. Accreditation Guide for Day Care Centres" (AELCS); "ACCAP Quality Standards with Indicators for Child Care Centres," October 2004 (AELCS); "Getting Started" (ARCQE); "ARCQE—The Benefits of Mentoring" (ARCQE); "Caregiver Interaction Scale Workshops and Observations a Huge Success!" (ARCQE Newsletter, Summer 2006); and "Facts About Caregiver Interaction Scale," September 2006 (ARCQE).

15 "Accreditation Stats" at www.aelcs.ca.

16 Government of Alberta News Release, "New Child Care Agreement Respects Parents' Rights to Choice and Flexibility," 7 July 2005; "Moving Forward on Early Learning

and Child Care. Agreement-in-Principle Between the Government of Canada and the Government of Alberta," 7 July 2005; "Alberta Spends Less on Daycare Than It Gets in Federal Funding," *Edmonton Journal*, 7 March 2008, B5.

17 "Nearly Thirty Children Are Being Taken Care of in Day Nursery," *Edmonton Bulletin*, 24 February 1917.

18 Luzon B. Davis, letter to the editor, "Why Do Governments Neglect Crucial Educational System?" *Edmonton Journal*, 10 March 2002, A13; "Childcare Worker Agitates for Union: She Insists Staff Deserve Double What They're Paid," *Edmonton Journal*, 26 February 2002, B3. See also "Low Pay Creates Revolving Door at Day Cares: Alberta's Turnover Rate Is Double the National Average," *Edmonton Journal*, 5 March 2002, B1.

19 Alberta Children's Services News Release, "Alberta Expands Programs, Adds New Services to Benefit Kids Six and Under," 14 October 2005; Alberta Children's Services, *Our Children Our Future: Alberta's Five-Point Investment Plan*, brochure, November 2005.

20 These statistics are from "What We Heard: Alberta's Consultation on the Creation of Child Care Spaces," September 2006, 5.

21 Government of Alberta News Release, "Provincial Child Care Plan Will Create More Quality Child Care Spaces for Children up to 12 Years of Age," 9 May 2008.

22 In early 2010, the monthly fees at a respected not-for-profit centre in Calgary were $1,170 for an infant and $890 for a preschooler. In comparison, the monthly fees at reputable, unregulated FDHs were estimated to range between $500 and $750 per month.

23 "Alberta Crying for Child Care."

24 In its 2003–4 budget year, Alberta spent $104 per child aged zero to twelve years on regulated child care compared to Quebec's spending of $1,448 (CRRU 2005, 209). In 2007–8, after Alberta had begun its new investments, it spent $195 per child aged zero to twelve compared to Quebec's spending of $1,694 (CRRU 2009, Big Picture, table 12). Alberta's new spending commitments to day care and out-of-school care in 2008 and 2009 likely increased this figure to approximately $350 in the 2009–10 budget year. A further five-fold increase would be required to put Alberta's spending on regulated child care in the same league as that of Quebec. Fiscal conservatives and the pro-family movement would both strongly mobilize against any increase of this magnitude in the public subsidization of child care.

25 "Supply Still Falls Far Short of Child-care Demand," *Edmonton Journal*, 15 April 2008, B5; Government of Alberta News Releases, "New Initiatives Target More Staff and the Creation of Child Care Spaces," 1 May 2007; "Provincial Child Care Plan Will Create More Quality Child Care Spaces for Children up to 12 Years of Age," 9 May 2008; "Year One of Provincial Child Care Space Creation Initiative Sees Great Success"; and "Improving Access to Quality, Affordable Child Care—Progress Made to Date," 12 May 2009.

26 In 2005 there were fifty-six separate OOSC programs throughout Alberta. Municipalities had the authority to develop their own OOSC regulations that must be followed for an organization to be eligible to enrol subsidized children, and Alberta's largest five cities had developed such regulations ("Family and Community Support Services: Annual Overview 2005," Alberta Children's Services, December 2006, 19; "Review Could Debase City's After-School Care," *Edmonton Journal*, 10 June 2005, B3).

27 "Family and Community Support Services Association of Alberta, 2004 Annual Report," n.d., 16.

28 "Tories Promise Child-care Cash," *Calgary Herald*, 28 March 2008, A4.

29 Government of Alberta News Releases, "Provincial Child Care Plan Will Create More Quality Child Care Spaces for Children up to 12 Years of Age," 9 May 2008, and "New Accreditation Program Supports Children Attending Out-of-School Care," 14 April 2009.

30 "U.S. Day-care Firm Got Cold Response to Building Proposal," *Edmonton Journal*, 6 March 2009, B4; Leslie Wulf, letter to the editor, "Investment Fund Wants to Bankroll Day Cares," *Edmonton Journal*, 10 March 2009.

31 Marketwire News Release, "San Anton and Edleun Announce Proposed Business Combination," 18 November 2009 (available online). For an update on Edleun's first four months of operation, see "Coming Soon: Big Box Babycare," *Fast Forward Weekly*, 29 July–4 August 2010, 4.

32 "Supply Still Falls Far Short of Child-care Demand"; "New 900 Child-care Spots Ease Crisis," Calgary Herald, 15 April 2008, B1; "Making Spaces for Children: Child Care Space Creation Innovation Fund 2008–09" (available from the author; accessed at www. child.alberta.ca/childcare on 1 January 2010 but no longer posted at that URL).

33 Jane Hewes, "Future of Child Care Deserves Our Attention," *Edmonton Journal*, 11 August 2008, A14; "Chair's Message" and "Apprenticeship Fast Facts," *Alberta Child Care Association Newsletter*, Spring 2009, 1, 8.

34 Outline for a new "Child Day Care Act" (AAYC Archives, 1974).

35 "Memorandum," Maria David-Evans to K. Barnhart and J. Lackey, 23 June 1992 (ECFS, file 2.1, Children's Services, 1991, box 1); "More Non-profits Can Run Casinos, Bingos, Raffles: Sports, Child-care Groups Now Eligible," *Edmonton Journal*, 22 August 2003, B4; Alberta Gaming and Liquor Commission, *Charitable Gaming*, sec. 3.6, "Children's Groups—Eligibility," issued 21 August 2003.

36 "Alberta Lottery Fund—Quick Facts (February 2007)" (accessed at www. albertalotteryfund.ca/aboutthealf/quickfacts.asp on 8 July 2007; active 1 August 2010). The data on Alberta Lottery Fund grants were generated from the database accessed at http://albertalotteryfund.ca/whobenefits.asp. The list of organizations in the database was searched using four terms: child care, childcare, day care, and daycare. A few not-for-profit day cares do not have one of these terms in their name and therefore would have been missed in the search.

37 Wayne Maki, letter to the editor, *Edmonton Journal*, 11 February 2008, A19; "NDP Pushes Province: Build Schools with Day-care Areas," *Edmonton Journal*, 29 April 2008, A4.

38 Beverley Smith, letter to the editor, *Edmonton Journal*, 11 February 2008, A19; Sonny Pawhuck, letter to the editor, "Let Funds Follow Child," *Edmonton Journal*, 5 May 2008; editorial, "Mixed Praise for Child Care Plan," *Calgary Herald*, 15 May 2008, A16.

39 "Alberta's Commission on Learning. Status of Recommendations: April 2006" (available from the author; accessed through www.education.gov.ab.ca/commission on 4 March 2007 but no longer available at that URL).

40 "Alberta Profile: Of Historical Note, 2004," CUPE Public Child Care website, http:// cupe.ca/child-care/child-care-profile--alberta (active 1 August 2010). The Medicine Hat School District's programs are described at http://nf.sd76.ab.ca (active 1 August 2010). The document consulted in January 2010 was www.sd76.ab.ca/departments/ early_childhood_services/full-day-kindergarten.pdf.

41 "Full-day Kindergarten Comes into Play," *Globe and Mail*, 16 June 2009, A16.

42 *Our Children Our Future*, 3; "Stay-at-Home Parents Support," Alberta Children's Services website, http://www.parentlinkalberta.ca/publish/611.htm (active 1 August 2010); "What We Heard," 5.

43 "Martin Aide Apologizes for Child-care Comment," *Globe and Mail*, 12 December 2005, A4; "Daycare Expansion at Risk, Groups Say," *Globe and Mail*, 9 February 2007, A4; "Call It Many Things, but Not a 'Child-care' Policy," *Globe and Mail*, 21 April 2006, A19. "Canada's Universal Child Care Plan: Choice, Support, Spaces," advertisement, *Globe and Mail*, 26 July 2006, A9; "Critics Blast Harper over Waiting Times," *Globe and Mail*, 9 January 2007, A4; "Tories Scrap Plan for Businesses to Create New Child Care Spaces," *Calgary Herald*, 15 March 2007, A10. Since the UCCB is taxed, its total cost was less than the $2.4 billion investment claimed by the government (Monte Solberg, minister of Human Resources and Social Development Canada, "Generous," letter to the editor, *Calgary Herald*, 26 April 2007, A19).

44 "Child Care," *Globe and Mail*, 14 January 2006, A5; "Call It Many Things, but Not a 'Child-care' Policy"; "Parents, Seniors to Save Most from Changes in Tax Structure," *Globe and Mail*, 30 December 2006, A16.

45 "Families Applaud Tax Breaks," *Calgary Herald*, 20 March 2007, A5; "F-rated Budget: A Friend to All with Families," *Globe and Mail*, 20 March 2007, A13; "Tax Break up to $310 to Be Given for Children Under 18," *Globe and Mail*, 20 March 2007, A17; "Tax Cuts Target Suburbs Where Tories Hope to Win," *Globe and Mail*, 20 March 2007, A1, A19; "Impact on Taxpayers" and "What a Relief," summary tables, *Globe and Mail*, 20 March 2007, A13.

46 "Super Mario Adds a Certain je ne sais quoi," *Calgary Herald*, 28 March 2007, A17; "A Modern-Day Duplessis? Only Dumont Knows for Sure," *Globe and Mail*, 28 March 2007, A1; "Income-Splitting off the Table—Tories," *Edmonton Journal*, 2 February 2007, A6. The latter article notes, "Supporters say income-splitting would help families, stimulate the country's lagging birth rate, and encourage stay-at-home parents." "Splitting Incomes Divides Parents: Move Would Help Single-Income Couples, but Greatest Benefits Likely Reaped by Wealthy," *Edmonton Journal*, 5 February 2007.

47 "ABC Learning's Debt Revealed as Rival CFK Childcare Centres Collapses," *The Australian*, 22 November 2008; "ABC Learning List a 'Death Sentence' for Childcare Centres," *The Australian*, 27 November 2008; Press Release, "Leading Charities Provide a New Start for ABC Learning," 9 December 2009. The press release stated, "GoodStart spokesperson Maree Walk said the company will operate the centres to the highest standards of education and care, with financial surpluses reinvested back into programs that improve childcare access and quality."

48 "Poor Day Care Centre Can Leave Lasting Effects on Young Child," *Edmonton Journal*, 28 February 1970 (PAA, 83.386, file: Newspaper Clippings).

References

Abbott, Andrew. 1992. "What Do Cases Do? Some Notes on Activity in Sociological Analysis." In *What Is a Case? Exploring the Foundations of Social Inquiry*, eds. Charles C. Ragin and Howard S. Becker, 53–82. Cambridge: Cambridge Univ. Press.

ADCTF [Alberta Day Care Task Force]. 1977. *Report of the Day Care Task Force to the Honourable W. Helen Hunley, Minister of Social Services and Community Health*. Edmonton: Province of Alberta.

Alberta. 1978. "Alberta Regulation 104/78." *Alberta Gazette*, 31 March, 312–318.

———. 1981. "Alberta Regulation 144/81." *Alberta Gazette*, 30 April, 633–40.

———. 1982. "Alberta Regulation 131/82." *Alberta Gazette*, 15 April, 633–40.

———. 1983. "Alberta Regulation 276/83." *Alberta Gazette*, 30 July, 1005–6.

———. 1991. *Day Care Regulation: Alberta Regulation 333/90 with Amendments up to and Including Alberta Regulation 246/91*. Edmonton: Alberta Queen's Printer.

———. 1994. "Alberta Regulation 344/94." *Alberta Gazette*, 15 December, 1063–64.

———. 1995. "Alberta Regulation 137/95." *Alberta Gazette*, 15 July, 785–86.

———. 1998. "Alberta Regulation 30/98." *Alberta Gazette*, 28 February, 93–96.

———. 2003. *Early Childhood Development in Alberta. Investments and Outcomes. Annual Report 2002/2003*. Edmonton: Government of Alberta.

———. 2004. *Early Childhood Development and Child Care. Our Children, Our Future. Annual Report 2003–2004*. Edmonton: Government of Alberta.

———. 2007. "Alberta Regulation 81/2007." *Alberta Gazette*, Part 2, 30 April, 219–20.

———. 2008. *Child Care Licensing Regulation: Alberta Regulation 143/2008 (consolidated up to 185/2008)*. Edmonton: Alberta Queen's Printer.

Alberta Bureau of Statistics. 1950. *Alberta Facts and Figures*. Edmonton: Government of Alberta.

———. 1967. *Population—Alberta: Census Divisions, Cities, Towns, Villages, Municipal Districts, and Improvement Districts, 1941, 1946, 1951, 1956, 1961, and 1966*. Edmonton: Government of Alberta.

———. 1981. *An Historical Profile of the Alberta Family*. Edmonton: Government of Alberta.

Alberta Children's Services. 2004. *Family and Community Services Annual Overview 2003*. Edmonton: Alberta Children's Services.

Alberta Commission on Learning. 2003. *Every Child Learns, Every Child Succeeds: Report and Recommendations*. Edmonton: Alberta Learning.

Alberta FSS [Family and Social Services]. 1990a. *Meeting the Need ... A Fairer, Better System for Albertans: A White Paper on Reforms to the Alberta Day Care Program*. Edmonton: Government of Alberta.

————. 1990b. *Alberta Day Care Reforms: A Fairer, Better System for Albertans*. Edmonton: Government of Alberta.

Alberta Office of the Ombudsman. 1994. *Own Motion Review. Alberta Family and Social Services Investigations of Licensed Day Care Centres*. Edmonton: Province of Alberta, Office of the Ombudsman.

Alberta SSCH [Social Services and Community Health]. 1976. *Proposal for Day Care Standards and Licensing*. Edmonton: Government of Alberta.

Alberta Tax Review Committee. 1998. *Final Report and Recommendations: Future Direction for Personal Income Taxes in Alberta*. Edmonton: Alberta Tax Review Committee.

Alex, Brown & Sons. 1988. *Kinder-Care Learning Centers, Inc.—Company Report*. Investext database.

Anderson, Gillian. 1998. "A Multi-Organizational Analysis of the Pro-Family Movement in Calgary: An Anti-Feminist Backlash?" Master's thesis, Univ. of Calgary, Calgary.

Anderson, Gillian, and Tom Langford. 2001. "Pro-Family Organizations in Calgary, 1998: Beliefs, Interconnections and Allies." *Canadian Review of Sociology and Anthropology* 38(1): 37–56.

Anderson, Lynell. 2005. *Lots to Build on, More to Do: Blueprint for Community Architecture for Early Childhood Learning and Care*. Vancouver: YWCA Canada.

Andrews, Kenneth T., and Bob Edwards. 2004. "Advocacy Organizations in the U.S. Political Process." *Annual Review of Sociology* 30: 479–506.

Bagley, Christopher. 1986. "Daycare in Alberta: A Review, with National Implications." Calgary: Faculty of Social Welfare, Univ. of Calgary.

Bella, Leslie. 1978. *The Origins of Alberta's Preventive Social Service Program*. Edmonton: Dept. of Rec. Admin., Univ. of Alberta.

————. 1980. *Alberta's Preventive Social Service Program. A Case Study of Preventive Social Service Development in Calgary*. Edmonton: Dept. of Rec. Admin., Univ. of Alberta.

Bella, Leslie, and Norma Bozak. 1980. *Evaluation of Alberta's Preventive Social Service Program. Case Study No. 3: Social Service Planning in Lethbridge*. Edmonton: Dept. of Rec. Admin., Univ. of Alberta.

Blain, Christine. 1985. "Government Spending on Child Care in Canada." In *Background Papers for Report of the Task Force on Child Care. Series 1. Financing Child Care: Current Arrangements*, 166–231. Ottawa: Status of Women Canada.

Blau, David M., ed. 1991. *The Economics of Child Care*. New York: Russell Sage Foundation.

Blumer, Herbert. 1956. "Sociological Analysis and the 'Variable.'" *American Sociological Review* 21(6): 683–90.

Boychuk, Gerard William. 1998. *Patchworks of Purpose: The Development of Provincial Social Assistance Regimes in Canada*. Montreal & Kingston: McGill-Queen's Univ. Press.

Broberg, Anders, and C. P. Hwang. 1991. "Day Care for Young Children in Sweden." In *Day Care for Young Children: International Perspectives*, eds. Edward C. Melhuish and Peter Moss, 75–101. London: Tavistock/Routledge.

Brouwer, Ada, and Howard McDiarmid. 1970. "The Founding of a Day Care Programme: A Documentation of the States of Development of the Bowness-Montgomery Day Care Association." Calgary: School of Social Welfare, Univ. of Calgary.

Burawoy, Michael. 1998. "The Extended Case Method." *Sociological Theory* 16(1): 4–33.

Bushnik, Tracey. 2006. *Child Care in Canada.* Catalogue no. 89-599-MIE2006003. Children and Youth Research Paper Series. Ottawa: Statistics Canada.

Calgary. 1990. *Charting Calgary's Future: Council's Strategic Plan.* Calgary: City of Calgary.

Campbell, Sheila D. 1997. "The Importance of the Early Years: The Beginnings of AAYC." *Altachild* 10(3): 1, 7–8.

———. 2001. "Acting Locally: Community Activism in Edmonton, 1940–1970." In *Changing Child Care: Five Decades of Child Care Advocacy and Policy in Canada,* ed. Susan Prentice, 81–95. Halifax: Fernwood.

Canada, Dominion Bureau of Statistics. 1953. *Ninth Census of Canada, 1951,* vol. 1. Ottawa: Queen's Printer.

Cavanagh, J. C., Flora J. Allison, and Ernest E. McCoy. 1983. *Board of Review: The Child Welfare System.* Edmonton: Court of Queen's Bench of Alberta.

Chief Electoral Officer of Alberta. 1983. *A Report on Alberta Elections, 1905–1982.* Edmonton: Government of Alberta.

Church, Sylvia. 1998. *Choices, Chances, and Child Care in Alberta: Results from a Provincial Survey of Daycare Parents.* Edmonton: Greater Edmonton Area Child and Family Resource Association.

Cleland, Jordan. 2002. *Supporting Day Care Professionals: Issues and Options.* Edmonton: KPMG Consulting.

Cleveland, Gordon, and Michael Krashinsky. 1998. *The Benefits and Costs of Good Child Care: The Economic Rationale for Public Investment in Young Children.* Toronto: Childcare Resource and Research Unit, Univ. of Toronto.

Clifford, Howard. 1993. *On the Road for Quality Child Care: A Vision Quest.* Self-published.

———. n.d. [1972]. *Let's Talk Day Care.* Edmonton: Canadian Mental Health Association.

Cohen, Jacob L. 1927. *Mother's Allowance Legislation in Canada: A Legislative Review and Analysis, with a Proposed "Standard" Act.* Toronto: Macmillan.

Connell, R. W. 1987. *Gender and Power.* Stanford, CA: Stanford Univ. Press.

———. 1990. "The State, Gender, and Sexual Politics." *Theory and Society* 19: 507–44.

Corsaro, William A. 2005. *The Sociology of Childhood.* 2nd ed. Thousand Oaks, CA: Pine Forge.

Cowern, Jocelyn. 1986. "Mini-Skool Ltd.—A Division of KinderCare." Presentation to the Special Committee on Child Care, 11 June, Toronto, Ontario.

CRRU. 1994. *Child Care in Canada: Provinces and Territories 1993.* Toronto: Childcare Resource and Research Unit, Univ. of Toronto.

———. 1997. *Child Care in Canada: Provinces and Territories 1995.* Toronto: Childcare Resource and Research Unit, Univ. of Toronto.

———. 2000. *Early Childhood Care and Education in Canada: Provinces and Territories 1998.* 4th ed. Toronto: Childcare Resource and Research Unit, Univ. of Toronto.

———. 2005. *Early Childhood Education and Care in Canada 2004.* 6th ed. Toronto: Childcare Resource and Research Unit, Univ. of Toronto.

———. 2007. *Early Childhood Education and Care in Canada 2006.* 7th ed. Toronto: Childcare Resource and Research Unit, Univ. of Toronto.

———. 2009. *Early Childhood Education and Care in Canada 2008.* 8th ed. Toronto: Childcare Resource and Research Unit, Univ. of Toronto.

Doherty, Gillian, Donna S. Lero, Hillel Goelman, Annette LaGrange, and Jocelyne Tougas. 2000a. "Summary of Findings." In *You Bet I Care! A Canada-Wide Study on: Wages, Working Conditions, and Practices in Child Care Centres,* xiii–xxvii. Guelph, ON: Centre for Families, Work, and Well-Being, Univ. of Guelph.

Doherty, Gillian, Donna S. Lero, Hillel Goelman, Jocelyne Tougas, and Annette LaGrange. 2000b. "Working Conditions, Wages, and Benefits: Teaching Staff and Directors." In *You Bet I Care! A Canada-Wide Study on: Wages, Working Conditions, and Practices in Child Care Centres,* 85–96. Guelph, ON: Centre for Families, Work, and Well-Being, Univ. of Guelph.

Dubashi, Jagannath. 1993. "Once Burned ... Twice Shy. That Might Be Good Advice on KinderCare, Just out of Chapter 11." *Financial World* 8 June, 32–33.

ECFS [Edmonton Community and Family Services]. 1995. *Reaching Out to Children in Poverty: Preschool Task Force Final Report.* Edmonton: City of Edmonton.

Englade, Kenneth F. 1988. "The Bottom Line on Kinder-Care." *Across the Board* 25(4): 44–53.

Erwin, Lorna. 1993. "Neoconservatism and the Canadian Pro-Family Movement." *Canadian Review of Sociology and Anthropology* 30(3): 403–20.

Esbensen, Steen B. 1983. *Day Care in Scandinavia: Denmark, Sweden and Norway.* Ottawa: Health and Welfare Canada.

Esping-Andersen, Gøsta. 1989. "The Three Political Economies of the Welfare State." *Canadian Review of Sociology and Anthropology* 26(1): 12–36.

———. 1999. *Social Foundations of Postindustrial Economies.* Oxford: Oxford Univ. Press.

European Commission Network on Childcare. 1994. *Men As Carers: Towards a Culture of Responsibility, Sharing and Reciprocity Between Women and Men in the Care and Upbringing of Children.* Regione Emilia-Romagna, Italy: Assessorato alla formazione Professionale, Lavoro, Scuola e Universita and European Commission Network on Childcare.

———. 1996. *A Review of Services for Young Children in the European Union, 1990–1995.* Brussels, Belgium: European Commission Directorate General V, Equal Opportunitie Unit.

Figart, Deborah. 2005. "Gender as More Than a Dummy Variable: Feminist Approaches to Discrimination." *Review of Social Economy* 53(3): 509–36.

Finkel, Alvin. 1989. *The Social Credit Phenomenon in Alberta.* Toronto: Univ. of Toronto Press.

Friesen, Bruce. 1995. *A Sociological Examination of the Child Care Auspice Debate.* Occasional Paper No. 6. Toronto: Childcare Resource and Research Unit, Centre for Urban and Community Studies, Univ. of Toronto.

Goodwin, Mark, Simon Duncan, and Susan Halford. 1988. "Policy Variations in Local States: Uneven Development and Local Social Relations." *International Journal of Urban and Regional Research* 12: 108–28.

Goyette, Linda. 1981. "Kentucky Fried Day Care." *Perception* (Jan–Feb): 47–48.

Guest, Dennis. 1980. *The Emergence of Social Security in Canada.* Vancouver: UBC Press.

Gunnarsson, Lars. 1993. "Sweden." In *International Handbook of Child Care Policies and Programs*, ed. Moncrieff Cochran, 491–514. Westport, CT: Greenwood Press.

Hamilton, Ian. 1970. *The Children's Crusade: The Story of the Company of Young Canadians*. Toronto: Peter Martin Associates.

Harder, Lois. 1996. "Depoliticizing Insurgency: The Politics of the Family in Alberta." *Studies in Political Economy* 50: 37–64.

Hayden, Jacqueline. 1997. *Neo-Conservatism and Child Care Services in Alberta: A Case Study*. Occasional Paper No. 9. Toronto: Childcare Resource and Research Unit, Centre for Urban and Community Studies, Univ. of Toronto.

Health and Welfare Canada. 1985. *Notes on Welfare Services Under the Canada Assistance Plan*. Ottawa: Health and Welfare Canada.

———. 1987. "National Strategy on Child Care." Ottawa: Health and Welfare Canada.

Heckman, James. 2006. "Skill Formation and the Economics of Investing in Disadvantaged Children." *Science* 312: 1900–1902.

Hwang, C. P., and Anders G. Broberg. 1992. "The Historical and Social Context of Child Care in Sweden." In *Child Care in Context: Cross-Cultural Perspectives*, eds. Michael E. Lamb, Kathleen J. Sternberg, Carl-Philip Hwang, and Anders G. Broberg, 27–53. Hillsdale, NJ: Lawrence Erlbaum Associates.

Jensen, Jytte J. 1996. *Men as Workers in Childcare Services: A Discussion Paper*. European Commission Network on Childcare and Other Measures to Reconcile Employment and Family Responsibilities for Women and Men. Brussels: European Equal Opportunities Unit..

Jenson, Jane. 2001. "Family Policy, Child Care and Social Solidarity." In *Changing Child Care: Five Decades of Child Care Advocacy and Policy in Canada*, ed. Susan Prentice, 39–62. Halifax: Fernwood.

Jessop, Bob. 1982. *The Capitalist State*. New York: New York Univ. Press.

Kahn, Alfred J., and Sheila B. Kamerman. 1987. *Child Care: Facing the Hard Choices*. Dover, MA: Auburn House.

Kalbach, Warren E. 2000. "A Demographic Overview of Racial and Ethnic Groups in Canada." In *Race and Ethnic Relations in Canada*, ed. Peter S. Li, 18–47. Toronto: Oxford Univ. Press.

Kloosterman, Robert. 2000. "Immigrant Entrepreneurship and the Institutional Context: A Theoretical Exploration." In *Immigrant Businesses: The Economic, Political and Social Environment*, ed. Jan Rath, 90–106. Basingstoke, UK: Macmillan.

LaGrange, Annette V. 1991. "The Early Childhood Services Diploma: A Case Study in Early Childhood Teacher Certification." PhD diss., Univ. of Alberta, Edmonton.

Langford, Tom. 2001. "From Social Movement to Marginalized Interest Groups: Advocating for Quality Child Care in Alberta, 1965–1986." In *Changing Child Care: Five Decades of Child Care Advocacy and Policy in Canada*, ed. Susan Prentice, 63–79. Halifax: Fernwood.

———. 2002. "Does Class Matter? Beliefs About the Economy and Class in Postindustrial Canada." In *Political Sociology: Canadian Perspectives*, ed. Douglas Baer, 307–24. Don Mills, ON: Oxford Univ. Press.

———. 2003a. "What Constitutes Child Neglect? The Tragic Story of the Boutique Children's Hotel, 1971." *Alberta History* 51(3): 16–25.

———. 2003b. "Why Alberta Vacillated over Wartime Day Nurseries." *Prairie Forum* 28(2): 173–94.

Langford, Tom, and Neil J. MacKinnon. 2000. "The Affective Bases for the Gendering of Traits: Comparing the United States and Canada." *Social Psychology Quarterly* 63(1): 34–38.

Lelveld, Joseph. 1977. "Drive-in Day Care." *New York Times*, 5 June, 110.

Lewin, Tamar. 1989. "Small Tots, Big Biz." *New York Times Magazine*, 29 January, 30–31, 89–92.

Lynn, Larry. 1978. "Father Goose in Day Care." *The South Magazine* August, 18–19.

Mahon, Rianne. 1997. "'Both Wage Earner and Mother': Women's Organising Around Child Care Policy in Sweden and Canada." Paper presented at the Canadian Political Science Association annual meeting, St. John's, Newfoundland.

———. 2008. "Varieties of Liberalism: Canadian Social Policy from the 'Golden Age' to the Present." *Social Policy and Administration* 42(4): 342–61.

Maloney, William A., Grant Jordan, and Andrew M. McLaughlin. 1994. "Interest Groups and Public Policy: The Insider/Outsider Model Revisited." *Journal of Public Policy* 14(1): 17–38.

Mansell, Robert L. 1997. "Fiscal Restructuring in Alberta: An Overview." In *A Government Reinvented: A Study of Alberta's Deficit Elimination Program*, eds. Christopher J. Bruce, Ronald D. Kneebone, and Kenneth J. McKenzie, 16–73. Toronto: Oxford Univ. Press.

McAdam, Doug. 1996. "Conceptual Origins, Current Problems, Future Directions." In *Comparative Perspectives on Social Movements: Political Opportunities, Mobilizing Structures, and Cultural Framings*, eds. Doug McAdam, John D. McCarthy, and Mayer N. Zald, 23–40. Cambridge: Cambridge Univ. Press.

McAdam, Doug, John D. McCarthy, and Mayer N. Zald. 1988. "Social Movements." In *Handbook of Sociology*, ed. Neil J. Smelser, 695–737. Newbury Park, CA: Sage.

McCain, Margaret, and J. F. Mustard. 1999. *Early Years Study: Reversing the Real Brain Drain.* Toronto: Ontario Children's Secretariat.

McDaniel, Susan A. 2001. "Born at the Right Time? Gendered Generations and Webs of Entitlement and Responsibility." *Canadian Journal of Sociology* 26(2): 193–214.

McKeen, Wendy. 2007. "The National Children's Agenda: A Neoliberal Wolf in Lamb's Clothing." *Studies in Political Economy* 80 (Autumn): 151–73.

Medicine Hat. 1992. *Footsteps to the Future: Day Care Policy Review.* Medicine Hat: City of Medicine Hat.

Michel, Sonya. 1999. *Children's Interests/Mother's Rights: The Shaping of America's Child Care Policies.* New Haven: Yale Univ. Press.

Miles, Robert. 1989. *Racism.* London: Routledge.

Moody's Investors Service. 1999. *Kinder-Care Learning Centers—History and Debt Report*, February 13. Investext database.

Morgan, Gwen G. 1992. *A Hitchhiker's Guide to the Child Care Universe: A Tour for New Policy Makers.* Washington, DC: National Association of Child Care Resource and Referral Agencies.

Munck, Ronaldo. 2002. *Globalisation and Labour: The New "Great Transformation."* London: Zed Books.

National Day Care Information Centre. 1984. *Status of Day Care in Canada 1984. A Review of the Major Findings of the National Day Care Study 1984.* Ottawa: Health and Welfare Canada.

Neugebauer, Roger. 1988. "How's Business? Status Report #4 on For Profit Child Care." *Child Care Information Exchange* 59: 29–34.

———. 1989. "Child Care 1989: Status Report on For Profit Child Care." *Child Care Information Exchange* 65: 19–23.

———. 1994. "KinderCare Looks to the Future: An Interview with KinderCare's CEO." *Child Care Information Exchange* 99: 89–94.

Olsen, M. I. 1955. "The Development of Play Schools and Kindergartens and an Analysis of a Sampling of these Institutions in Alberta." Master's thesis, Univ. of Alberta, Edmonton. Cited in Prochner 2000, 37.

Orloff, Ann S. 1993. "Gender and the Social Rights of Citizenship: The Comparative Analysis of Gender Relations and Welfare States." *American Sociological Review* 58(3): 303–28.

Pierson, Ruth. 1986. *"They're Still Women After All": The Second World War and Canadian Womanhood.* Toronto: McClelland and Stewart.

Prentice, Susan. 1999. "Less, Worse and More Expensive: Childcare in an Era of Deficit Reduction." *Journal of Canadian Studies* 34(2): 137–58.

Price Waterhouse Associates. 1982. *Interprovincial Comparisons—Day Care Facilities, Full-Day Programs.* Edmonton: Alberta SSCH.

Prince, Michael J. 2001. "Canadian Federalism and Disability Policy Making." *Canadian Journal of Political Science* 34(4): 791–817.

Prochner, Larry. 2000. "A History of Early Education and Child Care in Canada, 1920–1966." In *Early Childhood Care and Education in Canada,* eds. Larry Prochner and Nina Howe, 11–66. Vancouver: UBC Press.

Read, Malcolm, Margo Greenwood-Church, Lynn Hautman, Eva Roche, and Chris Bagley. 1992. "An Historical Overview of Child Care in Alberta." In *British Columbia, Alberta, Saskatchewan, Manitoba, Ontario, Yukon.* Vol. 1 of *Canadian National Child Care Study. Canadian Child Care in Context: Perspectives from the Provinces and Territories,* ed. A. Pence, 131–48. Ottawa: Statistics Canada and Health and Welfare Canada.

Red Deer and District PSS. 1976. *Annual Report, 1976.* Red Deer: City of Red Deer.

Ribbens, Jane. 1994. *Mothers and Their Children: A Feminist Sociology of Childrearing.* London: Sage.

Roche, Eva. 1983. "The Underlying Issues." *First Reading* (a publication of the Edmonton Social Planning Council) 2(9): 2–3.

Rooke, Patricia T., and R. L. Schnell. 1982. "Charlotte Whitton and the 'Babies for Export' Controversy 1947–48." *Alberta History* 30(1): 11–16.

———. 1987. *No Bleeding Heart: Charlotte Whitton, A Feminist on the Right.* Vancouver: UBC Press.

Saunders, Peter. 1986. *Social Theory and the Urban Question.* 2nd ed. London: Hutchinson.

Seager, Charles A. 1981. "A Proletariat in Wild Rose Country: The Alberta Coal Miners, 1905–1945." PhD diss., York Univ., Toronto.

Seguin, J. J. 1977. "Public Policy Planning in Education: A Case Study of Policy Formation for the Early Childhood Services Program in Albera." PhD diss., Univ. of Alberta, Edmonton. Cited in Prochner 2000, 37.

Shearson Lehman Hutton Inc. 1989. *Kinder-Care Learning Centers: Company Report.* 16 February, Investext database.

Shedd, M. S. 1997. "Family and Social Services, the Alberta Deficit Elimination Program, and Welfare Reform." In *A Government Reinvented: A Study of Alberta's Deficit Elimination Program*, eds. Christopher J. Bruce, Ronald D. Kneebone, and Kenneth J. McKenzie, 250–74. Toronto: Oxford Univ. Press.

Stevenson, Michael D. 2001. *Canada's Greatest Wartime Muddle: National Selective Service and the Mobilization of Human Resources During World War II*. Montreal & Kingston: McGill-Queen's Univ. Press.

Tarrow, Sidney. 1998. *Power in Movement: Social Movements and Contentious Politics*. 2nd ed. Cambridge: Cambridge Univ. Press.

Turcott, Garth. 2002. "Eight Months in Office." In *A World Apart: The Crowsnest Communities of Alberta and British Columbia*, eds. Wayne Norton and Tom Langford, 120–24. Kamloops, BC: Plateau Press.

Van der Gaag, Jacques. 2002. "From Child Development to Human Development." In *Investing in Our Children: From Early Child Development to Human Development*, ed. Mary E. Young, 63–78. Washington: World Bank.

White, Linda A. 1997. "Partisanship or Politics of Austerity? Child Care Policy Development in Ontario and Alberta, 1980 to 1996." *Journal of Family Issues* 18(1): 7–29.

Williams, Colin C. 2009. "A Capitalist World? Mapping the Limits of Market-Ism." *Theory in Action* 2(4): 66–76.

Wrigley, Julia. 1999. "Hiring a Nanny: The Limits of Private Solutions to Public Problems." *Annals, AAPSS* 563: 162–74.

Yates, Charlotte. 2000. "Staying the Decline in Union Membership: Union Organizing in Ontario, 1985–1999." *Relations Industrielles* 55(4): 640–74.

Yin, Robert K. 2009. *Case Study Research: Design and Methods*. 4th ed. Vol. 5 in Applied Research Methods Series. Thousand Oaks, CA: Sage.

Young, Claire F. L. 2000. "Women, Tax and Social Programs: The Gendered Impact of Funding Social Programs Through the Tax System." Ottawa: Policy Research Fund, Status of Women Canada.

Zwicker, Donna J. A. 1985. "Alberta Women and World War Two." Master's thesis, Univ. of Calgary, Calgary.

Index

C

"Cadillac" day care metaphor, 87, 307

CAFRA. See Child and Family Resource Association

Calgary: day care in, 1, 21, 24–26, 30, 39–40, 42–43, 46–47, 67–70, 86, 96–106, 114, 120, 136, 140–41, 151, 159–60, 164, 169, 175, 178–82, 184–85, 203, 215, 224, 248–50, 263–70, 286, 294, 295, 297–98, 307, 318, 343n15, 344n37, 345n56, 363n2, 366n40, 366n44, 382n104, 385n22 (see also Bowness-Montgomery Day Care Association; Bridgeland Day Care; Charleswood Day Nursery; Connaught Day Care; Educentres; Fairyland Day Care; Marlborough Day Nursery; Mother Duck's Day Cares; Mount Royal College Day Care; Panda Child Development Centres; PLAY Day Care; Providence Cay Care; Shaganappi Day Care); FDH programs in, 46, 76, 96–97, 101, 104, 106, 144, 159, 239–41, 248–51, 254, 285, 294, 304, 330, 332, 385n22; municipal day cares in, 62, 178, 248–50, 263–69, 272, 304, 377n27; and OOSC programs, 238–41, 253, 378n32; policy debates (1971), 66–67, 77–78, 80–81, 97–99, 102; policy debates (1974–75), 104; value-for-money audit (1993–94), 264, 266. See also Calgary Day Nursery Committee; Day Care Association of Calgary; Early Childhood Academy (of Calgary); Junior League of Calgary; University Women's Club of Calgary

Calgary Day Nursery Committee (CDNC), 23, 345n56

Campbell, Sheila, 14, 43–44, 50–51, 64, 77–78, 82, 85, 88–89, 152–53, 183, 339, 342n6, 347n11, 352n25, 362n71, 375n1

Canada Assistance Plan (CAP), 13, 51, 53, 73, 90–91, 99, 143, 192–96, 241–44, 247, 250–52, 256, 262, 273, 281, 284, 306, 357n98, 367n2, 369n14, 378n34

Canada Childcare Act (Bill C-144): Securing Alberta's support for, 195, 200, 209, 369n14

Canada Health and Social Transfer (CHST), 195

Canadian Education Property Fund, 317

Canadian Kindercare Ltd. See Kindercare

Canadian Union of Public Employees (CUPE), 165–66, 178–80, 260, 269, 364n11; opposition to KinderCare Learning's move into Canada, 165–66; union drive in Calgary, 178–80, 269, 366n44

CAP. See Canada Assistance Plan

CAPC. See Community Action Program for Children

Capithorn, Nora, 269, 339

Cardinal, Mike, 215–17, 224, 226

Catholic Women's League (CWL), 30, 34

CCFRC. See Child Care Family Resource Centres

CDI College, 234–35, 375n96

CDN. See Community Day Nursery

CDNC. See Calgary Day Nursery Committee

chain day care. See corporatization of day care

Charleswood Day Nursery (Calgary), 100, 185–87

Charlton, Karen, 110, 339

Child and Family Resource Association (CAFRA) (Edmonton), 218

Child Care Family Resource Centres (CCFRCs), 244–45

child care funding. See day care funding

Child Care Licensing Regulation (2008), 211

child care standards. See day care standards and regulations

Child Welfare League of America: and day care standards, 44, 59, 68

CHST. See Canada Health and Social Transfer

class struggles in day care, 9

Clifford, Howard, 2, 54–55, 58–65, 77–78, 85, 87–88, 255, 287, 339, 349n54,

Edmonton Independent Day Care Operators Association, 127, 147

EDNA. *See* Edmonton Day Nursery Association

Educentres (Calgary), 160, 175, 184

ELCC agreement. *See* Early Learning and Child Care (ELCC) agreement

Evans, Iris, 383n1

F

Fairyland Day Care (Calgary), 47, 82, 100, 163, 363–64n4

Family and Community Support Services (FCSS), 124–25, 239–41, 246–47, 249, 254, 258, 273, 277–78, 280–81, 284, 286, 316, 376n12, 377n23, 378n35, 378n38, 382nn96–97, 382n99, 382nn103–4, 385nn26–27

family day home (FDH) programs, 86, 132, 239, 382n99: administrative (agency) fees, 143–44, 204–5, 208, 215, 333–35, 375n3, cut to agency fees, 1990s, 215; operating allowance plan, 137–38, 144–45, 170, 191, 205–6, 208, 209, 212, 213, 216–17, 238, 295–96, 309, 315, 327, 333–36, 338, 361nn48–49, 364n21

family day homes (FDHs), unregulated, 8–9, 46, 58, 60, 70, 79, 84, 86, 96, 97, 111, 117, 119, 132, 142, 144, 156, 159, 204–5, 208, 215, 221, 226–27, 251, 253–54, 259, 282, 284, 288, 293–94, 308, 313, 317, 329–30, 332, 338, 341n3, 351n9, 372n41, 374n79, 375n3, 382n99, 385n22

Family Employment Tax Credit (Alberta), 374n91,

Family Service Association (FSA) of Edmonton, 50–51, 57–58, 348n27, 348n30, 348nn42–43

FCSS. *See* Family and Community Support Services

FDH. *See* Family day home (FDH) programs

FDHS. *See* Family day homes (FDHS), unregulated

federal-Alberta conflict over day care, 20, 26, 72, 306-7, 369n14

federal-provincial collaboration, 13

Federal/Provincial/Territorial Working Group on Child Care, 193–94, 199, 334, 338, 368n6, 370n25, 372n43

feminism, 8, 37, 74, 156, 196

First Nations. *See* Aboriginal child care programs

for-profit day care. *See* commercial day care

Fort McMurray: child care in, 121, 294, 383n5

free enterprise conservatism, 289, 319, 324–25, 327

Friesen, Julie, 14, 257, 339, 379

FSA. *See* Family Service Association (FSA) of Edmonton

G

gender and day care, 7–8, 10–12, 34–35, 37, 39, 50, 72–73, 88, 118, 191, 196, 288, 313–14, 319

generational inequalities, 10, 312–13

Getty, Don, 199, 206, 306

Gilbert, David, 93, 127, 131, 133, 281, 339, 353n35, 353n39, 358nn17–19

Glengarry Day Care (Edmonton), 60–62, 66, 72–73, 87, 96, 99, 128, 239, 243–44, 264, 278, 281, 375n5, 377n22

Gomberg, Tooker, 274, 277

Grande Prairie: day care in, 75–76, 112, 115–20, 250–51, 254, 282–85, 290, 378n38, 382n99: establishes day cares in Hythe and Beaverlodge, 117–20; municipal family day home project, 117, 119, 251, 253, 282–84, 303; out-of-school care (OOSC) in, 238, 253; privatization of city services, 283–84

Great West Garment Company (GWG), 20, 57

Griffiths, Dr. Audrey, 147–48, 361n55, 365n30, 367n53

Local Council of Women, Edmonton, 15, 17–18, 21, 69, 99

Lougheed, Peter, 77–78, 80–81, 85, 108, 123, 126–28, 133–34, 141, 152, 167, 239–40, 302, 315

M

Macken, Christine, 203

MADC. See Edmonton: Municipally Approved Day Cares (MADCs)

Maier, Dennis, 159, 197, 209–11, 219, 339

Manitoba: child care in, 17, 19, 29, 32, 155, 166, 193, 232, 293–94, 368n9

Manning, Ernest, 20–23, 30–33, 35, 37, 60–62, 72–73, 256, 287, 342n13, 349n54: view of the CBC 62, 349n54

Manning, Preston, 256

Mansbridge, Stanley, 95–96, 133

Marlborough Day Nursery (Calgary), 106, 138, 180, 185–87, 367n54

McCalla, Enid, 72, 342n13

McKibben, Sherry, 274, 277

Medicine Hat: day care in, 2, 66, 75, 106–12, 241, 247, 251–63, 277, 298, 321–22, 356n78, 378n34, 378n38, 379n46; Day Care Policy Review, 1992, 258–59, 379n46; kindergarten (early childhood services) in, 111, 321–22; maximum family payment of 15% of net income, 252; municipal day cares, 111, 251–253, 256–57, 259–63, 268, 377n27; out-of-school care (OOSC) in, 86, 111, 238, 253–54

Medicine Hat and District Chamber of Commerce (MHDCC), 257–58, 379n46

Medicine Hat and District Independent Day Care Operators' Association, 256

Medicine Hat Day Care Centre, 356nn74–77, 356nn83–84

Meguinis, Violet, 299

MHDCC. See Medicine Hat and District Chamber of Commerce

MLA Review Committee, 125, 132–36, 138–39, 141–42, 359n21, 359n27

model programs. See lighthouse programs

Moritz, Ann, 147, 152–54, 362n71

Mother Duck's Day Cares (Calgary), 101–2, 168

mothers' allowance, 17, 342n7

mothers' employment, 1, 6, 20, 25, 87

Mount Royal College Day Care, 69, 88, 96–97, 110, 146, 149–50, 187, 234, 267

municipal involvement in day care, 55, 121, 128, 132–36, 138, 142, 239, 253, 265, 268: rejection of, 24

municipal-provincial conflict over day care, 13, 95, 127–36

Murphy, Noreen, 201, 207, 266, 339, 370n29, 371n32

N

nannies, 8–9, 65, 159, 243, 294, 308, 311–12, 323

National Child Benefit (NCB), 219–20, 301, 338, 373n77, 374n91

National Longitudinal Survey of Children and Youth (NLSCY), 292–93

NCB. See National Child Benefit

Nelson, Jean, 58, 77, 79, 351n4

Ney, Dr. Philip, 198

NLSCY. See National Longitudinal Survey of Children and Youth

Norquay, Marg, 44–45, 346n8

not-for-profit day care, 1, 12, 51, 58, 60, 91, 95, 101–2, 106, 121, 127, 138, 143, 151, 155, 158–61, 164, 169–70, 192–95, 218, 240–42, 257–59, 296–98, 319, 325–26, 348n26, 356n90, 363n74, 366n44, 368n7, 368n9, 369n12, 385n22 gaming licenses, 320, in Sweden, 158, operating allowances freeze, 206–7, 213, 216, out-of-school care (OOSC) provided by, 247, 249

Notley, Grant, 123, 139, 241

O

Oberg, Lyle, 217–18

Oldring, John, 195, 201, 209–13, 216–19

Olds, Alberta: 1970 Day Care Seminar in, 77

123 Busy Beavers, 186, 294, 317–18

Ontario: child care in, 2, 4, 19–20, 125, 139,
155, 174–77, 192, 232, 292–94, 322,
342n13, 365n37

OOSC. See out-of-school care

operating allowances, 135, 143–45, 151,
157, 159, 161, 163, 167, 169–71, 188–89,
191, 230–31, 238–39, 242, 248, 273,
278, 291, 294–96, 301–4, 327, 333–38,
359n21, 361n48, 364n21: cost-sharing,
193–94, cutbacks to, 163, 170–71, 215,
elimination of, 189, 202-20, increase
of, 138, 144, 170, infant spaces, 315–16,
introduction of, 123, 137–38

Osterman, Connie, 194–95, 198–202, 206–
11, 216, 218, 371n32, 371n34

out-of-school care (OOSC), 8, 22, 86, 171,
186, 238, 242, 246, 288, 336, 338,
363n74, 375n6, 376nn12–14, 377nn22–
23, 377n25, 378n29, 378nn30–33,
379n38, 385n24, 386n29: accreditation,
304–6, 316–17, 321, 334, 384n12,
384nn14–15, 386n29; modular building
grants, 317; provincialization, 316, 321;
wage enhancements, 8, 151, 191–92,
287–88, 300, 302, 304–5, 308–9, 315–
18, 321, 327, 334, 384n13

P

Padua, Judy, 270, 273, 276, 282, 339

Panda Child Development Centres (Calgary),
102, 140–41, 160–61, 173, 175, 294

Pardee, Marjorie, 27–28, 30–31

parental responsibility, 208, 222–23: belief in,
34–35; mandatory parent checklist, 223

patriarchal gender order, 37, 73

patterning mechanisms, 3, 288, 299

pay equity in child care, 108, 314

physical mistreatment of children in day
cares, 154, 359n17

PLAY Day Care (Calgary), 102

policy initiatives to quell opposition, 273

post-Fordism and child care, 311–13

Preschool Task Force (PTF) (Edmonton),
272, 274–77

Preventive Social Service (PSS) day cares,
51–62, 65–71, 75–77, 83–87, 89–121,
127–130, 132, 192, 237–39, 241–42,
244–45, 263, 269, 298–99, 301, 307,
310, 329, 333, 335–36, 348n26, 349n43,
354n50; compared to Sweden day care
system, 157–58; compared to Texas day
care system, 155, 158

Preventive Social Services Act, 51, 329

Primrose Place Day Care (Edmonton), 58, 77

Private Day Care Society. See Day Care Society
of Alberta

privatization, 7, 189, 192, 220, 223, 226,
235, 268, 284, 288, 292, 294, 303, 315:
changes to Alberta tax system, 230-31

pro-family conservatism, 289, 319, 322,
324, 327

pro-family movement, 7, 12, 159–60, 189,
191, 196–203, 210, 228, 293, 306, 322,
324, 327, 385n24

Proletarian day care (Drumheller), 18

Providence Day Care (Calgary), 67

PSS. See Preventive Social Service (PSS) day
cares

PTF. See Preschool Task Force

Q

Quebec: child care in, 2, 19–20, 85, 193, 232,
291–94, 304, 310, 324, 342n13, 369n12,
385n24

R

Rainbow Day Cares (Edmonton), 183–86,
201, 367n51

Red Deer: day care in, 75–76, 112, 114–16, 118, 120, 210, 238, 247, 250–54, 284–85, 360n45, 378n38; supplementary municipal standards, 1979, 116; vote to eliminate quality subsidies, 1999, 285. *See also* Red Deer Day Care Centre

Red Deer Day Care Centre, 356n88

Regehr, Wally, 257, 259, 339

regulations. *See* day care standards and regulations

Reid, Wendy, 201, 222, 339, 370n29, 371n32, 371n33, 372n51, 373n61

Reimer, Jan, 240, 243, 275, 277

reprivatization. *See* privatization

Riley, Maude, 26, 28, 344n30

Ringdahl, Brenda, 197–98

Roche, Eva, 202–3, 276, 282, 371n37, 383n1

Rogers, Duncan, 49, 51–53, 131

Ryan, Bruce, 59, 63, 339, 349n47

S

SAHPS. *See* Stay-at-Home Parents Support

Sampson, Lana, 271, 273–74, 277–78, 339

Scott, Barbara, 67–69, 102–4, 106, 137, 250–51, 263–69, 272, 339, 350n66, 355n65, 355n68

Shaganappi Day Care (Calgary), 84, 96, 248, 267

Sheppard, Christine, 269, 339

Smith, Beverley, 198–99, 202, 340, 370n24

social liberalism, 7, 157, 289, 318–21, 325–26

Sorensen, Dennis, 102, 140, 167–74, 183, 187, 204, 325, 364n17

space creation start-up grants, 316, 318, 325

Speaker, Ray, 67

special committee on child care, 198

standards. *See* day care standards and regulations

stay-at-home mothers, 35, 44, 53, 60, 107,

191, 197–200, 226, 228–29, 259, 291–93, 300, 306, 319, 322–24, 327, 334, 383n1

Stay-at-Home Parents Support (SAHPS), 322–23, 334

Stelmach, Ed, 294, 301, 315, 325

Stepping Stones Day Care (Grande Prairie), 118–19

subsidies, portable, 86, 93, 106, 111, 115, 121, 127, 133, 136, 159, 192, 247–48: maximum subsidy rate, 309

Sweden: day care in, compared to Alberta, 4, 124, 156–58, 314

Syvenky, Sylene, 339

T

Task Force on Child Care, 197, 368n7

Texas: day care in, compared to Alberta, 1, 4, 124, 155–56, 158, 352n25

U

UCCA. *See* United Child Care Association

UCCB. *See* Universal Child Care Benefit

undervaluing of child care labour, 308, 311–15

unions in day care, 165–66, 174, 176–80, 188, 243, 248, 256, 260, 269, 308, 314, 365nn37–38, 366n44: decertification of unions, 179–80, 269

United Child Care Association (UCCA), 207, 209, 218

Universal Child Care Benefit (UCCB), 323, 387n43

University Women's Club of Calgary, 31, 34, 44–45, 56, 69, 72, 73

University Women's Club of Edmonton, 31, 43–45, 344n44

W

wage enhancements, 8, 151, 191–92, 287–88, 300, 302, 304–5, 308–9, 315–18, 321, 327, 334